GENDER AND GERMANNESS

Cultural Productions of Nation

Edited by
Patricia Herminghouse and Magda Mueller

Berghahn Books
Providence • Oxford

First published in 1997 by

Berghahn Books

© 1997 Patricia Herminghouse and Magda Mueller

Library of Congress Cataloging-in-Publication Data

```
Gender and Germanness : cultural productions of nation / edited by
  Patricia Herminghouse & Magda Mueller.
      p.   cm. -- (Modern German studies ; v. 4)
    Includes bibliographical references and index.
    ISBN 1-57181-112-5 (alk. paper)
    1. German literature--History and criticism.  2. Gender identity
in literature.  3. Nationalism in literature.  4. Germany--In
literature.  5. Arts, German.  6. Gender identity in art.
I. Herminghouse, Patricia.  II. Mueller, Magda.  III. Series.
PT111.P37  1997
830.9--dc21                                              97-23739
                                                            CIP
```

British Library Cataloguing in Publication Data

A catalogue record for this book is available from the
British Library.

Printed in the United States on acid-free paper.

GENDER AND GERMANNESS

Modern German Studies
A Series of the German Studies Association

This series offers books on modern and contemporary Germany, concentrating on themes in history, political science, literature and German culture. Publications will include original works in English and English translations of significant works in other languages.

CONTENTS

Lorenz Clasen, *Germania auf der Wacht am Rhein,* 1860. Courtesy of the Krefelder Kunstmuseen.

Introduction

LOOKING FOR GERMANIA
Patricia Herminghouse and Magda Mueller

A s Cultural Studies on both sides of the Atlantic have become increasingly preoccupied with questions of national identity and cultural representation, feminist studies have been insisting upon the entanglement of gender with issues of nation, class, and ethnicity. Particularly in the wake of German unification, the editors of the present volume sensed the need for an interdisciplinary, international attempt to reassess the nexus of gender, Germanness, and nationhood by pursuing strands of cultural debate in literature, history, the visual arts, and language from the eighteenth century to the present. Before German unification, such an attempt to examine the connection between gender and concepts of nation might have been considered a curiosity. The dismantling of the highly fortified border between the two German states and the Berlin Wall in particular changed not only the German landscape, but also disrupted the general silence regarding concepts of national identity that had prevailed since the founding of the two German states in 1949. While the inhibitions that surrounded reflections about German nationhood had marginalized the topic to the right of the political spectrum since the end of World War II, a process of re-evaluation was set in motion with the unexpected events of 1989-90.

Situated among feminist debates on gender and critical studies of German culture, the original essays we have selected for this focus on *Gender and Germanness* deal with a wide range of cultural productions, including minority discourses, post-colonial theory, film and cinema studies. Before introducing them, a discussion of certain presuppositions may prove useful. Even at the planning stage, Eva Kaufmann drew the editors' attention to the problematic nature of that word "German-ness." Faced with the difficult task of rendering it in German, one quickly discovers that it is basically untranslatable. If one were to select *Deutschtum* for "Germanness" one would be caught up in a web of associations and connotations that evoke images of traditional costumes and folk music such as were promulgated during the Nazi dictatorship – or, more recently, the nostalgia in circulation at the political rallies of the so-called *Vertriebenenverbände* (associations of ethnic German exiles from areas belonging to Czechoslovakia, Poland, and the former Soviet Union after World War II). In such contexts, *Deutschtum* conveys a static notion of historic rights for land and a not-yet-resolved longing for a place that one belongs [*Heimat*] that is connected with these claims for ownership. As the present anthology suggests, Germanness so understood is definitely not what the editors had in mind. Should we ever be faced with the task of publishing these essays in German, the title of the volume would certainly have to be changed.

Numerous commentators have noted that within the discourse of unification the German Democratic Republic (GDR) was often caricatured with female images, characterized by naiveté, dependency, and weakness, whereas the Federal Republic of Germany (FRG) was depicted as strong, male, and aggressive. The tradition of using female bodies or representations of woman as metaphors and allegories for nations and states is hardly new, however. The allegorical Germania of art, music, and poetry has Latin roots in Tacitus's *Germania* (A.D. 98). The reception of his account of the tribes living on the other side of the *Limes*, the "Wall" of Roman times that marked the border along the Rhine of Tacitus's *Germania*, led to a long tradition of art and literature depicting Germania and Arminius (Hermann, the Cheruscan chief, whom Tacitus called the "liberator of Germany"). Later, in early emblematology, Germania as mother of Germany was represented as one of the twelve daughters of Europe. In her analysis of how the details of representations of the figure and its historical context function to identify her meaning, Kerstin Wilhelms has shown that Germania can be an allegory for a geographic space, a state system, or an ideal (38).[1]

1. Wilhelms suggests something of the range of attributes that we will note in the following discussion: "Germanias Kopfbedeckung kann eine Mauerkrone sein, mit der sie z.B. für das Territorium des Hl. Röm. Reiches deutscher Nation steht oder ein Eichenlaubkranz, der sie 'herrschaftsneutral' als Deutsche identifiziert, oder auch die Kaiserkrone ... Herrschaftsinsignien wie Szepter und Reichsapfel, ein Schild mit einem (doppelköpfigem) Adler, ein Schwert oder ein Friedenszweig werden ihr als Accessoires mitgegeben und signalisieren Germanias Beziehung zur Macht und ihre jeweilige 'politische Verfassung.' Häufig erscheint sie als passive in Ketten gefesselte Frau, die zu ihrer Befreiung männlicher Hilfe bedarf; liegen die Ketten am Boden, so waren ihre Befreier erfolgreich" (38).

Given the historical tradition in which she became entangled, however, it is perhaps not surprising that, with few exceptions, feminist
artists and critics alike have not been inclined to pay very much attention to Germania in recent decades. The most (in)famous recent interpretation occurs in Heiner Müller's complex drama *Germania Death in
Berlin (Germania Tod in Berlin)*, where "Mama" Germania functions as
midwife in a grotesque scene in which Joseph Goebbels gives birth to
Hitler's child, a misshapen wolf.[2] And there is the deconstruction of the
word "Germania" that forms the editor's epigraph to *Germania*, a recent
anthology of Müller's essays and interviews: "**Ger**: Spear. [OLD GER-
MAN] **mania**: A form of insanity characterized by great excitement [*sic*],
with or without delusions, and in its acute stage by great violence."

It thus may be worth recalling that allegorical invocations of Germania
in connection with hopes for unification of the German nation prior to
1870 reflected emancipatory, not reactionary sentiments.[3] In the absence
of a political nation, the idea of a cultural nation took on increasing
importance within the nineteenth century. Of course, allegories can be
employed in the service of various political interests, and representations
with an emancipatory intent can be re-interpreted in the service of oppressive and chauvinistic politics. This can be seen, for example, in Heinrich
von Kleist's 1809 poem, "Germania an ihre Kinder," (Germania to Her
Children) where Germania is a strong, belligerent mother, protecting her
children from the Rhine to the Oder River, the Baltic to the Mediter-
ranean Sea, especially in the insistent question of its refrain: "Stehst du
auf, Germania? / Ist der Tag der Rache da?" [Germania, will you now
arise? / Is the day of vengeance nigh?]. By contrast, in his 1844 *Deutschland. Ein Wintermärchen (Germany: A Winter's Tale)* Heine constructs a
completely different image of "Die teure, wundersame, / Goldlockigte
Jungfrau Germania" [the dear, strange, / golden-haired virgin Germania,
Caput XIV] caught in the midst of Barbarossa's bellicose troops.

Numerous critics have traced the subsequent evolution of this image
in the visual arts, for example in paintings by Philipp Veit, comparing
the Germania panel of his fresco triptych for the Städelsches Kunstinsti-
tut in Frankfurt am Main, *Die Einführung der Künste in Deutschland
durch das Christentum* (Christianity Introduces Art to Germany, 1834-
1836) to his later *Germania* (March 1848) for the Paulskirche in the
same city. In the earlier work Germania is seated under an oak, the holy
tree of the Germans,[4] with the sheathed sword of the empire and the

---

2. For a useful commentary and interpretation, see Schulz (129-38) and Mieth.

3. See especially the essays in *Trophäe oder Leichenstein*.

4. In the process of national cultural formation, the oak became the sign of Germanness. According to Germanic mythology, the strongest and most beautiful tree (an

Golden Bull in her lap and a shield bearing the imperial eagle in her right hand. She gazes contemplatively at the crown of the Holy Roman Empire of the German Nation, which had been dissolved in 1806, now lying on the ground next to her. Her regal robe and the coats-of-arms of the seven electors (Kürfürsten, to whom the Bull grants the right to elect the emperor) on the pediment of her throne further enforce the political implications of the image (Hoffmann 123). In the 1848 painting, the same Germania, now displaying the imperial eagle on her gown, is depicted standing erect, looking straight ahead with her unsheathed sword poised and a banner with the national colors held aloft. The crown is missing but a pair of unshackled handcuffs is visible on the ground to her right (129). Most telling, as Lothar Gall has pointed out, is that the setting sun which cast the 1836 Germania in shadow has yielded to the bright light of the rising sun (17). In the Niederwald monument constructed after the war of 1870, depicting Germania with a wreath of oak leaves around her head and the sword in her left hand, the crown of the Holy Roman Empire of the German Nation is finally displaced by the crown of the new empire held aloft in her right hand.

Still more influential than Veit's depictions of Germania was Lorenz Clasen's 1860 painting "Germania auf der Wacht am Rhein" (Germania on Watch at the Rhine) for the Krefeld town hall. Here Germania, sword drawn, shield at the ready, reconnoiters the Rhine valley from on high in an allusion to German patriotic responses to Louis Adolphe Thiers's claim to the Rhine as the French border in 1840. Even though Germany was not a nation until 1871, the French provocation to national consciousness was reflected in numerous poems and songs of the 1840s, such as "They shall not get it" ("Sie sollen ihn nicht haben") by Nikolaus Becker – also known as "Der deutsche Rhein" (The German Rhine) or just "The Rhine Song" ("Rheinlied") – "Der Rhein" by Robert Prutz or, most enduringly, "Die Wacht am Rhein" (On Watch at the Rhine) by Max Schneckenburger (1840). Schneckenburger's song summoned not only patriots of the Vormärz but also German soldiers of later eras "zum Rhein, zum Rhein, zum deutschen Rhein," with its assertion:

---

oak) was consecrated to Donar, the God of thunder and lightning. During the period of Christianization, Boniface and other missionaries cut down oaks in the hope of ending pagan rituals, but to no avail: pagan tradition and Christian belief continued to exist side-by-side. Since the time of Klopstock, the oak appears to be increasingly associated with patriotic concepts of freedom and unity (Hürlimann 62 f.). See Hermand for an analysis of the sturdy, gnarled oaks that are a familiar presence in the paintings of Caspar David Friedrich. All of these cultural meanings are contained in the wreath of oak that often adorns Germania.

Solang ein Tröpfchen Blut noch glüht,
Noch eine Faust den Degen zieht,
Und noch ein Arm die Büchse spannt,
Betritt kein Welscher deinen Strand.[5]

"Die Wacht am Rhein" became the most popular song of the nineteenth century. Printed in more than 140 musical versions, it reached the epitome of its popularity in the wars of 1870-71 (Gast 84) and was reappropriated in the National Socialist era. The Rhine controversy is later reflected in the conflicting interpretations of the most famous monument to Germania, known as the Niederwalddenkmal, erected above Rüdesheim on the Rhine in 1883 in commemoration of Bismarck's 1871 triumph. The debate that erupted as to whether Germania's gaze was directed hostilely toward the French enemy across the river or benevolently upon the happily united citizens in the valley below continues to this day.

Some critics, such as the historian Lothar Gall, see in Johannes Schilling's monument a peaceful representation of the politically powerful empire that resulted from Bismarck's consolidation of the many German states and principalities, with the laurel-entwined sword now rests on the ground as a sign that peace prevails (25).[6] In large measure, interpretations that assert the bellicose quality of the Germania of the Niederwalddenkmal derive from the hundreds of jingoistic Germania poems that were produced during this period. In her survey of the enormous output of the era, Angelika Menne-Haritz identifies several thematic strands, beginning with the flag-waving patriotism in the vein of Ferdinand Freiligrath's famous 1870 poem, "Hurrah, Germania." But even here, Germania also continues in her motherly function: "Auf meine Kinder, alle Mann! / Zum Rhein! Zum Rhein! Zum Rhein! / Hurrah, hurrah, hurrah! / Hurrah, Germania!" [Arise my children, all men arise / To the Rhine! etc., (54)]. As mother of the nation, however, she is often simultaneously a virgin – representing less the ideal of the Virgin Mary than the armored strength of a Joan of Arc or Penthesilea (Menne-Haritz 57).[7]

In a peculiarly mixed metaphor, an article on "Germania" in *Meyers Konversationslexikon* summarizes the interpretation of Germania that

5. "As long as a drop of blood can yet warm our veins, / A fist yet draw a dagger, / An arm yet load a muzzle, / No Frenchy's foot shall touch thy shore."
6. In support of his interpretation, Gall cites Schilling's own 1876 statement: "Nicht dem besiegten Feind, dem deutschen Volk zeigt sie die Krone, die ihr Haupt zu schmücken bestimmt ist ... Der Krieg ist beendet. Germania überschaut das deutsche Vaterland, dessen schönster Vordergrund der gerettete Rheingau" (26).
7. See also Pape's more recent survey.

occurs in the course of the consolidation of German power after 1871: "This Germania is a conjoining of the warrior virgin (Valkyrie) with the German mother who symbolizes the all-embracing fatherland" (402).

The monument at Niederwald, created by Johannes Schilling, was only the most popular of the dozens representations of Germania that proliferated in the wake of national unification in 1871. Among the best known of these were the Germania of Rudolf Siemering's victory monu-

ment in Leipzig, R. Henze's marble sculpture on the Altmarkt in Dresden,[8] and of most interest here, two representations of Germania in the new Reichstag, designed by Paul Wallot in 1882. Both Reinhold Begas's copper sculpture of an equestrian Germania above the main portal of the Reichstag and the enormous stained glass window inside the building now depict Germania wearing the new imperial crown. While, according to Gall, Begas's sculpture alludes to Bismarck's 1867 pronouncement, "Put Germany, so to speak, in the saddle! She will know how to ride," Bismarck himself – who had refused to take part in the dedication ceremonies for the Niederwald monument – abjured the "idolization of the idea of nation" that Germania cult represented. He

Monument Niederwalddenkmal

also questioned the embodiment of the idea of nation in such a female figure: "A woman *(weibliches Wesen)* with a sword in this aggressive posture is unnatural. Every officer will feel the same way as I do about this" (quoted in Gall 27-29). His reservations, however, appear to have had little effect on the continuing appropriation of the image for nationalistic purposes: Germania entered currency as an adornment to the new 100 Reichsmark bills, replete with crown, sword and shield – but also with plow, anvil, and the ships of the imperial navy in the background. By 1914 she had become the fiercely vengeful warrior against a flaming background in Friedrich August von Kaulbach's *Deutschland – August 1914.*[9]

8. See Bauer, Mosse, and *Wahrzeichen und Denkmäler.*

9. All of these images are reproduced in Gall's fascinating survey of the iconography of Germania.

With Hitler's loss of World War II, Germania – like his plan to rename the capital of Germany after her – seems to have disappeared from the scene. Standing on a forlorn site that was no longer the center of divided Berlin, the ruin of the Reichstag came to symbolize a discredited idea of nation. Following unification in 1990, however, it was not only the plan to restore the building as the seat of German government, but Christo's and Jeanne-Claude's much publicized "Wrapping of the Reichstag" in 1995 that once again focused public attention on its symbolic meaning. The heated political debate in the German Bundestag (25 February 1994) about Christo's plan, dating back to 1971, for veiling the Reichstag culminated in a decision to allow the spectacle. The controversy in the German parliament, which was solemnly pronounced a question of national identity, and the exuberant public reception of Christo's project in the following year were of a different nature.

Magic happened. Christo's present to the citizens of Germany evoked multicultural understanding. A love parade of not only techno freaks and fans but of people from all walks of life and many nationalities, people turning to each other smiling, enjoying each other's company, and re-enacting some of the joy and enthusiasm that existed during the night of 9 November 1989, the fall of wall. Singers, musicians, jugglers, buffoons, illusionists, clowns, and drummers momentarily constructed the new German society as a postnational one in a *fête-champêtre* that utilized the veiled moment of history to drum out the mean spirits of nationalism that still nestled in far-away corners of the run-down, brittle edifice of power. This playful postmodern happening united the multicultural crowd in front of Reichstag, converting the formerly forlorn space into a festive arena of spontaneous communication and human encounter.

An article in *Der Spiegel* covering the veiling of the Reichstag entitled "Germanias Geisterhaus" (Germania's Haunted House) might, however, also serve to evoke associations of this historic symbol of German national ambitions with a haunted house, where she is still spooking around, where the old spirits of nationalism (which still surface from time to time in Germany) have yet to be exorcised. But perhaps during that summer of 1995, something more happened: what the international press referred to as Christo and Jeanne-Claude's "wrapping" of the Reichstag was in fact a veiling of what that edifice had come to stand for. Did its shimmering rainment, alluding as it did to the graceful folds of classical statuary, not somehow feminize that formidable hulk? Would the veiling and unveiling of a monumental statue of Germania ever have had such national and international impact in the past? Why then was this the case with the Reichstag? Had Germania been thus displaced?

Might the Germania who once inhabited the Reichstag, have done as some of the birds there did, and just disappeared under the veil for the interim? Or did she react like that irritated kestrel, who refused to retreat into the special shelter that was installed there for an endangered species? And where is she now?

Christo recycled all the material used for the veiling of the Reichstag and we are tempted to ask whether his art recycled certain perceptions about Germania. In response to a question about what they had learned from the Reichstag project, Christo's partner Jeanne-Claude echoed Bundestag speaker Rita Süssmuth's sentiments that the project symbolized Germany as an open society and an intact democracy when she replied:

> We learned that Germany is a truly democratic country. It was the first time in the world that a parliament debated and voted on art. That is democracy. Willy Brandt told us that the Germans would be able to understand who they are in the veiled Reichstag. But everyone sees something different. There will be 80 million different ways of seeing it ("Wann verhüllen Sie").

* * *

Not surprisingly, but indeed indicatively, most contributors to our project focus not on the central national emblems and allegories we have been discussing, but rather on texts from the margins. This for several reasons, one of which is surely the current ascendancy of German Studies and Cultural Studies approaches in the field today. Contributions to this anthology suggest something of the range of possibilities these approaches offer for an examination of cultural constructions of nation.

Although contemporary Anglo-American work on the intersecting discourses of race, class and gender has tended to locate the advent of racism in the Darwinist, antisemitic, and colonialist mentalities of the late nineteenth century, Susanne Zantop argues that closer examination will reveal that the beginnings of biological racism in Germany lie in the previous century. Concentrating on the eighteenth-century philosopher Christoph Meiners, whose speculations on the "nature" of Africans, Asians, and Native Americans link details of anatomy and physiology with conjectures about intelligence and morality, Zantop highlights his conclusions about the superiority of Germans, "the whitest and most beautiful of them all," and suggests that his definition of what is "un-German" helped to lay the groundwork for an understanding of national identity based on difference and exclusion, an identity that supported the idea of a superior (male) German racial identity.

Helga Watt's examination of the striking combination of patriotism and internationalism in the fiction and essays of Sophie La Roche also locates the roots of German patriotic nationalism in an earlier tradition associated with the names of Klopstock and Lessing. While attacking slavish admiration of all things foreign and attempting to further virtues and customs that she regards as characteristically German, LaRoche also advocated a kind of patriotism that recognized the good qualities of other countries. A Swabian middle-class Protestant married to a French-oriented Catholic in the service of aristocrats and princes of the church in the Rhineland, she also lived between two languages: she started writing in French and had to learn to write in German in her late thirties. In this very lack of a ready-made identity Watt sees the key to LaRoche's unique way of being female and being German.

A character who is female and *not* German, the title figure of Achim von Armin's 1812 novella "Isabella of Egypt" is an orphaned Gypsy princess, who thwarts a Romantic fantasy of German nationhood by spiriting her son, the future heir to the Holy Roman Empire, back to her native Egypt. Reading beyond the traditional emphasis on supernatural and bizarre elements of this tale, Sara Friedrichsmeyer argues that it intends more than the antidote to German rationalism and sterility that Heinrich Heine saw in Isabella. Her analysis of the conflicting interests of the present and future rulers of the empire demonstrates the need for close attention to the ramifications of linking the threat to an ethnically pure German nation not just to Gypsies, but specifically to a Gypsy *woman.*

Demonstrating that there is a place for poetry in German Studies approaches, Russell Berman focuses his analysis on Heinrich Heine's famous poem "Night Thoughts" ("Nachtgedanken"), where he uncovers a dramatic opposition of political criticism and personal anxiety that ultimately structures national identity around gender positions. Thus the exiled speaker, the lyrical ego who has left his home, has also left his mother, and an implied connection and competition between fatherland and mother ensues. Even more important, however, is the contest between the two women, mother and wife, allegories of Germany and France, darkness and light, and the complex web of loyalty and betrayal that characterizes the relationship of the poet to each. In a provocative conclusion, Berman argues that German Studies may have more to learn from exceptional products of German culture, such as Heine's poetry, than through the current vogue for the popular and "the ordinary."

The first section concludes with Brent O. Peterson's essay demonstrating that even while "history" in the nineteenth century was a male preserve, the discourse of "Germanness" articulated in historiographic and fictional texts of that century was predicated on specific models of femininity and family. His analysis examines how gender was encoded in the historical fiction that confronted the exclusion of the private sphere (love, marriage, family) from academic history (great men, great events). Focusing on representations of German women during the so-called Wars of Liberation (1812-1815), Peterson examines five novels published between 1824 and 1871 in order to challenge conventional wisdom about the liberal, progressive character of early German nationalism. His reading of the complex interdependence between women and the nation demonstrates the constructedness and the gendered underpinnings of the nationalist narrative, where women's relegation to the margins enabled the male center to hold.

* * *

Elke Frederiksen opens the following section on "Rethinking History and Canons" by problematizing assumptions about cultural as well as sexual differences that inform considerations of canon. If the traditional canon of German literature in both Germany and the United States persists in ignoring feminist contributions, she asserts, it runs the risk of being further marginalized in view of the ongoing "feminization of the profession," particularly in the U.S. Within the new feminist canon, however, Frederiksen points to the contradictory tendency to assert the multiplicity of both female and minority writers, on the one hand, and the inclination to set up new figureheads, such as Ingeborg Bachmann and Christa Wolf, on the other. German literary studies, including feminist scholarship, might overcome its present isolation, she suggests, by shifting from its traditional focus on German authors, periods, and genres to a thematic examination of issues that are of greater concern to the international community. In this, gender remains a decisive, although certainly not the sole category of literary and cultural analysis.

Within feminist movements, no issue has given rise to more ambivalence, intellectual and emotional, than ideologies that glorify motherhood as the basis of women's claim to dignity and equality in both the public and private spheres. Ann Taylor Allen's exploration of feminist maternalism as a construct that provided a framework for new forms of self-consciousness and activism challenges tendencies to dismiss it as merely backward and conservative. In its earliest phase, feminist maternalism ascribed an ethical rather than a merely biological function to "spiritual motherhood" by insisting that training for responsible citizenship took place in the mother-child relationship. With advancing industrialization and urbanization, "social motherhood" became the metaphor for the philanthropic but nonetheless hegemonic relationship of middle and upper-class women to the lower classes. In the turn to "eugenic motherhood" at the end of the century, maternalist feminism soon proved itself vulnerable to misogyny and ideologies of biological determinism. The ensuing National-Socialist mobilization of maternalist discourse in the service of war and genocide continues to overshadow the discussion of motherhood in Germany.

Stefana Lefko examines the ill-fated strategies of the bourgeois women's movement during the Weimar Republic in *Die Frau*, the official magazine of the Bund Deutscher Frauenvereine (BDF). Here, too, questions of nation became entangled with definitions of woman's "essence." Starting from the assumption that the sexes were diametrically opposed in essence, the journal resisted the position of liberal women who believed in equality of the sexes, criticizing their efforts toward women's rights as "mere feminism" and preferring to press claims for women's right to vote and work by pointing to their contributions to the *Volksgemeinschaft* [national community]. By arguing on the basis of their uniquely female capacities to help the entire society, bourgeois women attempted to defend themselves against accusations of selfishness and "unwomanliness," but also created role expectations that would soon be invoked by the National Socialist state to limit their rights.

In the closing essay of the historically oriented section, Patricia Herminghouse analyzes the ways in which the national narrative that sustained the construction of literary histories and the rise of German literary studies as an academic discipline in the nineteenth century also contributed to the exclusion of women writers. In her examination of some influential literary histories of the period, she identifies some of the factors that defined women out of the canon of serious literature and literary history: the rise of national consciousness, the influence of the natural sciences, and the potentially threatening increase in the number of women who were actually engaged in the literary enterprise. The cultural assumptions to which she points in this study persisted well into the latter half of the present century.

* * *

The section devoted to visual culture reflects contemporary tendencies to extend our exploration of "texts" to more than printed documents. In his analysis of the precarious construction of gendered identities and pleasures in Nazi mass culture, Lutz P. Koepnick focuses on the paradoxical promotion of Zarah Leander to star status beginning in 1936 as well as on the representation of the *femme fatale* in the melodramas of Detlef Sierck (later known as Douglas Sirk). In these films, Leander's body became a site at which both the ideological guardians of Nazi culture and cinematic audiences engaged in a complex, albeit mostly unarticulated, discourse about the role of mass culture in Nazi Germany, the question of "Germanness" vis-á-vis the utopian promises of Americanism, and, most importantly, the meanings of sexual difference and gender identity. Contrary to the intentions of the film industry, Koepnick argues, Sierck's use of Leander's star appeal indicates the relative failure of German fascism to contain the popular imagination and to forge spectatorial desires into an autonomous German culture industry. Contrary to the intent of Nazi cinema, Sierck's films are shown to stage a curious destabilization of male identity that potentially undermined the Nazi vision of a new man in the service of a new order.

Nazism as *femme fatale* and the resulting contradictory constructions of masculinity in post-World War II cinematic representations of Berlin are the focus of Barton Byg's examination of *film noir* and the various national "new waves." Both have been seen as ways of recuperating masculinity in the wake of the war and the abdication or disgrace of the "fathers." In analyzing why this did not occur, Byg's gendered reading of film movements considers the contradictory cultural and historical situation in East and West Germany compared with *film noir* in the U.S. In the GDR, *film noir* had to be mitigated with the "feminine" voice of socialist optimism, while attempts at a West German new wave were marked by various masculine melancholy obsessions. If the Cold War was partly a war against the "other" as Jew/homosexual/woman, the attempted recuperation of masculinity in postwar film sought the origins of cultural instability and the cinematic means to combat it in images from Weimar Berlin culture.

In her examination of images of madonnas and mourning mothers, Mariatte Denman delineates how concepts of gender and nationhood intersect during Germany's immediate postwar era, and how postwar ideals of femininity trace back to the discourse of womanhood and family of the National-Socialist era, while assigning responsibility for that era to men. Such visual representations of gender, she shows, contributed to a discourse of victimization and to intense debates about women's role in a postwar German society. Focusing particularly on the way in which the discourse of motherhood established the parameters of what Alexander and Margarete Mitscherlich later called Germany's "inability to mourn," Denman asks why and how representations of mourning mothers became so ubiquitous. In Barthes' terms, she suggests, motherhood became a myth, that is, a concept devoid of history, as can be seen in the 1993 staging of the nexus of motherhood and German nation in German Chancellor Helmut Kohl's choice of a Pietá by Käthe Kollwitz for the redesigned war memorial at the Neue Wache in Berlin.

Exploring another one of those untranslatable cultural terms, *Heimat*, and its connection to the Freudian "*unheimlich*," Ingeborg Majer O'Sickey argues that postwar *Heimatfilm* represents a seamless continuity with the genre as it existed in the Nazi era – not only in its use of the same actors and directors, but in its maintenance of the ideology of an organic, homogenized German culture. Using cinema's frame-up of Bambi as feminine principle in films following the publication of Felix Salten's novel *Bambi: A Life in the Woods* (1926), she analyzes how the culture industry exploited Bambi's qualities as a creature in need of protection to make her into an symbol that satisfies dominant cultural notions of femininity. She shows how a number of *Heimat* films of the 1940s and 1950s as well as the soft porn of the so-called *Lederhosen Sex* films instrumentalized the deer hunt and Bambi myth in order to represent women as sexual prey and men as sexual predators, until the celluloid hunt on women was finally challenged in the *Antiheimat* films of the late 1960s and early 1970s. The essay concludes with a look at Percy Adlon's 1990 *Salmonberries* as a deconstruction and Michael Verhoeven's *The Nasty Girl* of the same year as a reconceptualization of *Heimatfilm*.

The conflation of nation and female bodies is at the heart of Barbara Kosta's critique of Helke Sander's controversial 1992 documentary *BeFreier und Befreite (Liberators Take Liberties)*. Sander's attempt to excavate women's long-repressed stories of the mass rapes that occurred in the last days of World War II is shown to be problematic because of her inability to rethink the interrelation of war, nation, and sexual violence. Without denying the need to challenge the silence that has prevented working through the experience of wartime rape, Kosta suggests that Sander's interpretive framework perpetuates the very structure that initially produced it and inhibits its articulation rather than providing new lenses through which these testimonies might be read. Kosta criticizes the narrative of rape that Sander constructs by focusing on its preservation of a political stance that unwittingly resonates with right-wing representations of the mass rape of German women.

* * *

The last major section of the volume focuses on some of the "others" of German self-understanding. Drawing upon Ama Ata Aidoo's 1977 novel, *Our Sister Killjoy*, and Chantal Akerman's 1978 film, *Meetings with Anna*, Barbara Mennel shows how these works reflect questions of identity from specific non-German cultural positions in which the question of Germanness is imbricated on the level of formal, linguistic, literary, and visual devices. Akerman's film portrays a Jewish film-maker traveling through Germany while the main character of *Our Sister Killjoy* is a young Ghanian woman who becomes involved with a married German woman. In the light they shed on the interconnectedness of national and transnational histories and desires, these texts offer a gendered perspective on the nation that entails post-Holocaust and post-colonial experiences of diaspora. Mennel's examination of the complicated relationship of gender, race, and desire in these texts demonstrates their power to highlight issues that are usually silenced and marginalized in cultural representations of the German nation.

Denis Sweet examines the belated way in which the long-silenced gay (male) body entered general public consciousness in the GDR, culminating in Heiner Carow's 1989 film, *Coming Out*. Hitherto a taboo topic in the state-controlled media of the GDR, homosexuality entered into the public realm in 1987 with a spectacular media blitz. In these depictions the gay male was uniformly perceived as endangered – by his own hand – and the public response was pity. The Stasi, however, relied upon a more sinister reading of gay men that had recourse to older constructions of homosexuality as the site of both actual (syphilis, AIDS) and ideological (Western) contagion in order to codify the gay man as a security risk who required systematic surveillance. Self-representations by gay men themselves thus sought to elide difference through representations of bodies that were indistinguishable from the rest of the GDR population: assimilated, proper, and respectable. Whether pitiful, subversive, or adapted, gay bodies were engineered for certain political ends.

The relationship between patterns of consciousness that inform the ideologies of nation and gender is the focus of Karin Bauer's analysis of the prose of Herta Müller, a Rumanian-born German writer. Within Müller's notion of *Heimat*, Bauer explores the taboos and the structures of power through which both the Rumanian state and the conservative German community glorify national and male identity and relegate women's bodies to the realm of reproduction and commodity exchange. Yet while Müller's texts, in their resistance to the conformity and censorship that characterize the collective subject, represent the "Better" characterized by Theodor W. Adorno in his essay "On the Question: What is German?" her narrative strategies tend to reproduce the taboos of the German community. Bauer's analysis opens the question of whether such narrative reproduction of the repression, marginalization, and self-consumption of women perpetuates the cycle of self-destruction or opens up the potential for an Adornoean trace of "the Better."

Tracing the labile character of contemporary German identity to the persistence of unresolved feelings of guilt for the aberrations of National Socialism, Magda Mueller highlights the resultant contradictions in current German responses to two major groups of newcomers to German society: the asylum seekers who were granted specific rights in the German Basic Law of 1949 and the ethnic Germans, who are able to "come back" to Germany because of their German ancestry. She contrasts the well-intentioned tendency of liberal German women to focus on the dilemma of asylum-seeking women, who are marked by language and skin color as "non-German," while ignoring the plight of ethnic German women whose anachronistic understanding of their own Germanness, even when they do not know the language, is incompatible with the liberal desire to challenge traditional notions of German identity. The state, on the other hand, seems eager to promote the traditional values of hearth and family that the ethnic German women represent and much more concerned about the "otherness" of foreigners who might further undermine an already weak sense of national identity. Mueller shows how these contradictory concepts ultimately sustain anti-emancipatory discourses by their construction of the "other" as exotic and non-German.

Focusing on the years 1989-1996, Eva Kaufmann examines the role of "Germanness" in the poetry of the younger generation of East German women writers, delineating a changed relationship to "Germany" that has also been inflected by issues of gender in recent years. While for the older generation the question of nation was less central than fundamental social issues, the notion of Germanness in more recent writers was shaped by their own interests in other countries and other nationalities. With the rise of xenophobia since 1989, however, the work of the youngest generation – especially the poets – seems to have entered into a polemic engagement with limiting notions of "Germanness."

With a provocative comparison of issues of gender and nation in the writings of Franz Schönhuber (founder of the right-wing *Republikaner* party, known for its anti-immigration platform) just prior to unification and in essays of the German feminist Alice Schwarzer, Leslie Adelson sets the stage for a revised look at Aysel Özakin's novel *Die Preisvergabe* (1982). One of the most frequently reviewed and studied Turkish women authors of German literature, Özakin has consistently rejected both the national (Turkish) and the gendered (female) optics through which virtually all her works have been read by scholars and critics alike. Adelson's analysis explores what can be gained if, instead of arguing that Özakin denies the obvious, one considers some of the blind spots regarding gender and Germanness that feminist discussions of Turkish-German culture have helped to produce.

* * *

The volume concludes with two brief contributions by the feminist linguist Luise Pusch, who, with her usual combination of sharp wit and apt criticism, reminds us of the gendered nature of the relationship between fatherland and mother tongue. Asserting that the transformation of language introduced by women in the last two decades is the most pervasive and significant linguistic change of this century, Pusch points out that this development is not unique to Germany. Nor, she asserts, is it over. Arguing that language determines reality, Pusch demonstrates that the marginalization of women depends on the power of the linguistic structure of German, particularly in its plural forms, to put them under erasure. Women may not yet have access to power, but they do have access to language and in changing it, they affect reality in ways that again change language.

Taking a sharp look at the latest, most controversial official attempt to change language, the German spelling reform, Pusch finds more material for her serious-humorous critique in the authoritative guide to the new rules, the *Rechtschreibungs-Duden* (Spelling Duden) of 1996.

* * *

Unlike Christo and Jeanne-Claude, who hoped to open up one particular artifact of German culture to 80 million different perspectives, our ambitions as editors of this volume are far more modest. But we do hope these attempts to explore some of the problematic connections between *Gender and Germanness* in a wide range of topics will indeed open up some new perspectives on the work that remains to be done.

Note

Unless otherwise indicated, all translations from German are our own.

Bibliography

Bauer, Franz J. *Gehalt und Gestalt in der Monumentalsymbolik: Zur Ikonologie des Nationalstaats in Deutschland und Italien 1860-1914.* Munich: Historisches Kolleg, 1992.

Becker, Nikolaus. "Der deutsche Rhein." *Der deutsche Vormärz.* 128.

Bouffier, Franz. *Das National-Denkmal auf dem Niederwald: Litterarisch-topographischer Führer.* Wiesbaden: A. Gestewitz 1883.

Der deutsche Vormärz: Texte und Dokumente. Ed. Jost Hermand. Stuttgart: Reclam, 1967.

Gall, Lothar. *Germania: Eine deutsche Marianne? Une Marianne allemande?* Bonn: Bouvier, 1993.

Gast, Wolfgang, ed. *Politische Lyrik: Deutsche Zeitgedichte des 19. und 20. Jahrhunderts.* Stuttgart: Reclam, 1991.

"Germanias Geisterhaus." *Der Spiegel* 25 (1995): 174-84.

Heine, Heinrich. *Sämtliche Schriften.* Ed. Klaus Briegleb. Vol. 7. Frankfurt a. M.: Ullstein, 1981. 609.

Hermand, Jost. *Sieben Arten an Deutschland zu leiden.* Königstein: Athenäum, 1979. 172-241.

Hoffmann, Detlef. "Germania zwischen Kaisersaal und Paulskirche: Der Kampf um Vergangenheit und Gegenwart." *Trophäe oder Leichenstein?* 85-134.

Hürlimann, Annemarie. "Die Eiche, heiliger Baum deutscher Nation." *Waldungen: Die Deutschen und ihr Wald.* Berlin: Nicolaische Verlagsbuchhandlung, 1987. 62-68.

Kleist, Heinrich von. *Sämtliche Werke.* Ed. Curt Grützmacher. Munich: Winkler, 1967. 838.

Menne-Haritz, Angelika. "GERMANIA: die deutsche Nationalallegorie in den Kriegsgedichten von 1870/71." *Carleton Germanic Papers* 8 (1990): 47-63.

Meyers Konversationslexikon. Leipzig: Bibliographisches Institut, 1897.

Mieth, Matias. *Die Masken des Erinnerns: Zur Ästhetisierung von Geschichte und Vorgeschichte der DDR bei Heiner Müller.* Frankfurt a. M.: Peter Lang, 1994.

Mosse, George. *Die Nationalisierung der Massen: Politische Symbolik und Massenbewegungen in Deutschland von dem napoleonischen Krieg bis zum Dritten Reich.* Frankfurt a. M.: Ullstein, 1976.

Müller, Heiner. *Germania.* Ed. Sylvere Lotringer. Trans. and annotated Bernard and Caroline Schütze. New York: Semiotext(e), 1990.

―――――. *Germania Tod in Berlin.* Berlin: Rotbuch, 1977. 35-78.

Pape, Walter. "'Hurrah, Germania – mir graut vor dir': Hoffmann von Fallersleben, Freiligrath, Herwegh und die deutsche Einheit von 1870/71." *Oxford German Studies* 22 (1993): 134-67.

Prutz, Robert. "Der Rhein." *Der deutsche Vormärz.* 131-34.

Schneckenberger, Max. "Die Wacht am Rhein." *Der deutsche Vormärz.* 130-31.

Schulz, Genia. *Heiner Müller*. Stuttgart: Metzler, 1980.

Steen, Jürgen. "Nationalfeste – Geschichte als reale Utopie (1838-1862)." *Trophäe oder Leichenstein?* 135-94.

Cornelius Tacitus. *The Agricola and The Germania*. New York: Penguin, 1970. 101-60.

Tacke, Charlotte. *Denkmal im sozialen Raum: Nationale Symbole in Deutschland und Frankreich im 19. Jahrhundert*. Göttingen: Vandenhoeck and Ruprecht, 1995.

Tittel, Lutz. *Das Niederwalddenkmal 1871-1883*. Hildesheim: Gerstenberg, 1979.

Trophäe oder Leichenstein? Kulturgeschichtliche Aspekte des Geschichtsbewußtseins in Frankfurt im 19. Jahrhundert: Eine Austellung des Historischen Museums Frankfurt. Frankfurt a. M.: Historisches Museum, 1978.

Wagner, Monika. *Allegorie und Geschichte: Ausstattungsprogramme öffentlicher Gebäude in Deutschland. Von der Cornelius-Schule zur Malerei der Wilhelminischen Ära*. Tübingen: Ernst Wasmuth, 1989.

Wahrzeichen und Denkmäler in Deutschland: Bauwerke, Mahnmale und Monumente aus alter und neuer Zeit. Munich: Orbis, 1992.

"Wann verhüllen Sie den Mond, Herr Christo?" (Interview with Christo and Jeanne-Claude). *Der Tagesspiegel* (Beilage June/July 1995): B1.

Wilhelms, Kerstin. "Michel und Germania – ein deutsches Geschlechterverhältnis." *Der weibliche multikulturelle Blick*. Ed. Hannelore Scholz and Brita Baume. Berlin: trafo, 1995. 36-51.

Part I

EIGHTEENTH AND NINETEENTH CENTURY

Chapter 1

THE BEAUTIFUL, THE UGLY, AND THE GERMAN

Race, Gender, and Nationality in Eighteenth-Century
Anthropological Discourse

Susanne Zantop

> The Germans have always been one of the noblest people and were always
> recognized as such, and they are now undoubtedly the most powerful of all
> nations which – if it were to unite all its forces, like the Romans, to the detri-
> ment of others – could overwhelm the whole world.
>
> (Christoph Meiners, *Briefe über die Schweiz*, 1791)

istories and theories of race tend to locate biological racism in the
second half of the nineteenth century (Appiah). They associate it
with names such as Charles Darwin, Arthur Gobineau, or Houston
Stewart Chamberlain; with the rise of antisemitism, and the European
scramble for colonies. While Philip Curtin or George Mosse have
pointed to racism's roots in earlier discourses, even the most recent works
on colonialism and race relations repeat the by now conventional wisdom. Thus, in his recent study entitled *Colonial Desire*, Robert Young
speaks of "*new* racial theories based on comparative anatomy and cran-
iometry" *after* 1840 (11, emphasis added). And Anne McClintock, in
Imperial Leather (1995), locates the conflation of race, class, and gender
in Victorian England "*after* 1859 and the advent of social Darwinism"
(44, emphasis added). Neither casts more than a fleeting glance at Ger-

many and at earlier expressions of racism. Germany, which did not become a unified nation until 1871 and did not actively engage in colonialism until 1884, does not figure much in postcolonial theory. Not even among German scholars who, under the impact of the Holocaust, have tended to focus on antisemitism and the late nineteenth century rather than on precolonial race theories.[1] Yet a modern, biological concept of race as the *"ultimate, irreducible difference* between cultures, linguistic groups, or adherents of specific belief systems" (Gates 5) emerged in Germany as early as the 1770s and 1780s. Arguably, there are even earlier roots of modern racism in the *pureza de sangre* debate in sixteenth- and seventeenth-century Spain.[2] Ironically, however, it is in the anthropological-philosophical discourse on human races developed by Enlightenment philosophers that the supposed links between skin color, physiognomy, and anatomy on the one hand, and moral stature, intelligence, or economic status on the other, were systematically explored and given "scientific" currency. What is more, in their attempt to determine the "nature" of Black, White, Yellow, and Red Skins and their relative positions in cultural hierarchies, some German academics went so far as to speculate on the ultimate, irreducible difference between Germans and all others. In other words, they imbued the national-political category "German" with racial overtones.

One pivotal figure in this process of self-definition in terms of race was the Göttingen professor of philosophy Christoph Meiners (1747-1810). Today virtually unknown, this "ordentlicher Professor der Weltweisheit" (literally, *professor ordinarius of world wisdom*) established his reputation with a slew of studies in cultural history ranging from a *Revision der Philosophie* (Revision of Philosophy, 1772) and a *Grundriß der Geschichte der Menschheit* (Sketch of the History of Mankind, 1785/1786, 1793), to a four-volume *Geschichte des weiblichen Geschlechts* (History of the Female Sex, 1788-1800) – to name just a tiny portion of the mind-boggling production of this academic over-

---

1. So far, the impulse to study German antisemitism in the context of earlier manifestations of racism has come from outside Germany (see Gilman or Mielke). The recent "resurgence" of racism in Germany and the emergence of minority literatures claiming their own "German" traditions has led to a reexamination of Germany's racist traditions before colonialism (see Lennox et al.).

2. "Purity of blood" *(pureza de sangre)* had served as metaphor for racial purity since sixteenth-century Spain. While the fear of contamination with Moorish or Jewish blood was pervasive throughout the sixteenth and seventeenth centuries, "blood" lost its genealogical/class connotation in the eighteenth, gaining a biological grounding instead – which was then used to confirm cultural or economic superiority (see Kamen). The continuities between the Spanish *pureza de sangre* tradition and German race theories are spelled out in Meiners, "Ueber die Natur der Germanischen ...."

achiever.[3] It was not just Meiners's academic publications, however, that made an impact on the literate public, but the 160 essays in comparative cultural anthropology that he published in the *Göttingisches historisches Magazin,* a journal he founded and co-edited with the historian L. Th. Spittler from 1787 to 1794. Indeed, the journal served as his main vehicle for the propagation of a very special brand of what one might call "national racism."

In his *Grundriß der Geschichte der Menschheit* of 1786 Meiners had divided humankind into two basic races [*Hauptstämme*]: the "Caucasians" and the "Mongols" (Vorrede). Although he subdivided the former, again, into two, namely the so-called Celtic and Slavic peoples, Meiners makes clear that the world is, in fact, constituted by only two kinds of humans: the culturally superior, "beautiful" ones – the Europeans – and all others who are "mongolized" [*mongolisirt,* 32] to varying degrees and hence "ugly" and inferior – Asians, Africans, Americans. All of Meiners's subsequent publications are variations on the same theme. The "monomania" with which he tries to "enlighten" his contemporaries does not extend so much to history, as his biographer Prantl claims (*ADB* 224-26), as to reinforcing over and over again the racial, aesthetic, moral, and cultural boundaries between "us" and "them."

In a series of articles that appeared in 1790, Meiners elaborates on the "natural inferiority" of all peoples of color. The articles' titles and their date of publication establish the context or subtext for his investigations: the slave uprisings in the French colony of St. Domingue, the first serious challenge to European colonial rule.[4] From references to European conditions, however, it is clear that Meiners's antirevolutionary colonialist discourse also extends to "colonial" relations closer to home.

In his articles, Meiners attempts to link physiology to cultural behavior and political power. After emphatically pronouncing his support for

3. The secondary literature on Meiners is relatively small. Ihle, while critical of Meiners's theories, provides only summaries; Wenzel gives a short introduction to Meiners's tracts on religion; Mühlmann places him as a minor figure among the founders of classical anthropology; only the ethno-anthropologist Britta Rupp-Eisenreich takes a critical look at the long-term implications of Meiners's racial theories and their reappropriation by Nazi anthropology (133). It is not surprising that her article appeared in a French journal: As she suggests, Meiners's theories must have appeared too embarrassing to German intellectual historians, particularly after 1945.

4. These articles, again, constitute only a small selection of the total output. Meiners's obsession with peoples of color is apparent from the journal's inception – already in 1788 he wrote about the particular "irritability" [*Reizbarkeit*] of the "weak peoples," the slave trade, the "peoples of America," the food and drink habits of Mongolian peoples, etc. From 1790 onward, however, his interest in others is directly tied to political developments. For the impact of the Haitian Revolution on German literature, see Zantop, *Colonial Fantasies,* chapter 8.

the "growing enlightenment" [*wachsende Aufklärung*] and the emancipation of Jews and black slaves on the first pages of "On the Nature of the African Negroes, and the Subsequent Liberation or Subjection of Blacks," he retracts: the revolutionary fervor has gone too far in its demand for equality – an equality that is not just "impossible" but "unjust" (386). Some people are born inferior, he maintains, and the rulers are now called upon to restore the privileges to those with inborn superiority. Meiners's list of the naturally inferior links blacks with children, women, servants, criminals, and Jews. All these must not, and cannot, he says, aspire to equality with their natural superiors, the white male Christian masters. Clearly, racial difference becomes a metaphor for other power differentials. The supremacy of whites is premised on patriarchy and the alleged natural superiority of the white "race." In Meiners's wishful thinking, any challenge to the domestic and international power structure is "un-natural."

In the subsequent seventy pages of the article, Meiners sets out to "prove" the Africans' "natural predisposition to slavery" (436) by resorting to the analogy between blacks and animals introduced in 1785 by the anatomist Samuel Thomas Sömmerring. Sömmerring's observation about similarities between the jawline of a simian and an African skull serves Meiners as positive evidence and as starting point for a whole series of conjectures regarding the Africans' inborn abject racial character (430). Their insensitivity to beatings and torture, he says, their laziness, cowardice, lack of genius, tendency towards violence and treachery, their irritability, promiscuity, agility – all of which can be explained by their anatomy – require that whites exert tight control over them, Meiners concludes (419).

Meiners's sources are a few, selected travelogues, eyewitness reports of Caribbean plantation owners, and anatomical studies which he exploits for his own purposes. Theories or observations that contradict his apodictic statements are dismissed[5] on the grounds that positively described Africans cannot be "real Negroes" – they must be products of miscegenation with Arabs or Indians (441). Often, he resorts to circular reasoning to negotiate his point around opposing arguments. For example, moved by Blumenbach's caveat (directed at Sömmerring)[6] that one can-

5. See, for example, the twisted argument with which Meiners tries to counter Blumenbach's critique of Sömmerring (406-8). He admits that one cannot judge a people by one physical property alone and that one would have to examine many different specimens before making any conjectures. But since this is physically impossible (407), he has to resort to (selected) eyewitness reports by others, all of which support his contentions.
6. The anthropologist/physician Johann Friedrich Blumenbach also taught at Göttingen. Sömmerring, who worked in Mainz, responded to Blumenbach's cautionary note in the introduction to the second edition of his "Über die körperliche Verschiedenheit."

not deduce moral character from physical properties, Meiners seemingly dismantles, then rebuilds his own position:

> I am not, by any means, adducing the verdicts of the common spirit of observation and of common sense concerning the significance of certain physical characteristics as evidence that the Negroes must be as limited in understanding and inferior in good nature as they are ugly; I merely bring it up in order to show that it is not altogether novel or unheard-of to consider certain general and uniform formations or malformations of entire peoples not merely fortuitous and immaterial matters (408).

He then returns to his original position on natural inferiority, supporting it now not with observations of physical properties, but with observations of cultural differences:

> But even if we had no idea that the Negroes are uglier in body and countenance than the Europeans, and that they have smaller skulls, a smaller and less pliant brain and coarser nerves than these, we *would still be bound to conclude from their entire mode of living and acting* that Negroes are significantly less sensitive and more irritable than whites (409, emphasis added).

Although circular reasoning, frequent internal contradictions,[7] and incessant repetitions disqualify the text in the eyes of any critical reader, these very stylistic strategies enhance its pernicious impact on the general public. Under the guise of science, Meiners reintroduces and reaffirms handed-down observations (often taken out of context), which he constructs into a system of mutually reinforcing racial stereotypes. With rhetorical tricks he manipulates his readers into accepting this construction as truth. The many footnotes and the seeming openness to debate lend scientific credibility and legitimacy to the enterprise, as do references to respected scholars such as Sömmerring, Blumenbach, and Herder. The repetitions and causal/associative chain that link one physical property to all others – physical, moral, aesthetic, and intellectual alike – create an avalanche of determinacy or inevitability. Even on the rhetorical plane, anatomy becomes destiny. After having been repeated over and over again, in one or another constellation, any conjecture turns imperceptibly into "fact." The initial observation of a similarity of jawlines is used as the foundation for a whole host of analogies with the animal world that assign the African a position not just of inferiority but

---

7. In one instance, Meiners talks about the Africans' lack of fear of death (411); in another, he speaks about their fear of death (417); in one, he affirms the women's lack of motherly love for their offspring – they even eat their children (437) – in another; he claims that their often observed motherly love, a natural instinct, associates them with animals (453).

of natural service, as beast of burden, to "humans," that is, white Europeans. The purpose of Meiners's rhetorical tour de force is apparent in the questions and answers with which he closes his article:

> Before I continue, I ask those who know mankind and advocate justice whether they believe that such insensitive, excitable and phlegmatic, dumb and evil-minded people as the Negroes should be given such rights and such liberty, for their own good and that of others; that one could entice them with such goals to do good, and keep them under threat of punishment from doing bad; and that one could impose the same duties on them as on Europeans? I would be surprised if there was even one among my readers who would answer this question differently from the way in which all European nations who own slaves and who have slave legislation have answered it. (456)

A similar rhetorical appeal to the public's judgment opens the article on the nature of the American Indians. Here Meiners is even more defensive and cautious. He does not want to create the impression, he says, that he is out to manipulate his audience. The final decision about the truth of his proposition is up to the readers, he concedes (103) – a proposition that, again, claims to prove "natural" inferiority scientifically.

His first major point addresses the supposed physical uniformity of all Indians. Any observable differences are subsumed into a unified picture of the American: "he" is small or medium-sized; has a weak, plump body, big "shapeless" head, a flat narrow forehead, small eyes, high cheekbones, straight, coarse hair, no beard, and hands that are "either too small or too large" (114). Either way, he exceeds normalcy, that is, European norms established by Meiners.

This exterior supposedly matches and reveals the Americans' inner qualities. The characteristics that Meiners stresses correspond almost verbatim to those he claims to have discovered among Africans: an insensitivity to pain that "almost" surpasses the insensitivity of European domestic animals or of blacks (114); a high irritability based on weakness that "almost surpasses that of sickly children and hysterical women among the white peoples" (117); a taciturn, melancholy, suicidal personality (116); the ability to ape European customs without understanding them (118); a natural phlegm when it comes to working for Europeans (122), and so forth. On the positive side, Meiners registers the Indians' agility, manual dexterity, physical endurance, sharpness of senses and acuteness of memory. While Indians may not be able to serve as slaves because of their physical weakness, they might be useful as scouts or as artisans (130), he implies. The red thread in this wholesale condemnation of Native Americans is the insistence on their evasive tactics:

they refuse to be trained, used, abused. They do not reveal their secrets, nor do they obey: they dodge or withdraw. The ultimate sign of their "immense imbecility" is, Meiners asserts, that unlike Blacks or Southern Asians, they do not recognize the superiority of the Europeans ... (154).

As the two articles on Africans and Indians indicate, Meiners's characterizations of these colonized peoples are solely guided by considerations of their economic use value to Europeans. After having established the natural and permanent inferiority of both "races" vis-à-vis the European "race," and, implicitly, the right of the latter to use and abuse the former, he focuses exclusively on supposed physical, mental, or moral characteristics that serve or impede colonial exploitation. The Africans' superior physical strength and resilience "predestine" them to menial work, while their resistance to forced labor and "insensitivity" to corporeal punishment require ever greater brutality to keep them at bay. The physical weakness of the Americans disqualifies them as slaves, but their agility and dexterity, superior hunting and tracking skills "predestine" them to serve whites as guides, scouts, or workers in manufacture. Their resistance, Meiners suggests, has to be met not so much with brutal punishment – the Indians would just die from melancholy – but with greater cunning, for "all Europeans" know that "the more you are on your guard, the kinder and more willing the Americans are to serve you" (156).

Meiners's articles are all designed to naturalize colonial rule as the right of the racially superior and to legitimize the violent repression of resistance to European dominion. The colonial powers cannot grant emancipation to Indians, blacks, and other peoples, he reasons, because these are biologically incapable of being free – and if they try to emancipate on their own, colonizers must hold them back by force. The theories are thus clearly self-serving: *Weltweisheit,* world wisdom, becomes the handmaiden of *Weltherrschaft,* world dominion.

Meiners's insistence on racial difference and brutally enforced hierarchies raises a number of questions: Why would a well-established professor in Göttingen in 1790 come up with a justification for colonialism? What is the "German" interest in race theories – when Germany is neither a nation nor a colonizer, nor has any business with Africans or Native Americans? Do the few German planters in the Caribbean need Meiners's ideological backing? Is it European solidarity that moves him? Is he cozying up to the colonial powers in the hope that Germany, one day, will be given a piece of the pie? Or are there other motives? The next series of articles on race, published in 1791 and 1792, provides us with some tentative answers.[8]

8. Again, the transitions are flowing: Late in 1790, Meiners already began his series on European peoples with "Ueber die Natur der Slawischen Völker in Europa," which he

While the former articles concentrated on the colonies, Meiners now focuses his attention on Europe, northern Europe, to be more precise. In his earlier articles on peoples of color he had considered first of all size, then strength, and finally skin color as the principal markers of difference. Now it is hair, then skin color, then size that distinguish the beautiful from the ugly: "On the Growth of Hair and Beards among the Ugly and Dark-Skinned Peoples," "On the Colors and Shades of Different Peoples," "On the Differences in Size Among Different Peoples." The presence of a beard serves above all as an indicator of sexual, physical, moral, and cultural eminence. While all whites have beards (all, of course, except for women and children), the lack of a beard is the distinctive feature of *all* dark-skinned races (485). As history has taught us, Meiners recapitulates, the "smoothest," "weakest," and "most cowardly" of all ugly peoples, the beardless Americans, could not withstand the manly bearded beautiful Europeans (496, 502). And beards, he states, come with "better blood" (500). Blood, rather than anatomy, causes intellectual, moral, or economic differences between the races. Blood divides nations into manly and effeminate, civilized and uncivilized.

Blood causes variations in skin color, another exterior indicator of cultural superiority. Like facial hair, skin color divides the world into strong and weak, moral and immoral, hard-working and lazy (658). Yet while all Europeans are white, not all are equally white: "Lapps, Finns and some of their descendants, furthermore some herders of Hun descent living between the Danube and the Dnjeper, finally Jews, Armenians, Turks, and Gypsies" must be excluded (667) on account of their different shade – which Meiners circumscribes as "dirty-white" [*Schmutzig-weiß*] – and hence inferior physical or mental abilities. Those with the "whitest, most blooming and most delicate skin" are of Germanic stock; "they live in Northern Germany, Denmark, Sweden, Norway, Holland, Great Britain and the adjacent islands" (668). Greek women may be superior to Slavic women if we judge them by the "beauty of their countenance and even the vivacity of their color," Meiners concedes, "but rarely or never do they attain, as to delicacy and whiteness of skin, the pink cheeks of beautiful Englishwomen or German women and maidens" (668). When it comes to beards and to whiteness, blond, blue-eyed Northern Europeans are unsurpassed.

Meiners's third article in the series pushes the analogy between white, bearded, and beautiful one step further: if "tall is beautiful," it is Germany that has produced the "tallest and most beautiful" men in all of Europe

---

continued in 1791 with "Ueber die Natur der Germanischen und übrigen Celtischen Völker." The bulk of his articles on Europeans, however, appears in 1792.

and the whole world (700). By implication, small and "ugly" mountain dwellers in the German or Swiss Alps are probably not of German blood (701), nor are the Wends, Slavs, Jews, Gypsies and other "non-German" *Fremdlinge* (strangers, or foreigners, 702) living in German states.

What we can observe in these essays is thus a curious process of exclusion and narrowing down: after establishing first a European "racial" solidarity vis-à-vis all "ugly peoples" – the colonized – Meiners now differentiates among Europeans, creating a scale on which Germans, or the "Germanic type," not only excel over other Europeans, but over German "minorities" – linguistic, religious, ethnic groups on German soil, all of whom are excluded under the term *Fremdlinge*. Meiners thus creates categories for a German racial identity based on "purity of blood," and for German superiority within Europe based on supposedly superior biological, moral, and intellectual qualities.

As the final passage of "On the Difference in Size" shows, however, Meiners is not thinking of his compatriots, but of the old *Germanen,* who, "strong like oak-trees" and sustained by meat, milk and beer, lived on the rich soils and under the blue skies of the fatherland, engaging in martial arts. "Spices" and artful concoctions, he says, were as foreign to those Germans as corrupting luxuries, "lascivious books and plays" (703). Today's Germans, Meiners admits, are less tall and less strong; they have degenerated, become smaller and weaker (707), because they indulge in culinary and sexual excesses and lack physical exercise. However, what they have lost in size, they can make up through military drill. If Germans practice martial arts, Meiners prophesies, and if they educate their minds, "they will become not only richer and more enlightened, but also more powerful and invincible than ever before" (710).

The three physical properties then – dense beards, white skin, and tall size – only function in combination. Together, they convey racial superiority, unless body and mind "degenerate" [*ausarten*]. While Germans naturally excel, according to Meiners's racial hierarchy, they have to work hard to attain a position of supremacy in Europe, for there are others – the British, the Danes, the Dutch, the Scandinavians – whose racial makeup makes them natural competitors for political power. Germans can only succeed if they do not indulge, if they control their urges for physical gratification, and discipline, militarize their bodies.

As the insistence on beards and physical strength implies, Meiners's theories of racial superiority are intimately tied to a gendered conceptualization of nations: superior nations are strong, "masculine"; inferior ones "weak," effeminate. Their weakness is evident both in their response to other nations – they surrender to European conquest and colonization – and in that they permit the "rule of women" (*Geschichte des weiblichen*

Geschlechtsm 61f).[9] If, for the earlier articles, the context was the revolutionary uprisings in the colonies, in 1792 it is clearly the French Revolution and the threat of revolutionary ideas and armies that might spill across the Rhine. The description of frenzied revolutionary masses as "feminine" evident in much of the German eye-witness reports from France, and the fear of becoming "feminized" through the French "rape" of German territories seems to have preoccupied not just Meiners, but many German intellectuals of the time.[10] The remasculinization of the Germanic body that Meiners advocates thus has both an international and a domestic component: to (re)assert male prerogative over uppity "women" – within the family, within the nation, and within the "family of nations."

It is easy to dismiss Meiners's anthropological theories as reductive, shrill, absurd. And indeed, they seemed to have generated much criticism and scorn among his contemporaries, above all Georg Forster, who, in 1791, published a scathing critique of the first series of articles in the *Allgemeine Literatur-Zeitung*.[11] Yet while Forster chastises Meiners for his one-sidedness (238), arbitrariness in the interpretation of texts (238, 242), internal contradictions and circular nature of his argument (243), and lack of critical evaluation of sources (245), he also credits him with immense erudition and sharpness of mind (238), comparing him to none less than Albrecht von Haller. Similarly, Forster's father-in-law, Christian Gottlob Heyne, while ridiculing Meiners in his correspondence, continues to supply him with review assignments for the reputable *Göttingische Anzeigen von gelehrten Sachen,* thus providing him with a forum for the propagation of his racist theories. Upon Meiners's death in 1810, Heyne composes a long obituary for the Göttingen Royal Academy of Science, in which he praises, again, the vastness of Meiners's knowledge and publications, while expressing guarded reservations about his tendency to jump to false conclusions and stick to them in the face of evidence to the contrary.[12]

9. The latter reproach, although directed at distant peoples, resonates with a commonly heard critique of *ancien régime* France, according to which courtisans and *salonnières* dominated over "effeminate" men.

10. For a discussion of this overlap of metaphors, see my articles "Crossing the Boundaries" and "Dialectics and Colonialism."

11. Meiners had published a critique of Forster's *Voyage around the World* in the *Göttingische Anzeigen von gelehrten Sachen* in 1778; Forster a response in the same journal. Forster's feud with Meiners continued throughout Forster's career. See the detailed *Einführung* to the volume of reviews by Horst Fiedler, particularly 393 ff. and 415. On the recent reception of Meiners among anthropologists, see also Rupp-Eisenreich: "c'est un nom qui hante, tel un spectre, la plupart des ouvrages consacrés à l'histoire de l'ethno-anthropologie" (132).

12. "He recognized the diversity of talent and character of diverse peoples, although this diversity seemed to happen for many reasons partly known and partly unknown, natural, and ethical and political: He was drawn towards certain types of human beings

A pattern emerges: whereas many intellectuals such as Herder, Wieland, Heyne, Sömmerring, Kant, or Lichtenberg produce flippant asides against Meiners in private – Lichtenberg and Wieland go so far as to call him "Mongol Meiners" (Forster 18:453; Starnes 554)[13] – in public they refer to him with deference, as an authority, a scholar. As Herder writes to Forster on 26 December 1791: "what one cannot change, one must tolerate" (Forster 18: 482). In fact, as a professor of philosophy and comparative anthropology at the elite university of Göttingen, as a member of the Illuminati,[14] and as "Hofrat" of Great Britain and Braunschweig, the "unendurable Meiners" (Schlosser 339) enjoyed not just toleration, but public recognition (Wenzel 3-7).[15] His scholarly fame was such that Tsar Alexander asked him to organize the Russian university system. In recognition of his achievements, he became honorary member of the University of Moscow (1804), and pro-rector of his university (1805-06). His works were reprinted and widely discussed. "German" skulls appeared on anatomical tables, in direct contrast to skulls by Africans, Calmucks, Americans, and "Caribs" (Wünsch).[16] It is only fitting that the renowned anatomist Johann Friedrich Blumenbach, in his survey of contemporary theories of race, would include Meiners's bipolar division between "the handsome" and "the ugly" – "the first white, the latter dark" (268) – without so much as adding a critical word.[17]

---

who were established by nature with certain (individual) strengths of spirit and bodies and limits, where, by the law of nature, they had to confine themselves; he placed the Negroes in the lowest place from which there was no possibility of rising. Although he could be easily led in some other matters of investigation, he never allowed himself to be led from *this* judgment; no doubt he would have moved on to a truer estimation of things, if he had considered the Negroes later in life" (17-18). I wish to thank my colleague in the Classics Department, Phyllis Katz, for providing a translation of Heyne's Latin text.

13. The adoption of racist terminology even by critics of Meiners's theories is an indication of the pervasiveness of "physiognomical" discourse.

14. For his status and role among the Illuminati order, and his counterrevolutionary stance, which allied Meiners (code name "Dicearch") with Herzog Ernst II. Ludwig von Sachsen-Gotha, see Wilson 264.

15. Rupp-Eisenreich traces his influence on French anthropology and on subsequent race/culture theorists in France (Jauffret, Volney, Gobineau, Comte) and Germany (Klemm, Carus, Menzel, Oken, Mühlmann, and Egon von Eickstedt), 132-36.

16. Wünsch (1744-1828), Professor of Mathematics and Physics at Frankfurt a. d. Oder, shares many characteristics with Meiners – his autodidactic education, his delight in bizarre theories, his notoriety in academic and his popularity in middle-brow circles, and a considerable literary output.

17. As Rupp-Eisenreich points out, Blumenbach undercuts this seeming acceptance of Meiners's ideas by adding that Caucasians are more beautiful "according to *our* ideas of beauty" – while "our" suggests an awareness of positionality, it does not make the statement any less problematic.

The inclusion of Meiners into public discourse on race and his influence, perhaps not on the intellectual elite, but on the rulers and on
wider segments of society[18] may have had to do with the esteem that
university professors and *Hofräte* enjoyed in eighteenth-century Germany (and not just then). As Heyne's exasperated comments suggest,
once one was in the system, protected by powerful sponsors, one could
not be ignored. Furthermore, while his "new science" was controversial,
the ground for its (partial) acceptance had been prepared by previous
debates, particularly those surrounding the publication of Corneille de
Pauw's *Recherches philosophiques sur les Américains* (Philosophical Investigations on the Americans, 1769) in Prussia, and by the physiognomic
craze generated by Lavater's theories (Gerbi; Zantop, *Colonial Fantasies*;
Schlosser 293).[19] The division of the world into two opposed camps of
strong and weak, civilized and barbarian, progressing and decaying
nations had become a topos in cross-cultural comparisons from Buffon's
Natural History (new ed. 1769) onward; to judge humans' moral or
intellectual status by the shape of their skull or the size of their nose had
become a popular pastime. As I suggested earlier, Meiners's popularity
may, however, have had to do with the particular historical events during which his "national racism" emerged: the Haitian and the French
Revolutions. If read against this backdrop, theories that affirm the natural superiority of the white race – and the superiority of the Germanic
male to boot – can be read as compensatory *fantasies* rather than scientific conjectures: fantasies of strength in view of an attack on white dominance; fantasies of *Ausgrenzung* (exclusion) in view of physical and
metaphoric border crossings; fantasies that serve to assuage the frustration felt by many Germans in the 1790s over the fragmentation and
weakness of "the German nation." The pervasive sense of victimization
and national "impotence" among the German bourgeoisie explains the
urgency with which Meiners theorizes national remasculinization: Ger-

18. Bitterli (118) notes Meiners's popularity, yet emphatically rejects any connection
with contemporary racism or overlap with his more respectable contemporaries. Rupp-
Eisenreich, on the other hand, insists on Meiners's wide-spread acceptance, despite the
controversial nature of his writings. As the *Grande Encyclopédie de France* (1885-1902)
formulated this paradox: "Son enseignement et ses ouvrages accessibles au grand public
lui valurent une véritable et longue popularité. Mais il n'a rien laissé qui mérite de sur-
vivre" (quoted by Rupp-Eisenreich 137).

19. Meiners called his comparative cultural anthropology a "neue Wissenschaft" in
his introduction to the *Grundriß der Geschichte der Menschheit*. On the de Pauw controversy, see Gerbi and Zantop, *Colonial Fantasies*, chapter 3. Meiners frequently alludes to
that tradition when he mentions de Pauw as one of the three "great writers" (Goguet and
Montesquieu are the other two) who profoundly influenced his own work. On physiognomy as popular "science," see Schlosser (2:290 ff).

many must become a man – strong, tall, bearded – in order to rebuke its imperialist neighbor. It explains at least in part why despite all criticism, Meiners's "bafflingly modern" theories – as a critic of 1931 called them (Ihle 8) – enjoyed an underground existence throughout the nineteenth century, and why they would reemerge whenever political and/or socio-economic crises warranted national reaffirmation. Theories of the superiority of beautiful "male" Germanicity over ugly, effeminate Latin races were one way to turn the tables, if only in theoretically.

Bibliography

Appiah, Kwame Anthony. "Race." *Critical Terms for Literary Study*. Eds. Frank Lentricchia and Thomas McLaughlin. Chicago: U of Chicago P, 1990. 274-87.

Bitterli, Urs. *Die Entdeckung des schwarzen Afrikaners: Versuch einer Geistesgeschichte der europäisch-afrikanischen Beziehungen an der Guineaküste im 17. und 18. Jahrhundert*. Zürich: Atlantis, 1970.

Blumenbach, Johann Friedrich. "On the Natural Variety of Mankind." *The Anthropological Treatises of Johann Friedrich Blumenbach*. Trans. Thomas Bendyshe. London: Longman, 1865.

Curtin, Philipp D. *The Image of Africa: British Ideas and Action, 1780-1850*. Madison: U of Wisconsin P, 1964.

Forster, Georg. "Göttingisches historisches Magazin, von C. Meiners und L. T. Spittler. Vols. 4-7." *Georg Forsters Werke*. Berlin: Akademie, 1977. 11: 236-52.

Frank, G. "Christian Ernst Wünsch." *Allgemeine Deutsche Biographie*. Leipzig: Duncker & Humblot, 1898. 44: 317-20.

Gates, Henry Louis. "Writing 'Race' and the Difference It Makes." *Critical Inquiry* 12.1 (Autumn 1985): 1-20.

Gerbi, Antonello. *The Dispute of the New World* (1955). Rev. and enl. ed.. Trans. Jeremy Moyle. Pittsburgh: U of Pittsburgh P, 1973.

Gilman, Sander. *On Blackness without Blacks: Essays on the Image of the Black in Germany*. Boston: Hall, 1982.

Heyne, Christian Gottlob. "Memoria Christophori Meiners Collegae et Sodalis Soc. R. Sc. Gott." *Commentationes societatis regiae scientiarum gottingensis recentiores*. Göttingen, 1808-1811. 3-18.

Ihle, Alexander. *Christoph Meiners und die Völkerkunde*. Göttingen: Vandenhoek & Ruprecht, 1931.

Johnston, Otto W. *The Myth of a Nation: Literature and Politics in Prussia under Napoleon.* Columbia, S. C.: Camden House, 1989.

Kamen, Henry. "America and its impact on racial attitudes and 'blood purity'." Presentation at the 1991 "Conference on America in European Consciousness" (John Carter Brown Library), unpublished manuscript.

Lennox, Sara, Sara Friedrichsmeyer, and Susanne Zantop, eds. *The Imperialist Imagination: German Colonialism and Its Legacy* (forthcoming)

McClintock, Anne. *Imperial Leather: Race, Gender and Sexuality in the Colonial Contest.* New York: Routledge, 1995.

Meiners, Christoph. *Geschichte des weiblichen Geschlechts.* 2 vols. Hannover: Helwing, 1788.

———. *Grundriß der Geschichte der Menschheit..* Lemgo: Meyer, 1786.

———. "Historische Nachrichten über die wahre Beschaffenheit des Sclaven-Handels, und der Knechtschaft der Neger in West-Indien." *Göttingisches historisches Magazin* 6 (1790): 645-79.

———. "Ueber die Farben und Schattierungen verschiedener Völker." *Neues GHM* I (1792): 611-72.

———. "Ueber den Haar- und Bartwuchs der häßlichen und dunkelfarbigen Völker." *NGHM* I (1792): 484-508.

———. "Ueber die Natur der Afrikanischen Neger, und die davon abhangende Befreyung, oder Einschränkung der Schwarzen." *GHM* 6 (1790): 385-456.

———. "Ueber die Natur der Americaner." *GHM* 6 (1790): 102-56.

———. "Ueber die Natur der Germanischen und übrigen Celtischen Völker." *GHM* 8 (1791): 1-48 and 67-124.

———. "Ueber die Verschiedenheit der cörperlichen Größe verschiedener Völker." *NGHM* I (1792): 697-762.

———. "Von den Varietäten und Abarten der Neger." *GHM* 6 (1790): 625-45.

Mielke, Andreas. *Laokoon und die Hottentotten: Oder über die Grenzen von Reisebeschreibung und Satire.* Baden-Baden: Koerner, 1993.

Mosse, George. *Nationalism and Sexuality: Respectability and Abnormal Sexuality in Modern Europe.* New York: Fertig, 1985.

Prantl. "Christoph Meiners." *Allgemeine Deutsche Biographie (ADB).* Leipzig: Duncker & Humblot, 1898. 21: 224-26.

Rupp-Eisenreich, Britta. "Choses occultes en histoire des sciences humaines: le destin de la 'science nouvelle' de Christoph Meiners." *Ethnographie* 90-91 (1983): 131-83.

Schlosser, F. C. *History of the Eighteenth Century and of the Nineteenth Till the Overthrow of the French Empire.* 2 vols. Trans. D. Davison. London: Chapman and Hall, 1844.

Sömmerring, Samuel Thomas. *Über die körperliche Verschiedenheit des Mohren vom Europäer* (1784); 2nd. ed.: *Über die körperliche Verschiedenheit des Negers vom Europäer.* Frankfurt a. M., Mainz: Varrentrapp, 1785.

Starnes, Thomas. *C. M. Wieland, Leben und Werk.* Sigmaringen: Thorbecke, 1987.

Wenzel, Herbert. *Christoph Meiners als Religionshistoriker.* Diss. Tübingen, 1917.

Wilson, W. Daniel. *Geheimräte gegen Geheimbünde: Ein unbekanntes Kapitel der klassisch-romantischen Geschichte Weimars.* Stuttgart: Metzler, 1991.

Wünsch, Christian. *Unterhaltungen über den Menschen.* 2 vols. Leipzig: Breitkopf, 1796.

Young, Robert. *Colonial Desire: Hybridity in Theory, Culture and Race.* New York: Routledge, 1995.

Zantop, Susanne. *Colonial Fantasies: Conquest, Family, and Nation in Precolonial Germany, 1770-1870.* Durham: Duke UP, 1997.

_____. "Crossing the Boundaries: The French Revolution in the German Literary Imagination." *Representing Revolution: Essays on Reflections of the French Revolution in Literature, Historiography, and Art.* Ed. James Heffernan. Hanover: UP of New England 1992. 213-33.

_____. "Dialectics and Colonialism: The Underside of the Enlightenment." In *Impure Reason: Dialectic of Enlightenment in Germany.* Ed. W. Daniel Wilson and Robert C. Holub. Detroit: Wayne State UP, 1994. 301-21.

Chapter 2

SOPHIE LA ROCHE AS A GERMAN PATRIOT

Helga Schutte Watt

In an essay on the marginal position of German women writers, Ruth Klüger asks what kind of social and intellectual conditions helped a few women develop independent thinking and become creative when their culture was determined to keep them from any ambition outside of the traditional role of subservient wife and selfless mother. She finds that productive women typically came from different social backgrounds than productive men. While Martin Luther's Protestantism created the mental space where middle-class men could develop their minds, it did not provide the same benefits for aristocrats and women. Klüger explains that advances for "mankind" did not necessarily mean advances for women and that creative women found special niches in times and places that may appear "reactionary" to scholarship centered on the male experience. This paradox can help us understand an eighteenth-century woman's perspective on patriotism.

Sophie La Roche (1730-1807) carved out her identity as a writer between the social, political, and religious factions of her day. In numerous novels, short stories, essays, travelogues and memoirs, she endeavored to broaden the mental horizons of women within the limits of an established gender-based protocol. This apparent compliance with the rules of her society allowed her to be published, thereby achieving more freedom for herself while educating her female readers. La Roche's evolving patriotic commitment to German culture, which she shared with many contemporary male writers, confronted her with another dilemma:

she saw the cause of patriotism in conflict with the striving for self-realization of women. She could not resolve this tension without breaching the ideal of German women voluntarily sacrificing personal independence to support their families and fatherland.

An adherent of the Enlightenment, La Roche was influenced by French, English, and German writers and thus schooled in a broader European cultural context. The books she read, her international correspondence, and her own travels abroad gave her a European, even cosmopolitan outlook, but she was also a German patriot, proud of her cultural heritage and committed to advancing the welfare of the German states, which then comprised the Holy Roman Empire. Her German identity becomes most apparent in her reaction to France in the period before and after the French Revolution of 1789.

Scholars have traced the genesis of a German consciousness, i.e., the examination and affirmation of a separate language-based cultural identity, back to the humanists of the late fifteenth century (Dörner 130 f.), describing a process which intensified in the second half of the eighteenth century and culminated in Klopstock, the poets of the Storm and Stress and the Göttinger Hain.[1] The scholarship, however, deals only with the patriotic sentiments of male writers. While La Roche had less influence on public opinion than Klopstock or Herder, her comments on the political events of her time reveal the perspective of a well-read, mature woman.

The daughter of a Protestant physician who later became dean of the medical school in Augsburg, La Roche grew up in Upper Swabia, moving from Kaufbeuren to Lindau, Biberach, and Augsburg. She remained proud of the republican traditions of the free imperial cities of that region (e.g., Biberach and Augsburg), perceiving in them a pale image of the greater freedom she would discover on journeys to Switzerland and Holland. At the age of seventeen, she became engaged to a Catholic physician, an Italian who did not speak German. She conversed with him in French and learned Italian from him. Her father broke this engagement, very much against her own wishes, because of a dispute over the religious affiliation of any future children. Her second fiancé was her cousin, the later famous writer Christoph Martin Wieland, who in the distant future would edit her first novel. In 1753 she broke their increasingly awkward engagement, in order to marry Frank La Roche, the protégé (possibly the natural son) of a prominent reform-minded Catholic diplomat, Count Friedrich von Stadion. Her husband and five children were Catholic – this time her father did not impose any condi-

---

1. See Fischer 54-130.

tions – while she remained Protestant. Repeated moves, two broken engagements, religious confrontation and accommodation – the early life of this future writer was certainly not quietly conventional.

For the next twenty-seven years, La Roche supported her husband in his career, first with Count Stadion at the court of Kur-Mainz, then at Stadion's residence at Warthausen (near Biberach). From 1770 to 1780 (after the count's death), Frank La Roche held increasingly important positions in the service of the prince bishop of Kur-Trier who resided at Koblenz-Ehrenbreitstein. Kur-Mainz and Kur-Trier were the seats of Catholic governments; their prince-bishops were *Kurfürsten*, i.e., electors of the emperor. It cannot have been easy for the Protestant commoner La Roche to adjust to this aristocratic and Catholic environment, where she had to be careful about what she said and how she acted. Her husband was widely admired for his administrative and diplomatic skills, as well as for his progressive views; in 1775 Emperor Joseph II raised him to the nobility, and in 1778 the prince bishop named him chancellor of Kur-Trier. Within two years, however, a conservative Catholic backlash caused his sudden dismissal from office, reducing the family to very modest means. This change in fortune ended Sophie La Roche's social obligations; she was at last able to devote herself almost entirely to her literary activities, and she began to count on her income as a writer. After her husband's death in 1788, she had even fewer resources; in 1794 she lost her small widow's pension in the turmoil following the French Revolution.

In addition to contending with different religions and social classes, La Roche also lived between languages. For her first novel, published when she was forty years old, she had to learn to write in German because, before this time, most of her correspondence, as well as some unpublished short stories, had been composed in French. Her Swabian dialect did not make the transition to an increasingly standardized literary German any easier, but La Roche wanted to be more "German."

In the eighteenth century, the German Empire, also known as the Holy Roman Empire of the German Nation, consisted of more than 300 principalities and had no national or cultural center. Protestant Prussia and Catholic Austria were the leading states, but while La Roche admired Frederick the Great and Joseph II, she was neither Prussian nor Austrian. She considered herself German, a tradition based on German culture and language. Friedrich Carl von Moser summarized the idea of the German nation in his work, *Von dem Deutschen Nationalgeist* (On the German National Spirit, 1766): "We are one people, of one name and language, under a common leader, subject to the universal laws which determine our Constitution, and connected by a great common interest in liberty" (5 f.). Moser lamented the dismal state of the empire and urged his compatriots to put the nation ahead of particularistic interests. Irmtraud Sahmland describes the impact of this book and similar works, concluding: "Patriotism is recognized as a means to effect a feeling of connectedness among Germans, to produce a unity even if it is limited to mentality and ideas" (125). La Roche attempted to contribute to a German mentality, partly modeled on the supposedly related English culture, when she created her most famous literary character, Sophie von Sternheim.

* * *

Her first novel, *Geschichte des Fräuleins von Sternheim* (*History of Lady Sophia Sternheim,* 1771), demonstrates an incipient pride in German literature and a move away from French influences. In one scene La Roche contrasts a noble German writer (a thinly disguised Wieland) with a minor French author who is, however, preferred by the German nobility. The Frenchman is characterized as a lackey of the rich and powerful; he entertains his audience with Parisian gossip and compliments his hostess on her person and soul which he declares to be "not at all German" (117).[2] The distinguished German writer, who admires "France's great sons," treats this fool with courtesy while Sophie von Sternheim is offended by the little man's vanity and the shallow minds of those who listen to him. Her own partly English ancestry contributes to a decided preference for that language and culture.

The heroine, an orphan, describes her life at the court of a small German principality, simply referred to as "D." Ruthless aristocratic relatives have brought her here and expect to gain personal advantage by offering her as a mistress to the weak and immoral ruler of this state. Her aunt criticizes Sternheim's professed love for Germany: since patriotism is identified with the educated middle class, the heroine's sentiments reveal that she is the granddaughter of a professor. Sternheim is happy whenever she can escape the artificial life at court. On one of her outings, she gives us a sympathetic description of poor rural Germany: "The road we traveled showed me much of our German countryside, sometimes consisting of a rough, niggardly piece of land that was patiently cultivated by its suffering, emaciated inhabitants with their bare hands" (90). One observer attempts to separate Sternheim's English and German traits: "A charming seriousness in her face, a noble, well-bred courtesy in her expressions, the utmost tenderness toward her friend, a kindness worthy

---

2. Quotes for *Sternheim* from the English translation by Britt.

of reverent admiration, and the most delicate sensibility of soul. Is not this the greatness of the English inheritance from her grandmother?" (95). On the German side he lists the following qualities: "She has a mind adorned with learning and proper concepts and without the slightest prejudice, the courage of a man in averring and defending her principles, and many talents combined with the most engaging modesty" (95). We note delicate sentiments on the English and moral courage, a supposedly male quality, on the German side. Lack of prejudice, also defined as admiration for foreign countries, will return as typically German in later works. This novel takes us from Germany to England and Scotland; there is a faint stirring of German patriotism and some anti-French sentiment associated with life at the German court in D.; the heroine's bitter experience with a villainous lord temper her original passion for England.

Sternheim provided her author with sudden fame and adulation. For a few years, La Roche's home became a magnet for young writers, including Goethe, the Jacobi brothers, Johann Heinrich Merck, and J.M.R. Lenz. This exposure had an effect on her self-image and sense of mission. During the 1770s anti-French sentiment and German patriotism became more evident in young writers, culminating in the Göttinger Hain's glorification of "the bard" Klopstock and condemnation of Wieland as a Francophile and lascivious disciple of Voltaire.[3] Inspired by her young admirers and increasingly distanced from Wieland, La Roche adopted a distinctly more German tone.

Her second novel, *Rosaliens Briefe an ihre Freundin Mariane von St.* (Rosalie's Letters to her Friend Mariane von St., 1779-1781), features a middle-class German heroine. Rosalie and her friends "carefully avoid the use of foreign words" and "like to be entirely German" (3: 169). This heroine also has a social conscience, giving us a sympathetic description of the poverty in rural Germany reminiscent of the passage cited from *Sternheim*. Rosalie writes not only of poor soil, but also of grief and poverty caused by little despots, "since wilted cheeks show the cares of the women, and down-cast, ill-humored expressions show the hard life of the men as clearly as their dilapidated dwellings and miserable garments" (1: 17).

Ursula Naumann justly claims that "despotism, the great subject of the political writers of the Enlightenment, is the central grievance ... in Sophie La Roche's work" (497). While in *Rosalie* most of this despotism is exercised in personal relationships, especially by men over women, La Roche is also concerned with its political and social manifestations. The

---

3. See Sahmland, who argues that Wieland only became a patriot in the late 1780s and 1790s (170).

"domestic despot" (3: 87) makes life difficult for his wife, while despotic princes are directly responsible for the miserable living conditions of their subjects.

This novel focuses on the middle class, how it can better itself and contribute to the well-being of the country as a whole. We see model administrators conscientiously serving the interests of their masters as well as of the clerks, laborers, craftsmen, and farmers in their charge. But La Roche also keeps larger cultural issues in mind. Thus she addresses what she perceives as a national weakness, a lack of proper self-respect and a tendency toward slavish imitation of French customs and fashions. She deplores how Germans emulate the French in little things rather than learn from what is truly superior, such as respect for good craftsmen and artisans. The French enjoy products of higher quality and better design than those made in Germany. Their centralized government and culture give them many advantages: "They feel that they are one. For us the time when we enjoyed this blissful feeling is long gone. Germany! Oh, what can the most beautiful and grandest amount to when it has been torn into pieces and then patched together in a haphazard fashion" (1: 449). Here La Roche exhibits nostalgia for the time before the Thirty Year's War. Since Germany's glory is supposed to lie in the past, inherited customs, old-fashioned clothing and furnishings are valued and old German virtues recalled. For men German virtues comprise seriousness, honesty, and valor although "a zeal for justice and the welfare of humanity" gives contemporary German men the reputation of being querulous, violent, and obstinate (3: 265). For German women traditional virtues mean frugality, marital devotion, and good housekeeping skills: "The limited number of dishes at the noon and evening meals, the frankness with which we show our love for our husbands, the modest pride and zeal with which we conduct our housekeeping tasks are German" (1: 169). That German housewives excel over their European sisters is a common perception, also advanced by Herder: "Housewifely activity, sexual purity, faithfulness, and honor have been distinctive traits of the female gender in all German tribes and nations" (4: 419 f.). Rosalie's husband, Cleberg, explains why she makes him happy:

> Because you are a German wife, because in addition to the shining qualities which would grace a French, English, or Italian woman, you know what our men's cloth coats, your taffeta skirts and linens consist of; you know that cotton is not made, wine not brewed, and paper not woven; you can teach your cook how to make soup, bake bread and cakes, how to roast meat and prepare vegetables; your home is more important to you than anything else; you like to please me; you take care that I never see you unkempt, unclean, or unattractive; you can sew, knit, embroider, and even mend (3: 81 f.).

The shining qualities – Cleberg is probably referring to Rosalie's accomplishments in music, drawing, and languages – are not enumerated, only the skills required for running an efficient household. This super-house-wife has to worry about the impression she makes on her husband: she cannot ever afford to show distress, fatigue or the dishevelment caused by hard work, but must be sure to please him at all times. Rosalie is fortunate to want to do of her own accord what her demanding husband expects. A witty and unconventional woman friend, however, frequently mocks Cleberg and men in general for being tyrannical and presumptuous. Rosalie likes and respects this woman, but she herself does not challenge the wishes of the men in her life. La Roche thus allows questioning of male authority and cheerful compliance to stand side by side, a typical example of her ambivalent messages. She recommends to German women the learning and achievements more commonly found in France and England, but not at a cost to their domestic virtues.

Rosaliens Briefe introduces us to a circle of congenial families living in the countryside and improving their immediate environment. While this may suggest a withdrawal from the larger society and its problems, the friends also discuss what could be achieved beyond their own domain. Public schools are recommended over private tutoring to cultivate general taste and thus raise the level of arts and crafts. For girls there would be public sewing schools to teach domestic skills, but all the schools would nurture a patriotic spirit in both sexes (3: 325). There are dreams of a better national future: "Perhaps a ruler over the greatest part of our motherly land will arise from royal German blood; inspired by a patriotic spirit, he will examine and sift customs and mores. Then the chaff and all that is mere ape-like imitation will be discarded; a particular mode of dress may even be introduced" (1: 458). If Germans, like the French and British, would prefer and improve their own products and way of life, then they could achieve a happiness of their own. German women are advised to dress tastefully and to follow foreign fashions with moderation. As it is, fewer German men can afford to get married because of the increased costs of supporting a family in the expected style influenced by France. The author finds a fitting image for the high cost of foreign imports: "We burn half a German forest to have a few sickly foreign plants in our green houses" (1: 459).

Characteristically, La Roche combines anti-French sentiments with criticism of the aristocracy, contrasting the artificial and constrained French world with English ideals of noble simplicity, natural grace, and increased social mobility. Despite its German tone, this novel also aims to further international connections and understanding. One friend prefers the French mode; another favors English customs; Rosalie herself is happily German, but her home displays artwork from England, France, Italy, and Germany. Germans, La Roche suggests, should value what other nations have produced without, however, loosing sight of their own heritage.

From 1783 to 1784 La Roche published a journal for women, *Pomona für Teutschlands Töchter* (Pomona for Germany's Daughters). Pomona is the goddess of the harvest – the author/editor was then in her fifties – and the rest of the title indicates the ambitious goals of her enterprise: the education of young women as good housewives and intelligent companions to their husbands, but also as citizens of Germany and Europe. La Roche publishes articles on France, England, Italy, and Germany that emphasize the accomplishments of outstanding women. For Germany, she needs to rely heavily on representatives of the aristocracy, although she had asked her learned correspondents for suggestions. One explanation she offers for the apparently smaller number of talented German women is that they are modest and embarrassed by public praise. She generalizes that German women do more for others while their sisters abroad know more. Ultimately, she holds men responsible: in England and France they have a higher regard for their wives and daughters than in Germany.

La Roche teaches respect for foreign merit, but she also lets her compatriots appreciate their own strengths and weaknesses. Germans tend to be industrious and eager to learn; they recognize the worth of other countries. This virtue, however, has a negative corollary: "No other nation has this degree of complaisance and self-degradation as we do" (1: 729). She believes that Germany is now one of the great nations of Europe: "The genius of her scientists, merchants, and artists has risen to the same height as that of other nations, and since Frederick of Prussia, they surpass all others in the art of war" (1: 838), a superiority that turned out to be a highly problematic asset in the course of the nineteenth and twentieth centuries. Her apparent endorsement of militarism here conflicts with the abhorrence of war expressed in her late novels.

In her efforts to raise the appreciation for literature among her readers, La Roche publishes excerpts from James Thomson's *Seasons* and then has to defend herself against charges of Anglophilia. Since her critics are learned men, she comes up with a clever response: men form their minds according to Greek and Roman models; they study dead languages and imitate dead civilizations while she tries to learn from what is superior in a related living people (1: 836). In a letter of 12 July 1783, Gottlieb Pfeffel of Strasbourg claims to speak for several men in advising her to be more German. He is worried about the effect that idealized English heroes and customs might make on impressionable female minds: "For the noble La Roche it would be a worthy task to collect the basic traits of the German character, to cleanse it of all excesses due to Francomania and Anglomania, and to present the German beauties with German ideals of both sexes" (Hassencamp 493 f.). In thus urging her to create a national taste and to hide or naturalize anything borrowed from abroad, Pfeffel, however, also reveals how highly he estimated La Roche's influence on her readers.

Pomona is open to the world, but written for German women with hopes of a better German future, inspired by Joseph II. La Roche admires the emperor's reforms in Austria and wishes his example to move other German states toward greater religious tolerance, improved order and industry, and simple taste in clothing, thereby awakening the noble patriotism Germans used to have (1: 837). Again she suggests that men choose a national costume to further a national mentality (1: 839) and that women return to the simple dress and high-minded morality of former days: "Demeanor and clothing without artifice should even now distinguish from all others the women of a nation once respected abroad for the brave courage and honesty of its men and the charming modesty of its women" (2: 918).

In her articles on France and England, La Roche attempts to bring German women closer to French and English models, such as Mme. de Sevigné, Mme. de Lambert, Lady Mary Wortley Montagu, and Fanny Burney. However, she still finds virtue in contentment and modesty, even asserting that her female compatriots deserve praise for voluntarily accepting their second-class status (1: 931). Here she gets caught in the contradiction posed by her desire for greater emancipation and the perceived need to remain within the acceptable limits set by her culture. If she wants to accomplish anything at all, she must not go too far. We are reminded of the gentle Rosalie, who represents an ideal German woman, but is, nonetheless, supportive of her women friends who transgress against the conventions of their society. La Roche's heroines, with minds of their own and determination to match, tend to identify themselves as English; the choices for German women appear much more limited.

* * *

Although many German writers admired the first stage of the French Revolution and saw in it some hope for Germany, La Roche could not sympathize with violence, regicide, and rule by terror. She did, however, have several friends among enthusiastic democrats: Georg Forster in Mainz, Gottlieb Pfeffel in Strasbourg and Georg Wilhelm Petersen in Speyer. In June of 1791 she wrote to a friend: "I was in Mainz, stayed with democrats and spent the days in the home of the von Steinbergs [aristocrats]. Something ominous is happening in our Germany, and the behavior of our courts leads me to believe that Divine Providence wants a change; the courts must act as though they are deaf and blind to bring about this change all the sooner, otherwise this behavior does not make any sense" (*Ich bin mehr Herz als Kopf,* 328 f.). La Roche felt caught between opposing factions. This statement, addressed to a countess, is less indicative of her religious views than of her impatience with despotism. Opposed to any violent change, she fears that the German princes and their entourage may be provoking the populace through stupidity and arrogance. She is not deaf and blind to the occurrences around her and attempts to learn all she can about the latest events and discussions in France.

The French Revolution provides the background for two novels, *Schönes Bild der Resignation* (Beautiful Image of Resignation, 1795-1796) and *Erscheinungen am See Oneida* (Phenomena at Lake Oneida, 1798), both written from the perspective of victims or opponents of the Revolution. In the first novel, a young English aristocrat travels to France because he is inspired by the royalist rebellion in the Vendée of 1793. He describes the life of a virtuous French countess who has found refuge with her former servants while her husband has fled abroad. This lady educates her son and does embroidery to obtain some income, demonstrating that true nobility resides more in the soul than in the title. The Englishman conquers his passion for this woman and leaves France for Germany. Here he admires Baden, where a wise prince has created a model state. "If it were possible for Englishmen to wish to have another country, they would choose Baden" (2: 222), an indication of La Roche's endorsement of reforms from above. The protagonist's parting wish summarizes her patriotic sentiments of that time: "May Germany soon be freed from the misery and ruin that the New Franks brought to a great number of her inhabitants. For all of them I wish the old national spirit of valor and fidelity, which inspired Hermann's sons at all times and through great men made them into a glorious and honored nation, giving them Leibniz and Frederick the one and only" (2: 228).[4] The message of the novel is anti-Revolution, but not anti-French.

In *Erscheinungen am See Oneida*, a young man and his wife, both aristocrats, escaped from persecution in France to live on a deserted island in upstate New York, supporting themselves with their own labor. About to give birth, the heroine seeks the help of kindly native American women,

4. Hermann refers to Arminius, who defeated the Romans in A.D. 9. There were several literary works by eighteenth-century writers about this "German" hero (who became a symbol for German patriots), including a fragmentary epic by Wieland and three plays by Klopstock. See Dörner.

while her husband listens to a noble brave relate his encounters with cruel white men. Eventually they join a new democratic community, which also shelters a Dutchman who left Europe to escape the tyranny of princes. The German narrator wonders how the horrors of the French Revolution could have been perpetrated by the most civilized nation in Europe (3: 28).[5] He states that it took Europeans many centuries to achieve civilization, but that the French Revolution destroyed all that had been won to arrive at a bestiality unknown to the American Indians (2: 163). Injured pride and lust for revenge made former members of the third estate applaud cruelty instead of feeling pity for the victims. "This unfortunate spirit of proud self-love transformed half of the otherwise charming inhabitants of France into unfeeling tigers" (3: 110). La Roche often refers to the carefree attitude or native recklessness of the French and implies that this makes them more vulnerable to evil passions.

The more upset she becomes with events on the continent, the more she turns to England, wanting at times to read only English books. In 1798 she writes to a friend: "Oh God! What a sight! Prostrated Germany being kicked around! But I am a sentimental old fool to speak of Germany as one; since that most barbaric and inhumane of all treaties, the Westfalian Peace, Germany does not exist anymore" (*Ich bin mehr Herz als Kopf*, 370). La Roche seems to have forgotten about her former dissatisfaction with political and social conditions in the German states; now she tends to idealize the time before the Revolution, especially the reign of Frederick the Great, envying those family members and friends who did not live to see the cruel present. In *Mein Schreibetisch* (My Desk, 1799), she expresses renewed optimism when she reports on efforts to collect the remnants of Northern mythology, another supposed link to a glorified German past: "Good men hope to rekindle the almost extinguished old German spirit by reviving these genuinely German ideas and images" (2: 136). Like most of her compatriots, she is extending the term "German" into times and places where one could at best speak of various Germanic tribes.

* * *

Michael Maurer emphasizes that La Roche's knowledge of history and her political consciousness were rare for a woman of her time (131). He claims that her German patriotism and Francophobia increased with the course of the French Revolution (136) and places her somewhere on

---

5. In her letters La Roche sometimes refers to the French armies as "Frankenhorden." Friedrich Leopold von Stolberg went further by calling the French "Westhunnen" (Fink 114).

the spectrum between reformist and reactionary conservatives (148 f.). Monica Nenon, on the other hand, stresses La Roche's critical and reformist thinking in an article on her political stance (159). Advocacy of a constitutional monarchy for France and reforms from above for Germany does not make La Roche any more conservative than the majority of German writers of the time. She condemns despotism, but she counsels patience to its victims, believing that different social classes are necessary, that each has its own merits and advantages, and that the poor and oppressed should try to be content with their lot.

When La Roche needs models for the advancement of women, she usually turns to women abroad. She makes her readers aware of French, English, Italian, and other outstanding women of the past and present; in a spirit of international sisterhood, she recommends their books and their example. When it comes to German patriotism, however, La Roche expects leadership from German men. If they determine what should be done, German women will do their part and even be content with their inferior status. In her travelogues La Roche states repeatedly that she considers politics a male domain, although she herself clearly has political interests and opinions. She abhors violence and war, which she also considers part of the male sphere. Thus she declares in *Briefe über Mannheim* (Letters about Mannheim, 1791) that women of her time strove to achieve the learning of men without adopting their murderous spirit of revenge and other destructive passions (193). In *Liebe-Hütten* (Loving Homes, 1803), one of her late works, a hymn to the humble sewing needle leads to the following exclamation: "How happy for humanity if Venus' husband, who for the past ten awful years has forged the thunderbolts for the infuriated sons of the earth, would devote the strength of his arm to the peaceful tool of earthly goddesses!" (1: 271f.).

As a writer La Roche hopes to contribute to her nation by furthering the intellectual, moral, and emotional education of the individual. In a preface to her *Moralische Erzählungen* (Moral Tales, 1799), she reaches for such a goal without her usual modesty, turning to an imagined past, which could, however, prefigure a better time to come: "I ask fate to grant me the wish that this second edition will bring a closer connection of the sympathetic bond between my readers and myself, so that the love for truth, beauty, and goodness, for knowledge and fatherland will inspire all Germans and bring back the golden age of the ancients when truth, fidelity, justice, and love of humanity were recognized."

In works published after 1800, there are relatively few anti-French sentiments, and these are balanced by a continuing recognition of exemplary French men and women. In her late years, La Roche resigns from the turmoil around her, hopes and prays for peace, and turns to the world of books and flowers. She died in February 1807, after Napoleon defeated Austria and Prussia, and before there was any prospect of a just peace or a future for Germany. Although it has been asserted that La Roche did not progress after her first novel,[6] most recent critics disagree.[7] She not only experimented with new literary forms, but also faced the issues of her time with frankness and intelligence.

Looking at her entire oeuvre, we see an advocate for the education of women and a patriot seeking political and social reforms as well as increased national self-respect. The Germany she envisioned would have been an equal among other European nations. The problematic aspects of this vision derive from particular gender-based traditions deemed an essential part of a distinctly "German" culture, which assigned women a severely restricted supporting role. In so far as La Roche upheld these traditions, she educated Germany's daughters to understand their peculiar dilemma and make a willing sacrifice of their independence for the benefit of the fatherland. Since La Roche herself had broken out of the prescribed role, she could not be entirely comfortable in advising her readers to perfect the art of minding hearth and home. By writing with admiration about the achievements of individual women throughout history and all over the world, and by creating strong and intelligent heroines capable of shaping their own lives, she also pointed the way towards happier options for self-realization of women.

Note

The original La Roche editions cited here are located at the Deutsches Literaturarchiv, Marbach/Neckar. Translations are my own unless otherwise indicated.

6. See Langner's summary of research on La Roche (4-8). *Sternheim* was her only great success and it is also the only work discussed by most critics. Traditionally, scholars who consider her entire oeuvre tend to disqualify all or most later novels and mine the non-fiction only for biographical information.
7. See Maurer, Nenon, Loster-Schneider, and Langner.

Bibliography

Dörner, Andreas. *Politischer Mythos und symbolische Politik: Sinnstiftung durch symbolische Formen am Beispiel des Hermannsmythos.* Wiesbaden: Westdeutscher Verlag, 1995.

Fink, Gonthier-Louis. "Die Französische Revolution im Spiegel der deutschen Literatur und Publizistik (1789-1800)." *Die Französische Revolution und der deutsche Südwesten.* Ed. Hans-Otto Mühleisen. Munich, Zurich: Schnell & Steiner, 1989. 60-147.

Fischer, Bernd. *Das Eigene und das Eigentliche: Klopstock, Herder, Fichte, Kleist: Episoden aus der Konstruktionsgeschichte nationaler Intentionalitäten.* Berlin: Erich Schmidt, 1995.

Hassencamp, Robert, ed. "Aus dem Nachlaß der Sophie von La Roche: Briefe von E. M. Arndt, G. Forster, W. Heinse [et al.]." *Euphorion* 5 (1898): 475-502.

Herder, Johann Gottfried. *Ideen zur Philosophie der Geschichte der Menschheit.* Vol. 4 of *Herders Werke.* Ed. Theodor Matthias, 5 vols. Leipzig, Vienna: Bibliographisches Institut, n. d.

Klüger, Ruth. "Zum Außenseitertum der deutschen Dichterinnen." *Untersuchungen zum Roman von Frauen um 1800.* Ed. Helga Gallas and Magdalene Heuser. Tübingen: Niemeyer, 1990. 13-19.

La Roche, Sophie von. *Briefe über Mannheim.* Zürich: Orell, Geßner, Füßli & Co., 1791.

_____. *Erscheinungen am See Oneida.* 3 vols. Leipzig: Gräff, 1798.

_____. *Geschichte des Fräuleins von Sternheim.* Ed. Barbara Becker-Cantarino. Stuttgart: Reclam, 1983.

_____. *The History of Lady Sophia Sternheim.* Tr. Christa Baguss Britt. Albany: SUNY Press, 1991.

_____. *"Ich bin mehr Herz als Kopf": Ein Lebensbild in Briefen.* Ed. Michael Maurer. Munich: Beck, 1985.

_____. *Liebe-Hütten.* 2 vols. Leipzig: Gräff, 1803.

_____. *Mein Schreibetisch.* 2 vols. Leipzig: Gräff, 1799

_____. *Moralische Erzählungen.* 1799. Mannheim: Bender, 1850.

_____. *Pomona für Teutschlands Töchter.* 1783-84. 4 vols. Munich: Saur, 1987.

_____. *Rosaliens Briefe an ihre Freundin Mariane von St.* 1797. 3 vols. Eschborn: Klotz, 1994.

_____. *Schönes Bild der Resignation: Eine Erzählung.* 2 vols. Leipzig: Gräff, 1798.

Langner, Margrit. *Sophie von La Roche: Die empfindsame Realistin.* Heidelberg: Winter, 1995.

Loster-Schneider, Gudrun. *Sophie La Roche: Paradoxien weiblichen Schreibens im 18. Jahrhundert.* Tübingen: Narr, 1995.

Maurer, Michael. "Sophie von La Roche und die französische Revolution." *Wieland-Studien* 2 (1994): 130-55.

Moser, Friedrich Carl von. *Von dem deutschen Nationalgeist.* 1766. Selb: Notos, 1976.

Naumann, Ursula. "Das Fräulein und die Blicke: Eine Betrachtung über Sophie von La Roche." *Zeitschrift für deutsche Philologie* 107 (1988): 488-516.

Nenon, Monika. "Social Theory and Human Welfare: The Political Stance of Sophie von La Roche in Her Novels." *Lessing Yearbook* 23 (1992): 159-74.

Sahmland, Irmtraud. *Christoph Martin Wieland und die deutsche Nation: Zwischen Patriotismus, Kosmopolitismus und Griechentum.* Tübingen: Niemeyer, 1990.

Chapter 3

ROMANTIC NATIONALISM

Achim von Arnim's Gypsy Princess Isabella

Sara Friedrichsmeyer

𝕴f literary historians still debate Achim von Arnim's position along the continuum from Romanticism to Realism,[1] it is not his "Isabella of Egypt" ("Isabella von Ägypten") that has them perplexed. Published in 1812 in a collection with three other texts and dedicated to the Grimm brothers, it displays humor, some irony, and a distinctly nonrational tinge – so distinct in fact that the unwary reader is quickly disoriented. The present and past, the natural and the supernatural, the mimetic and the imaginative flow into one another free of authorial markers. "Romantic" elements – such as ghosts, the occult, the night, mistaken identity, disguises – abound along with the grotesque and the fantastic.

And then the characters: assembled in the novella along with an *Alraun*, a little mandrake root-become-man, are an old Gypsy woman who choreographs the seduction scene and who looks, quoting Heine, like "the fairest of the seven deadly sins" (95); a fat corpse clad in a bearskin who has risen from his grave in his quest for money; and a golem, a soulless figure of clay shaped like the beautiful Isabella. As Heine commented in *The Romantic School (Die romantische Schule),* this novella could teach even the French a lesson in the terrible, the uncanny, the gruesome, and the ghostly (95). Within the context of Heine's essay, these words, of course, should be understood as less than unbridled applause.[2]

---

1. For the scope of the discussion, see Haustein (v-xi); see also Hoffmann.
2. He advises his French audience to "[l]eave all these horrors of insanity, hallucination, and the spirit-world to us Germans," where they are at home. He has found at the

The novella's structure is also typically Romantic in its assiduous avoidance of formal structuring principles, in part because von Achim refused to subject his works to conscious shaping (Hoermann 1-2). This homage to his own creative genius, however, did not serve him well. While von Arnim's friend Wilhelm Grimm had praise for "Isabella" – he counted it "among the most beautiful and unique" of all von Arnim's works – he also admitted to being disturbed by the author's insistence on opening hidden doors that allowed the action to escape in all directions (III: 188).[3]

Von Arnim garnered little attention as a writer until Heine hailed him a "great poet" and "one of the most original minds of the Romantic School" (90). Heine's essay – in which he also complained that von Arnim was usually "as serious as a dead German" (91-92) – helped to awaken interest especially in "Isabella," which he singled out for special praise (94). Subsequent generations of scholars have concurred with this judgment, and the novella is today discussed as belonging to the canon of the genre (Hoermann, Preface n.p.) and one of the "exemplary literary texts" of German Romanticism (Seyhan 107).[4]

Rather than examining further the novella's status within a canon or its paradigmatic Romanticism, I am interested here in von Arnim's treatment of Isabella and the Gypsies, and in how that treatment reflects von Arnim's own hopes for a German nation. On one level this is Isabella's story. And – for readers who like a Romantic story – it is quite intriguing. We meet Isabella in a haunted house in Ghent after her father has been falsely executed for stealing. Von Arnim introduces her and continues to speak of her in terms of her physical attributes and even more often of her innocence. She possesses "a beauty that unfolds more gloriously every day" (491); she is "saintly" (556) and is eulogized in her coffin as "the Pure One" (555).[5] We are also meant to be persuaded of her uniqueness. Living at a time when Gypsies could be killed on sight (455), she can emerge only after dark. Just as von Arnim thus carefully sequesters her from bourgeois society, he also separates her from the Gypsies, whom she considers "rough" (453). Treated by the Gypsies as a "higher being," she has come to think of herself as such (464).

French border, he reports, that "the sight of the tricolored flag frightens away ghosts of every sort" (98).

3. A reference with Roman numerals refers throughout this study to one of the 3 volumes of *Achim von Arnim und die ihm nahe standen.*

4. In 1960, Heinrich Henel commented that, had von Arnim been able to maintain the style and force of the first twenty pages, he would have written a masterpiece (91).

5. Parenthetical references to the novella are from the Migge edition. I have used the Pierce and Schneider translation where possible; other translations from the novella are my own.

Isabella controls the romantic plot devices and drives the action: she reads occult manuscripts, learns many secrets of the universe, and creates the miniature man, the *Alraun*. She is also the pivotal figure in the legend von Arnim retells, according to which the Gypsies have been forced to wander in a diaspora as punishment for the refusal of their ancestors to grant refuge to the Virgin Mary on her flight to Egypt.[6] In von Arnim's version the parallels to the Biblical salvation story are stressed, and Isabella's link with the Virgin Mary positions her as a mediator for her entire people (534). It is she who in a "dream of annunciation" (Hoermann 95) is told by her dead father that she will bear a son who will lead her people back to Egypt to reclaim their rightful homeland (520).[7]

The subtitle, however, points to another level for reading the story: "The First Love of Emperor Charles V" ("Kaiser Karl des Fünften erste Jugendliebe"). The Holy Roman Emperor Karl V ruled over a vast Hapsburg empire in the early sixteenth century, but not over a German nation.[8] By choosing this setting, von Arnim directs his reader's attention to the Reformation and the ensuing peasant wars that could have resulted in a move toward political unity for the German-speaking lands. This part of the story belongs not to Isabella, but to Karl, and von Arnim tells it in high moral terms. As the novella has it, the drive to nationhood was thwarted because the emperor lacked a strong ethical dimension. He betrayed Isabella because of his inability to distinguish between spiritual love and the sensuality of the golem. And because he lacked "pious harmony" and proved so vulnerable to "contemptible greed," he was unable to inspire any movement toward national unity, the lack of which is cited as a source of great unhappiness even for the narrator's own generation (552).

Von Arnim's Karl V has found nothing to replace the lost spiritual harmony of the Middle Ages; he is materialistic, opportunistic, haughty, and given to sensuality. Isabella therefore leaves him to fulfill her own destiny; she gives birth to their son Lrak (the narrator carefully informs

6. Most critics cite Grellmann as von Arnim's main source for his eccentric "history" of the Gypsies (cf. Schürer; Neumann). In von Arnim's telling, the Jews have for centuries passed themselves off as Gypsies, resulting in great damage to the Gypsies' reputation (453-54). Few critics comment on the antisemitism of the novella.

7. Actually this prophecy is not fulfilled. It is Isabella who leads her people back.

8. Karl V (1500-58), well known from the equestrian portrait by Titian, was crowned Holy Roman Emperor in 1520 in Aachen. He was not successful in suppressing Protestantism, in part because he was continually drawn away from Germany by, among other pressures, the rivalry with France. He abdicated after the Religious Peace of Augsburg (1555), leaving the throne of Spain to Philipp II and the imperial crown to Ferdinand I, and withdrew to a monastery in Estremadura.

the reader to note the reversal of letters) on her peregrinations to Egypt. Von Arnim is little interested in the lives of the lovers after their separation, but by the end of the novella he has them dying on the same day, Isabella in Egypt and Karl in the monastery to which he has retreated after giving up his empire. And by this time, the emotional and structural emphasis of the narration has shifted to Karl. Isabella's death is related solely through his vision; its importance is measured in terms of its effect on Karl during his final earthly moments. Lying in his coffin, he glimpses a vision of an ethereal Isabella. "She waved to him and he followed her ... and saw a bright morning light in which Isabella was showing him the way to heaven" (552). The eternal feminine has brought redemption to one more erring striver.

* * *

During his European travels from 1801 to 1804,[9] von Arnim acquired the notion of distinct peoples with distinct folk traditions. Much of his early collaborative work with Brentano was consequently aimed at documenting and then propagating a specifically German tradition and national character, a "Volksgeist."[10] Many of his later works, including "Isabella," maintained this concentration. His focus in "Isabella" on the development, or in this case nondevelopment, of the German nation has not been overlooked by critics. The *völkisch* elements of the novella were fastened on by scholars in the 1930s and early 1940s (cf. Lenz). Since then, however, and perhaps therefore, they have been rather studiously ignored.

In von Arnim's own time, friends and critics, especially those who shared his patriotic values, often directed their comments to his flagrant merging of history and fiction. In his dedication to the collection in which "Isabella" appeared,[11] the author alluded to his differences with the Grimm brothers:

In eurem Geist hat sich die Sagenwelt
Als ein geschloss'nes Ganze [sic] schon gesellt,
Mein Buch dagegen glaubt, daß viele Sagen
In unsern Zeiten erst recht wieder tagen,
Und viele sich der Zukunft erst enthüllen,
Nun prüfet, ob es Euch das kann erfüllen. (447)[12]

9. Riley's biography is the most recent.
10. They were so dedicated to promoting national unity that they refused, for example, to distinguish in *Des Knaben Wunderhorn* between songs from various geographic regions.
11. See Schürer and Haustein for a discussion of the novella in the context of the entire collection. The frame story establishes the connection to von Arnim's own day.
12. "*In your* minds the world of legend / Comes together as a complete whole, / My book on the contrary believes that many legends / Come back to life again in our times, / And many reveal themselves only in the future, / Now see if that can be the case for you."

The dedication, however, did not placate Jacob Grimm. Von Arnim's willful tampering with history, he scolded after reading "Isabella," could create an "untrue" reality, causing confusion and even false conceptions of the past (III: 191-94; III: 99-100).[13] This topic continued to be a focus of von Arnim's correspondence with the Grimms over many years. In a manifesto of sorts written during their discussion of *Die Kronen-wächter* (The Crown Guardians), von Arnim maintained that his friends' convictions concerning history and poetry contradicted his own in a most dramatic way. The impetus for writing, he claimed, "whether provided by 'real' history ... or by one's own life, seems ... completely immaterial." As a justification he added: "Unless Homer was crazy, he could not possibly have believed his yarns of the Trojan War anymore than Klopstock the speeches of the angels," except, he insisted, that both have an "inner" truth (III:401).

The "inner truth" von Arnim constructs in "Isabella" blends history with legend, fact with fiction, and the old with the new in an attempt to draw attention to the issue of German national identity. He has no illusions about writing a serious history, at times urging the reader's acceptance of his version, at others warning against it. Upon the appearance of the tiny *Alraun*, the mandrake man given the imposing Roman name of Fieldmarshal Cornelius Nepos, the narrator interrupts to caution against connecting him with any historical person of that name (475). Yet at other times the same narrator strives to create at least an illusion of historical authenticity, as when, late in the novella, he claims Zacharias Taurinius as a source for his account of Isabella's death. Scholars have ascertained that, although in 1799 and 1800 Taurinius did publish a travelogue in two volumes titled *Beschreibung einiger See- und Landreisen nach Asien, Afrika und Amerika* (Description of Several Ocean and Land Trips to Asia, Africa, and America), Isabella's story has no place in it (Moering).

Most critics today, persuaded by Benedict Anderson's influential work, understand the concepts of nation and nationalism as "ideas," as imaginary constructs. As a spate of recent works attest, it was during the late eighteenth and early nineteenth centuries that the "idea" of nationhood took hold among German intellectuals.[14] In her comparison of five different forms of nationalism, Liah Greenfeld describes the German variant as an ethnic nationalism, a conception of belonging based on such factors as blood, common traditions, language, and religion rather

13. See Kiermeier-Debre for a discussion of von Arnim's views on the limits of history vis-á-vis fiction; the study is based on the debate von Arnim and the Grimm brothers carried on in their letters after the publication of "Isabella."

14. In addition to Greenfeld, see, for example, Hobsbawm, Ignatieff, Brubaker, Connor.

than on a political constitution or other political forms of unification. Although she does not cite von Arnim, his "Isabella of Egypt" lends credence to her thesis. Von Arnim and those among his contemporaries who did provide her examples abhorred the long tradition of French cultural supremacy and were, especially after the Prussian defeat at Jena, increasingly driven to establish a German national identity in its stead. Lacking a political nation-state, however, they were forced to construct that identity according to ethnic rather than political criteria.[15] As the editors of *Nationalisms and Sexualities* conclude, "nationality is a relational term whose identity derives from its inherence in a system of differences ... National identity is determined not on the basis of its own intrinsic properties but as a function of what it (presumably) is not" (5). In the Gypsies and their history, von Arnim found an element of alterity, that is, a mirror to help his German-speaking contemporaries define their own national characteristics and reflect on their dreams of a nation-state. In the "Ariel" frame to his 1809 novella collection *Der Wintergarten* (The Winter Garden), von Arnim's poet despairs: "We had hoped for a wonderful era for Germany ... like a wonderful prismatic mirror she was to unite the whole world. But ... the war came [and] shattered our mirror" (345). Von Arnim continued constructing mirrors, but instead of Germany as a grand mirror for the rest of the world, he found himself forced to create one for the Germans themselves.

* * *

Since the late eighteenth century, cultures have never been described merely in terms of their variety, but within a hierarchy based on Western notions of developmental stages. They have been ranked according to their perceived ability to overcome a "natural" state and enter history as "developed" cultures. Gypsy culture has never been perceived as "developed" in the sense understood by Western critics. Especially since the Enlightenment, with its stress on values such as reason, progress, permanence, property, and the development of nations, Gypsies have come to be essentialized in the popular imagination as an ethnic group for whom these concerns matter little. They have come to be seen as a group out of time and out of history (Trumpener).[16] As such, they have been readily

15. On von Arnim's politics, see Knaack.
16. Acton, Hancock, Fraser, and Fonseca are perhaps the most important of recent writers to speak out against the prevailing representations and the homogenization such representations require. Although nomenclature remains problematic, Fonseca reports increasing acceptance of the term "Gypsy" by the people themselves (228) and uses it herself. I have chosen to use it because the other all-embracing term, "Roma," is confusing in a German context where it is used as the designation for a single Gypsy group.

available to writers as an idealized or despised other, as a mirror through which writers can document their own opposition or allegiance to Western culture and its manifestations.[17] In either case, the writer has little interest in the Gypsies per se or in presenting anything resembling a balanced depiction of their actual existence or their very complex history.

As with the vast majority of other writers who have idealized Gypsies, what von Arnim idealizes in "Isabella" and elsewhere is a totalizing image he himself has created. In an essay published along with *Des Knaben Wunderhorn* (The Boy's Magic Horn) titled "Von Volksliedern," he provides a prototypical example of what Edward Said has referred to as Orientalism, insisting, for example, on the Gypsies' child-like goodness, and claiming as well that although we unjustly persecute them, we owe the Gypsies "so many good and beneficial things ... . Despite all their love, they find no home [*Heimat*] among us" (451-52). In other works of fiction, such as his novel *Die Kronenwächter*, he expresses a comparable understanding. Thus in "Isabella" the Gypsies are loyal to the wandering tribe; they are close to the organic processes of nature; their traditions are intact. Throughout, they are incorporated as a uniform representation of the more "natural," more mystical and spiritual aspects of human existence, the very aspects lacking in von Arnim's Karl V. Had Karl possessed them, the novel seems to infer, history might have been different. And were von Arnim's own compatriots possessed of these virtues, the inference continues, nationhood for Germans would be possible.

The categories von Arnim chooses for describing Gypsy existence are certainly not unfamiliar to feminist critics. They are by and large the same as those applied to women since the sex roles polarized toward the end of the eighteenth century: a spiritual, non-rational principle close to the processes of nature in contrast to the notions of progress, culture, and rationality typically associated with males. This role division also had implications for nationalist strivings. As the editors of *Nationalisms and Sexualities* phrased it in their introduction, crediting both George Mosse and Benedict Anderson, "nationalism favors a distinctly homosocial form of male bonding" (6). Nineteenth-century rhetoric generated a hierarchy that valued nations and the males who created them over females and "feminized" non-nations.

The rhetoric, however, also specified a role for women. A spiritual and maternal presence was also required as an accompaniment to the political male, if for no other reason than to secure a male-directed his-

17. Thomas Mann's caveat about the "gypsies in a green wagon" in "Tonio Kröger" is perhaps the best-known example of the former; Nicolaus Lenau's 1838 poem "Die Drei Zigeuner" illustrates the latter. Numerous other works are listed in Trumpener. See other examples in Djurić.

tory (*Nationalisms*, 6). In von Arnim's case the evidence suggests that his glorification of women in "Isabella" was also an exuberant response to his 1811 marriage to Bettina Brentano. All three of the other works contained in the collection of 1812 in which "Isabella" appeared have female title characters.[18] The context is provided by the narrator's poem in the conclusion to "Isabella":

> Wo große Zeichen hin zur Zukunft deuten,
> Da wollen wir nicht stets nach Männern schauen,
> Es ändern sich auch einmal wohl die Zeiten:
> Vielleicht beginnt nun bald die Zeit der Frauen!" (557)[19]

Von Arnim's Isabella exhibits ideal love: she is "the only one in centuries" capable of a spiritual devotion devoid of the "lustfulness of her sex" (464). Even after her sexual encounter, actually seduction, of Karl V, she is touted as "deeply and profoundly innocent" (509). By the time of her death, she has been able to create something akin to an earthly paradise in Egypt, an accomplishment about which the narrator waxes particularly eloquent: through her efforts, there had emerged fertile gardens where happy children could play; there were now leaping fountains and brightly plumed birds where once crocodiles had basked in the sun and only the hissing of snakes had been heard (555).

This trope of the idealized, mediating female figured prominently in the works of other Romantic writers such as Novalis and Friedrich Schlegel, philosophers such as Franz von Baader, and artists such as Caspar David Friedrich, many of whom described their hopes and ideals in the language of androgynous perfection. Deploring their own one-sidedness, which they understood as a too strict adherence to the rational precepts of the Enlightenment, and premising their theories on the notion of rigidly polarized sexes, they posited in women all they deemed lacking in themselves. Thus glorified, women became the ideal partners through whom many early nineteenth-century artists and thinkers believed they could regain their own wholeness. Although their ideas were theoretically applicable to women's perfection as well, their works make clear that the wholeness they sought was for males alone; the female partners of their male protagonists often died or simply disappeared (see Friedrichsmeyer).

18. The others are: "Melück Maria Blainville, die Hausprophetin aus Arabien: Eine Anekdote," "Die drei liebreichen Schwestern und der glückliche Färber: Ein Sittengemälde," and "Angelika, die Genueserin und Cosmus, der Seilspringer: Eine Novelle."

19. "Where great portents point to the future, / We do not want to focus constantly on men, / The times will probably be changing: / Perhaps the era of women will soon begin!"

Isabella serves a similar utilitarian purpose for von Arnim. And just as von Arnim created her to reflect the spiritual love and the connection to the organic world missing in Karl's being, so did he attribute these same "female" qualities to the entire world of the Gypsies, who serve then as a mirror for a prospective German nation. But unlike many other writers, von Arnim does something else with his idealized mirror: he scratches and clouds it. In various ways he undercuts his idealization of the feminized and exotic Gypsies and their female redeemer, deliberately conditioning his reader to the impossibility of any lasting union between Karl and Isabella and attesting to the unbridgeable chasm separating Germans from Gypsies.

In addition to his narrator's partiality for Karl, von Arnim incorporates frequent, not so subtle reminders to his German-speaking audience of Isabella's and the Gypsies' fundamental otherness; frequently this is accomplished in terms of language, a key category in von Arnim's own understanding of what constitutes a *Volk*.[20] By the time Isabella forsakes Karl's bedroom, leaping out the window into the arms, literally, of her waiting people, they have sworn her their allegiance. Before repeating their song, however, the narrator interrupts the flow to delineate a linguistic boundary between the Gypsies and Isabella on the one hand and the Germans – author, narrator, and readers alike – on the other. For purposes of the story, he says, he will try to translate their "heartfelt greeting" (547). Her death scene, too, he feels moved to translate "into our German mother tongue" (555). Even in some of the most lyrical passages intoned to define Isabella's perfection, von Arnim inserts reminders of her difference, by linking her as she leaves Karl, for example, to *her* people, not to the Germans: "She belonged to the species of birds that, despite the tender care and loving attentions at the hands of kind people, cannot resist taking wing when it hears the call of its kin ..." (548). We are assured that Isabella's "counterfeit marriage" – a misstep female literary characters have only in the late twentieth century been able to survive – did not disturb "the purity of *her* moral code" (548, my emphasis). In case we as readers have any lingering tendencies to look to Isabella as the nucleus of the story or as a model, the narrator intervenes quite directly to persuade us differently: the legends revolving around Isabella's life and death are acknowledged as "educational" (553), but, we are cautioned, "they do not belong in our European world" (553).

20. He believed, for example, that the German language should be standardized and spread through Europe as the *lingua franca* that could unite popular culture with the arts and sciences. See discussion in Hoermann (20).

Von Arnim also provides his readers with the necessary insights to challenge Isabella's oft-proclaimed virtue. Thus, although Isabella is the titular and emotional center through much of the work, and although von Arnim is suggesting that at least some of the qualities associated with her Gypsy essence would have made Karl the kind of ruler who could have forged the all-important German nation, the reader is never allowed to settle into a fantasy of Isabella as the model for German womanhood. For that we have only to look to *Die Gräfin Dolores* (1810), where he preached his ideal of marital, monogamous, Christian love as a counter to Friedrich Schlegel's *Lucinde*. In addition to Isabella's distinctly unbourgeois sexual behavior, this supposed paragon is not adverse to the kind of material corruption von Arnim feared.[21] Although she lauds the poverty of her people (548), her whole purpose in creating Cornelius Nepos had been to get help in amassing the money necessary to attract Karl. Typically critics have blamed these and other blemishes on Braka, a judgment von Arnim encourages.[22] His narrator, for example, lingers on details as the old Gypsy woman instructs Isabella in the art of seduction. Similarly, it is Braka who convinces Isabella of the importance of money in attracting Karl and of her consequent need for the *Alraun* (463). But Isabella has other flaws too, and Braka cannot be implicated in all these thematic lines. She knowingly sacrifices her nearly human guard dog in the process of creating the *Alraun* (463-64), and later, when he is hungry, drowns a nursing kitten to make room for her tiny creation (472, 546). Thus, despite its idealization of Isabella, this novella should in no way be construed as intimating that von Arnim is dreaming of a woman to lead the German-speaking peoples to their destiny as a nation-state.

Nor, of course, are we to assume that the Gypsies are thoroughgoing models for Germanness. Although von Arnim idealizes the Gypsies, we know – as did readers of his day – that he is not recommending the Gypsy life style as a behavioral model for respectable Germanness. By presenting the Gypsies as so fairytale like, so much the outsiders, and so feminized, he infers the impossibility of anyone's taking them too seriously; by presenting them as exotic and childlike, he further removes them from the dimensions of history. Von Arnim, as his nonfictional writing makes clear, was a Prussian with a Protestant sense of morality,[23] dedicated to preserving the nonurban, noncapitalist, and male-oriented

21. Haustein links these fears to von Arnim's antisemitism (39-40).
22. Hoermann's comments are typical: when Karl strays into the neighborhood, "Braka quickly maneuvers the completely innocent Isabella into Charles's bedchamber" (92).
23. Von Arnim's Faust, for example, saves himself from the devil by printing the Bible and turning his back on fame (Streller).

way of life he considered inherently German at a time when the upheavals following the French Revolution were threatening its demise. As such, his hopes fit the well-known pattern documented by Mosse, according to which nineteenth-century nationalism in Germany was very much in league with a desire for bourgeois morality and respectability. There was nothing nomadic, childlike, ahistorical, or even remotely sensual about the German nation for which von Arnim longed.

* * *

Yet von Arnim succeeded in lulling successive generations of critics into an uncritical acceptance of his idealization of Isabella and the Gypsies. The trend was already there with Heine, who grounded his positive reception in part on his belief that "[t]his strange fairy-tale people, with their brown faces, friendly soothsayer eyes, and melancholy mysteriousness, comes to life … .Everything the excellent Arnim tells us about the gypsies is profoundly moving" (94-95). Even in 1992 Azade Seyhan wrote: "The exotic other, excuded and misunderstood, emerges as the representation of a higher truth" (129). Just as critics have generally accepted the exemplary nature of the Gypsies as von Arnim intended, so have they also taken von Arnim's word that Isabella is the pure and innocent redeemer. She is typically regarded as a utopian principle defined in opposition to Karl (Völker 118). Bernd Haustein's description of her as the perfect synthesis of saint and human being (40), Werner Vordtriede's declaration that she is not involved in the "fall from grace caused by the worship of money" that he sees as the crux of the story (264), and Roland Hoermann's assessment of her as perhaps von Arnim's most attractive human figure, a *femme spirituelle* (65), are representative. Scholars have not protested the idealization, nor have they recognized that Isabella is declared "saintly" precisely because she can be instrumentalized by others. Braka, for example, uses her as a way of obtaining her own financial security, and Karl values her physical presence in part as a way to keep the *Alraun* in his services (542-43). Another good example of her malleability is provided by her dressing and cross-dressing. She is the compliant one, allegedly uninvolved in any long range plans; others dress her as part of their own power machinations. Early in the story, Braka instructs her in the art of feminine attire in order to attract Karl. Later Karl's aged and celibate tutor dresses her as a boy so she can be inconspicuously removed from the palace without damage to his own reputation (525). Later Karl dresses her again as a boy as part of his own joke on his tutor (536-38). Still later Karl has her dressed by one of the ladies of the court as befitting a princess, a move that ensures the court's accepting her as such.

If critics have been able to accept the allegedly purifying love of a gypsy seductress in the work of a Prussian moralist, they have done so, as did von Arnim, by measuring her and her people on a different scale. Now in one sense this is generous. By acknowledging that Gypsies live according to another code, von Arnim is indicating that he, like Herder, sees the relative merits of various ethnic groups, of their folk traditions, their language, their culture. But this is not the author's final assessment and neither should it be ours.

Ultimately, von Arnim's depiction of Isabella and the Gypsies is of a racial group so homogenous, so exotic, so radically other, and so "female" that its members cease to exist as human beings or subjects of their own history. At the same time, this treatment reflects an ethnic nationalism mired in illusions of exclusivity. This has been ignored by the critics, by Heine, who was usually looking for conservative credos and finding them in most works of German Romanticism, as well as by more contemporary critics presumably versed in the analytic strategies of feminist literary criticism or the ideologies of nationalism. There can be no question but that von Arnim's dream of nation, based here on distinct moral codes for distinct peoples, requires separate destinies for separate peoples. Consequently, the Gypsies and Isabella resemble a collective *deus ex machina*; having failed to perform their wonders, they can be dispatched on their way to Egypt – where they belong. Isabella's decision to return to Egypt is sanctimoniously described as an inevitability: "In Europe she was like a rare flower that opened only at night, because day was then dawning in her homeland" (548).

Fiction then has its benefits: the Gypsies willingly disappear as does Isabella, leaving Karl to ponder and rue his youthful indiscretions. The novella presumably left von Arnim's nineteenth-century German readers to mourn their lack of nation, to contemplate just what it was about Isabella and those Gypsies that won them their fictional homeland, and – perhaps – to make some adjustments in their own national character that could lead them in a similar direction. It leaves a late twentieth-century reader with a story, perhaps benign in itself, that, when viewed in its cultural and historical contexts, is one more disquieting document of the German dream of an ethnically pure nation-state forged by like-minded and like-blooded men, a homogenous homeland – and one certainly without Gypsies.

Bibliography

Achim von Arnim und die ihm nahe standen. Ed. Reinhold Stieg and Herman Grimm. 3 vols. Stuttgart: Cotta, 1894-1913.

Acton, Thomas. *Gypsy Politics and Social Change: The Development of Ethnic Ideology and Pressure Politics among British Gypsies from Victorian Reformism to Romany Nationalism.* London: Routledge, 1974.

Anderson, Benedict. *Imagined Communities: Reflections on the Origin and Spread of Nationalism.* London: Verso, 1983.

Arnim, Achim von. "Isabella of Egypt." *Fiction and Fantasy of German Romance. Selections from the German Romantic Authors, 1790-1830.* Ed. Frederick E. Pierce and Carl F. Schreiber. Trans. Carl F. Schreiber. NY: Oxford, 1927. 171-243.

———. "Isabella von Ägypten, Kaiser Karl des Fünften erste Jugendliebe." *Achim von Arnim: Sämtliche Romane und Erzählungen.* Ed. Walther Migge. Munich: Hanser, 1963. II:452-557.

———. "Der Wintergarten." *Achim von Arnim: Sämtliche Romane und Erzählungen.* Ed. Walther Migge. Munich: Hanser, 1963. II:123-435.

———. and Clemens Brentano. "Von Volksliedern." *Des Knaben Wunderhorn.* Berlin: Haude and Spener, 1928. I: 435-84.

Brubaker, Rogers. *Citizenship and Nationhood in France and Germany.* Cambridge: Harvard UP, 1992.

Connor, Walker. *Ethnonationalism: The Quest for Understanding.* Princeton: Princeton UP, 1994.

Djurić, Rajko. *Roma und Sinti im Spiegel der deutschen Literatur: Ein Essay.* Studien zur Tsiganologie und Folkloristik 13. Frankfurt a.M.: Lang, 1995.

Fonseca, Isabel. *Bury Me Standing: The Gypsies and Their Journey.* New York: Knopf, 1995.

Fraser, Angus. *The Gypsies.* 2nd ed. Oxford: Blackwell, 1995.

Friedrichsmeyer, Sara. *The Androgyne in Early German Romanticism: Friedrich Schlegel, Novalis, and the Metaphysics of Love.* Stanford German Studies 18. Bern: Lang, 1983.

Greenfeld, Liah. *Nationalism: Five Roads to Modernity.* Cambridge: Harvard UP, 1992.

Grellmann, H.M.G. *Dissertation on the Gipsies.* 2nd ed. [Trans. of *Historischer Versuch über die Zigeuner.* 1783.] London: Ballantine, 1807.

Hancock, Ian. *The Pariah Syndrome: An Account of Gypsy Slavery and Persecution.* Ann Arbor: Karoma, 1987.

Haustein, Bernd. *Romantischer Mythos und Romantikkritik in Prosadichtungen Achim von Arnims.* Göppinger Arbeiten zur Germanistik 104. Göppingen: Kümmerle, 1974.

Heine, Heinrich. "The Romantic School." *The Romantic School and other Essays.* Ed. Jost Hermand and Robert C. Holub. Trans. Helen Mustard. The German Library. Vol. 33. New York: Continuum, 1985. 1-127.

Henel, Heinrich. "Arnims 'Majoratsherren.' *Weltbewohner und Weimaraner.*
Festschrift für Ernst Beutler. Ed. B. Reifenberg and Emil Steiger. Zürich:
Artemis, 1960. 73-104.

Herder, Johann Gottfried. *Reflections on the Philosophy of the History of*
Mankind. Chicago: U of Chicago P, 1968.

Hobsbawm, E.J. *Nations and Nationalism Since 1780: Programme, Myth,*
Reality. Cambridge: Cambridge UP, 1990.

Hoermann, Roland. *Achim von Arnim.* Twayne's World Authors Series. Ed.
Ulrich Weisstein. Boston: Twayne, 1984.

Hoffmann, Volker. "Die Arnim-Forschung 1945-1972." *Deutsche*
Vierteljahrsschift 47 (Sonderheft 1973): 270-342.

Ignatieff, Michael. *Blood and Belonging: Journeys into the New Nationalism.*
New York: Farrar, Straus and Giroux, 1994.

Kiermeier-Debre, Joseph. "' … was bloß erzählt und nicht geschehen …':
Dichtung und Geschichte: Achim von Arnims Poetik im Einleitungstext zu
seinem Roman *Die Kronenwächter." Grenzgänge: Studien zu L. Achim von*
Arnim. Ed. Michael Andermatt. Bonn: Bouvier, 1994. 117-46.

Knaack, Jürgen. *Achim von Arnim – Nicht nur Poet. Die politischen*
Anschauungen Arnims in ihrer Entwicklung. Darmstadt: Thesen, 1976.

Lenz, Hans-Uffo. *Das Volkserlebnis bei Ludwig Achim von Arnim.* Germanische
Studien 200. 1938. Nendeln: Kraus, 1967.

Moering, Renate. "Fremdsprachige Quellen zu Arnims Erzählungen." *Beiträge*
eines Wiepersdorfer Kolloquiums zu Achim und Bettina von Arnim. Ed.
Heinz Härtl and Hartwig Schultz. Berlin: de Gruyter, 1994. 103-16.

Mosse, George L. *Nationalism and Sexuality: Middle-Class Morality and Sexual*
Norms in Modern Europe. Madison: U of Wisconsin P, 1985.

Nationalisms and Sexualities. Ed. Andrew Parker, et al. New York: Routledge,
1992.

Neumann, Peter Horst. "Legende, Sage und Geschichte in Achim von Arnims
'Isabella von Ägypten': Quellen und Deutung." *Jahrbuch der Deutschen*
Schillergesellschaft 12 (1968): 296-314.

Riley, Helene M. Kastinger. *Achim von Arnim.* Reinbek bei Hamburg:
Rowohlt, 1979.

Said, Edward. *Orientalism.* New York: Vintage Books, 1979.

Schürer, Ernst. "Quellen und Fluß der Geschichte: zur Interpretation von
Achim von Arnims Isabella von Ägypten." *Lebendige Form: Interpretationen*
zur Deutschen Literatur. Festschrift für Heinrich Henel. Ed. Jeffrey Sammons
and Ernst Schürer. Munich: Fink, 1970. 189-210.

Seyhan, Azade. *Representation and Its Discontents.* Berkeley: U of California P,
1992.

Streller, Dorothea. "Achim von Arnim und 'Auch ein Faust.'" *Jahrbuch der*
Sammlung Kippenberg 1 (1963): 150-62.

Trumpener, Katie. "The Time of the Gypsies: A 'People without History' in
the Narratives of the West." *Critical Inquiry* 18.4 (Summer 1992): 843-84.

Völker, Ludwig. "Naturpoesie, Phantasie und Phantastik: Über Achim von Arnims Erzählung *Isabella von Ägypten*." *Romantik: Ein literaturwissenschaftliches Studienbuch*. Ed. Ernst Ribbat. Königstein/Ts: Athenäum, 1979. 114-37.

Vordtriede, Werner. "Achim von Arnim." *Deutsche Dichter der Romantik*. Ed. Benno von Wiese. Berlin: Schmidt, 1971. 253-79.

Chapter 4

HOW TO THINK ABOUT GERMANY

Nationality, Gender, and Obsession in Heine's "Night Thoughts"

Russell A. Berman

he conceptual redefinition of literary studies as "Cultural Studies," of which "German Studies" has come to represent one particular variant, appears to have induced a preference for the study of novels or other prose genres and a relative reluctance to engage in lyric poetry. The contemporary thematization of material culture certainly points a critic toward the stuff of everyday life, which is typically displayed to a much greater degree in prose fiction, while the sparse abstractions of verse are presumed to have less capacity for the sorts of political claims that current critical discussions address. To the extent that Cultural Studies involves the constitution and contestation of collective identities, then the novel becomes a privileged genre due to underlying assumptions about its scope, whether these assumptions derive from Lukács' paradigm of totality or Bakhtin's model of dialogism (Berman 10). Conversely, the suggestion that poetry may have less to say directly about political or social concerns reflects the consequences of the autonomy of aesthetics in the early nineteenth century that still structure standard expectations regarding literature. Even when Adorno tried to demonstrate the social substance of lyric, he had to begin precisely from his public's assumption that poetry has little to do with society (73-74). In the age of Cultural Studies, then, with critical attention devoted increasingly to questions of politics in literary representation, a shift away from poetry becomes a fact of scholarly life. Film – a modern expansion of the realist novel – is in; verse is out.

This hierarchy of taste, away from the traditionally "high" form of poetry and toward the popularity of the novel, is not a matter of any logical necessity; there are plenty of examples of political or public poetry that might be cited as likely evidence for the cultural-studies readership. The bias itself may however be taken as a sort of evidence of the practices that underpin contemporary efforts to read other cultures, that is, to read them as novels rather than as poems, whereby the generic opposition is intended to point toward alternative theorizations of culture. A novelistic Cultural Studies examines identity formation against a background of existing structures, that frame, if not determine, the vicissitudes of the subject: as if the anatomical eye of the critic was already anticipated in the voice of the narrator, who prereads the world for the recipient. A security of judgment results, reserving little room for ambiguity, and perhaps even less for innovation. The artifacts of another culture are collected, classified, and preserved, but a recognition of the alterity of culture as a possible source of qualitatively new experience, a specifically poetic project, is missing. Cultural Studies approaches culture as a collection of ethnographic facts within which identities are constructed, rather than as a realm of creativity in which individuals invent new forms. The problem with Cultural Studies is not that it is "Marxist," as polemical opponents of the academy would have it, but rather that Cultural Studies, like orthodox Marxism, is slipping toward a deterministic and conformist model of culture, which, for all of its verbal radicalism, remains constitutively inimical to change.

How to think about another culture, how to think about Germany: the focus on the construction of identities, intended to demonstrate the non-naturalistic and therefore presumably malleable character of subjectivities, can metamorphose quickly into a simplistic analysis of subsequentiality that may trivialize the material. The preestablished epistemic horizons of discourse are unfortunately understood to set the limits and perhaps even define particular instances or concretizations of fundamental patterns. Nothing new ever happens in an obsessive repetition of the always already given: structuralism had problems with history, and they are inherited, via poststructuralism, in much of Cultural Studies. Yet precisely this determinism undercuts the self-definition of Cultural Studies as radical – when all is said and done, it may only be reductionistic, an illustrated cultural history – unless it can outline alternative approaches to culture that allow for precisely the alterity, as innovation, that repetition proscribes.

Thinking about Germany and thinking differently about Germany are the topics of Heine's "Night Thoughts," ("Nachtgedanken"), one of the best known poems of the German canon, especially its opening verses: "Denk ich an Deutschland in der Nacht, / Dann bin ich um den Schlaf gebracht".[1] Written early in 1843, it appeared as the last of the twenty-four "Political Poems" *(Zeitgedichte)* that constitute the final section of the volume *Neue Gedichte (New Poems)*, published in the autumn of 1844. In this concluding section, the poem gains saliency as a programmatic statement, although the thematic ambivalence of the text has historically elicited a contradictory reception. The initial reference to Germany, as well as later, decidedly ironic pointers, invite the reader to attribute the poet's sleeplessness to conditions in Germany, in which case the text is cast as a political poem with a critical message. This account is however immediately modified by the poet's explanation that his long separation from his mother produces his sorrow. The political question recedes behind the privacy of filial love or, rather, the two become inextricably linked, especially in light of the biographical context: Heine's exile from Germany, his residence in Paris, and, hence, the distance from his mother in Hamburg were themselves results of political conditions. Thus, with reference to "Night Thoughts," Max Brod wrote in 1934: "The love for his mother remained one of the most solid bases of Heine's love. It mixes in a touching way with his homesickness for Germany" (25, my translation). Sixty years later, Jost Hermand similarly suggests an overlap of the personal and the political: "His criticism of Germany, no matter how sharp or malicious or perhaps even just witty, was always based on the yearning of an unloved son, who would have much rather stayed at home with 'mother' than to wander around in foreign countries" (270, my translation).

Brod's sentimentalist insistence on Heine's yearning leads him to overlook the critical tones in the poem; Hermand maintains an ear for the criticism, while recognizing Heine's own identification of mother and Germany. This antinomic tension traverses the reception history. Like Brod, Joachim Müller also presents a sentimentalist account: "The yearning for the mother is the yearning for Germany, and the yearning for Germany is the yearning for the mother. Wherever Heine loves most ardently, from a natural tie, that is his Germany" (425). In contrast (and explicitly critical of Müller), Werner Psaar foregrounds the political material by pointing out how the yearning was an expression of exile's bitterness: "'Night Thoughts' demonstrates better than any other poem

---

1. "Thinking of Germany in the night, / I lie awake and sleep takes flight" (Draper 407).

in German the real misery of exile, the suffering in the nights, the anxiety about returning, yearning and fear, engagement and denial, allegiance, despair, and the search for comfort" (114). While the critics vary,
then, on the precise balance of the personal and political, they do all
agree that the poem gives sincere and mournful expression to Heine's
concerns with Germany, be they merely personal or of a wider scope.
Nor can there be much doubt that the poem does indeed thematize
Germany and asks questions about the constitution of national identity.
Yet the focus on the question of the relationship between the representations of Germany and motherhood has distracted attention from
another tension in the poem.

The ten stanzas of the published poem announce the poet's noctural
worries about Germany and his mother, tracing his thought processes or
rather staging the processes of obsession that beset the lonely subject. Yet
as the poet's reverie grows increasingly anxious, the final stanza releases
him as the sun breaks in, his wife enters the room, and the geographical
setting returns emphatically to Paris:

> Gottlob! durch meine Fenster bricht
> Französisch heit'res Tageslicht;
> Es kommt mein Weib, schön wie der Morgen,
> Und lächelt fort die deutschen Sorgen.[2]

German worries are banished with French sunlight: the passage suggests
that the standard question of the reception history regarding the relationship of the political topic of Germany to the private concerns with
the mother may give way, by the final stanza at the latest, to a contrastive staging of national identity characteristics, in particular the tension between the two women, the German mother and the French wife.
In other words, the topic of the poem is not the poet's distance from his
mother but the distance between the alternatives of mother and wife,
Germany and France.

"Night Thoughts" should therefore be read as an opportunity to consider the substance of Cultural Studies – "Denk ich an Deutschland" –
and the conditions, limits, and possibilities of such thinking. In particular, the poem raises questions regarding the mediation of gender and
nationality as an available topic of such thinking. The reception history
of the poem, in contrast, has focused primarily on the relationship
between homeland and mother, surely a conventionally conservative def-

---

2. "Thank God! my window's shining bright / With France's cheerful morning
light; / My wife comes in, fair as the morrow, / And smiles away this German sorrow."
(Draper 408)

inition of the issues at stake, rather than addressing the competition between female figures and between nationalities. The appearance of the French material only in the final stanza is surely no evidence of its marginalization, as Müller claimed (425). For the conclusion of the poem and of the volume is hardly an unmarked location; on the contrary, one can more convincingly claim that it represents the conclusion of the whole book which leads, so to speak, from German Romanticism to French light. It is hard not to conclude that sentimentalizing readings of the poem have hesitated to address the role of France and of the wife due to a sense of standard piety toward the tropes of filial homesickness, even though the poem labors to overcome precisely such nostalgic devotion; the reception of the poem, in other words, still has to catch up with the poem itself.

Heine inherits the project of a contrastive staging of France and Germany from Madame de Staël's *De l'Allemagne* (1810). As early as 1831, just after his arrival in Paris, he deploys the imagery of a sleeping Germany and an active France, as the location of a revolutionary politics, in his introduction to Kahldorf (114). Harald Weinrich refers to this as Heine's "parallel thinking" of the two countries, a term effectively borrowed from Heine, who wrote of the "eternal parallelism" between the two (116).

The parallel in the poem, however, involves less identity and similarity than contrast, most obviously in the visual imagery: Germany is the locus of darkness and nocturnal brooding, while France is associated with the arrival of morning's light. This implies a shift away from the cultural codes of German Romanticism, as exemplified by Novalis's "Hymnen an die Nacht" (Hymns to the Night), which had themselves entailed a rejection of the rationalism of the Enlightenment. That Enlightenment, in the form of the metaphor of light, is reestablished at the poem's end, although now with a new set of associations. The sensuality of the wife and her smiling optimism banish the obsessions of the night, initiating a new and, in this context surely, revolutionary day: While the Germans sleep, the French act. Elsewhere Heine associates the revolution with the crowing of "der gallische Hahn," [the Gallic cock], and Marx, whose acquaintance Heine would make in the autumn of 1843, would soon conclude his introduction to the *Critique of Hegel's Philosophy of Right*, which appeared in the *Deutsch-Französische Jahrbücher* in 1844, with the same metaphor: "When all the inner conditions ripen, *the day of German resurrection* will be proclaimed by *the crowing of the Gallic cock*" (Weinrich 112; Tucker 65).

Given the extensive and often emphatically political tone of the *Neue Gedichte*, it is arguable that Marx's engaged deployment of the metaphor is quite consistent with its significance in Heine's poem of the same period. It is not merely a matter of a contrast between Germany, asleep, benighted, and romantic, with a France of Enlightenment rationality. Dreaming Germany is not only being awakened to the light of reason; it is also being freed from its nightmares by a female enfigurement of revolution. Yet because the nightmares concern the memory of the mother, evidently misread by the sentimentalist tradition, and the revolutionary woman is linked intertextually to a trope of national arousal, the Gallic cock (which may have a phallic resonance but is clearly transgendering by casting the woman as a rooster), any inquiry into nationality in the poem necessarily involves an exploration of the implicit terms of gender identity.

"Night Thoughts" evokes a competition for the attention of the male poet, torn between devotion to his mother and the reveille of his wife; his concern for the mother has occupied him through the night, kept him away from his wife, and trapped him in a trancelike obsession: "die alte Frau hat mich behext."[3] The allusion to witchcraft indicates how the mother is located within the tropes of German Romantic poetry and its dependance on folk traditions. Indeed the first verse of the fifth stanza – "Die Mutter liegt mir stets im Sinn" – uses a phrasing reminiscent of the second of the "Heimkehr" poems of Heine's first poetry volume, *The Book of Songs (Das Buch der Lieder),* the so-called "Lorelei," in which an old legend is described as "Das kommt mir nicht aus dem Sinn."[4] Both Lorelei and mother seize possession of the lyric subjectivity and represent a mortal danger: in the former case the boatsman sails to his death, while in the latter, the poet loses himself in morbid thoughts. Of course some twenty years separate the two poems; if, however, Heine's self-citation indicates that the mother in "Night Thoughts" can be taken as a recurrence of the Lorelei, then she assumes all the features of uncanny threat associated with the siren figure of the earlier poem, and the Marianne of revolution emerges as a genuine competitor, arriving in the morning to rescue her lover from the mother/sorceress with whom he had spent the night. The competition between the women consequently implies a tension within the poet, wavering between alternative definitions of masculinity, as son and as husband.

Heine's adulation of his mother, Betty van Geldern, has frequently been noted by his biographers; it stands out as a conventionally *Bieder-*

3. "The dear old woman has cast a spell" (Draper 407).
4. "Will not depart from my mind." (Draper 76). The original version of the verse from "Night Thoughts" reads "Sie kommt mir nicht mehr aus dem Sinn" (Heine:1983, 770), which differs from the "Lorelei" verse only in the pronoun and the inclusion of the temporal adverb.

meier aspect of a poet more often judged as radical and audacious. Yet this devotion was, at least in the view of Wolfgang Hädecke, not without negative consequences. Betty's ambitions for her son's professional career were never met by his literary pursuits, eliciting a sense of failure and frustration, as Heine described: "I followed obediently her expressed wishes, but I must confess that she was guilty for the fruitlessness of my attempts and efforts in bourgeois positions, since they never corresponded to my own nature" (Hädecke 39, my translation). While the path of his success would draw him away from the worlds of business and law that his mother had wished for her son, a residue of guilt and obligation remained, to which he would return repeatedly: the same structure of obsession recorded in "Night Thoughts." Hädecke conjectures that his "tie to his mother is on a very different level than his intellectual and artistic interests; it is a relationship of hidden eroticism, of which Betty was quite unconscious, but which Heine understood quite well" (41). The most telling evidence is the second of the two sonnets dedicated to his mother in the *Book of Songs*, "Illusion-mad," ("Im tollen Wahn"), in which the poet speaks of his poor decision to leave his mother and to seek love elsewhere, a love that ultimately he can only find with her:

> Doch da bist du entgegen mir gekommen,
> Und ach, was da in deinem Aug geschwommen,
> Das war die süße, lang gesuchte Liebe.[5]

"Night Thoughts" still draws on the image of the mother whom the poet cannot leave, but, unlike the Biedermeier tone of the early poem, casts her as a threat, an uncanny figure of nocturnal suffering, a vampire who disappears only at the break of day. The mother he cherished so much in the *Book of Songs* has grown into a lugubrious threat in the *New Poems*, but, in Paris two decades later, he can envision an alternative to his youthful romanticism.

Heine visited his mother in Hamburg before leaving for Paris in 1831, and when writing "Night Thoughts" in 1843, he had not seen her for the twelve years mentioned in the second stanza. In Paris in October of 1834, he had met Crescentia Mirat, whom he came to call Mathilde, and they began to live together in 1835. Hädecke comments that Heine's "sensitive mother-dependency" prevented him from developing a sexual relationship with the intellectual women with whom he interacted, such as Princess Cristina von Belgiojoso-Trivulzio or George

---

5. "But there you came to welcome me again, / And oh! within your eyes I saw it then – /There was the sweet, the long-sought love at last" (Draper 46).

Sand. Instead he finds Heine writing to his friend Heinrich Laube on 27 September 1835: "I am damned to love only the low and the foolish" (319, my translation). We know that Mathilde knew no German, and there is no evidence that she and her husband shared parts of his literary or intellectual life.

We nevertheless also know of his devotion to her and of his concern for her well-being; in the midst of the controversy with Salomon Strauss in the wake of the Börne polemic, the couple married on 31 August 1841 in Saint-Sulpice. Yet there is ample evidence of tension in the marriage and a certain tone of defensiveness creeps into Heine's letters when he reports on Mathilde. To his sister Charlotte he confesses that they married even though they "had previously quarreled daily for more than six years," and to his friend August Lewald he used the image of a "matrimonial duel, which will not end till one of us be slain." Most telling, though , is a letter to Betty of 8 March 1842, hardly half a year after the wedding:

> My wife is – God be praised! – quite well. She is a most excellent, honorable, good creature, without deceit or malice. But, unfortunately, her temperament is very impatient, her moods unequal, and she often irritates me more than is good for me. I am still devoted to her with all my soul; she is still the deepest want of my life; but that will all cease some day, as all human feelings cease with time, and I look forward to that time with terror, for then I shall have to endure the burden of the caprices without the alleviating sympathy. At other times I am tormented with realizing the helplessness and want of decision in my wife in case I should die, for she is as inexperienced and senseless as a three-year-old child (von Embden 56).

As much as Heine surely loved Mathilde, the relationship was deeply troubled, as the letter to the mother indicates. If, in "Night Thoughts," the poet has spent the night with his mother rather than his wife, who only enters in the morning, Heine's private circumstances may be the source of the depiction. "After only a few years," writes Hädecke, "the two seemed to have largely refrained from sexual relations, certainly also a consequence of Heine's progressive ailment – in 1844 he wrote to Charlotte that they had maintained separate bedrooms for years and that there was no prospect of children" (323). The point is not to reduce the poem to the biographical facts, but to invoke the biography in order to illuminate problems in the text. Just as the evidence of Heine's strong attachment to his mother can be cited to relativize the sentimentalist understanding of the figure of the mother in the poem, so too does the nature of his relationship to Mathilde provide a new perspective on the conclusion. Surely his own anxieties regarding the intellectual and social mismatch contribute to the representation, which is, in effect, an introduction of Mathilde to his German family and public, i.e., Heine is insisting on the grace and virtue of his "Weib," until only recently his mistress, no matter what class prejudices might be operating against her.[6] At the same time, the opposition between mother and wife, in particular the manner in which the wife supersedes the memory of the mother in the historical progression of the poem, concedes the actuality of the very tensions which Heine's gesture of introduction is designed to overcome.

In any case, Heine's celebration of his wife is surely not naive or devoid of complex motivations. The twenty-fourth and final text in the "Political Poems" is intended certainly to resonate with the twenty-fourth and last of the "Romanzen" in the same volume of *New Poems*: "Unterwelt" ("The Lower World"), in which Pluto regrets his marriage to Prosperine and longs for the joys of his bachelor years. As in "Night Thoughts," a realm of darkness contrasts with a realm of light, but the valorization is reversed: Pluto is only too happy to give Prosperine leave to spend half the year on the surface of the earth with her mother, while he can indulge in the pleasures of forgetfulness far away from the light of day:

Süße ruh! Ich kann verschnaufen
Hier im Orkus unterdessen!
Punsch mit Lethe will ich saufen,
Um die Gattin zu vergessen.[7]

The dovetailing of the two poems is complex: in "Lower World," the desire to forget the wife contrasts with the obsessive memory of the mother in "Night Thoughts," and the polarization of light and darkness is inverted. Yet the structure of "Lower World" is ironized further, in so far as it is none other than the god of the underworld who is celebrating Hades, the corollary to Germany in "Night Thoughts." With this in mind, one might take the romance as a back-handed confirmation of the validation of the world of light, which in turn would draw the positionings of the two poems quite close together as expressions of a programmatic Enlightenment. Yet as convincing as such an account of the *New Poems* may be, there remains much evidence of Heine's constant attrac-

6. "It may be observed that Heine – often very naively – did his best to praise his wife, or, to express it plainly, endeavored to vindicate his marriage to his mistress; but, making every allowance, he was evidently most sincerely devoted to her, and it is in this, as in many things, he shows the extraordinary attachment to domestic life and family ties, which is characteristic of the Hebrew race" (von Embden 84).

7. "Ah, sweet peace! Go take your daughter – / I'll enjoy an easylife, / Mixing punch with Lethe water / To forget I have a wife" (Draper 384).

tion to Germany and to the complex of nocturnal tropes as the source of his artistic creativity: "Anno 1839" of the same collection is perhaps the most salient example.

Considerations of Heine's relationships to Betty and Mathilde therefore make a reading of "Night Thoughts" more complex without providing any definitive conclusion. What has conventionally been taken to be a loving portrait of his mother turns out instead, in light of biographical conjectures, to depend on a more problematic network of Romantic images. Meanwhile, the apparently triumphal entry of the wife in the final stanza may relate less to the victory of the Enlightenment and revolution and more to the exigencies of Heine's efforts to legitimate Mathilde to Betty. He would visit his mother in Hamburg in the autumn of 1843, on his first trip back to Germany; he would not introduce Mathilde to Betty personally until the second and last trip in the summer of 1844.

If standard readings of the poem have focused on the nature of the homesickness and the balance between private and political elements, this interpretation has sought to demonstrate some internal tensions within the imagery: Germany and France, mother and wife, realms of darkness and light. To navigate among these polarities entails the recognition that the poem concerns the reciprocal definitions of gender and nationality, which can lead to at least three distinct conclusions. The first involves the manner in which gender roles and sexualities are mobilized as parts of national definitions. For Heine, Germany seems to suffer from a deficient masculinity. According to Lucienne Netter, Heine appreciated a bellicose and conventionally masculine element in the French character, insisting on "the positive aspect of this burning impatience: courage," while he shared with other Emigrés a sense of disappointment that none of the Germans in Paris had participated in the fighting of July 1830 (66): it would have been an opportunity to demonstrate a heroic manliness, not typically associated with Germany. This may have been a more widely held belief in the nineteenth century: Nietzsche would conclude the 209th aphorism of *Beyond Good and Evil* with a vignette from the sexual competition between France and Germany: "[…] it was not so long ago that a masculinized woman [Mme. de Staël – RB] could dare with unbridled presumption to commend the Germans to the sympathy of Europe as being gentle, goodhearted, weak-willed, and poetic dolts. At long last we ought to understand deeply enough Napoleon's surprise when he came to see Goethe: it shows what people had associated with the 'German spirit' for centuries. *'Voilà un homme!'* – that meant: 'But this is a *man*! And I had merely expected a German" (Nietzsche 323). "Night Thoughts" therefore stages a passage from a Germany of deficient manliness to an implicitly normative sexuality of France. Interestingly Nietzsche's account implies the importance for Germany to overcome the legacy of a transgendered de Staël, i.e., to overcome its romanticism, a positioning he shares with Heine.

In this context it is important to recall a poem written during Heine's studies in Bonn when the reactionary weight of the Karlsbad Decrees of 1819 put an end to the progressive aspirations shared by many at the end of the Napoleonic Wars. It was published in 1822 with the title "Germany. A Fragment" ("Deutschland. Ein Fragment"); in its description of counter-revolutionary Germany, the image of "mothers' boys" ("Muttersöhnchen") figures prominently, anticipating the similar configuration in "Night Thoughts" of maternal dependency and retrograde politics: genuine freedom, by extension, is a matter for grown men. In the early poem, the agonistic heroism is more sharply contoured, however, as the poet, claiming a vantage point of superiority, looks down on the degraded country: "Schau' ich jetzt von meinem Berge / In das deutsche Land hinab" (Hädecke 109-10).[8] By the time of the supposedly more radical *New Poems*, Heine had developed a more acute awareness of his own imbrication in the structures of backwardness he chose to attack. "Night Thoughts" does describe a passage from filial subordination to phallic masculinism, but it is not a simple or irreversible transition, given the degree to which it concedes the poet's own nocturnal anxieties.

In addition to the sexual history of the poem, a second line of inquiry proceeds from the first verse and its announcement of thinking about Germany in order, however, to draw out of the text a distancing from the particular mode of thought. On one level this involves the implied transition from the obsessive profundity of a melancholy German mind, and its awakening to a Saint-Simonist celebration of life and flesh in France. This is surely a familiar paradigm, contrasting romantic Germany with rational France and bemoaning what would come to be called Germany's *Sonderweg*, its special path, different from the implicity normal path of France and England. Consequently the paradox of the poem would be the congruence of a foregrounded homesickness, a looking backwards, so to speak, and an historical imperative pointing in a quite different direction: an obligation to leave Germany or, at least, to leave the culture of backwardness it was taken to represent.

The cognitive reconfiguration implied by the poem, however, is not limited to the national transition, nor is it correctly grasped as a displacement of a German thinking by a French alternative. What is at

8. "Look now from my mountain station / Down on Germany's sad waves" (Draper 300).

stake rather is a staging of the limitations of an initial logocentricity, the project of merely thinking about Germany, which remains deficient as long as it is not conjoined with the possibility of action. The curse of the poet in "Night Thoughts" is the inadequacy of philosophy and idealism, overcome only at the end by the entry of the wife representing a very different set of principles: sensuality, of course, in her beauty, but also a postidealism to the extent that her mere smile – and not a word or logos – overcomes the convoluted thoughts of the troubled night and breaks the spell of the sorceress/mother: woman as postlogocentricity. Her smile is an emblem of existentialist affirmation of the possibility of action. As a passage to the materialism of the deed, this final "Political Poem" repeats and reasserts the promise of the first in the collection, "Doktrin," which is organized around the image of waking people from sleep; the poet in "Night Thoughts" has no sleep, but he too is caught in an inadequate consciousness from which he is awakened only at the end.

The first hypothesis regarding the poem posited a context of a presumed masculinity-deficit in Germany, corrected by the passage of the poem; the second repeats the argument with regard to the contrast between idealist thinking and materialist practice. Both approaches certainly highlight aspects of the text, but one should not lose sight of the fact that both are also themselves thematic components of the poem and therefore not strictly valid as explanations. In other words, the binary opposition performed by the juxtaposition of mother and wife within the poem should be taken more as a device rather than the meaning, a device to underscore the deficiencies in particular thought patterns and not as a programmatic assertion of French reason or Saint-Simonist materialism.

"Night Thoughts" shows how the poet, worrying about his mother, proceeds to worry about all his loved ones in Germany and, from there, quickly forges ahead to a compulsive counting of cadavers, a sort of unproductive worry that keeps him awake until his wife arrives to put an end to his melancholy. This debilitating mentality is the concern of the poem, rather than the German reality which underlies the insomniac's concerns: the topic of the poem is not Germany but thinking about Germany, "Denk ich an Deutschland," and "deutsche Sorgen" or, in other words, Cultural Studies. The text in fact demonstrates how the poet's thinking of a proleptically generalized Germany, the "Deutschland" of the first verse, sets him on an erroneous path that necessarily magnifies anxiety and distorts his affection for his mother: his legitimate concern for her well-being disappears behind images of mass death: "Mir ist als wälzten sich die Leichen / auf meiner Brust [...]."[9] An affect of longing

---

9. "As if the dead host pressed unknowing / upon my breast [...]" (Draper 408).

slips into anticipatory mourning that then explodes into a full blown melancholic disorder. Put differently, the problem of the poem is not Germany but a particular mode of thinking about Germany. There is some evidence that Heine codes this mode as feminine: it includes the mother's writing described in the poem, and it may also involve Heine's underlying resistance to de Staël, as Diana Justis has argued (9). Yet there are plenty of German Romantics in *Die romantische Schule*, who could serve as examples of Heine's male targets.

More importantly the neurotic exaggerations that devolve from the imagery of Germany are themselves dismantled by the text through its representation of a complex arrangement of gender and sexuality. The representation of gender, therefore, functions as a corrective to the negative nationalism of the poetic verse, i.e., a Romantic rhetoric that stages Germany as a site of infinite threat, a threat which the text exposes and critiques. Gender operates in a complex way on two different levels: the misogynist desire to overcome Germany's deficient masculinity and thereby escape the political reaction is undermined by the poem's depiction of gender complexity in the tension between wife and mother. In other words, if German backwardness appeared to entail a threat of effeminization, Heine demonstrates that progressive France, the political alternative, is equally a site of female agency. In turn, the Romantic characterization of lugubrious Germany loses its legitimacy; by implication, the poem posits a German Studies that, rather than repeating "Märchen aus alten Zeiten" [old fairy tales], might study Germany instead of its traditional representations, no matter how seductive these noctural thoughts and horror stories might still be to the willing executors of the romantic legacy.

In "Night Thoughts" and in general in the *New Poems*, Heine was returning to poetry for the first time since his first volume, the *Book of Songs* of 1822. Most of his work in the intervening years had been in prose, particularly his travelogues and his reports from Paris; this generic choice was quite consonant with prevailing aesthetics, which claimed that contemporary society could best be captured in prose, while poetry was treated as nearly obsolete. Reclaiming poetry, Heine raises an issue at the core of Cultural Studies, the relative values of the accumulation of material in the prose text and the alternative possibility of concentrated expression and formal innovation in verse. "Night Thoughts" parodies obsessive concern with preservation, a sentimentalism toward the past, and a self-deceptive exaggeration of suffering and threat, and it attempts to clear the way for an alternative approach to Germany, one that could focus on the possibility of human action and innovation, rather than on the ineluctable and structural. It demonstrates the trap of a premature generalization of Germany, therefore eliciting a distance from the total-izing aesthetic of the novel as form. Finally, it directs us away from mere documentations of conditions or discourses presumed to shape lives and allegedly construct identities, while demonstrating instead the capacity of human action, even as subtle as a smile, to announce the possibility of freedom, which ought to be the topic of studies of culture.

The morning and the night, the wife and the mother, are poised in the fragile crystal of the poem, freezing, for a moment, antipodal possi-bilities: writing and vision, age and youth, myth and enlightenment. Mathilde's triumphalism hardly erases Betty, preserved in the anamnesis which, of course, predominates in the reception history attuned to a remembering of the past more than to the accomodations of exile, which memory may condemn as treasonous betrayals. Yet this poetic territory of lamentation conjoined to redemption is nothing other than the landscape of German poetry, at least between Luther's mighty fortress, embattled but preserved, to Celan's "Death Fugue," entwining Faustian crime with the *Song of Songs*. To speak of these voices – Gun-dolf's phrase "Schicksalsprache eines Volkes" [the language of destiny of a people] comes to mind – implies several cultural claims, including of course the possibility of culture, poetic culture, and its urgency for his-tory, and, with regard to Germany, the constitutive status of Jewish tra-ditions (Gundolf 31). For this is not only an intriguing subtext in "Night Thoughts," it also takes issue with claims of ultimate incompatibility, e.g., in Gershom Scholem's dismissal of the "German-Jewish symbiosis" or, more recently, the thesis that an eliminationist antisemitism is the defining feature of modern German culture, or that German identity necessarily and with an internal logic led to the Holocaust. Daniel Gold-hagen's thesis is relevant to Cultural Studies (and not only to historians, narrowly defined) because his fundamental cultural contentions are based on the same ethnographic turn underlying much of the Cultural Studies movement: witness his repeated reference to the perspective of an "anthropologist," his interest in antisemitism as a "cultural axiom," descriptions of the "common sense" of a culture, and ultimately the focus on the "ordinary," as in "ordinary Germans." (Goldhagen 1, 9, 14, 15, 419, 460). If it is not exactly the standard Cultural-Studies vocabu-lary, it rings quite familiar after Geertz, Foucault, popular culture. What sets it apart from Cultural Studies as currently practiced is of course the remarkable gender-blindness of the treatment, as if Germans were "ordi-narily" mainly men.

Antisemitism was not some litmus test of authentic Germanhood, not in historically distant periods, not in the nineteenth century, and not in 1933: not even, for that matter, in 1943, as evidenced by Victor

Klemperer's reports from wartime Dresden (Klemperer II: 387). Such a pejorative evaluation of Germans may be part of the "common sense" of our culture, but that is another matter that leads to questions regarding the function of American German Studies. For Cultural Studies, the question is whether "common sense" is an adequate object of investigation. Heidegger's *Gerede*, Adorno's *Verdinglichung*, Arendt's "banality": are these the domain of culture or are they not, like the "ordinary," the very problem to which culture is the answer. Consider the thought experiment: is the goal of education, especially but not exclusively literary education, "ordinariness"? Do we teach our students to be "ordinary"? Is the point of the project some fundamental compliance in an administrative logic of conformism? Surely not, surely it involves aspirations of exceptionality (alterity, if you prefer), and this is the home territory of the poem. How to think about Germany? Cultural Studies stands at a cross roads between aesthetic and ethnographic models of meaning. The choice of direction remains open. We have a choice. But we should not delude ourselves into thinking that the choice is inconsequential, for our institutions, for education, or for our culture, both national and personal.

Bibliography

Adorno, Theodor W. *Noten zur Literatur I*. Frankfurt a.M.: Suhrkamp, 1958.

Arendt, Hannah. *Eichmann in Jerusalem: A Report on the Banality of Evil*. New York: Viking, 1963.

Berman, Russell A. *Cultural Studies of Modern Germany: History, Representation, and Nationhood*. Madison: U of Wisconsin P, 1993.

Brod, Max. *Heinrich Heine*. Leipzig and Vienna: E.P. Tal, 1934.

De Stael-Holstein, Anne Louise Germaine (Necker) Baronne de. *De l'Allemagne*. Paris: Hachette, 1967.

Embden, Ludwig von. *The Family Life of Heinrich Heine*. London: William Heinemann, 1893.

Goldhagen, Daniel Jonah. *Hitler's Willing Executioners: Ordinary Germans and the Holocaust*. New York: Knopf, 1996.

Gundolf, Friedrich. *Hutten, Klopstock, Arndt: Drei Reden*. Heidelberg: Weiss'sche Universitätsbuchhandlung, 1924.

Hädecke, Wolfgang. *Heinrich Heine: Eine Biographie*. Munich: Carl Hanser, 1985.

Heidegger, Martin. *Sein und Zeit*. Tübingen: Max Niemeyer, 1986.

Heine, Heinrich. *Neue Gedichte*. Ed. Elisabeth Gernot. *Historisch-kritische Gesamtausgabe der Werke*. Vol. 2. Ed. Manfred Windfuhr. Hamburg: Hoffmann and Campe, 1983.

_____. *The Complete Poems of Heinrich Heine: A Modern English Version*. Trans. Hal Draper. Boston: Suhrkamp/Insel, 1982.

Hermand, Jost. "Der 'deutsche' Jude H. Heine." *Dichter und ihre Nation*. Ed. Helmut Scheuer. Frankfurt a.M.: Suhrkamp, 1993. 257-72.

Justis, Diana Lynn. "The Feminine in Heine's Life and Oeuvre: Self and Other." Dissertation Cornell, 1993.

Klemperer, Victor. *Ich will Zeugnis ablegen bis zum letzten: Tagebücher*. Berlin: Aufbau, 1945.

Müller, Joachim. *Wirklichkeit und Klassik*. Berlin: Verlag der Nation, 1955.

Netter, Lucienne. "Heine et les Français: Histoire d'une Amitié." *Recherches Germaniques* 15 (1985): 63-86.

Nietzsche, Friedrich. *Basic Writings of Nietzsche*. Ed. Walter Kaufmann. New York: Modern Library, 1992.

Novalis (Friedrich von Hardenberg). *Hymnen an die Nacht. English and German*. Trans. Dick Higgins. New Paltz, NY: McPherson, 1984.

Psaar, Werner. "Zur Deutung Heinescher Gedichte in Deutschunterricht: Probleme und Versuche." *Heine Jahrbuch* 6 (1967): 81-123.

Scholem, Gershom. *On Jews and Judaism in Crisis: Selected Essays*. New York: Schocken, 1976.

Tucker, Robert C., ed. *The Marx-Engels Reader*. New York: W. W. Norton, 1978.

Weinrich, Harald. "Heinrich Heines deutsch-französische Parallelen." *Heine Jahrbuch* 29 (1990): 111-28.

Chapter 5

THE FATHERLAND'S KISS OF DEATH

Gender and Germany in Nineteenth-Century Historical Fiction

Brent O. Peterson

Women were usually relegated to supporting roles in nineteenth-century historical fiction – even in works by women authors; the period's historical novels depended on swashbuckling heroes to attract readers, in much the same manner as its popular and academic history focused on the actions of "great" men in politics and on the battlefield. History, which was invented as both a "scientific" discipline and a literary genre at the beginning of the nineteenth century, was mainly national history and an unabashedly male preserve, but as it was defined and popularized in both fictional and non-fiction histories, the German nation depended on specific models of femininity and the family. Thus, to understand "Germany" as a discursive formation, i.e., as a set of ideas rather than merely a place or a political entity, one needs to examine how gender was encoded in the emerging nationalist narrative. Historical fiction, where women were at least included, if seldom accorded a central position, provides unparalleled access to the gendered construction of the German nation.

The nineteenth-century historical novel is a vast and largely unexplored corner of German literary life.[1] While only a few historical nov-

1. In the past twenty-five years there have only been four full-length studies of historical fiction, none of which was concerned with the issues raised here. See Eggert, Geppert, Limli, and Sottong.

els have achieved anything close to canonical status, Norbert Eke describes historical fiction during the first third of the century as "the leading form of the novel, pure and simple" (301).[2] He also credits a woman, Wilhelmine von Gersdorf, with having written the first German novel to bear the title "historical," *Aurora Gräfin von Königsmark: Ein historischer Roman* (Aurora, Countess of Königsmark: An Historical Novel), while Denis Sweet claims that the early German author of historical fiction, Benedikte Naubert, influenced Sir Walter Scott, rather than having been influenced by him (204). More importantly, the historical fiction that Gersdorf, Naubert, and hundreds of other male and female writers produced was predominately concerned with German history and culture, and it can scarcely have been accidental that the historical novel and the academic discipline of history both came into being simultaneously with German nationalism. Narrative discussions of the past were one of the primary sources of information about what Prussians, Saxons, and Anhalt-Zerbstians had to learn in order to become Germans, and, to judge by the holdings of the private, for-profit lending libraries that mirrored the period's literary tastes, for most of the nineteenth century historical fiction was the most popular literary genre in Germany.[3] The same narratives that articulated and popularized this new national consciousness were also filled with gender-specific role models. While the subject of women and the German nation in nineteenth-century historical fiction is too vast to cover in a single essay, a small sample of thematically linked texts can help elucidate what was at stake in representing both women and Germany in historical fiction.

For this purpose, novels set in the so-called Wars of Liberation (1812-1815) are particularly useful, because it is during that extended conflict that German national consciousness is supposed to have come into full flower. If one believes the myth, perpetrated in large part by nineteenth-century historians and the authors of historical fiction, "the German people" – students, shopkeepers, and peasants alike – arose to the last "man" in order to throw out the foreign invaders; whether popular German nationalism really developed during the struggle to free "Germany" from Napoleon is unclear. No such country as Germany existed either before or after the conflict, and none of the individual German governments wanted to see themselves united into a single political entity. Just who the Germans were remained a contentious issue, in part because potential Germans seem to have retained regional or caste identities when they were supposed to be acquiring a national orientation. Speak-

---

2. All translations from this and subsequent German texts are my own.
3. See Martino.

ing of one particularly crucial constituency, the historian Hans Ulrich Wehler estimates that fewer than five percent of university students participated in the struggle against the French, and participation was likely to have been even lower in other segments of the population (I, 525). The story of German resistance to Napoleon was, nevertheless, a very useful fiction in constructing a common German past, and shared histories continue to be an important part of what it means to belong to a national community. How writers treated the Napoleonic era is therefore especially revealing, and those treatments are also typical of how they dealt with other people and events from history.

Particularly in novels written during the first third of the nineteenth century the heroes and heroines tended to be aristocrats, whose allegiance was a matter of caste rather than nationality. Two examples, briefly treated, will have to suffice before turning to the far more interesting cases of bourgeois characters. One of the first novels to deal with the wars against the French was Friedrich de la Motte Fouqué's *Der Refugié* (The Refugee), which appeared in 1824. The book's confused hero, who is both bourgeois and aristocratic, as well as Prussian, French, and German, dies along the Rhine River, unsure of his national identity and unable to marry his beloved Countess Maria von Hohenstein, because she is unaware of his noble lineage.[4] Since she knows nothing of the hero's conflicted heritage, the question of nationality never arises for this otherwise well-read and insightful young woman, and she eventually marries someone else.

Of interest here is not simply how little attention Fouqué's text pays to its female characters, who make only brief appearances in the novel's three substantial volumes. More puzzling, and therefore more revealing, is the fact that women in these novels apparently pay no attention to politics and the events that threaten their brothers, sons, and lovers. For example, once the French invade Prussia, Maria von Hohenstein temporarily enters a nunnery, where she seems to have spent her time waiting to marry whoever survives the conflict. Hers is the typical fate of aristocratic women in historical fiction. She represents the opportunity for an idyllic retreat from the world of war and nationalist tensions, but her offer can only be accepted after the fighting has stopped. Essentially, domesticity is suspended until the book's men work out whatever problems exist in the public sphere, while the women disappear from the plot, because there is nothing for them to do – and "no place" for them to do anything either. In ideological terms, women occupy a literal utopia, an empty space, blissfully but unrealistically free of nationalist tensions. Men might agonize

---

4. See Peterson for a reading that concentrates on the hero of this and other novels.

over their own loyalties, but, unless they suffer the tragic fate of Fouqué's hero, they eventually marry their comrades' sisters or cousins. For no other reason than their mutual availability, Maria von Hohenstein marries a Count von Sternberg; they retire to a world of society balls; and the novel ends. Not once does the author or narrator allow her to become involved in the struggles that animate the book's male characters.

The situation is somewhat more complex, but just as limited for the main female character in the second example of early historical fiction, H. E. R. Belani's 1829 novel, *Die Demagogen* (The Demagogues). That book's main character, Baron Hermann von Rosenberg, also waits until the conflict with Napoleon is over before marrying his Italian cousin, the Countess Monta Rosa. She is more involved in the plot details than Maria von Hohenstein; at times Carla Monta Rosa even assumes a male identity in order to take part in her cousin's schemes. In the end, however, she marries for love, while Hermann views marriage as an act of renunciation. He gives up his dream of a liberal revolution in Germany, decides that his love for a German woman was a fantasy, and settles for Carla. Adding insult to injury, Hermann then describes himself as "homeless" – as if his new wife were not just as uprooted, both in Germany and in New York's Hudson River valley, where the two of them finally settle (II, 245). In fact, since the marriage fulfills a contractual obligation to unite two branches of the family, it satisfies caste loyalties about which only Hermann is aware. Once again, the woman is an unthinking object of male attention. Neither Carla Monta Rosa nor Maria von Hohenstein is allowed to decide her own fate, although they accept their lot by justifying it in terms of the strictly "female" private sphere.

Of course, for either of these women to have made their own choices about issues in the public sphere would have raised the spectre of conflict not only with foreign invaders, but also, and more problematically, with their potential husbands. Significantly, it is mainly the bourgeois heroines of novels from later in the century who explore the possibility of women's nationalism. Again, two examples will have to suffice, but since they both place their female characters in far more complex situations, rather than sending them to nunneries or relegating them to the margins of the plot, they require a more detailed treatment. The novels are Ludwig Rellstab's *1812*, which was published in 1834, and Julius von Wickede's *Der lange Isaack* (Tall Isaack) from 1863, but, to show that these themes were not limited to male authors, a very brief look at Louise von François' 1871 novel, *Die letzte Reckenburgerin* (The Last Reckenburgerin) will also be included.

Like most nineteenth-century historical novels, *1812* is not only long but also immensely complicated. Half a dozen major characters become involved in innumerable plot twists and turns, and the author needs more than a few unlikely coincidences to keep his whole intricate construction from collapsing. Although readers can assume there will be some sort of happy ending, in part because they are aware of what happened in Germany after 1812, Rellstab's novel nevertheless raises a number of troubling issues. It is not the simple panegyric to German nationalism that someone unfamiliar with the genre might expect; indeed, by representing the effects of history on ordinary men and women, historical fiction is in a position to make its accounts far more nuanced than academic history, which concentrates on the affairs of states and the "great men" who ran them. For example, as the book opens, "a young German," Ludwig Rosen is returning to Dresden from Italy in order to fulfill his duty to his mother and his "fatherland," both of whom are threatened by a renewed French invasion. Ludwig's obligation to his mother seems straightforward, because she is a widow living with his younger sister, but what he owes the fatherland is far less clear, and the text immediately calls the categories "German" and "fatherland" into question. If it were up to him, Ludwig would remain in Italy with its warm climate and friendly inhabitants, and he also knows that Dresden will be welcoming Napoleon, with whom Saxony has long been allied. In fact, the book's young hero is himself an admirer of the French emperor, because he sees in Napoleon the one possible solution to "the German problem" of small states and corrupt princes. As reluctant as he is to be "home" in the first place, Ludwig decides that he can only fight for Germany by leaving it, so he joins a Franco-Polish regiment whose officers he met during his return from Italy. The news sends his sister into despair, and the reader encounters, perhaps for the first time, an openly patriotic German woman. Not for nothing is she also bourgeois.

Marie Rosen knows that her brother's absence will be hard for their mother to bear, but the prospect is even more difficult for Marie to accept. Ludwig is aware that his sister has "a true German heart" (101), but she, too, is torn by conflicting desires. Marie has fallen in love with one of Ludwig's Polish officer friends, Count Rasinski, and he returns her affections. Indeed, he offers to marry her, once the war is over, despite their very different class and national backgrounds. Unlike the aristocratic heroines of the previous two novels, whose allegiances are more to caste than country, and whose spheres of opportunity are decidedly domestic, Marie refuses. She even argues with Rasinski about politics, and the narrator takes great pains to explain her dilemma: "He was allied with someone she could only view as the enemy of her fatherland; she could honor him as a noble man, love him as a generous friend, but never belong to him, fuse her whole being with his without neglecting duties whose sacredness completely pervaded her soul" (111). In other words, unlike the typical women of historical fiction, Marie ventures far enough into the public sphere both to have an opinion on the day's burning issues and to accept the painful consequences of her beliefs. The choice she makes is difficult and groundbreaking. Renouncing romance was traumatic for anyone coded "female" in nineteenth-century fiction, and by choosing "the German nation" over domestic bliss, Marie essentially accepts the nation's masculine values. Unfortunately for her, and even more so for the novelist, the heroine's "male" decision raises innumerable narratological problems; in essence, by allowing Marie Rosen to break the narrative convention of female passivity in national issues, Rellstab severely limits his options for writing a plausible happy ending. Indeed, his novel requires all manner of contortions to end at all.

One might, however, forgive an author a great deal for daring to let women pose serious questions. For example, although it strains the reader's credulity to believe that Ludwig Rosen would encounter and help rescue a beautiful young woman along the road over the Simplon pass, later to be saved by her from the flames of Moscow, only to discover that she is really the long-lost sister of his best friend, and a German rather than a Russian, the woman in question does raise the issue of nature vs. nurture with regard to national identity. Similarly, the Polish countess who "accidentally" meets Marie Rosen at a spa and offers to protect her from the French secret police turns out to be Count Rasinski's sister, but she also lends validity to claims of Polish national feelings that contrast sharply with Marie's German convictions. In short – and there are far more startling coincidences than those just listed – if one allows Rellstab such improbabilities, his novel can show just how complicated and contentious the issue of national identity must have been for him and his readers. His utterly unrealistic plot permits three women characters to become involved in very realistic dilemmas, each having to do with a different aspect of national identity.

Ludwig is the first to encounter Polish nationalism, and he declares himself happy to be in a Polish regiment, because their struggle is "unquestionably just" (121), but it is Countess Micielska who lends the cause genuine nobility. To begin, the narrator describes her as having a "tall, majestic physique" (119); a page later he terms her figure "tall and noble" (120). The countess also fares well in a direct comparison with Marie, even though one might expect the German woman to be more positive:

> The countess showed an active, intellectual interest in public affairs; ... she read the newspapers and the day's political tracts eagerly; she was familiar with the history of events, followed them with acumen, and was able to connect distant incidents intelligently with the fate of her fatherland. Marie by

contrast simply loved her home and the people to whom she belonged above all else; her language and mode of thought made her a German ... . Once the fatherland was liberated, her interest in public affairs would disappear or at least recede into the distance as it did for all women (376).

The "all women" at the end of this passage is troubling, and it also contradicts what the narrator has just said about Countess Micielska. On the one hand, the phrase certainly reflects an underlying patriarchal attitude, but on the other, it shows how difficult it was for writers to deal realistically with strong women. Since Poland, despite the nobility of both its cause and its supporters, is not freed in the Wars of Liberation, since the countess cannot really settle for the diminished life available to her in Europe after 1815, and since she is also denied a heroic death in the struggle that claims her brother, Countess Micielska appears in the novel's final scene and announces that she is emigrating to America, where she hopes to die – soon, but nevertheless breathing the sweet air of freedom. It is as happy an ending as is possible, given her impassioned support for a doomed cause.

Rasinski's death, by contrast, means that Marie must have made the right choice. She ends up marrying her brother's German friend, and the reader hears nothing more of her German patriotism. The third woman, however, raises another set of complex issues. Ludwig knows her as Bianka, the mysteriously beautiful figure who appears and disappears so frequently that she seems to haunt his life like a ghost. Meanwhile, the reader encounters a Russian countess, Feodorowna, who is unexpectedly critical of her own national origin. Although Russia soon becomes Germany's most important ally in their common war against Napoleon, Feodorowna's father is presented as a particularly galling example of "eastern barbarism." He is dishonest, treats his servants like cattle, and tries to marry his daughter to an odious but rich prince. She rebels and even tells the family's German gardener to flee: "Woe to anyone who has to call [Russia] fatherland; blessed are they who have a different home!" (182). Feodorowna seems resigned to accepting the country of her birth; for her, national origin appears to be an inescapable, if also tragic fate.

Identity in this novel has gone beyond allegiance and crossed the boundary to an essentialism that is ultimately based in blood. It is therefore not surpriing, given the new discursive framework of national identity, that on her wedding night, this Russian countess finds out that she is actually German. The reader eventually learns – or immediately guesses – that she is actually Bernhard's sister. If that coincidence were not enough, Rasinski's troops storm the family castle before her marriage is consummated; Feodorowna turns out to be not only German but also the beautiful bourgeois Bianka, a character as pure (white) as her name has always suggested; and, since they are no longer separated by national identity, Bianka and Ludwig marry near the novel's end. Thus, the two happy couples are completely German. They can experience the book's happy ending because, and only because, there are no national encumbrances to their love, which also means, in narratological terms, that the two women can be relegated to lesser roles. The novel's penultimate chapter has the four main characters back in Germany, where the war is not quite over. In fact, it is only 1813, and the two men answer the fatherland's call to arms. Ludwig and Bernhard march off, this time as Germans in an ostensibly German army, while Marie and Bianka retreat to the countryside near Dresden. They, too, are German patriots, but as women they have to stay home. In short, Bianka and Marie pay a double price for their eventual happiness: They have to ally themselves with their fellow Germans, rather than marrying the foreigners with whom they initially fell in love – Rasinski and Ludwig, who was a foreigner until Bianka's mistaken identity was resolved; these women are only able to observe from a distance the dreams of national unity and freedom that they share with their husbands. To be sure, their fate is better than the death or exile visited upon the women of other countries, but the German fatherland has still forced "his" women to pay dearly for their reward. Neither Bianka nor Marie is as interesting or as fully developed a character as Countess Micielska.

The toll that Rellstab's novel extracts from its heroines is made both possible and necessary by the women's national origins, so it should not be surprising that Julius von Wickede raises the stakes considerably by placing a Jewish family at the center of *Tall Isaack*. The book is one of the very few philo-Semitic works of nineteenth-century fiction, particularly patriotic fiction, and there are certainly a disturbing number of counter examples in the corpus of German literature, such as *1812*, which features a Lithuanian Jew who is a double agent and, perhaps, a murderer, although he at least speaks coherent German rather than the pidgin usually associated with Jews in these works. He also only appears twice, whereas Wickede's main characters are all Jews. Chief among them are the peddler Isaack and his daughter Rebekka. The novel takes place in the countryside around Lüneburg in 1813, and it opens by contrasting Isaack's hard life, as he hikes from farm to farm selling needles, fabric, and whatever else people need, with that of the Bruhn family. They used to be prosperous yeoman farmers, but while war, taxes, and the cost of quartering French forces have taken their toll on the family's wealth, they remain solid citizens and staunch Germans. One day Isaack knocks on their door and hears the following, profoundly mixed greeting: "Really and truly, Isaack, to be sure you are only a Jew, and I actually can't stand Jews, but there is not a man in all of Hannover who has a more honest heart in his chest than you do" (I: 49). Isaack, for his part, claims to have made his most recent trip "so that he could render an important service to the cause of the fatherland" (I: 50). In fact, at the cost of considerable personal sacrifice and danger, he provides crucial information about the movement of the French army to the German population and the troops who are just beginning to defend them, but what his daughter does is far more interesting.

Rebekka lives in Lüneburg in a house that is described, in another example of faint and demeaning praise, as "unusually clean for Jews" (109). Among its decorations are busts of Schiller, Lessing, and Mendelssohn, appropriately, because the young woman has inherited her mother's love of German literature. Actually, it was Rebekka's maternal grandfather, "a learned rabbi, ... who first revealed the rich treasures of our best German authors" to the family (I: 117), and Rebekka herself can scarcely read enough of these classic works. She also longs for someone, presumably a man as intelligent and as well read as she is, so the two of them can talk about literature. When she offers to nurse a wounded Prussian officer back to health, she initially thinks her prayers have been answered. Rich, noble, and patriotic, Fritz von Dassow appears to be an ideal romantic hero, and he is also fresh from the university, i.e., presumably a reader. Although the irony may not have been intended, the narrator terms Rebekka's care "true Christian charity, a purer and nobler example could not be found on earth" (II: 8); she also reads aloud to him from Goethe, Schiller, and Klopstock. The scene is too good to be true, especially, as skeptical readers will note, this early in a three-volume novel.

As a character, Rebekka anticipates almost all the tensions and difficulties associated with German-Jewish assimilation throughout the nineteenth and on into the twentieth century; she allows Wickede to explore a strategy that actually served German Jews quite badly, even in 1863, more than seventy-five years before the Holocaust. Rebekka is educated, beautiful, sensitive, and more committed to German culture than many Germans. She has also adopted what the book codes as German traits, for example, cleanliness and Christian charity. Moreover, although she refuses to renounce the religion of her forebears, Rebekka eagerly reads a New Testament that a theology student friend has given the wounded officer, while at the same time she wonders why Jews support Germany when most Germans reject them as compatriots. Wickede uses Rebekka to show how Germans, who are often no more positive than Fritz von Dassow, viewed this remarkable woman and her father – first, foremost, and last – as Jews whose German patriotism remained incomprehensible. While the Jews in this novel are unable to fashion an alternative identity, neither can they understand the Germans' unyielding rejection of their German-Jewish orientation. *Tall Isaack* is a prescient examination of the small tragedies that presaged Germany's greatest disaster, and its troubled philo-Semitism is particularly remarkable in an overtly patriotic treatment of the Wars of Liberation.

Fritz von Dassow, meanwhile, is grateful for the care he receives but bored by the German classics that Rebekka reads him. The contrast between the two characters could scarcely be greater: "The books that the young lieutenant ordered from a lending library in the city during the course of his gradual recuperation, books that were more to his taste, were either so trivial or so risqué that [Rebekka] scornfully threw them aside after reading only a few pages" (II: 31). As the son of an ancient noble family Fritz knows that unbridgeable caste differences separate him from the daughter of a Jewish peddler, while Rebekka has long since lost interest in her dashing dolt, except when he talks of doing battle with the French:

> In his moments of military enthusiasm the lieutenant appeared to the Jewish woman again in the ideal light in which she had first seen him after he was wounded ... . [but it] remained an inexplicable mystery to her that the same man who was open to such noble emotions, who continually showed himself ready to shed his heart's most intimate blood gladly for the liberation of the fatherland, would also show so little interest in every higher intellectual calling, indeed, would exhibit a taste for trivialities to which she was indifferent or even contemptuous. But Rebekka also felt the bitterest pain at defeats suffered by the allies, and she, too, loved her great German fatherland, for although she was a Jew, she was, at the same time, a true and genuine German ... (II: 39-40).

What is really at issue in this passage is what it means to be German. The book questions the concept of the *Kulturnation* by asking to what extent the nation's vaunted high culture links the vast majority of Germans, including German aristocrats, who neither read nor understand the "nation's" artistic heritage, and the narrative voice also doubts the sufficiency of patriotic enthusiasm as a foundation for the national project. Most important, Wickede wonders who the real Germans are, and whether they include women and Jews.

The question of identity for women and Jews appears in a different guise when one of the local noble-women, who had earlier turned down an offer of marriage from a solidly German farmer, is forced to marry a French officer. She finds herself isolated in occupied Hamburg, where she reluctantly visits the German-speaking mistress of the French military governor. For an aristocrat, even one whose husband could use a few favors, calling on this "fallen woman" and "notorious Jew" is a bitter pill to swallow, and her dismay is complete when she recognizes her as Isaack's older daughter, Sara. Although she was carried off by French officers in 1806, Sara seems to have made the best of a bad situation. She is as intelligent and as cultured as her sister Rebekka, and, according to rumor, has had an affair with Napoleon himself. In effect, Sara represents one of the few choices available to a strong female character other than a submissive marriage, but for her the wages of freedom include, first, a reputation for immorality, second, the hatred of her German compatriots, because she is both a traitor and a Jew, and, third, the scorn of her father and sister. Sara's only friend, if one can use the term so loosely, is the French officer's wife, for although the two women despise each other immediately and instinctively, neither of them has a better option. While readers are probably not disturbed by the sad fate accorded to an opportunistic and not particularly intelligent German countess, the fact that Sara ultimately fails to find happiness could be troubling. In narratological terms, however, the author has run out of alternatives. Renouncing France and freedom, even if it earned a reconciliation with her father, would put Sara back into the same set of dilemmas that her sister faces, on the one hand, the multifaceted conflicts between German high culture, a cruder form of German patriotism, and anti-Semitic prejudice, and, on the other hand, Rebekka's own incompatible loyalties. What, one might wonder without too much irony, is an intelligent German-Jewish woman to do?

Rebekka finds herself forced by circumstances to lodge with a slovenly aunt, a woman whose lack of household skills apparently make her more Jewish in one of the book's few slips into caricature. Not surprisingly, Rebekka sits with her favorite book, Lessing's *Nathan the Wise*, a play about religious tolerance. In its famous ring parable Lessing's play suggests that the Muslim, Christian, and Jewish religions are equally valid variations on a single theme, but Rebekka is to be sadly disappointed if she expects her reality to conform to one of the classic texts of the German Enlightenment. In fact, she and Fritz von Dassow's theologian friend fall deeply in love, but their relationship is hopeless in the sense that the two can never marry without one of them converting, presumably Rebekka, whose gender and religion both mark her as weaker. Although drawn together by their shared intellectual interests, mainly their love of German literature, these two characters are simultaneously repelled by their differing and deeply held religious convictions. Here too, Wickede stages an interesting confrontation, which is all the more telling because he seems to have shared Lessing's enlightened perspective, but was unable or unwilling to concoct the kind of implausibly happy ending that rescues the playwright's idealism. Whereas Lessing reveals his play's young lovers to be siblings of such mixed parentage that the question of religion is obviated, while marriage becomes impossible, Wickede refuses to stoop to such coincidences. Whether his "realistic" high-mindedness was intended as a claim on literary quality is probably beside the point, even though the book raises the issue of high culture so relentlessly that it has to be reflecting on its own status as well as on the political questions that it poses. In any case, just as he is about to march off to fight the French, the theologian informs Rebekka that he will marry her after the war is over if she becomes a Christian. She refuses, saying: "God's will ordained that I was born a Jew … . If I had been born a Christian, I would certainly have become a true adherent of your religion" (II: 321-25). In essence, Wickede represents religion as an accident of birth, not unlike national origin, and the student, for all his Protestant convictions, has no choice but to respect Rebekka's decision. The only question is what will, or, in structural terms, what can become of these two ill-matched lovers.

It takes a great deal of plot before they are reunited, but Rebekka eventually learns that her beloved theologian was mortally wounded in the allies' victory over Napoleon at Leipzig. He wants to see her before he dies, so Rebekka hurries off to the hospital. Of course, the young man dies in her arms, and, just as predictably, Rebekka succumbs to her own feverish nerves and dies, too, but at home and in Isaack's warm embrace. Even so, the melodrama is not quite complete; it needs the narrator's final, lame assessment: "The souls of the two lovers were now in that better, eternal beyond, where no religious difference could ever separate them" (III: 340-41). Actually, allowing religious differences to be overcome anywhere, even in heaven, is probably progressive on Wickede's part, and it is difficult to see what else he could have done with these two characters. The student might have lived happily ever after with some patriotic German woman, but Rebekka's plight is irresolvable. In addition, the conflict between these two lovers gives the novel considerable narratological interest. Had Rebekka simply been a staunchly supportive German, she could scarcely have had a larger role than that played by the farmers' stalwart daughters who marry various soldiers. These women tend to appear once, simply to let the reader know of their existence; they then suffer some minor tragedy or threat that shows their prospective husband in a favorable light; and they marry in the novel's final chapter. *Tall Isaack* contains two such women whose virtual invisibility, for which they are rewarded, contrasts starkly to Rebekka. She dies not only because of her religious convictions, but also because there is not yet an acceptable role for strong female characters. One simply cannot imagine her following Countess Micielska into exile or suddenly becoming a housewife. Rebekka has to die, and the fatherland seals her doom.

Having killed off his heroine, Wickede still has a few loose ends to tie up. Isaack, not surprisingly, dies alone, revered by the Bruhn family and rewarded for his service to the fatherland but a tragic figure nonetheless. Although he is memorialized in the novel, the fictional Isaack's legacy was probably shared by "real" people in his circumstances: "In the course of time remembrance [of Isaack] disappeared completely" (III: 345). He is allowed to enjoy something of a reconciliation with his daughter Sara, who manages to rescue him from imprisonment and death in Hamburg, but she, too, pays a heavy price for her independence. In many respects Sara's ultimate sin is not disloyalty to her father and fatherland but her active sexuality, which might be construed as the supreme affront to them both. It certainly makes Sara ineligible for a traditional happy ending. Once she manages to set her father free, Sara resolves "to renounce future sins and to end her relationship" with Hamburg's military governor (III: 312), and she is last seen in Strasbourg in charge of a home for orphaned girls. Hers is, to be sure, a better fate than Rebekka's, at least in this world, but doing penance on the border between France and Germany, far from her father and far from the successful life that she had led is scarcely a reward.

The aristocrat's daughter, who is just as "guilty" as Sara, initially appears to do well. After her first husband dies, she marries into a family from the old French nobility, moves to Paris, and turns militantly Catholic. In the broader scheme of things, however, she falls victim to the novel's thoroughly antiaristocratic tenor, and her becoming French and Catholic is scarcely positive. The two conversions are mainly a sign of how shallow her convictions are, and the book ends by condemning her indirectly as her mother chokes to death on too large a serving of Strasbourg liver paté. Other aristocrats, for example, doltish Fritz von Dassow fare no better, and the novel is filled with asides lamenting those German princes who live in wasteful splendor and side with the French rather than pursue policies for the benefit of Germany and their subjects. This is not to say that Wickede's novel is republican. At one point the narrator calls for German unity under a Prussian king, a remarkably prescient view in 1863, some eight years before it came to pass (II: 78), and he also regrets the failure of the Congress of Vienna to deal with Schleswig-Holstein, which would lead to war between Prussia and Austria in 1866 (II: 183-84). In symbolic terms, the monarchy functions as a guarantee that the old order will survive the transformation from what people believed was still an intact organic community [*Gemeinschaft*] into the new nation; the role accorded to the king is a sign of how anxiously yeoman farmers, here symbolized by the Bruhns, and the old middle class, mainly craftsmen in outmoded guilds, viewed encroaching modernity. Thus, for all its progressive impetus, Wickede's novel actually looks to the past for its solutions. Its backwards glance encompasses both a subordinate position for women and a very ambiguous German identity.

Louise von François' novel, *The Last Reckenburgerin*, also seems to move forward into the past, as its heroine turns the countryside around Reckenburg into a patriarchal utopia. To be sure, her reforms and control become far gentler once she adopts an orphaned girl, but Eberhardine von Reckenburg twice calls herself "fritzian" in an obvious reference to Frederick the Great's rebuilding of Prussia after the Seven Years' War (385, 391). She also chooses not to marry, perhaps because she describes the relationship to one prospective husband in terms of the equality "between man and man" (397). Hardine faults him for his lack of compassion, a female virtue, but the novel seems aware that her strength can only exist in the private sphere. It is, therefore, scarcely surprising that the Napoleonic wars are not central to the book's plot. When war does impinge on the action, it shows how even a woman author was unable to carve out a more active role in the public sphere for her otherwise strong heroine. "During my 'fritzian' activities I remained a sympathetic observer of public life, whose catastrophes coincided with those of my own new life" (390). After a page or two the armies move on, while Hardine can only enter into "a sort of connection with the patriots who were secretly spinning their webs in Prussia and Austria" (390). Clearly, it is not patriotism alone that condemns this woman to spinsterhood, but her patriotism is one more sign of how strength – paradoxically, yet just as surely as weakness – condemns women to the domestic sphere or worse. Eberhardine von Reckenburg is too strong to marry but not strong enough to answer when Germany calls; outside of Reckenburg, in other words, outside of their homes, the fatherland has no use for women.

In the case of Tall Isaack's daughter Rebekka the fatherland's kiss of death has to be understood literally; there is simply no way for her to survive the conflict between religion, culture, and the nation. She takes Germany's culture too seriously to be merely patriotic, and she holds her own beliefs too firmly to sacrifice them on the altar of Prusso-German Protestantism. For the other women discussed here, the fatherland's kiss of death is more figurative. It either condemns them to traditional female roles or prevents them from achieving even that modicum of happiness. On the one hand, passive women invariably marry within the nation, which basically means that they are subject to their husbands' beliefs and political orientation. Marrying across national borders is unthinkable, and once that temptation has been eliminated, these women recede into the background. On the other hand, active women are condemned to spinsterhood, banished from the nation, or forced to endure both punishments. The two sexually active women are dealt particularly harsh fates, no doubt, because they surrendered their virtue to foreigners. Good German men, a category that excludes Jews and most aristocrats, do battle with the French invaders, and they expect to find and marry the wholesome daughters of yeomen farmers when they return home. Women who are too strong, too intelligent, or too independent might confuse these sturdy soldiers, and the nation prefers its children to be born and raised by more conventional heroines. In short, fictional accounts of the Wars of Liberation sent a double message. These novels, and hundreds like them, propagated a myth of national ideological unity, and they modeled male and female roles for the new nation that was being built upon a foundation of this shared and often mythic history. The only safe place for women was on the margins of Germany's emerging national narrative, where they enabled its male center to hold.

Bibliography

Belani, H. E. R. [Karl Ludwig Häberlin]. *Die Demagogen: Novelle aus der Geschichte unserer Zeit.* 2 Vols. Leipzig: Wienbrack, 1829.

Eggert, Hartmut. *Studien zur Wirkungsgeschichte des deutschen historischen Romans 1850-1875.* Frankfurt a. M.: Klostermann, 1971.

Eke, Norbert Otto. "Eine Gesamtbibliographie des deutschen Romans 1815-1830. Anmerkungen zum Problemfeld von Bibliographie und Historiographie." *Zeitschrift für Germanistik* Neue Folge 2 (1993): 295-308.

Fouqué, Friedrich de la Motte. *Der Refugié oder Heimat und Fremde: Ein Roman aus der neueren Zeit.* 3 Vols. Gotha and Erfurt: Hennings'sche Buchhandlung, 1824; reprint *Sämmtliche Romane und Novellenbücher.* Ed. Wolfgang Möhrig. Hildesheim: Olms, 1989. 10.1-3.

François, Louise von. *Die letzte Reckenburgerin.* 1871. Bonn: Latka, 1988.

Geppert, Hans Vilmer. *Der andere historische Roman: Theorie und Struktur einer diskontinuierlichen Gattung.* Tübingen: Niemeyer, 1976.

Gersdorf, Wilhelmine von. *Aurora. Gräfin von Königsmark: Ein historischer Roman.* 2 Vols. Quedlinburg and Leipzig: Basse, 1817.

Limlei, Michael. *Geschichte als Ort der Bewährung: Menschenbild und Gesellschaftsverständnis in den deutschen historischen Romanen (1820-1890).* Frankfurt a. M.: Lang, 1988.

Martino, Alberto. *Die deutsche Leihbibliothek: Geschichte einer literarischen Institution (1756-1914).* Wiesbaden: Harrasowitz, 1990.

Peterson, Brent O. "German Nationalism after Napoleon: Caste and Regional Identities in Historical Fiction: 1815-1830." *German Quarterly* 68.3 (Summer 1995): 286-303.

Rellstab, Ludwig. *1812: Ein historischer Roman.* 1834, Leipzig: Reclam, 1914.

Sottong, Hermann J. *Transformation und Reaktion: Historisches Erzählen von der Goethezeit zum Realismus.* Munich: Fink, 1992.

Sweet, Denis, "Introduction to Naubert's *The Cloak.*" *Bitter Healing: German Women Writers 1700-1830.* Ed. Jeannine Blackwell and Susanne Zantop. Lincoln: U of Nebraska P, 1990.

Wehler, Hans Ulrich. *Deutsche Gesellschaftsgeschichte.* Munich: Beck, 1989.

Wickede, Julius von. *Der lange Isaack: Historischer Roman aus der Zeit des deutschen Befreiungskrieges.* Jena: Costenoble, 1863.

Part II

RETHINKING HISTORY AND CANONS

Chapter 6

THE CHALLENGE OF "MISSING CONTENTS" FOR CANON FORMATION IN GERMAN STUDIES

Elke Frederiksen

> As one who was trained – and well-trained, too – in the canonical tradition, and who loves a good deal of it, I must nevertheless say that what has kept me intellectually alive as I enter my fifth decade of teaching have been the challenges of feminism and multiculturalism. It has not simply been the need to learn new texts, new histories, new conceptions of culture but more my need constantly to rethink my ideas about cultural norms, social values, categories of experience, and analyses of race, gender, and class. What I have found, contrary to the late Allan Bloom, is not that feminism and multiculturalism have closed the American mind, but that they have opened it (Lauter 14).

This 1994 comment by the American Studies scholar Paul Lauter is provocative and critical at the same time. It emphasizes feminism and multiculturalism as the decisive intellectual impetus for an ongoing questioning of cultural norms, in particular the categories of ethnicity, gender and social class, as impetus for movement and change. And Lauter does not speak alone. Well-known literary and cultural critics such as Jonathan Culler, Stuart Hall and Frank Trommler are fully aware of the contributions of feminist studies in the United States and in Europe. With regard to the impact of feminist German Studies, Trommler states that "since 1976, the group 'Women in German' has provided an important stimulus, far exceeding the limits of *Germanistik* in the United States" (30).

"Missing contents," dynamic challenge, and canon formation, the three key ideas in my discussion that are implicitly contained in Lauter's quote, require closer examination. The notion of "missing contents" is inspired by Ellen Friedman's essay "Where are the Missing Contents? (Post)Modernism, Gender and the Canon" (1993). At the beginning of her essay, Friedman refers to the French philosopher Jean François Lyotard, who writes about "missing contents" in the literature of modernity in *The Postmodern Condition* (240). What is "missing" and what this literature expresses nostalgia for, according to Lyotard, are the master narratives that sustained Western civilization in the past and have now been called into question (78-81). In his introduction to the English translation of Lyotard's text, Fredric Jameson goes a step further by positing "not the disappearance of the great master-narratives, but their passage underground as it were, their continuing but now *unconscious* effectivity as a way of 'thinking about' and acting in our current situation" (xii). Friedman identifies the "yearning for fathers, for past authority and sure knowledge that can no longer be supported" (240) in works by contemporary male authors such as Donald Barthelme and Thomas Pynchon, as well as in texts by William Faulkner, T. S. Eliot, Ernest Hemingway, Ezra Pound, and James Joyce, and she concludes that "the oedipal preoccupation with fathers – missing, lost, or otherwise inaccessible – is a compulsive theme in male modernism" (241). Quite in contrast, Friedman's analysis of texts by female authors such as Gertrude Stein, Djuna Barnes, H. D., Anaïs Nin, Jane Bowles, Kathy Acker, and Joyce Carol Oates leads her to observe that "women's works of modernity, however, show little nostalgia for the old paternal order, little regret for the no longer presentable" (242). Her reading of these texts through the lens of gender reveals rather different male and female paradigms of "missing contents." It is to this difference that she attributes the exclusion of most female modernists and postmodernists from the canon:

> Modernism and postmodernism reveal a pattern of bifurcation: two unpresentables, two sets of missing contents. As male texts look backward over their shoulders, female texts look forward, often beyond culture, beyond patriarchy, into the unknown, the outlawed (244) … . They – Stein, Barnes, Bowles, Nin, Acker – remain outlaws, outside the canon because there is little in the backward, oedipal glance for them. Instead they aim their gaze unabashedly and audaciously forward (251).

Friedman's theses offer a useful starting point for problematizing traditional as well as feminist concepts of canonical thinking and for questioning reasons for the exclusion of women from the canon within German Studies. Differences, however, that inform canon formation are not only gender- but culture-based, a premise which significantly expands Friedman's gender-based concept of canon. In spite of certain concessions made to texts by women writers in the last ten years, the traditional German literary canon at most universities in the United States still consists primarily of texts by male authors, as evidenced by reading lists, seminar titles and dissertation topics.[1] The situation in German-speaking countries seems to be similar, if one considers Wulf Segebrecht's reading suggestions in *Was sollen die Germanisten lesen?* (What should Germanists read? 1994), or Sigrid Weigel's critical comments in *Topographien der Geschlechter* (Topographies of Gender, 1992) and the numerous reports of female colleagues and students from universities in Germany.[2]

Discussions concerning problems of the canon are not new. Nonetheless, the debates regarding a theoretical understanding of canons, in connection with practical recommendations for reading, have intensified within the last five years both in the United States and in German-speaking countries, not only in German Studies but also in other languages and cultures such as French Studies, English and American Studies, as well as in other disciplines such as the social sciences. Two volumes, which appeared almost simultaneously, may serve as examples in German Studies: *Rethinking Germanistik: Canon and Culture* (1991), an innovative project of cooperation between students and professors at various universities in the western United States, and *Literaturdidaktik – Lektürekanon – Literaturunterricht* (Didactics of Literature – Literary Canon – Teaching Literature, 1990), a collective project by scholars from Switzerland, Austria, the Federal Republic, and the former German Democratic Republic.[3]

Despite the extremely broad spectrum of viewpoints regarding the problem of canon formation – its contents, function, effects and ramifications, the concepts of a para-canon (Stimpson), an anti- or alternative canon (Gugelberger, Kolodny), and even an elegy for the western canon (Harold Bloom) – the common goal of the most recent German

---

1. Jeannine Blackwell conducted surveys in 1983 and in 1993, which focused on the inclusion of women writers in reading lists for M.A. and Ph. D. students of German literature. Texts by authors such as Christa Wolf, Ingeborg Bachmann, and Annette von Droste-Hülshoff appeared most frequently.

2. The lack of texts by female authors read in seminars was pointed out to me during visits at universities and at conferences in Berlin, Hamburg, Kassel, Münster, and Stuttgart in the late 1980s and early 1990s. My colleague Simon Richter reported similar comments from the University of Würzburg in 1996.

3. For a discussion concerning problems of canon in Germany, the essays by Renate von Heydebrand are particularly useful.

Studies discussions, at least among younger scholars in the United
States, seems to be the wish to open up traditional canons. The editors
of *Rethinking Germanistik*, for example, describe the main premise of
their essay collection:

> Their [the included essays'] similarity lies first in a dedication to the prob-
> lematic of "rethinking": identifying structures, unearthing fundamental
> assumptions, making critiques more precise. On a less conscious level ...
> they all share in their orientation the desire to break down notions of cen-
> trality. These can be found in heterosexual white, Western, male discourse;
> they can also be inscribed in our institution's history and in our own discur-
> sive use of the past (ix).

This volume contains important theoretical considerations and practical
suggestions for change which is still slow in coming at many universities.
And even though the editors of the *Women in German Yearbook (1997)*
emphasize the significant changes in research and teaching that feminism
has inspired at American universities (Friedrichsmeyer Clausen 169),
Ruth-Ellen B. Joeres effectively points out the persistence of a problematic
relationship in the United States between traditional male-dominated German Studies on the one hand, and feminist orientations, predominantly
practiced by women, on the other: "My present thinking is that *Germanistik* and feminism are reasonably unrelatable. *Germanistik* is mostly a male
domain; feminism is mostly the province of females. Although that would
not necessarily imply alienation, there seem to be very few connections"
(248). Interestingly enough, she remarks that such a dichotomy seems to
be less prevalent in other languages, such as French and Spanish (250).

Joeres correctly warns that ignoring the insights provided by feminist
literary and cultural studies on the part of German Studies scholars will
most likely lead to isolation in the future (255). In its one-sidedness such
a *Germanistik* runs the risk of marginalization in a transcultural and
interdisciplinary dialogue. In view of the so-called "feminization" of our
field (Finney, Nollendorfs) and the tendency of female students to turn
increasingly towards feminist scholarship, the persistent distance
between traditional and feminist German Studies could have far-reaching consequences, aside from the obvious intellectual loss. Barbara
Becker-Cantarino argues for "integrative research on gender roles and
gender relationships in a social and historical context, which also takes
into account power relations and signification processes" (228), and one
can only hope that traditionally-oriented German Studies scholars take
serious note of these insights.

Given the necessity of integrating the results of feminist scholarship
into constantly changing canons of German literature and culture, it is

also important to examine critically the new and still evolving feminist canon in the field of German Studies in the United States. Regarding discussions of canon, Joeres remarks:

> Feminism urges us to question the canon or any other form of canonic thinking that hides behind absolute concepts of "good," "beautiful," "bad" in order to make us assume that the dominant modes of thinking are not only correct, but inevitable and eternal … . Feminism looks not only back, not only to the present, but thinks in utopian ways about the future. Feminism will insist on rebutting the pessimism that sees no future, no possibility for change (253).

As early as 1981, the French author and theorist Hélène Cixous had insisted, "There's work to be done against *class*, against categorization, against classification … against the pervasive masculine urge to judge, diagnose, digest, name" (61). Much earlier, the Austrian writer Ingeborg Bachmann had pointed out in her essay "Literatur als Utopie" (Literature as Utopia, 1959) that literature is "an ideal we shape to suit our imagination, preserving certain facts and discarding others" (257).

For decades, even in the 1960s and 1970s, a firmly rooted traditional literary canon has existed in the United States which, in contrast to Germany, hardly changed, even during the student movements of the late 1960s and early 1970s. In order to counteract what Silvia Bovenschen has called the "Geschichte weiblicher Geschichtslosigkeit" (history of women's missing history, 15), feminist literary scholars in the United States as well as in the Federal Republic of Germany were initially concerned with a de- and re-construction of traditional canons. Efforts to change established perceptions of canon expressed themselves, first of all, in demands for access to the canon, in order to affect its reconstruction (Blackwell; Weigel 1983); secondly, in the formation of an alternative canon (Kolodny, Robinson) and, finally, in a critical discussion of the elimination of canons altogether (Lawrence, Vansant, Heydebrand/ Winko). This last approach met with minimal success, as some kind of canon structure – albeit an open and flexible one – seems to most American feminists necessary in order to provide some intellectual guidance (Gross, "In Defense of Canons," 109). An important first step has been the discovery of "lost" and "forgotten" texts by women writers, which, despite some reprintings and reissues, even today unfortunately remain largely inaccessible. The close rereading of these texts and the parallel development of various feminist theoretical approaches led to a questioning of the immutability of established (male) canons.

As a result of new insights gained through feminist literary scholarship, a number of publications appeared in the 1980s that reconstructed the history and the unique characteristics of literature by women writers. Important examples are the book-projects *Frauen Literatur Geschichte: Schreibende Frauen vom Mittelalter bis zur Gegenwart* (Women Literature History: Women Writers from the Middle Ages to the Present, 1985) and *Deutsche Literatur von Frauen* (German Literature by Women, 1988) that represent collaborations among feminist literary scholars from German-speaking countries and the United States. These volumes have been especially influential because they not only revisited texts by better-known authors, but introduced previously unknown texts, opened up traditional concepts of genre, utilized new feminist theoretical approaches, contributed significantly to the validation of texts by women, and exposed patriarchal and hierarchical assumptions about literature. Invaluable as they are for future research, they must be read as products of the 1980s because of their emphasis on the history of women's writing. In their various contributions they integrate theoretical feminist insights from the late 1970s and 1980s, ranging from gynocritical studies[4] of women's writings to scholarship that draws on cultural history, to other discussions (largely by scholars from the Federal Republic of Germany) that followed French theoretical models, viewing their "task as the deconstruction of a male discourse that has excluded female otherness" (Lennox 163).

By the end of the 1980s, Biddy Martin was calling for a more thorough examination of the mechanisms of exclusion, in order to "more completely highlight the problems of the relationship between center and margin instead of merely moving the previously marginalized to the center or simply replacing one focal point with another" (166). In the final analysis Martin is concerned with privileged Western feminism, which cannot afford to disregard developments outside its own sphere if it wishes to expose unexamined racism, ethnocentrism, antisemitism, and homophobia, within as well as outside of feminist academia. She calls into question the "coherence and unity of the category 'women' as a basis for scholarly analysis and political solidarity" (166). Appropriately, in the last five years, the interests of many feminists in German Studies in the United States have shifted toward researching *differences*, not only on a cross-cultural level, but also within their own cultural contexts. In a global context, feminist and multicultural discourses have

4. Elaine Showalter defined "gynocritics" as the study of "women as *writer* – with woman as the producer of textual meaning, with the history, themes, genres, and structures of writing by women. Its subjects include the psychodynamics of female creativity; linguistics and the problem of a female language; the trajectory of the individual or collective female career; literary history; and, of course, studies of particular writers and works" (Showalter 128).

recently moved increasingly to exploring the implications of "minority" cultures for the whole society (Lauter 10).

What implications and questions emerge for feminist German Studies scholars from these discourses? Will the field become involved in global discussions or remain on the sidelines, playing at best a marginal role? Several suggestions are appropriate here, which counteract a restricted and restrictive canonical gaze. Although one of the explicit goals of feminist literary and cultural studies has been to give voice to a multiplicity of both female and "minority" writers, much feminist research still seems to focus on texts by "major" authors such as Christa Wolf, Ingeborg Bachmann, and Bettina Brentano-von Arnim, or on certain periods in nineteenth- and twentieth-century German literature and culture (e.g., Romanticism, the Weimar Republic, the German Democratic Republic). With all respect for what has been achieved here, one has also to be aware of the danger of creating new figureheads that threaten to overshadow a difference of voices and to become the standard by which to judge a multitude of texts, which would ultimately create a new "inside" (Spivak) or "center" that would limit rather than widen our perspectives.

The social structure of Germany and the United States has been radically altered in recent years by the influx of millions of foreigners, and the contradictions between conventional concepts of society and a changed multicultural reality have created a crisis mentality in Germany with particular implications for the middle and working classes (Henderson 29). As a result, scholars of literature and culture are being challenged to find alternatives to traditional concepts of canon, which focus primarily on authors, periods, or genres. By shifting toward a critical thematic examination of issues it would become possible to emphasize a more flexible notion of canon formation as a continuous dynamic process (Gross, "In Defense of Canons," 111) and to overcome the current isolation of German Studies from the global dialogue.

Rubrics such as "Multiculturalism," or "Contemporary German Literature and the Third World" for example, could serve as overarching themes, which would treat in detail such questions as racism, Eurocentrism, ethnocentrism, the categories *Eigenbild* [self image] and *Fremdbild* [image of foreignness] among Germans, migration, and a multitude of differences including class, gender, religious, and national distinctions. In discussions of literary texts by authors such as Rafik Schami, originally from Syria, Libuše Moníková from the former Czechoslovakia, Aysel Özakin from Turkey, and the Afro-German poet May Ayim as well as of the theoretical and nonfiction texts which have appeared in large numbers since 1992 (Henderson, Arens), the gender component is a necessary element, although it alone is not sufficient. In addition to gender, class distinctions as well as ethnic, national, and religious differences are crucial categories of literary/textual analysis as ultimate determinants of literary and cultural activity. Accordingly, Leslie Adelson recognizes "the production of gender as simultaneously and inextricably intertwined with configurations of race, nationality, class, ethnicity, and other signifying social practices through which power is manifested" (*Making Bodies, Making History*, xiv). Literary products of so-called "minority" writers whose texts resist tradional as well as feminist concepts of contemporary "German" literature and culture necessitate a reconceptualization and re-evaluation of "German" literature and culture, which must recognize and include multiple differences as integral elements (Adelson, Arens). Methodologically, the discussion of "multiculturalism" requires an interdisciplinary, inter-and cross-cultural approach, which utilizes a variety of theoretical approaches (e.g., sociohistorical, feminist, poststructuralist) and which views different cultures side by side.

Such a refocussing of feminist canonical thinking, which can include other topics of international concern such as "Fascism," or "Concepts of Nation and/or Nationality," enables Germanists to participate in global feminist debates. Amy Kaminsky's comments are especially relevant here. In her article "Issues for an International Feminist Literary Criticism" (1993),[5] she pleads for a truly global perspective in feminist literary criticism that "presupposes multiple reference points. The globe is a geometric as well as a geopolitical figure whose surface has no fixed center but, rather, many sites for making meaning and interpreting reality" (215). Kaminsky links her arguments to criticism of the situation within feminist scholarship in general, which seems to have ignored such multiple reference points and fostered its own hierarchy with the fields of English and French Studies dominating theoretical discourses. She recognizes the increasing interdisciplinarity of feminist scholarship, which, on the one hand, utilizes knowledge developed in fields such as philosophy, history, psychoanalysis, sociology, and anthropology while, on the other, paying little or no attention to feminist work on and in other literatures such as Latin American, German, or South Asian (213-14). One might speculate about the reasons for such marginalization (e.g., language difficulties, politics), but the need for information remains. As Kaminsky phrases it:

5. My discussion of Kaminsky's article was inspired by Jeanette Clausen's and Sara Friedrichmeyer's editorial postscript in *Women in German Yearbook 10*.

We need to know what's going on beyond our precincts. We need, simply, data on which to ground and test our theories. Quite apart from an explosion in knowledge that makes it virtually impossible to keep up even with our own fields (however we define them), in the United States we are handicapped by a lack of knowledge of foreign languages that is simply unheard of among similarly educated people in the rest of the world (222).

In any case, the flow of information seems to be rather one-sided, since feminist German scholars have consistently integrated theoretical insights of Anglo-American and French feminist scholarship into their work. They have done so to the extent that names such as Kristeva, Cixous, and Irigaray, or Gilbert, Gubar, de Lauretis, Spelman, Spivak, Butler, Christian, and hooks are generally familiar and have become part of an implicit theoretical canon.

Nevertheless – since it is a one-sided flow of information – the editors of the recently published volume of the *Women in German Yearbook 10* (1995) ask self-critically:

Have we in WIG created a eurocentric or "germanocentric" feminist scholarship? ... How can we make our hard-won insights into German literary and cultural history accessible and useful to non-Germanists while also expanding our own horizons beyond the confines of German-speaking countries? If we agree that a global perspective in feminist literary criticism is our aim, how can we contribute to its definition as well as to its realization?" (Clausen and Friedrichsmeyer, "WIG 2000," 268).

In addition to the above suggestions for a general reorientation of feminist canonical thinking, one could envision an opening up of our most important scholarly means of communication, the *Women in German Yearbook*, toward issues of international concern. It could occasionally publish focus- or theme-oriented volumes, which would combine disciplinary as well as interdisciplinary and/or cross-cultural discussions. Feminist German scholars are active not only in the United States and in German-speaking countries, but all over the world, for example in South America, Eastern Europe, Australia, China, Japan, and India; their diverse research and life contexts could provide valuable insights and expand the views of American and European scholars. Inviting them to participate in trans- and cross-cultural discussions would be an attempt to globalize different perspectives which, in contrast to a universalizing view, does not assume the existence of a firm and fixed center, but rather, as Kaminsky formulates it, "presupposes multiple reference points ... [and] many sites for making meaning and interpreting reality" (215).

"Missing" or unknown contents as continuous and dynamic challenge to traditional notions of canon, but also as challenge to feminist reflections on canon formation, has become, if one follows Paul Lauter's argument, a postulate for survival:

"In this newly emerging world, being monocultural and patriarchal is as limiting – and ultimately as dangerous – as being scientifically and computer illiterate. You survive, but you don't know what's happening, do you, Mr. Jones?" (13)

Note

All translations from German are my own.

Bibliography

Adelson, Leslie A. "Migrants' Literature or German Literature? 'Torkan's *Tufan: Brief an einen islamischen Bruder'.*" *German Quarterly* 63.3/4 (1990): 382-90.
_____. *Making Bodies Making History: Feminism & German Identity.* Lincoln: U of Nebraska P, 1993.
Arens, Hiltrudis M. "Eine Herausforderung für die Germanistik: Kulturelle Hybridität und literarische Texte von Einwander [sic] Innen," Diss. U of Maryland, College Park, 1997.
Bachmann, Ingeborg. "Literatur als Utopie." *Werke.* Vol. 4. Ed. Christine Koschel, Inge von Weidenbaum, Clemens Münster. Munich: Piper, 1978. 255-71.
Becker-Cantarino, Barbara. "Feministische Germanistik in Deutschland: Rückblick und sechs Thesen." *Women in German Yearbook 8.* Ed. Jeanette Clausen and Sara Friedrichsmeyer. Lincoln: U of Nebraska P, 1993. 219-33.
Blackwell, Jeannine. "German Women Authors Presently on Reading Lists 1993." Unpublished manuscript.
Bloom, Harold. *The Western Canon: The Books and School of the Ages.* New York: Harcourt Brace, 1994.
Bovenschen, Silvia. *Die imaginierte Weiblichkeit: Exemplarische Untersuchungen zu kulturgeschichtlichen und literarischen Präsentationsformen des Weiblichen.* Frankfurt a. M.: Suhrkamp, 1979.

Cixous, Hélène. "Castration or Decapitation?" Cited in: Margaret J. M. Ezell. *Writing Women's Literary History*. Baltimore: Johns Hopkins UP, 1993. 161.

Clausen, Jeanette and Sara Friedrichsmeyer. "WIG 2000: Feminism and the Future of *Germanistik*." *Women in German Yearbook 10*. Ed. Jeanette Clausen und Sara Friedrichsmeyer. Lincoln: U of Nebraska P, 1995. 267-72.

Culler, Jonathan. *On Deconstruction: Theory and Criticism after Structuralism*. Ithaca, NY: Cornell UP, 1982.

Deutsche Literatur von Frauen. 2 vols. Ed. Gisela Brinker-Gabler. Munich: C.H. Beck, 1988.

Eagleton, Terry. "Introduction: What is Literature?" *Literary Theory: An Introduction*. Minneapolis: U of Minnesota P, 1983. 1-16.

Finney, Gail. "Iphigenie in *Germanistik*, or the Feminization/ Humanization of the Profession." *Rethinking Germanistik*. 31-43.

Frauen Literatur Geschichte. Eds. Hiltrud Gnüg and Renate Möhrmann. Stuttgart: Metzler, 1985.

Friedman, Ellen G. "Where Are the Missing Contents? (Post)Modernism, Gender, and the Canon." *PMLA* 108.2 (1993): 240-52.

Friedrichsmeyer, Sara and Jeanette Clausen. "What's Feminism Got To Do With It? A Postscript from the Editors." *Women in German Yearbook 7*. Ed. Jeanette Clausen and Sara Friedrichsmeyer. Lincoln: U of Nebraska P, 1991. 169-73.

Gross, Sabine. "In Defense of Canons." *Rethinking Germanistik*. 105-12.

_____. "Figurative Space and the Invisible Signifier." *Semiotica* 96.3/4 (1993): 363-79.

Gugelberger, Georg M. "*Germanistik*, the Canon, and Third World Pressure." *Rethinking Germanistik*. 45-56.

Hall, Stuart. "Cultural Studies and its Theoretical Legacies." *Cultural Studies*. Ed. Lawrence Grossberg, Cary Nelson, and Paula A. Treichler. New York: Routledge, 1992. 277-86.

Henderson, Ingeborg. "Multikulturalismus als Unterrichtsgegenstand." *Die Unterrichtspraxis* 27.2 (1994): 29-33.

Heydebrand, Renate von. "Probleme des 'Kanons' - Probleme der Kultur- und Bildungspolitik." *Kultureller Wandel und die Germanistik in der Bundesrepublik*. Ed. Johannes Janota. Tübingen: Niemeyer, 1991. 3-22.

Heydebrand, Renate von, and Simone Winko. "Arbeit am Kanon: Geschlechterdifferenz in Rezeption und Wertung von Literatur." *Genus - zur Geschlechterdifferenz in den Kulturwissenschaften*. Ed. Hadumod Bußmann and Renate Hof. Stuttgart: Kröner, 1995. 206-61.

Joeres, Ruth-Ellen B. "'Language is Also a Place of Struggle': The Language of Feminism and the Language of American *Germanistik*." *Women in German Yearbook 8*. Ed. Jeanette Clausen and Sara Friedrichsmeyer. Lincoln: U of Nebraska P, 1993. 247-57.

Kaminsky, Amy. "Issues for an International Feminist Literary Criticism." *Signs* 19.1 (1993): 213-27.

Kolodny, Annette. "A Map for Rereading: Gender and the Interpretation of Literary Texts." *The New Feminist Criticism*. 46-62.

———. "The Integrity of Memory: Creating a New Literary History of the United States." *American Literature* 57.2 (March 1985): 291-307.

Lauter, Paul. "Feminism, Multiculturalism, and the Canonical Tradition." *Transformations* 5.2 (1994): 1-17.

Lawrence, Karen R., ed. *Decolonizing Tradition: New Views of Twentieth-Century "British" Literary Canons*. Urbana: U of Illinois P, 1992.

Lennox, Sara. "Feminist Scholarship and *Germanistik*." *German Quarterly* 62.2 (Spring 1989): 158-70.

Literaturdidaktik – Lektürekanon – Literaturunterricht. Ed. Detlef C. Kochan. *Amsterdamer Beiträge zur neueren Germanistik* 30. Amsterdam: Rodopi, 1990.

Lyotard, Jean-François. *The Postmodern Condition: A Report on Knowledge*. Trans. Geoff Bennington and Brian Massumi. Foreword by Fredric Jameson. Minneapolis: U of Minnesota P, 1984.

Martin, Biddy. "Zwischenbilanz der feministischen Debatten." *Germanistik in den USA*. Ed. Frank Trommler. Opladen: Westdeutscher Verlag, 1989. 165-95.

The New Feminist Criticism: Essays on Women, Literature, and Theory. Ed. Elaine Showalter. New York: Pantheon, 1985.

Nollendorfs, Valters. "Out of *Germanistik*: Thoughts on the Shape of Things to Come." *Die Unterrichtspraxis* 27.1 (1994): 1-10.

Rethinking Germanistik. Canon and Culture. Ed. Robert Bledsoe, et al. New York: Peter Lang, 1991.

Robinson, Lillian S.. "Treason Our Text: Feminist Challenges to the Literary Canon." *The New Feminist Criticism*. 105-21.

Segebrecht, Wulf. *Was sollen Germanisten lesen? Ein Vorschlag*. Berlin: Erich Schmidt, 1994.

Showalter, Elaine. "Toward a Feminist Poetics." *The New Feminist Criticism*. 125-43.

Spivak, Gayatri Chakravorty. "Reading the World: Literary Studies in the Eighties." *In Other Worlds: Essays in Cultural Politics*. New York: Routledge, 1988. 95-102.

Stimpson, Catherine R. "Reading for Love: Canons, Paracanons, and Whistling Jo March." *New Literary History* 21 (1990): 957-76.

Trommler, Frank. "Einleitung." *Germanistik in den USA*. Opladen: Westdeutscher Verlag, 1989. 7-43.

Vansant, Jacqueline. "Wieviel Kanon braucht der Mensch?" *Die einen raus - die anderen rein. Kanon und Literatur: Vorüberlegungen zu einer Literaturgeschichte Österreichs*. Ed. Wendelin Schmidt-Dengler et al. Berlin: Erich Schmidt, 1994. 161-71.

Weigel, Sigrid. "Der schielende Blick. Thesen zur Geschichte weiblicher Schreibpraxis." *Die verborgene Frau: Sechs Beiträge zu einer feministischen Literaturwissenschaft*. Ed. Inge Stephan and Sigrid Weigel. Berlin:

Chapter 7

FEMINISM AND MOTHERHOOD IN GERMANY AND IN INTERNATIONAL PERSPECTIVE 1800-1914

Ann Taylor Allen

In the field of women's history there is no issue that gives rise to more ambivalence, both intellectual and emotional, than that of feminism and motherhood: specifically, the prominent role of discourses based on motherhood in feminist movements from their beginnings until the present day. Such discourses will be collectively designated "feminist maternalism," because they demanded the improvement of women's status through claims to a specifically female motherly character and role. The discomfort of present-day feminists with this aspect of women's history arises in part from the historical period – the 1960s and 1970s – in which the field of women's history in its present form originated. "Liberation" was first defined in opposition to domesticity and traditional roles such as motherhood. Seeking a "usable past," feminist historians looked in history for their own image. But they were often confronted with an alien reality; instead of demanding or exalting the liberation of women, as individuals or as a group, from maternal roles or values, feminists of the nineteenth and much of the twentieth century often glorified motherhood as the basis of women's claim to dignity, equality, or a widened sphere of action in both public and private spheres.

Many of the earliest feminist historians asserted that feminist maternalism represented a concession, even a sellout to prevailing patriarchal views of the world, and often dismissed all such ideas as simply not feminist. However, such a blanket rejection would require the historian to dismiss or to explain away much of the history of feminist movements, including most of the great pioneers: Elizabeth Cady Stanton, Helene Stöcker, Mary Wollstonecraft and many others, all of whom developed and emphasized maternalist ideas. Another response was to define maternalism as a characteristic of backward or conservative movements and to place it in opposition to allegedly more progressive ideologies based on equal rights and gender similarity. This attitude is particularly evident among some historians of Germany. The British historian Richard Evans attributed the maternalist emphasis of German feminist movements to the conservative and feudal attitudes of the German bourgeoisie. (Evans, *Feminist Movement;* Peters). Claudia Koonz assigned to German feminists, specifically because of their maternalist emphasis, a share of the responsibility for the eventual success of National Socialist reproductive policies; and more recently, Nancy Reagin has identified the maternalist emphasis of bourgeois feminist movements in Hannover at the turn of the century as inherently reactionary.

But any definition of maternalism as intrinsically reactionary, conservative, or protofascist simply fails to take into account its prevalence in all varieties of feminism, from radical to conservative, during the nineteenth and most of the twentieth century. More recently, some historians have taken a far more positive view of maternalist ideology and practice as they contributed to the development of modern welfare states. Some of these works tend to go to the opposite extreme; they give too little attention to the very real ethical contradictions and problems often posed by maternalist approaches to social policy (Koven and Michel; Bock and Thane).

Some of these problems posed by the historical assessment of maternalism arise from an over-literal interpretation of ideology, as a claim to literal truth (in this case, biological determinism: all women are, or should be, mothers). The American anthropologist Clifford Geertz has suggested that ideologies express not a literal, but a metaphorical truth[1] enabling groups to deal with social and economic change by using familiar aspects of their experience as a symbolic framework to respond to new and unfamiliar conditions. Thus the concept of motherhood or "motherliness," originally denoting a biological or familial role, took

---

1. By metaphor I mean (in the words of *Webster's Unabridged Dictionary*) a figure of speech "through which a word or phrase ordinarily and primarily used of one thing is likened to another, different thing by being spoken of as if it were that other."

on an expanded meaning including a much wider and more public sphere of responsibility for society as a whole. Three phases can be discerned in the development of maternalism in Germany and in comparative international perspective: the origins during the period 1800-1860; the development of broader forms of activism from 1860-1900; and the impact of public-health and eugenics movements from 1900-1914.

The emergence of maternalist ideologies in Germany and elsewhere, usually traced to the period immediately following the eighteenth-century revolutions, has often been interpreted as a conservative reaction to the disappointment of the hopes for more radical reforms raised by women activists of the French Revolution (see Kerber). But in fact such ideas represented less a retreat into conservatism than an exploration of some new possibilities; for the theory that the moral responsibility for child-rearing lay with mothers was not old but new during this era. Eighteenth-century laws allotted the legal, and religious teaching and custom the moral responsibility for child-rearing to fathers; the new pedagogy based on Rousseau likewise involved male teachers (Campe, Klattenhoff).

By asserting the importance of the mother-child bond as a source of knowledge and empowerment, feminist writers both protested the patriarchal organization of the family and commented on the pressing political questions of the postrevolutionary era. Because the events of the revolutionary period had undermined belief in traditional structures of deference and authority, theorists across the political spectrum asked how freedom and order might be reconciled and the bond of citizens to each other and to the state be created and maintained. In order to respond to these questions, early German feminist writers drew on the ideas of the Swiss pedagogue and educational theorist Johann Heinrich Pestalozzi. Pestalozzi believed that the source of all learning was in sense experience, and that the mother-child relationship, as the first context for such experience, was the beginning of both cognitive and moral development. From the moment the mother takes the child on her lap, he wrote, "the germs of love, trust, and gratitude soon grow" (Pestalozzi 285).

As the mother-child bond represented the first and most perfect of all social bonds, its breakdown brought individual and social catastrophe. The French Revolution, wrote Bremen teacher Betty Gleim, one of the earliest German feminist writers, had failed because changes in political constitution could not change the human heart. In her book on women's education, published in 1810, Gleim praised women as the source of the social and affiliative virtues, "warm participation in the troubles and joys of others: the strength of patience, love, hope and faith;" (Gleim 62).[2] Only through the spread of such virtues, she wrote, could society become "a great organic whole, in which each part is at the same time means and end." (Gleim 11; Allen, *Feminism and Motherhood*, 34). Thus feminist maternalism was less a conservative rejection of the revolution than an attempt to come to terms with its historical legacy by creating new forms of community that would resolve the tension between self and other, and between individualism and social order.

At least during its earlier phases of development, this kind of maternalism rather undermined than reinforced biological determinism. Physicians and moralists of the late eighteenth century, influenced by Rousseau, had ceaselessly emphasized a biological function, breast-feeding, as the mother's only important task. The definition of motherhood as a chiefly moral and ethical function was clearly in opposition to this dominant position. Moreover, Gleim and other early feminist writers used maternalist arguments to champion the cause of precisely those women who were not biological mothers, that is, the unmarried and childless women who were desperately in need of occupations. The analogy of household and society was used in the early nineteenth century chiefly to justify the expansion of these women's activities into occupations that were motherly in a figurative sense, including such professional and volunteer activities as teaching and various kinds of charitable work (Gleim 102-10).

The association of women with "motherly" traits has usually been interpreted chiefly in the context of a male-dominated discourse on the polarization of public and private spheres that confined women to the private sphere of the family, reserving the public sphere for men (Hausen). The public/private boundary was not stable, however, but fluid, affording feminists many opportunities to question and subvert it. The revolutions had shown the importance of teaching the duties of citizenship to the welfare, even the survival of the state, and therefore child-rearing was recognized not only as a private but as a public function (Allen, "Let us live for our Children").

A prime example of the relationship of child-rearing to feminism, and of both to politics, was the kindergarten movement, which first developed in Germany in the 1840s. Friedrich Froebel, an educator who is best known for developing a new form of early-childhood education, the kindergarten, in the 1840s, linked the female vocation for early-childhood education, which he termed "spiritual motherhood," to develop-

2. See Scott (4-7) and *passim* on the ongoing concern of French feminists to criticize individualistic ideas of citizenship.

ment of new forms of community and citizenship (Klattenhoff; Allen, *Feminism and Motherhood*, 39-45). Kindergarten pedagogy was based on Froebel's games or "gifts." Inspired by the central concepts of German idealist philosophy, these educational playthings included a ball representing the undivided wholeness of the universe, and blocks and sticks that could be put together in patterns. They thus symbolized the relationship of the whole to the parts. Kindergarten teaching methods were designated "motherly" partly in protest against the religiously orthodox and authoritarian methods of the traditional, church-sponsored day care centers, which at this time were taught by "fatherly" male teachers. The kindergarten emphasized respect for the child's individual development, an internalized rather than externally-imposed form of discipline, and a pedagogy emphasizing the membership of the individual in an organic social and natural world (Allen, "Gardens of Children"; Erning).[3]

The subsequent development of the kindergarten as a new kind of educational institution, and of a network of training institutes for kindergarten teachers, was largely due to the energy and commitment of women. In 1848, when the kindergarten idea first attracted a large group of female supporters, revolutionary uprisings and the removal of press censorship had shaken the German states as well as other European countries (Gerhard). The central political questions of this revolutionary period concerned new forms of authority, citizenship, and social harmony. French utopian socialism, which at this time was extremely popular among progressive German intellectuals, exalted motherhood as a force for social progress and called for the breakdown of public/private barriers and the infusion of familial love into public life (Scott 57). The kindergarten itself was a challenge to conventional public/private boundaries. It brought women and small children out of the home into an institution, but it also created an institutional culture based on private, or familial, values (Allen, *Feminism and Motherhood*, 58-78; Prelinger 139-44).[4]

These aspirations were expressed by the founders of the Hamburg Academy for the Female Sex [Hochschule für das weibliche Geschlecht], the first institute of female higher education in the German-speaking world, which opened in 1850 (Kleinau). The purpose of the institution, which in addition to a rather ambitious academic curriculum offered kindergarten teacher-training, was to develop specifically female, or "motherly" energies for the reform and regeneration of society. The

3. On the history of the kindergarten in Germany, see Erning, Neumann, and Reyer.
4. For more on the participation of women in the Revolutions of 1848 in Germany, see Gerhard, Hannover-Druck, and Schmitter.

school's founders, Carl and Johanna Küstner Froebel, looked forward to the transition from a period of revolutionary violence to a new period of love, harmony and cooperation (Kleinau; Prelinger 95-100). Henriette Breymann, Froebel's niece and student, was disturbed by the violence and hatred of the revolutionary uprisings in her area, and invoked "what up until now has been entirely lacking … the spirit of spiritual mother-hood in its deepest meanings and most varied forms" (Lyschinska, vol.1, 86). Among the complex implications of this statement were both con-servative fears of class conflict and utopian aspirations to new forms of community. Thus, during the revolutionary era of 1848, maternalism expanded to encompass a wide variety of ethical, social and political meanings, linking the cause of women to other progressive movements of the time (Prelinger, Paletschek).

Certainly the political importance of spiritual motherhood was known to the Prussian regime which in 1851, after the defeat of the 1848 revolution, forbade the Froebel kindergarten as "part of a conspir-acy to convert the youth of the nation to atheism" (quoted in Paletschek 216). Kindergartens were closed, some forcibly (Prelinger, 61-165; Allen, *Feminism and Motherhood*, 82-83). In 1860, however, with the succession of William I as regent (he became King of Prussia in 1861), the kindergarten ban was rescinded; in the middle of this decade the two major German women's organizations, the General German Women's Association (Allgemeiner deutscher Frauenverein 1865) and the Lette Association (Lette-Verein, 1866), named for its founder the philan-thropist Adolf Lette, were established (Bussemer). The later decades of the nineteenth century saw a broadening of maternalist ideology, hith-erto applied chiefly in familial or pedagogical contexts, to encompass much more extensive possibilities of social activism and reform.

In the German-speaking world and elsewhere, the forms of "social motherhood" that were first developed in the 1870s, the formative period of the united German state, may be understood as a specifically female response to the economic, political and cultural problems of a society undergoing rapid industrial and urban development. The metaphor of the "great social household" was expanded to deal with a new reality, that of urban society. In Germany, the pioneers of the kindergarten movement, Henriette Breymann (now Schrader-Brey-mann), Bertha von Marenholtz-Bülow, and Henriette Goldschmidt, were also among the earliest creators in the German-speaking world of a role for upper and middle-class women social reformers in the city. "We have our city fathers," said Henriette Goldschmidt, "but where are the mothers?" (quoted in Allen, *Feminism and Motherhood*, 111). The metaphor of motherhood in this context had several important meanings. Many city-dwellers, such as Schrader-Breymann herself, who had moved with her husband Karl Schrader to Berlin in 1872, came from smaller communities where bonds of long acquaintanceship and traditions of paternalism mitigated some of the harsh effects of class inequality. For women such as Schrader-Breymann and her colleague Hedwig Heyl, "motherhood" symbolized the recreation of these bonds of community in a big-city environment that they perceived as impersonal, heartless and dangerous. The Pestalozzi-Froebel House, which started as a kindergarten in 1873 and acquired its first permanent building in 1883, encouraged kindergarten trainees to establish personal relationships with the families of their pupils and to organize their classes into small groups of different ages to reproduce family life (Erning, Neumann and Reyer, 1: 54-57). Because small-town family life included a closeness to nature and to agriculture that was denied to city children, the Pestalozzi-Froebel House included gardening and field-trips to the country in its curriculum (Schrader-Breymann). Thus, like other urban reformers of their era in Germany and elsewhere, these women educators often expressed nostalgia for earlier forms of the family and community life (Allen, *Feminism and Motherhood*, 111-35).

However, in many other ways the practice of "social motherhood" was quite well adapted to the new social conditions – including those of proletarianization and class conflict. "Motherhood" symbolized the benevolent but nonetheless hegemonic relationship of middle and upper-class women to the lower class. For example, the kindergarten movement under the leadership of Bertha von Marenholtz-Bülow gave up the utopian vision of 1848, which had called for the admission of children of all classes to the kindergarten, and instead set up "Volks-kindergärten" specifically as remedial institutions for the children of the poor (Allen, *Feminism and Motherhood*, 86-87). Maternal solicitude was used to justify and reinforce new forms of class stratification and inequality.

However, female social activists (as exemplified by the kindergarten founders as well as many others) did not simply support the state in its projects of social control. The ideology of "social motherhood" also asserted specifically female ethical ideals that were often contrasted to the "fatherly" discipline of the state. Female philanthropists were thus often quite critical of state-sponsored welfare measures. Schrader-Breymann and her colleagues were at first opposed to Bismarck's social insurance programs because the abstract and rule-oriented male spirit of bureaucracy was alien to the female, or "motherly" spirit of individualized compassion and concern. In the opinion of Hedwig Heyl, an industrialists's wife who became a prominent figure in Berlin philanthropic and women's organizations, Bismarck's social insurance laws had undermined the voluntary responsibility assumed by conscientious employers for the welfare of their employees. She quoted the French philosopher Renan, "Bismarck has made German greater, but the Germans smaller" (Heyl 22).

A later generation of female reformers who came of age around the turn of the century, including for example Alice von Salomon, Frieda Duensing, and Anna von Gierke, were much more favorable to the involvement of the state in social welfare. They emphasized women's gift for "social motherhood" in order to argue for greater participation by women in state bureaucracies and for the founding of female professions such as social work (Zeller). However, they opposed the absorption of private female-dominated philanthropic organizations into state bureaucracies and insisted on a cooperative relationship between public and private philanthropy that preserved the independence of female-led organizations. "Social motherhood" as a metaphor for a specifically female approach to social reform thus proved useful and flexible: it expressed feminists' aspirations both to inclusion within, and to independence from, the developing bureaucracy of the welfare state in the early twentieth century (Allen, *Feminism and Motherhood*, 206-28; Sachsse; Meyer-Renschhausen; Stoehr).

Some historians of feminist movements of the nineteenth and early twentieth centuries have associated this maternalist form of feminism specifically with Germany (or with continental Europe) and have contrasted it to the supposedly more liberal and individualistic orientation of English-speaking feminists of the same era (Evans, "The Concept of Feminism"). It is certainly true that suffrage movements began earlier and had a much greater following and significance in the United States than in Germany or, in fact, in any continental European country. However, American women's movements did not use only, or even chiefly, individualist arguments – they too relied heavily on the idea of social motherhood to assert women's right to play a role in public life.

The success of the kindergarten movement when exported from the land of its origin to the United States testified to the strength of maternalist energies among American women activists. When the kindergarten was forbidden in Prussia and some other states in 1851, many of its German proponents were forced to go into exile in Britain and America, and they brought the kindergarten with them. In the latter half of the nineteenth century, the Froebel kindergarten found greater acceptance in these countries than in the land of its origin. For example, starting in 1877, kindergarten classes, specifically of the Froebelian type, were integrated into many urban school systems in the United States, and gained the enthusiastic support of the teaching profession (Shapiro). In Germany, by contrast, the kindergarten was never integrated into public-school systems, although it was supported by some municipalities as a custodial institution for the children of the poor, and not until our own era has it gained broad support among the middle class. The reasons for this difference are many and complex, but among the most important was simply the greater influence of American women – both volunteers and professionals – on public life, especially education. These women, whether belonging to the women's organizations that supported private and public-school kindergartens or to the largely feminized teaching profession, were much less inspired by equal-rights feminism than by "social motherhood." This and many other examples suggest that maternalist feminist ideologies were more rather than less influential in the English-speaking world than in Germany. Moreover, American suffrage movements, particularly toward the end of the nineteenth century, strongly emphasized "social motherhood" as an argument for women's right to vote, thus combining maternalist with equal-rights ideology (Allen, "Let us Live with our Children").

The aspect of German feminist maternalism that has been most disturbing to historians in the present has been the enthusiastic response of some German feminists, starting around 1900, to new hereditarian and biological theories of human development (Janssen-Jurreit; Evans, *The Feminist Movement in Germany*, 158-70). This response must be seen in its historical context. In all Western European countries (starting with France in the 1870s) the decline in birth-rates was hailed as a "crisis" threatening domestic prosperity and the military strength. The fashionable new field of eugenics provided a scientific justification for such pessimistic forecasts. Prominent devotees of this field asserted that modern urban civilization had created such a dysgenic environment that, unless the process of reproduction was controlled and modified, deterioration, decay and death would result. Moralists, politicians, and others used this as a justification for an attack particularly on the feminist movement, which they accused of discouraging child-bearing by advocating access to education and professional employment. The new wave of misogyny brought a clamor for stricter laws limiting women's access to abortion, contraception, and educational advantages (Bergmann, Janssen-Jurreit). This attack was also conducted on a symbolic level; in art and literature of the period the emancipated woman became a symbol of disorder, decadence, and physical and psychological disease.

But despite its misogynistic implications, this debate had one major advantage for feminists. Mainstream feminist organizations concerned for their respectable image had up to this time been reluctant to incorporate issues concerning sexuality and reproduction into their programs. However, in an era when reproduction became a topic of public discussion, feminist organizations were enabled – indeed forced – to develop public positions on such issues.

Such feminist positions were shaped by the new leadership of the women's movements, including the new umbrella organization, the Federation of German Women's Associations (BDF [Bund Deutscher Frauenvereine]), founded in 1894, the League of Progressive Women's Organizations [Verband fortschrittlicher Frauenvereine], founded in 1899, and the League for the Protection of Mothers (Bund für Mutterschutz), founded in 1905. Due to the development of female professionalism, many of the new leaders were academically trained lawyers, social workers, teachers, and physicians who greeted the fashionable scientific ideas of the day with much the same enthusiasm as many of their male contemporaries (Schwartz, "Eugenik und Bevölkerungspolitik"). New scientific views of sexuality as an entirely natural drive encouraged many feminists to reject traditional religious and cultural constraints on female behavior and to exult the power of female sexuality as a life-giving force. Eugenic theory clearly stated that genetic fitness depended neither on the class nor on the marital status of the parents. Some feminists used this theory to argue for the equalization of the status of legitimate and illegitimate children and for the recognition of non-marital relationships. Feminist sexual reformers at the turn of the century used biological theory to argue not for biological determinism but for women's reproductive self-determination. Particularly the image of the unmarried mother was remade to symbolize not sin and social marginalization, but the triumph of life-giving female energy over a discredited patriarchal morality (Allen, "Radical Feminism and Eugenics").

The metaphorical use of motherhood to signify life, health and the continuity of generations was central to some of the most important feminist campaigns of this era, including those for reproductive rights and for social benefits for mothers and children. On such issues, German feminists were among the most active in the Western world; for example, in 1908 the BDF held a full-scale debate on a proposal to recommend the abolition including the campaign of some German feminists for the complete elimination of Paragraph 218, which penalized both women who sought, and physicians who performed abortions. Opponents of the proposal argued that the abolition of the statute would harm the state by reducing birth-rates and undermining standards of sexual morality. Proponents argued on the contrary that mothers who controlled their own reproductive destiny would benefit the state by producing healthy and carefully nurtured offspring, thus compensating through better quality for lesser quantity. The defeat of the proposal showed that radical ideas on the reform of marriage and the family were confined to a minority of feminists. But there was a large area of agreement, for both sides had framed arguments linking the reproductive rights of women to the welfare of the state and of the new generation (Allen, *Feminism and Motherhood*, 188-205).

Both mainstream and radical feminists were instrumental at the turn of the century in taking the first steps toward a new kind of polity, the welfare state, in which the support of mothers and children became an explicitly public concern. Feminists such as the founder of the social-work profession, Alice Salomon, and the socialists Lily Braun and Henriette Fürth, as well as the major feminist organizations, took the lead in campaigns for state-sponsored benefits such as maternity insurance for working mothers, support for maternal and child health, and many others (Koven and Michel; Bock and Thane). In a widely-read book that was translated into many languages, the Swedish author Ellen Key hailed the new twentieth century as "the century of the child," and declared that "the right of the child to choose its parents" – that is, the child's right both to sound genetic heredity and to careful nurture – must be upheld both by individual parents and by national policies (1). In the developing welfare state, motherhood became a service to the state, and thus a basis for citizenship and entitlement.

Although the enthusiasm of some German feminists for eugenics was interpreted in some of the first historical accounts as a sign of typically German authoritarian, even protofascist tendencies, more recent research confirms the popularity of very similar ideas among feminists of other countries. British and American feminists also justified the legalization of birth control more often by invoking "population quality" and the welfare of the state than the individual rights of women; indeed the great American crusader Margaret Sanger was a eugenics enthusiast and thought of "race control" and "population control" before arriving at "birth control" as the name of her movement (Sanger 108).

In fact, maternalism everywhere had its authoritarian side; mothers enforce good conduct because they know better than their children what is best for them. In Germany as in many other Western countries, feminists worked closely with social purity movements designed to enforce moral conduct – including campaigns against the sale of alcoholic beverages, legalized prostitution, pornography and many other forms of vice. Feminist reformers had justified reproductive rights for individuals as a means toward public health for society as a whole, and had urged legalized voluntary sterilization as the only responsible choice for those afflicted with hereditary disease. For those who could or would not make that "responsible" choice, a few feminists advocated compulsory sterilization. Similarly, many who opposed the police regulation of prostitution nonetheless argued for various criminal penalties for infected persons who engaged in sexual activity, thus endangering future generations by the spread of venereal diseases. Such recommendations were not (as they have sometimes been pictured) reactionary lapses into patriarchal attitudes; they were in the logic of maternalist feminism itself. For if the aim of "social motherhood" was to promote social harmony and well-being, then it followed that offenders against these values, if they could not be won over, must be excluded from the community. Their conviction that maternal authority was always benevolent sometimes blinded feminists to authoritarian elements within their own thinking. In 1912, the German socialist feminist Adele Schreiber, a member of the League for the Protection of Mothers and a formidable activist on behalf of women and children, proposed at the annual meeting of the Federation of German Women's Association (BDF) that mentally retarded people should be confined to humane, but sex-segregated colonies, to prevent them from reproducing and transmitting their disability to the next generation. Although such a proposal might seem "monstrous," she explained, the sacrifice of reproduction was no heavier than similar sacrifices required by the state, such as military service that might mean death (Allen, *Feminism and Motherhood*, 202 and "Feminism, Venereal Disease and the State").

During the period before World War I, ideas such as those expressed by Schreiber were very controversial among feminists and accepted by only a minority, but in the 1920s they became much more prevalent. As Atina Grossmann and Cornelie Usborne have shown, most feminist reformers of the 1920s shared the belief of many male social reformers in compulsory sterilization of persons afflicted with some hereditary diseases, the requirements of health certificates for marriage licenses, penalties for the spread of venereal diseases, and other state-sponsored measures to ensure population quality.[5] Certainly the feminists did not intend, and could not have foreseen, the measures taken by the National Socialists, who instituted programs of compulsory sterilization and other forms of reproductive control starting in 1933. But feminists, along with many other progressive activists and intellectuals had played a role in creating a public climate that accepted such measures.

This complex history shows how important it is to view the ideas of feminists, not according to our own ideal definition of feminism, but in

5. For some revealing research into the popularity of eugenics, and specifically of compulsory sterilization, among left-wing and progressive circles, see the articles by Schwartz.

the context of the periods in which they developed. In all of these periods, feminists have based their claims to equality both on gender similarity and on gender difference, and have not regarded these arguments as contradictory (cf. Scott). Nor have definitions of female gender roles, including motherhood, been fixed and essentialist; in every period they have given rise to many and diverse personal, political and metaphorical meanings. In our own day, as in the past, the place of maternalist ideology within feminist movements is debated, but the difference between American and German debates indicates more general differences in the way feminists of these two nations have come to terms with their history. In the United States, feminist movements of 1980s were more open to theories of gender difference than those of the previous two decades. Some authors glorified motherliness and its associated nurturing and nonviolent qualities (Ruddick). The American psychologist Carol Gilligan, who asserted that women's ethical decisions were based more on interpersonal relationships and less on abstract principles than those of men, claimed that women spoke with a different, though equally authoritative voice. Although these authors were criticized for essentialism and for reviving outworn stereotypes of female behavior, their ideas have also proved quite influential (Kerber et al.).

In Germany, ideologies based on gender difference also became more popular in the 1980s than in previous decades. But feminists who advocate maternalism meet a still more serious rebuke, a reminder of the history of National Socialism, which mobilized women's enthusiasm for motherhood in the service of war and genocide (Windaus-Walser; Gravenhorst and Tatschmurat).[6] Thus in this as in many other cases, the discussion of gender issues in the German-speaking world is overshadowed by the history of the National Socialist era. But no more than any other major movement for social change should feminism be understood as part of a *Sonderweg* leading inevitably to National Socialism.[7] A history that now spans more than two centuries should be seen in its full diversity, moral ambiguity, and complexity.

6. See the extended comments on this controversy in Bock, "Gleichheit und Differenz."

7. See Bock, "Gleichheit und Differenz."

Bibliography

Allen, Ann Taylor. "American and German Women in the Kindergarten Movement." *German Influences on Education in the United States.* Ed. Henry Geitz, Jürgen Heideking and Jurgen Herbst. New Haven: Yale UP, 1995. 85-101.

————. *Feminism and Motherhood in Germany, 1800-1914.* New Brunswick, NJ: Rutgers UP, 1991.

————."Feminism, Venereal Diseases, and the State in Germany, 1890-1918. *Journal of the History of Sexuality* 4 (1993): 27-50.

————. "Gardens of Children, Gardens of God: Kindergartens and Day-Care Centers in Nineteenth-Century Germany." *Journal of Social History* 18 (1986): 435-50.

————. "German Radical Feminism and Eugenics, 1900-1918." *German Studies Review* 9 (February, 1988): 31-56.

————. "Let us Live for our Children: Kindergarten Movements in Germany and the United States." *History of Education Quarterly* 28 (1988): 405-36.

Bergmann, Anna. *Die verhütete Sexualität: Die Anfänge der modernen Geburtenkontrolle.* Hamburg: Rasch und Rohring, 1992.

Bock, Gisela. "Gleichheit und Differenz in der nationalsozialistischen Rassenpolitik." *Geschichte und Gesellschaft* 19 (1993): 277-310.

————, and Pat Thane, eds. *Maternalism and Gender Politics: Women and the Rise of European Welfare States, 1880s-1950s.* London: Routledge, 1990.

Bussemer, Herrad Ulrike. *Frauenemanzipation und Bildungsbürgertum: Sozialgeschichte der Frauenbewegung in der Reichsgründerzeit.* Weinheim: Beltz, 1985.

Campe, Joachim Heinrich. *Sittenbüchlein für Kinder.* Braunschweig, 1788.

Erning, Günter, Karl Neumann and Jürgen Reyer. *Geschichte des Kindergartens.* 3 vols. Freiburg i. Br.: Lambertus, 1987.

Evans, Richard. *The Feminist Movement in Germany, 1894-1933.* London: Sage, 1976.

————. "The Concept of Feminism: Notes for Practicing Historians." *German Women in the Eighteenth and Nineteenth Centuries: A Social and Literary History.* Ed. Ruth-Ellen Joeres and Mary Jo Maynes. Bloomington: Indiana UP, 1986.

Geertz, Clifford. "Ideology as a Cultural System." *The Interpretation of Cultures.* New York: Basic Books, 1973, 194-229.

Gerhard, Ute, Elisabeth Hannover-Druck, and Romina Schmitter, eds. *Dem Reich der Freiheit werb' ich Bürgerinnen: Die Frauen-Zeitung von Louise Otto.* Frankfurt: Syndikat, 1979.

Gleim, Betty. *Erziehung und Unterricht des weiblichen Geschlechts: Ein Buch für Eltern und Erzieher.* Leipzig: C.J. Goschen, 1810.

Gravenhorst, Lerke, and Carmen Tatschmurat, eds. *TöchterFragen: NS Frauengeschichte.* Freiburg: Kore, 1990.

Grossmann, Atina. *Reforming Sex.* New York: Oxford UP, 1995.

Hausen, Karin. "Die Polarisierung der Geschlechtscharaktere – Eine
Spiegelung der Dissoziation von Erwerbs- und Familienleben."
Sozialgeschichte der Familie in der Neuzeit Europas. Ed. Werner Conze.
Stuttgart: Klett, 1976. 363-93.

Heyl, Hedwig. *Aus meinem Leben.* Berlin: C.A. Schwetke, 1925.

Jansen-Jurreit, Marie-Louise. "National-Biologie, Sexualreform und
Geburtenrückgang: Über den Zusammenhang von Bevölkerungspolitik
und Frauenbewegung um die Jahrhundertwende." *Die Überwindung der
Sprachlosigkeit: Texte aus der neuen Frauenbewegung.* Ed. Gabriele Dietze.
Darmstadt und Neuwied: Luchterhand, 1978.

Kerber, Linda. *Women of the Republic: Intellect and Ideology in Revolutionary
America,* Chapel Hill: U of North Carolina P, 1980.

Kerber, Linda, et al., "On *In a Different Voice*: An Interdisciplinary Forum."
Signs: Journal of Women in Culture and Society 11 (Winter, 1986): 304-33.

Key, Ellen. *The Century of the Child.* New York: Arno Press, 1972.

Klattenhoff, Klaus. "Pädagogische Aufgaben und Ziele in der Geschichte der
öffentlichen Kleinkinderziehung." *Geschichte des Kindergartens.* 3 vols. Ed.
Günter Erning, Karl Neumann, und Jürgen Reyer. Freiburg i. B.:
Lambertus, 1987. Vol. I, 106-19.

Kleinau, Elke. "Die 'Hochschule für das weibliche Geschlecht' und ihre
Auswirkungen auf die Entwicklung des höheren Mädchenschulwesens in
Hamburg." *Zeitschrift für Pädagogik* 36 (1990): 121-26.

Koonz, Claudia. *Mothers in the Fatherland: Women, the Family and Nazi
Politics,* New York: St. Martins, 1987.

Koven, Seth and Sonya Michel. eds. *Mothers of a New World: Maternalist
Politics and the Origins of Welfare States.* New York: Routledge, 1993.

Lyschinska, Mary. *Henriette Schrader-Breymann: Ihr Leben aus Breifen und
Tagebüchern zusammengestellt und erläutert.* 2 vols. Berlin and Leipzig: de
Gruyter, 1922.

Meyer-Renschhausen, Elisabeth. *Weibliche Kultur und soziale Arbeit: Eine
Geschichte der Frauenbewegung am Beispiel Bremens, 1810-1927.* Köln:
Böhlau, 1989.

Paletschek, Sylvia. *Frauen und Dissens: Frauen im Deutschkatholizismus und in
den freireligiösen Gemeinden, 1841-1852.* Göttingen: Vandenhoek und
Ruprecht, 1990.

Pestalozzi, Johann Heinrich. *How Gertrude teaches her children: an attempt
to help mothers to teach their own children.* Syracuse, N.Y.: C.W. Bardeen,
1898.

Peters, Dietlinde. *Mütterlichkeit im Kaiserreich: Die bürgerliche
Frauenbewegung und der soziale Beruf der Frau.* Bielefeld: B. Kleine, 1984.

Prelinger, Catherine. *Charity, Challenge and Change: Religious Dimensions of
the Mid-Nineteenth-Century Women's Movement in Germany.* New York:
Greenwood, 1987

Reagin, Nancy R. *A German Women's Movement.* Chapel Hill: U of North
Carolina P, 1995.

Ruddick, Sara. *Maternal Thinking: Toward a Politics of Peace.* Boston: Beacon Press, 1989.

Sachsse, Christoph. *Mütterlichkeit als Beruf. Sozialarbeit, Sozialreform, und Frauenbewegung, 1871-1929.* Frankfurt a. M.: Suhrkamp, 1986.

Sanger, Margaret. *Margaret Sanger: An Autobiography.* New York: W.W. Norton, 1938.

Schrader-Breymann, Henriette. *Der Volkskindergarten im Pestalozzi-Froebel Haus.* Berlin: Leonhard Simion, 1890.

Schwartz, Michael. "Eugenik und Bevölkerungspolitik: Über neuere Beiträge zu einer problematischen Sozialtechnologie." *Archiv für Sozialgeschichte* 32 (1992): 426-44.

_____."Sozialistische Ursprünge eugenischen Denkens." *Vierteljahreshefte für Zeitgeschichte* 4 (1994): 537-70.

Scott, Joan Wallach. *Only Paradoxes to Offer: French Feminists and the Rights of Man.* Cambridge, MA.: Harvard UP, 1996.

Shapiro, Michael Steven. *Child's Garden: The Kindergarten Movement from Froebel to Dewey.* University Park: Pennsylvania State UP, 1982.

Stoehr, Irene. "Organisierte Mütterlichkeit: Zur Politik der deutschen Frauenbewegung um 1900." *Frauen suchen ihre Geschichte: Historische Studien zum 19. und 20. Jahrhundert.* Ed. Karin Hausen. München: C.H. Beck, 1982.

Usborne, Cornelie. *The Politics of the Body in Weimar Germany.* Basingstoke: Macmillan, 1992.

Wickert, Christl. *Helene Stöcker, 1869-1943: Frauenrechtlerin, Sexualreformerin und Pazifistin. Eine Biographie.* Bonn: Dietz, 1991.

Windaus-Walser, Karin. "Gnade der weiblichen Geburt?" *Feministische Studien* 1 (1988): 131.

Zeller, Susanne, *Volksmütter: Frauen im Wohlfahrtswesen der zwanziger Jahre.* Düsseldorf: Schwann, 1987.

Chapter 8

"TRULY WOMANLY" AND "TRULY GERMAN"

Women's Rights and National Identity in *Die Frau* [1]

Stefana Lefko

> There never was any chance under the Weimar Republic that the BDF's conservative orientation could be changed, its hostility to the Republic mitigated or its approach made more effective. (Evans 238)

Scholarship about the Federation of German Women's Associations (Bund Deutscher Frauenvereine or BDF) has generally emphasized the organization's lack of initiative in pursuing women's rights. The BDF is blamed for the decline of the bourgeois women's movement after the organization's refusal to support legalized abortion in 1908,[2] and accused of leading women to welcome National Socialism.[3] Pointing out its affinities to the most conservative strands of the nineteenth-century women's movement,[4] scholars emphasize the BDF's lack of innovation in the fight for women's rights at the time and its essentially patriarchal view of women, which would later supposedly be taken over by the

1. With the exception of the quote from Emma Enders, all translations from the German are my own.
2. See Evans.
3. See, for example, Wittrock 15-16, or Koonz's assertion that the middle-class women's movement welcomed the Nazis' antidemocratic stance: (144). For an excellent refutation of Koonz, as well as the assertions of Evans and other historians that "the women's movement could only extend a warm welcome to Adolf Hitler and the Third Reich" because the philosophies were so similar, see Bock.
4. See Bussemer.

Nazis. Yet these critiques often overlook both that which was new within BDF strategies and the complex and changing nature of its efforts during the Weimar Republic. In reality, opinion within the large and diverse membership of the BDF on how "woman," her rights, and her role in the public sphere were to be defined differed widely. Although the BDF, an umbrella organization sworn to political neutrality, tried to adopt an approach general enough for all of its members to accept, the task was daunting. The strategies utilized depended not only upon the organization within the BDF to which an individual belonged, but also upon that person's background, influences, and the time and particular political situation in question. An examination of the BDF journal *Die Frau* during the Weimar Republic demonstrates the complicated nature of the strategies employed on behalf of women's rights, and how the nature and meaning of "emancipation" is time- and place-specific.

Common to most contributions in *Die Frau* was the notion of the binary opposition of the genders. Women's more spiritual, idealistic nature was seen as complimentary to men's concrete, achievement-oriented nature, with both genders perceived as necessary for a properly functioning society. In order to improve and reconstruct a society damaged by war and lacking in important female contributions, arguments about expanding women's traditional role into the public sphere – borrowed from nineteenth-century discourses – were used to promote their involvement in legislation, law, finance, and nearly every other traditionally masculine field.[5]

Despite an ambitious program of demands for women's rights in 1907, the BDF put off its own cause in the name of national welfare during World War I.[6] In 1916, Helene Lange, editor of *Die Frau*,[7] even openly criticized those women willing to put women's rights ahead of national unity during the war.[8] But when in 1917 the Organization for the Fight against Women's Emancipation[9] wanted to legislate that no

---

5. Evans argues that the vagueness of the BDF description of specifically "womanly" activities which would help to bring female values into a new society would allow every "knitting circle" to see itself as feminist. Here he clearly overlooks the value of this strategy as a weapon which allowed women to claim the medical profession, law, university admission, all professions, and government – even national budget control – as within their sphere.

6. See Altmann-Gottheiner 70.

7. Lange served as head of the General German Teacher's Association (Allgemeiner Deutscher Lehrerinnenverein) as well as president of the General German Women's Association (Allgemeiner Deutscher Frauenverein or ADF). She was a member of the BDF executive committee from 1894-1904, after which time she continued to edit *Die Frau*. She belonged to the moderate faction within the BDF. See Evans 27-29, 145-53.

8. See Lange, "'Neuorientierung' in der Frauenbewegung" 1.

9. *Bund zur Bekämpfung der Frauenemanzipation.*

man could have a female superior, Lange did not hesitate to label this proposal as selfish and inimical to the nation in a time of national need.[10] After the Kaiser, under pressure from within Germany and abroad, promised suffrage reform in 1917, the BDF launched a major campaign for women's rights.[11] Articles in *Die Frau* specified ways in which women, as full citizens with active and passive voting rights, could help the nation, emphasizing that they had earned their citizenship rights with their efforts during the war.[12] It was pointed out that women had brought in the harvest while the men were at war and had thus defeated the "starvation plans of England,"[13] and that the war had demonstrated their ability to work in the public sphere. They suggested that the postwar surplus of single women be enlisted in the national interest instead of being doomed to a life of celibacy and inactivity.

In 1917, Camilla Jelinek invoked the often-utilized justification of women's entry into certain manufacturing fields – their flexibility and small motor skills – to suggest special womanly abilities for a future role in legislation, where they could help the nation in ways which men could not. "Woman," she claimed,

> instinctively transmits her methods of individual education, individual care of the poor, etc., to the general sphere ... With all her strength she wants to help work on the future of the state, and that means also through participation in legislation! She can feel that there are little springs and little wheels in the state machinery which are better set in motion by the tender fingers of the woman than by the stronger but less flexible fingers of the man (329).

The BDF also continued the prewar strategy of citing biological motherhood as proof that women possessed special life-giving instincts. Giving birth, however, was not required: women's motherly instincts could be employed within the public sphere even when they remained unmarried. Indeed, the need to utilize those gifts which might otherwise be wasted was one of the primary arguments for women's participation in the working world. Now, during the Weimar Republic, it was further proposed that, because of their special gifts, women should be able to direct girl's schools and participate in legislation, where their perspective would be substan-

10. See Lange "Neue Frauenfeindschaft" 290.

11. See Evans 224-25.

12. At the same time that the BDF fought for women's rights, it constantly emphasized the nationalism of the women's movement, defending against charges by opponents of women's rights that the movement was internationalist and pacifist. During the war, the BDF issued statements against Wilson's Peace Note of 1917, the Armistice Terms, the Treaty of Versailles, and the League of Nations. See Evans 211.

13. See Altmann-Gottheiner 74.

tially different than that of men. These unique talents could thus be brought into the public sphere to aid in the reconstruction of the nation.[14]

* * *

When women did receive both active and passive voting rights after World War I, *Die Frau* urged its readers to recognize the importance of political involvement. They were to educate themselves and take advantage of new opportunities by working constructively within already existing parties, not by forming a special party for women.[15] As the movement for voting rights had included many women of differing political orientations, a unified women's party would have been, at best, difficult to realize. The readership of *Die Frau* itself tended to be middle-class with democratic loyalties, and the leadership often had ties to the German Democratic Party (Deutsche Demokratische Partei or DDP). Indeed, Gertrud Bäumer[16] served not only as President of the BDF from 1910 to 1919 and editor of *Die Frau* throughout the Weimar Republic, but also as a DDP representative in the Reichstag from 1919 to 1932. In keeping with the political orientation of the BDF leadership, *Die Frau* fought the spread of Communism from the very beginning of the Weimar era, attacking it as a threat to the rights which they had just been given in the new constitution. This argument would also be used later against the Nazis.

During the upheavals of the early Weimar Republic, *Die Frau* argued, as it had in the prewar period, that women's participation within existing political structures would bring a special idealism and morality to the struggle to shape the new state. This special ability – and not women's claim to general human rights – was seen as the justification for their entry into the public sphere. When women sink to the level of men, Marianne Weber[17] argued in 1919, there is no point in their participation in politics, "because if we dull our moral feeling and allow our souls to be damaged, then our political importance remains limited to the rep-

14. Not only the conservative women's movement thought this way. Augspurg and Heymann, for instance, issued statements in 1914 declaring that men's politics had failed Europe and caused the war and that only women could reform society, as they stood closer to "true humanity." See Evans 218-19.

15. See Weber, "Die Beteiligung" 2.

16. Bäumer was elected president of the BDF in 1910 at the age of 36, after already having been on the BDF's executive committee for 10 years. After she stepped down in 1918, she edited *Die Frau* until publishing stopped in 1944. She served as a DDP representative in the Reichstag throughout the entire Weimar Republic, as well as a ministerial advisor in the Ministry of the Interior. After World War II, she was active in the Christlich-Soziale Union and Christlich-Demokratische Union.

17. Marianne Weber, widow of the sociologist Max Weber, was active in the DDP, referred to accurately by Wittrock as the "Sammelpartei des Bürgertums," as well as in the

resentation of our gender interests, and is unimportant for the reconstruction of the entire [nation]" ("Die Beteiligung," 3).

In the meantime, the fight for women's rights was carried on in ways
not always considered "progressive" today. The BDF opposed the legalization of abortion for moral and "cultural" reasons. Hilde Adler, for
example, stated in *Die Frau* in 1921 that "together with the cinema, the
romanticism of pulp literature, and the model of black market dealing, it
would just encourage the already sexually overstimulated public to an
unrestrained animalistic living out [of their desires]" ("Freigabe," 205-06).

Efforts by Helene Stöcker and her League for the Protection of Motherhood (Bund für Mutterschutz) to reform bourgeois sexual morals, to
make contraception widely available and to teach sexual education in the
schools were fought with the assertion that such measures would result
in "indiscriminate, wild sexual relations" and the further mistreatment of
women by men. The resulting decline in the number of abortions would
represent only an "apparent" control of sexual drives, not a real one.[18]
Instead, contributors to *Die Frau* argued that men should be taught to
exercise self-control and educated to the same moral standards as women.

In the first half of the Weimar Republic, *Die Frau* often emphasized
that men and women were guaranteed equal rights according to the new
constitution. Article 109 stated, however, that "men and women have
fundamentally the same rights and duties as citizens." The word "fundamentally" caused many problems in the struggle for women's rights
during the Weimar Republic: judges who had wide-ranging powers in
the interpretation of the constitution had, for the most part, been
appointed during the imperial era and had no particular loyalty to the
new state. In addition, most family and marital legislation was adopted
from the prewar period, even if it stood in direct conflict with the new
guarantees of equality.

After the initial euphoria wore off, *Die Frau* was filled with complaints about the situation for women. Emmy Beckmann's angry tirade
against sexist injustices is typical of the journal's response to the backlash.
She protested against unfair firings, against the fact that qualified women
were often not allowed to lead schools, and that women were often not
given proper access to education.[19] Gertrud Bäumer joined the outcry,
arguing that existing legislation had to be altered to give women better
legal protection ("Rede zum sozialen Teil," 202).

BDF. She was President of the BDF from 1919 to 1920, and served on the BDF executive committee during the Weimar Republic.

18. See Lange, "Die Frau und das neue Geschlecht," 300.

19. See Beckmann 26.

Such protests that the political process did not give women a fair chance continued throughout the Weimar Republic. Bäumer complained that women were often shunted off onto unimportant committees by virtue of their "special nature," and not allowed to work on more important ones where the chance for change actually existed. This, however, is seen as a purposeful male attempt to retain power, and not related to the effects of the theory of women's "special nature" which were continuously propagated within *Die Frau*.[20]

While authors in *Die Frau* were fighting the battle for women's rights using constitutional guarantees of equality, other strategies were also being pursued, including an updated form of the nineteenth-century idea of the special cultural mission of women. Although Germany could no longer be an imperial power, it could become a *Kulturstaat* [cultural nation], where women's gender-specific abilities would enable them to be the bearers of culture, re-forming men as well as women and creating a national atmosphere of spirituality and culture. Marianne Weber wrote in 1919 that women belonging to the propertied classes had been able to remain outside of the "struggle for existence" during the war and thus to retain their "spiritual capital." For this reason, they had a special responsibility for " the reconstruction of morality, the formation ... [of society] through love and beauty, through moderation and harmony, through dignity and refinement. This will happen through continued untiring work for the welfare of the possessionless classes, which were so much more damaged than we were" ("Die besonderen Kulturaufgaben," 137-38). Through a reference to the salon culture of the eighteenth century, Weber also implied later in the same article that men would benefit from an intellectual exchange with culturally educated women.

Eventually, it was even argued that the women's movement itself was a product of German culture. Helene Lange pointed out in 1923 that:

the German women's movement grew ... out of ... the deep and noble intellectual culture of our classical literature. Its first leaders ... had it to thank that next to an emphasis on human rights, a clear and secure feeling of female specificity remained and helped them to overcome that which was doctrinaire in that concept of the nation which was merely built upon theories of natural law. Thus, from the beginning, demands ... were not posed in the sense of mere feminism, but in the full consciousness of the importance of bringing the female kind, eternally different from men, to effectiveness in community life ("Phasen," 329).

Later authors would quote anthropological work by J.J. Bachofen on past matriarchal regimes to bolster their claim that women had indeed

---

20. See Bäumer, "Das Wichtige und das Unwichtige," 3-4.

exercised significant influence in the cultural and political spheres. Bachofen's theories were invoked to argue for the combination of marriage and profession for women, hotly debated during the Weimar Republic, as natural and "Germanic." Like their female Germanic ancestors and their male contemporaries, women should be able to fulfill themselves through marriage, motherhood, and work, if they wished. Yet, as Marianne Beth complained in 1929, a woman still confronted "a completely impossible choice: a profession with celibacy or marriage without her own income, in a perhaps unbearable situation as a housewife." In vain did the working woman seek the kind of professional satisfaction that would compensate her for the attendant sacrifice of love and family (11-13).

* * *

Adapting Oswald Spengler's claim that the West was in decline, some contributors saw the Weimar Republic as the last stage of a "male" age, incomplete and in need of female corrective influence. For evidence, "scientific" works like that of Dr. F. Landmann were quoted, which asserted that men were responsible for societal moral decline.[21] It was argued that the age of the machine, brought about by a predominance of men in the public sphere, would be tempered and altered by female influences, and that under this female guidance, everything from machines to apartments, to government structure and policy-making, could be redesigned from the standpoint of human welfare, not profit. Women's "culture" would counter the effects of men's "civilization." The women's movement was thus redefined as an idealistic, humanizing force engaged in a cultural struggle. Culture itself, as Bäumer remarked in 1927, could only be rescued when women participate:

> It doesn't just have to do with women and men, but with polarly opposed cultural values, of which one part has been repressed and stunted through one-sided development. And so the women's movement deepened into the cultural struggle about the rights of life and humanity against the power and influence of material goods, the exterior apparatus of civilization and superficially useful achievements ("Die Frau und das geistige Schaffen," 371-72).

Women argued against charges that they were becoming "masculinized" by pointing out that they did not want to imitate men or lose their specifically female qualities: on the contrary, they wanted to utilize them for the good of society. After economic and technical transformation in the second half of the nineteenth century had emptied and eliminated

21. See "Reine Mutterschaft," 701.

women's jobs at home, their "life strength," it was felt, had looked for, and found, new channels.

Dr. Lenore Kühn,[22] writing in 1927, felt that the cultural renewal which would come through women's participation in the public sphere would regenerate that which was "German" within culture, replacing the need for the "exhausted German culture" to turn to "Negro music, Charleston, jazz bands and all plebeian Americanisms" ("Die Krise des Intellekts," 334). Despite this last statement connecting women's rights and Germanness, women of other nationalities working for women's rights were generally portrayed positively in *Die Frau* , including Russian and American women. However, authors such as Guida Diehl,[23] who attacked the women's movement as too international and un-German – a charge it had been fighting since before World War I – were sharply criticized. For the BDF, which had been trying for several decades to define itself as both an integral part of the nation and an advocate of women's rights, this sort of attitude represented dangerous opposition. Diehl was attacked as unchristian, nationalist, and anti-Semitic.[24]

* * *

Although foreign women were often reported on in positive ways during the era of stabilization, a different strategy was pursued in the magazine during the economic crisis of the early 1930s. In the attempt to resist claims of the far Right that women's rights were imported from the capitalist West or the Bolshevist East, a certain image of woman and women's rights began to be defined as uniquely and truly German. In 1930, Gertrud Bäumer argued that the much referred-to Germanic ideal woman was not a Gretchen figure, but instead a strong woman who resisted an inferior position out of Germanic instinct. In her attempt to defend women's rights as inherently German, she performed a remarkable about-face from an earlier article of Marianne Weber's, asserting that:

> [it is] astonishing, when of all things from the nationalist, indeed, from the National Socialist side the German woman in her political effectiveness is relegated back to the political "salon" – a creation of French culture of a time

22. Dr. Lenore Kühn was associated with the Deutschnationale Volkspartei and served as speaker and editor of the party journal. She was elected to the executive committee of the BDF near the end of the Weimar Republic. Kühn wrote for Sophie Rogge-Börner's *Die Deutsche Kämpferin* as well as providing numerous articles for *Die Frau*, generally arguing for a synthesis of the conservative women's movement and fascism. See Wittrock 172-73.

23. Guida Diehl founded the *Neulandbewegung*, a right-wing protestant organization, which, by the late 1920s, had over 200,000 followers. She joined the NSDAP in 1930. See Koonz 80-85, Wittrock 115.

24. See Zahn-Harnack, "Frauen-erneuerung," 27.

and a social order in which politics was run by a small group and in which the woman for the most part won her influence through a clever combination of intellect and eroticism, which surely corresponds very little to the nature of Germanic women in general ("Stellungnahme," 6).

In contrast to this "French" model, the "Germanic" model, where women worked honestly and decently alongside their men in the public sphere for the *Volksgemeinschaft* was seen as preferable and historically justifiable. Germanic women, it was claimed, had made important decisions with the men in the early Germanic tribes and had even sometimes fought at their side. This model of the strong Germanic woman, who played an important part in governing the tribe, was seen as vastly preferable to Nazi proposals, which argued for excluding women from politics and public life. Even women's voting rights were described as uniquely Germanic. Bäumer pointed out in 1933 that, in the matter of women's rights, "the leading countries have been the Scandinavian and Anglo-Saxon ones ... there is a clear racial demarcation line between the Germanic countries with women's voting rights and the Latin countries without women's voting rights" ("Lage und Aufgabe," 388-89).

Fears about the spread of Communism also played an important role in the pages of *Die Frau* , even as the Nazi threat grew. The June 1931 issue criticized both movements as radical. The main difference between them in terms of women's rights, Charlotte Baenitz felt, was that the Communists did not recognize women as intrinsically different from men, or able to form society in gender-specific ways, while the NSDAP found important and essential differences between men and women, but nonetheless did not want women to participate in the formation of the state. Baenitz argued in response that, while there were differences between men and women, a "general human characteristic" existed as well which justified women's entry into the public sphere.[25]

The tactic of promoting women's rights as specifically Germanic was shared by early Nazi female reformers like Sophie Rogge-Börner,[26] who fought for a non-patriarchal fascism[27] in her magazine *Die Deutsche Kämpferin* (The German Female Fighter). Yet when the National Association of German Housewives' Societies (Reichsverband Deutscher

25. See Baenitz 683.

26. Despite her conservatism and nationalism, Sophie Rogge-Börner was never a member of the Nazi party. She served as editor of *Die Deutsche Kämpferin* from 1933 until it was banned by the Gestapo in 1937. See Wittrock 169-71.

27. Rogge-Börner's specific form of "non-patriarchal fascism" envisioned a society which, although repressing all but the racial "elite," would allow men and women equal rights, to the extent that anyone could speak of rights within the fascist political context envisioned. Women would also be trained for warfare.

Hausfrauenvereine or RDH) voted to leave the BDF in 1932, taking an estimated one-half to one-third of BDF members with them,[28] Leonore Kühn could claim that the real reason for the departure was that *Die Frau* was not politically neutral enough: that is, it was too inclined to favor liberalism over "völkisch" nationalism or National Socialism.[29]

Although *Die Frau* had always attempted to remain politically neutral and flexible enough to adopt new strategies for women's rights during the Weimar Republic, in the last years of the era its editorial staff did consistently campaign against the Nazis and for a parliamentary system. As Richard Evans remarks, although some BDF members wanted to attempt to alter the NSDAP from within rather than attempting a frontal attack, and although preserving the BDF's neutrality was important to everyone, the majority of members supported Emma Enders when she declared "National Socialism has grown big in its fight against Jews and women. It will not give this fight up. Today I am for struggle" (quoted in Evans 255). The National Socialists were criticized for both their opposition to women's rights and their antisemitism. In 1930, Dr. Dorothee von Velsen described Nazi goals as:

> the rule of men, the men of a certain race and culture, in a certain kind of state … This final goal is according to divine will, because it means the victory of light over darkness, of the creative Aryan spirit over the corroding Jewish one, as well as over the female principle, which is apparently to be regarded as matter (135-36).

But despite harsh criticism the threat dictatorship would represent to the struggle for women's rights, pro-Nazi articles, particularly by Dr. Leonore Kühn, were occasionally published in the journal under the guise of retaining political objectivity. However, such articles nearly always inspired debate or open attacks from other contributors. For instance, a 1930 letter from "Raba Stahlberg, stud. jur.," which argued that women should give up positions in public life and rely upon men to translate female political impulses into action in the public sphere, received a swift rejoinder from another student (Schwenk 175-76).

As the Weimar Republic drew closer to its end, articles in *Die Frau* became more outspoken in their attempt to draw voters away from the Nazis, often pointing to constitutional rights as the basis of women's demands for better treatment. *Die Frau* still defended democracy as the only type of governmental system which could ensure women's rights,

28. See Evans 252.
29. See Evans 251. At this time Kühn, well known for her Nazi sympathies, was on the BDF executive committee.

and encouraged, even pleaded with women to participate in the political process. The November 1932 issue urged citizens to vote for parties that supported women's rights, arguing:

> [We see] a serious danger for the entire nation in the reactionary prejudice with which employment and citizenship for women is regarded today ... we are convinced that the unfruitful and unnatural power struggle of the sexes in the economy and the state can only be overcome through the realization that an organically developed national state must be built upon the equal joint work of man and woman ("An die Wähler und Wählerinnen!" 66-67).

Too late did the BDF recognize that the factors pulling women apart were stronger than those which held them together. As a movement consisting of women of diverse political orientations, the BDF was unified around the idea of a polar difference of the sexes and a common idea of women's special essence. Despite repeated concessions to the right during the Weimar Republic, the BDF in general and its more liberal members in particular were increasingly accused by nationalists of individualism and valuing feminist interests over national welfare. In addition, having often referred to the Weimar constitution in their efforts for women's rights, they were identified with the much-loathed Weimar Republic itself.[30] When the time came for unified political action, the BDF was unable to come up with a strategy that all of its members could accept: their attempt to remain in the middle of the road satisfied no one. Correspondingly, as the Weimar Republic entered its last years, the BDF had internal difficulties, beginning with the loss of the RDH. In addition, the antisemitic viewpoints that the BDF tolerated in its debates and in the pages of *Die Frau* under its professed goal of "tolerance" and remaining "above politics" alienated and offended members of the Jewish Women's Association, long affiliated with the BDF.[31]

Simultaneously, *Die Frau* and the women's movement were also fighting a battle on many fronts against a variety of opponents who attacked women's rights as responsible for the ills of the nation. In a last-ditch effort to influence voting, a declaration and an election flyer were published in the March 1933 issue, imploring members to protect the "full claim to rights of women on the state" and to put all of their powers as

30. See Frevert 202.

31. The Jewish Women's Organization, an important part of the BDF despite the BDF's uneven record of support for its Jewish members, remained a part of the organization until its dissolution in 1933. For excellent accounts of the very complicated relationship between the JFB (Jüdischer Frauenbund), and the BDF, see Kaplan, *Die jüdische Frauenbewegung in Deutschland* and Kaplan, "Sisterhood under Siege: Feminism and Anti-Semitism in Germany 1904-1938" in Bridenthal.

women to work in the state, "the only way Germany will live." Despite this late attempt to represent a unified standpoint, the journal was not able to influence the political developments of the following year. The BDF voted to disband on May 15, 1933. In the next issue of *Die Frau*, an article by Dr. Agnes von Zahn-Harnack[32] listed the accomplishments of the organization. Among its important functions she mentioned the discussion evenings about antisemitism with Catholic, Protestant, and Jewish women. In the final analysis, however, she thought that the BDF had not been particularly effective in meeting its goals.

> With the greatest concern, the Federation saw how possibilities for the working woman, especially in higher positions, got worse from month to month. One "cutback" followed another; here it affected individuals, there whole groups. ... In the most varied forms and in the most varied places we attempted to stop this development; but we were successful almost nowhere ("Schlußbericht" 551).

Even in the months after the Nazi takeover in 1933, *Die Frau* still published articles opposing bookburning and advocating international understanding, minority rights, and women's right to work, to university education, and to political participation.[33] But political damage control had also begun. In a complete turnaround from her pre-takeover position that only democracy could protect women's rights, and that every tyranny threatened women, even if they participated, Gertrud Bäumer wrote in April 1933:

> How the state is created is ... in the last analysis unimportant for the problem which faces us ... whether it is a parliamentary, a democratic, a fascist state. For every construction, the question exists of how women will help shape [the new state], and the basic demand will always be the same ... to bring the cultural influence of women to full inner development and ... social effectiveness ("Lage und Aufgabe," 385).

But she also remained optimistic that extreme Nazi positions towards women would be tempered by those of their coalition partners, and that the constitution would be changed, if at all, only by democratic means. Meanwhile, not surprisingly, Dr. Leonore Kühn was loudly proclaiming an inherent affinity between the women's movement and Nazism:

32. Dr. Agnes von Zahn-Harnack was, like Bäumer and Weber, associated with the DDP. She was involved in the founding of the Deutscher Akademikerinnenbund. She was also president of the BDF from 1931-1933. See Wittrock 34-53, and Evans 237-38.

33. See Bäumer, "Zur Kanzlerrede," 527; and Hebestreit, "Jugend, Geist und Zeitgeist," 603.

German women themselves have prepared the way for this renewal with impassioned hearts and selfless desire; the will to true unity, to true social work for the whole of the people, to a greater proximity to life and a turning away from an intellectualism which had become sterile, to a calling out of the forgotten powers of the soul, of the German blood, the native soil, the religious engrossment – in short, the powers of life according to its physical and spiritual primal basis. Also her great hope is: renewal! ("Lebensraum," 515).

Even she, however, could see dangers for women's rights, and protested that women were also part of the nation and should be allowed to use their unique gifts in the service of the *Volksgemeinschaft* within the new state. Despite such articles, it must be remembered that the editorial position of *Die Frau* previous to the Nazi takeover was one of pro-Democratic political activism. Scholarship that quotes post-takeover articles or only the positions of Dr. Leonore Kühn as "typical" of the journal's stance during the Weimar Republic ignores the wide variety of political positions of its contributors, as well as the many phases of often internally contradictory theoretical arguments supporting women's rights within the magazine.

* * *

Although allowing women to claim such traditionally masculine fields as law, government or finance as their realm, and remaining flexible enough to keep most BDF members satisfied, the strategy of using traditional rhetoric about special womanly qualities rooted in a polar difference between the sexes helped to create a discourse about the "truly womanly" which could be, and was, used against women. In addition, the definition of women's rights as "truly German" was taken over and expanded by the early feminist fascists around Rogge-Börner in a racist and anti-semitic way, as a fight for rights for the "truly German woman" – a strategy which eventually led to the banning of *Die Deutsche Kämpferin* because of its emphasis on women's participation in traditionally male fields within the public sphere.[34]

34. One cannot really speak of "the" Nazi view on women due to the fact that, as many historians have pointed out, women's role was left purposefully vague so as to incorporate as many women as possible into the new state. This vagueness allowed competing versions of "the Nazi woman" to arise, which, however, generally excluded women from political and military life. The difference between Rogge-Börner's ideas about women's participation in the state and the traditional patriarchal images of women generally accepted by Nazis (also Nazi women) is shown clearly through the following excerpt from a letter from Nazi Käthe Ruppin to her *Gauleiter* after she had heard Rogge-Börner speak in 1933. She wrote that Rogge-Börner demanded "in a provocative form and manner: the military training and arming of women, admittance of women to the profession of judge, participation and decisive influence in domestic and foreign policy. I

Despite the anti-Nazi editorials of the late Weimar era, Gertrud Bäumer was allowed to continue publishing *Die Frau* until 1944. After the Weimar constitution had become meaningless, the journal was still free to continue its discussion of women's cultural gifts, a topic which would appeal to all of its readers and was considered politically safe. The strategy of *Die Frau* was to work for a concept of women's rights based on women's special essence while attempting to remain politically neutral enough to appeal to the broad membership of the BDF, a strategy which proved to have little effect on concrete rights for women once the possibility for organized political action no longer existed.

Bibliography

Adler, Dr. med. Hilde. "Freigabe der Vernichtung des keimenden Lebens?" *Die Frau* 28 (1920/21): 200-08.
Altmann-Gottheiner, Dr. Elisabeth. "Das Problem der Frauenberufsarbeit in und nach dem Krieg." *Die Frau* 23 (1915/16): 70-78.
"An die Wähler und Wählerinnen! An die künftige Volksvertretung!" Editorial. *Die Frau* 40 (1932/33): 65-67.
Baenitz, Charlotte."Gedanken über die Stellung der christlichen Frau in der Frauenbewegung." *Die Frau* 39 (1931/32): 681-84.
Bäumer, Gertrud."Die Frau und das geistige Schaffen, Teil III." *Die Frau* 34 (1926/27): 369-72.
———. "Geschlecht und Kultur." Review by Rosa Mayreder. *Die Frau* 30 (1922/23): 133-37.
———. "Lage und Aufgabe der Frauenbewegung in der deutschen Umwälzung." *Die Frau* 40 (1932/33): 385-92.
———. "Rede zum sozialen Teil des Regierungsprogramms – gehalten am 21. Feb. 1919 in der deutschen Nationalversammlung. "*Die Frau* 26 (1918/19): 197-205.
———. "Psychologische Bilanz der Wahlen." *Die Frau* 38 (1930/31): 4-7.
———. "Das Wichtige und das Unwichtige in der Politik."*Die Frau* 37 (1929/30): 3-8.
———. "Zur Kanzlerrede. Adolf Hitler im Reichstag 17.5.33."*Die Frau* 40 (1932/33): 526-27.

---

answered that for we National Socialists, a fundamental principle is that judge, soldier and state leader should be and remain the man" (Wittrock 170).

Beckmann, Emmy. "Der 'ewige' Mann." *Die Frau* 33 (1925/26): 26-32.

Beth, Dr. jur. et phil. Marianne."Von Schlagworten und Fiktionen in der Frauenbewegung." *Die Frau* 37 (1929/30): 9-18.

Bock, Gisela. "Rassenpolitik und Geschlechterpolitik im Nationalsozialismus." *Geschichte und Gesellschaft – Zeitschrift für Historische Sozialwissenschaft.*. 19.3 (1993): 277-310.

Bridenthal, Renate, et. al., eds. *When Biology Became Destiny: Women in Weimar and Nazi Germany.* New York: Monthly Review Press, 1984.

Bussemer, Herrad U. "Bürgerliche Frauenbewegung und männliches Bildungsbürgertum 1860-1880." *Bürgerinnen und Bürger: Geschlechterverhältnisse in 19. Jahrhundert.* Göttingen: Vandenhoeck und Ruprecht, 1988.

Evans, Richard J. *The Feminist Movement in Germany 1894-1933.* London: Sage, 1976.

Frevert, Ute. *Frauen-Geschichte zwischen bürgerlicher Verbesserung und neuer Weiblichkeit.* Frankfurt a.M.: Suhrkamp, 1986.

Greven-Aschoff, Barbara. *Die bürgerliche Frauenbewegung in Deutschland 1894-1933.* Göttingen: Vandenhoeck und Ruprecht, 1981.

Hebestreit, Gerda. "Jugend, Geist und Zeitgeist." *Die Frau* 40 (1932/33): 603-07.

Hübner, Friedrich M., ed. *Die Frau von morgen, wie wir sie wünschen.* Leipzig: Seemann, 1929.

Jelinek, Camilla."Die Frau und der Staatsgedanke. " *Die Frau* 24 (1916/17): 321-31.

Junge Mutter, Eine. "Das Weltbild der heutigen Jugend." *Die Frau* 40 (1932/ 1932/33): 608-10.

Kaplan, Marion A. *Die jüdische Frauenbewegung in Deutschland: Organisation und Ziele des jüdischen Frauenbundes 1904-1938.* Hamburg: Christians, 1981.

Koonz, Claudia. *Mothers in the Fatherland: Women, the Family, and Nazi Politics.* New York: St. Martin's Press, 1987

Kühn, Dr. Leonore. "Die Krise des Intellekts." *Die Frau* 34 (1926/27): 332-36.

———. "Lebensraum für die Frau in Staat und Kultur."*Die Frau* 40 (1932/ 33): 515-26.

Lange, Helene. "Die Frau und das neue Geschlecht." *Die Frau* 28 (1920/21): 299-306.

———. "Neue Frauenfeindschaft." *Die Frau* 24 (1916/17): 286.

———. "'Neuorientierung' in der Frauenbewegung." *Die Frau* 24 (1916/17): 1-4.

———. "Phasen des weiblichen Kulturbewußtseins: Die innere Geschichte der Frauenbewegung." *Die Frau* 30 (1922/23): 323-35.

———. "Steht die Frauenbewegung am Ziel oder am Anfang?" *Die Frau* 29 (1921/22): 33-46.

"Reine Mutterschaft." Book review of *Reine Mutterschaft* by Dr. med. F. Landmann. *Die Frau* 33 (1925/26): 701.

Schwenk, stud. rer. nat. Hanna. "Die Haltung der weiblichen Jugend in der NSPD." *Die Frau* 38 (1930/31): 175-76.

Velsen, Dr. Dorothee von. "Staatsbürgerin und Parteiwesen." *Die Frau* 38 (1930/31): 91-97, 135-42.

Weber, Marianne. "Die besonderen Kulturaufgaben der Frau, Teil II." *Die Frau* 26 (1918/19): 137-43.

_____. "Die Beteiligung der Frau am geistigen und sittlichen Wiederaufbau unseres Volkslebens." *Die Frau* 27 (1919/20): 1-7.

Wittrock, Christine. *Das Frauenbild in faschistischen Texten und seine Vorläufer in der bürgerlichen Frauenbewegung der zwanziger Jahre.* Frankfurt a.M.: Diss. 1982.

Zahn-Harnack, Dr. Agnes von. "Frauen-erneuerung." Review of *Deutsche Frauenwille* by Guida Diehl. *Die Frau* 36 (1928/29): 27-30.

_____. "Schlußbericht über die Arbeit des Bundes Deutscher Frauenvereine." *Die Frau* 40 (1932/33): 551-55.

Chapter 9

THE LADIES' AUXILIARY OF GERMAN LITERATURE

Nineteenth-Century Women Writers and the Quest
for a National Literary History

Patricia Herminghouse

$\mathcal{S}$ ince the 1970s German literary scholars have been increasingly
involved in attempts to render critical accounts of their discipline,
including analyses of the rise of literary history, the formation of a literary canon, and the institutions of literary criticism.[1] Concurrently –
and especially in American universities, where the impact of the "new
feminism" was initially greater – women scholars, growing increasingly
sensitive to the exclusion of women from most representations of the literary enterprise, began systematic searches in order to recover the "lost"
women of German literary history.[2] Rarely, however, with the exception
of Gisela Brinker-Gabler's pioneering 1976 essay, have there been fruit-
ful intersections of the two strands of investigation. The sheer magni-
tude of the task of documenting women's participation in the literary life
of nineteenth-century Germany has thus far probably been an obstacle
to large-scale analyses of the cultural assumptions that sustained the
construction of the literary histories from which women continued to be
excluded until late in the present century. Women, it should be remem-

1. See Peter Uwe Hohendahl's survey of the most recent studies of the history of the
discipline, "Germanistik als Gegenstand der Wissenschaftsgeschichte."
2. See, for example, the anthologies and bibliographies of Blackwell and Zantop,
Kord, Cocalis, Brinker-Gabler, among others.

bered, were also not admitted to the German universities and thus neither among the professors nor the audience for the lectures on literary history that began to gain in popularity after the Wars of Liberation.[3] The very social and political developments that led to the subsequent proliferation of published literary histories and the institutionalization of literary studies [*Literaturwissenschaft*, literally "literary science"] as an academic discipline in nineteenth-century Germany simultaneously supported a concept of literary history that served to exacerbate the marginalization of women in the cultural sphere. And if, as Jost Hermand recently asserted, the writing of literary history in the nineteenth century functioned as a sort of seismograph of the culture and mindset of an era (49), it may be possible to trace in its increasing professionalization and nationalism the roots of the tendency to devalue and debar literature written by women that has characterized German literary history since its beginning.

While it is not feasible here to undertake the kind of in-depth analysis that remains a desideratum of German feminist literary history, it is possible to identify at least some of the factors that underlay most conscious and unconscious attempts to locate women's proper sphere outside the realm of serious literature and literary history. These include the rise of national consciousness, developments in the natural sciences, and the cultural anxieties that accompanied dramatic increases in the number of women who were actually engaged in the literary enterprise – anxieties that are reflected in various attempts to contain the threats that they seemed to pose by defining women's "nature" as intrinsically unsuited for the creation of cultural products. Unsurprisingly then, German literary history can be seen to reflect dominant beliefs about the nature and function of women in the world. It may, in fact, be argued that implicit in the very framing of the aims and goals of nineteenth-century *Literaturwissenschaft* was a hegemonic presumption of homogeneity that precluded women's integration into the literary enterprise, resulting in what was at best a half-hearted attempt to append them as a sort of "ladies auxiliary" in an androcentric project of constructing national identity.

* * *

The connection between the discourse of nation and the development of *Germanistik* [the study of German language, literature, and literary history] as an academic discipline in the nineteenth century have been the subject of a number of recent studies.[4] Even before the establishment of

3. See Weimar for details of these developments.
4. See, for example, Hohendahl, *Building a National Literature;* Rosenberg; Weimar; Fohrmann; and Hermand.

university chairs in German literature, early literary histories written for a general public by men in disciplines such as history (Johannes Scherr), philosophy (Rudolf Haym), or philology (Robert Prutz) served a political/ideological function in channeling the reading interests of the educated German middle class in a national direction. Many of these works, which usually filled multiple volumes, were written for a general readership, including the large audience of women readers that had been growing steadily since the eighteenth century. The extent to which literary historians also sought to provide a scholarly foundation for the ideology of nation is already evident in the ubiquity of the term "Nationalliteratur" in the titles they gave to their works, most of which went through multiple editions over a period of several decades.[5]

Rainer Rosenberg goes so far as to assert that *Literaturwissenschaft* was more influential than literature itself in the development of German national consciousness in the second half of the nineteenth century, since the mission of providing the state with a sense of national identity belonged much more to the literary historians than to the writers (357). Statements by literary historians themselves seem to bear out this observation. Julian Schmidt, in his typical moralistic vein, faults Germany's poets for failing "to liberate our nation from the dull confines of middle-class atrophy, to imbue it with self-confidence, to awaken its dormant powers, and to introduce it as an equal into the ranks of European nations," before declaring – with false modesty – that his multivolume literary history will attempt to render a feeble sketch of "the intellectual life of the nation, past and present, which proves that the nation does not lack the necessary strength and ability for this task" (5: 599).

Literary histories themselves sometimes included an entire, separate unit on historiography, such as Rudolf von Gottschall's chapter on historiography and politics ("Geschichtsschreibung und Politik," 2: 465-524), into which he also inserts a survey of literary histories of the period. The self-identification of literary historians with the national cause is, not surprisingly, reflected in the literary history that they produced, including not only general perceptions that men make history, but specific convictions that women do not. In his immensely popular sociology of the family, first published in 1854, Wilhelm Heinrich Riehl adduced a grammatical proof for this state of affairs: "The state [*der Staat*] is masculine

5. Karl Barthel's *Die deutsche Nationalliteratur der Neuzeit*; Rudolf Gottschall's *Die deutsche Nationallitteratur des neunzehnten Jahrhunderts*; Ludwig Salomon's *Geschichte der deutschen Nationalliteratur des neunzehnten Jahrhunderts*; Friedrich Kirchner's *Die deutsche Nationalliteratur des neunzehnten Jahrhunderts*; Adolf Stern's *Die deutsche Nationallitteratur vom Tode Goethes bis zur Gegenwart* are just a representative sample of the many that appeared in the second half of the nineteenth century.

gender, and the social groups (the peasantry [*das Bauerntum*] and the bourgeosie [*das Bürgertum*]) are *generis neutrius*: what about women? They should remain in the 'family' [*die Familie*], which, after all, reflects its predominantly feminine character already in the gender of the noun" (13). The emancipatory vision of (male) bourgeois liberal ideology not only maintained, it actually proclaimed rigorous gender dichotomies. Such gender dichotomies may actually have been upheld by the maternalist arguments of educated middle class women who, as Ann Taylor Allen argues in this volume, employed the rhetoric of "spiritual motherhood" to ground their claims of a feminine contribution to the production of nation. Thus in his literary history, even a liberal like Julian Schmidt asserts explicitly and succinctly, "In matters of politics, women are on the outside and it cannot be any other way" (5:448). Both Schmidt and Gottschall bolster their argument that women are not able to write historical novels with arguments about the "nature of woman" that had been gaining currency since the eighteenth century. The link between the perceived ability of individuals to make history and their possession of the qualifications to write about it is evident in Gottschall's assertion that

> women writers [*schriftstellernde Frauen*] who turn their attention to the novel are only able to see in history chance materials for memoir-like chit-chat ... or for psychic portraits and suspenseful entanglements ... . [Their] entire nature appears to make women less inclined and less capable of gaining any distance to themselves and painting objective-historical portraits, in which questions of culture, of the state and of the church are not discussed in the boudoirs of sentiment, but at the bar of history (3: 378).

In their eagerness to advance the national agenda, literary historians were often initially reluctant to deal with more recent literature, which could not be readily integrated into such an emerging identity. Although this in itself explains the absence of many women writers from the canon that was in the process of being established, a few literary historians, including Gottschall and Schmidt, attempted to give some account of women's participation in literary life of the nineteenth century and to relate it to the rise of literacy among women. But they generally did so primarily through the establishment of gender dichotomies based on their perceptions of men's and women's differing relationship to the national question. In contrast to the "manly verse" [*Männerlyrik*] produced by writers of the Young German movement – "Poets who attempted to influence the nation itself through the general validity and intellectual significance of what they had to say" (2: 368) – Gottschall coins the expression "*Blumistik*" [flower verse] to describe, "the sweet and pretty, shallow literature of the day," which arose in conjunction with the emergence of a female reading and writing public in the first half of the nineteenth century. In his eyes, then, it was not surprising that "a race of men who had gone through the Wars of Liberation could only turn away from this trivia with contempt" (2: 362).

* * *

In addition to its preoccupation with German national identity, the subsequent development of German *Literaturwissenschaft* reflects advances in the prestige and influence of science and technology in the nineteenth century. In their establishment of a national professional organization in the first half of the nineteenth century – well before the Germanists established their own professional group in 1861 – German natural scientists and physicians saw a symbolic prelude to the longed-for unification of the nation; by 1865 the concept of "German science" had developed into what Jutta Kolkenbrock-Netz identifies as a "mythic macroconcept" in a mutually reinforcing exchange between scientific and nationalistic discourse (215 ff.).

Like the natural sciences, which attempted to provide a biological basis for claims for the historical destiny of the German people (Rosenberg 357), *Literaturwissenschaft* employed a characteristic mix of sober scholarship and popular science in service of national ideology. In the process, it also appropriated from the realm of the natural sciences a discourse that defined and delimited women's place in the literary enterprise, a discourse that enshrined social inequalities as laws of nature. The connection between *Naturwissenschaft* and *Literaturwissenschaft* came then to reinforce rather than to challenge the cultural assumption of dichotomous "laws of nature" regarding women's inferior status and man's sure destiny as "master over nature." Such ontologizing of gender polarities, with its emphasis on the "natural limitations" and "true nature" of women pervaded most spheres of society, so it is not surprising that literary historians, too, repeatedly insisted that the private and not the public realm is the proper sphere of female activity, thus defining women out of literary history. Notions derived from thinkers such as Herbert Spencer and Charles Darwin were also employed in support of arguments that women's mental capacity was circumscribed by the laws of both physiology and evolution. Since their biological constitution was thought to consume more "vital force" than men's, it was argued, "women had less energy for physical and mental development than men" (Newman 6). It followed then that their presumed limited mental capacity – deriving from their scientifically ascertained smaller brain size – would also make women intellectually incapable of the objectivity, rationality, and abstraction demanded of the men of science and letters.

The feminist critique of the modern ideology of science elaborated by Evelyn Fox Keller is strikingly applicable to notions that prevailed in German literary history, particularly her demonstration of "how much of the nature of science is bound up with the idea of masculinity" (3) and the acceptance of, indeed commitment to, "the deeply rooted popular mythology that casts objectivity, reason, and mind as male, and subjectivity, feeling, and nature as female" (6 f.). The more sweeping the actual transformations in scientific knowledge, the more intense became the efforts to shore up the ideology of gender dichotomies through recourse to scientifically ascertainable – and thus immutable – "facts" about the nature of gender differences. It is not stretching the point to claim the applicability for *Literaturwissenschaft* of Keller's assertion, with reference to the natural sciences, that "a circular process of mutual reinforcement is established in which what is called scientific receives extra validation from the cultural preference for what is called masculine, and conversely, what is called feminine – be it a branch of knowledge, a way of thinking, or woman herself – becomes further devalued" (92).

A perusal of the literary histories of the period yields ample evidence of the efforts of literary historians to legitimate their discipline by invoking the natural sciences. In a separate chapter entitled "Wissenschaft und Kritik" (Science and Criticism), Richard M. Meyer even went so far as to establish a genealogy of the virility contributed to the field of literature and literary criticism by some of the natural scientists themselves:

> These men ... contributed to poetry models of energy, of courage victorious, such as could not be found in any other domain of the public sphere at that time ... . This gave rise to a new kind of literary criticism which cast off atrophied lines of thought and helped to pave the way for new ones; it led to a new, critically oriented propagandistic literature akin to the Young German school; and this brought about, slowly, very slowly, the new realistic literature of the present, which promises such an auspicious renewal of the age-old relationship of science and poetry (583).

Schmidt and Gottschall likewise devote entire chapters or sections to the natural sciences, asserting the preeminent role of modern science not only for literary and cultural history, but for the form and content of literature itself. Thus Schmidt can argue that it is the very incapacity for scientific thought that makes women unable to write on political themes in their novels. They not only lack the elements of experience in this area, he asserts, "they also do not have the ability to ignore individual situations and to establish rules and principles. Even if a woman succeeds in informing herself about all important aspects of a political issue, her judgement will be less mature than that of a man with the same background" (5:447 f.). Ironically, Schmidt goes on to assert that *women* are too quick to form snap judgements and careless analogies!

The same pseudo-scientific perceptions of women's lack of intellectual strength that had kept them out of the schools until at least mid-century and out of universities until the end of the nineteenth century legitimated not only women's exclusion from the realm of *Literaturwissenschaft*, but in many respects from the realm of literature itself. The presumtion of male cultural dominance was grounded in a kind of literary Darwinism that presumed that only the fittest could survive the scrutiny of the arbiters of the new "national literature." The rare instances when literary historians wished to praise an individual woman writer posed a predicament, from which they usually attempted to extricate themselves by praising her un-womanly qualities. In the case of the poet Annette von Droste-Hülshoff, for instance, Gottschall emphasizes her opposition to all emancipatory tendencies as well as to "the mere play of emotions" (354); other critics typically praised her "harsh masculine style" [*männlich-herbe Art*] In any case, praise entails the need to position her outside the gender-specific norm.

The attempts of literary historians to create taxonomies to contain the ever-increasing number of women writers can sometimes border on the grotesque, as did Gottschall's attempt to categorize "die Sängerinnen" according to their marital status. Writing by these women can be divided into two classes, he asserts, the poetry of unmarried and the poetry of married women:

> The unmarried ones write pure moonlight lyrics full of endless longing, the most chaste love and most tender resignation; their main poetic operators are the zephyrs that play about the flowers and kisses that can only be kissed in verses; they tell us about what the forest and the little birds are saying … .
> Married women are more solid in their thoughts and feelings. Having learned the lessons of experience, they give wise rules for living, exhort us to be virtuous, write allegories and parables, idylls about the honeysuckle arbor and the mill in the vale, travel accounts in which they celebrate the old castles and the good beds in the inns. Sometimes they even sing the praises of many a notable personality, but never of their husbands (3: 350 f.).

It seems fair to suggest that these categories have less to do with the "real" women whose literary endeavors gave rise to such absurd taxonomies than with the real anxieties of men whose concepts of national emancipation could not accomodate the destabilization of gender roles that women's writing seemed to imply. This becomes evident in, for example, Gottschall's ambivalence towards the so-called *Frauenroman* [women's novel]. He concedes that while few literary sparks any longer rose from among the ashes of the domestic hearth cultivated in the con-

servative family novel, women writers who raised the flag of emancipation and stormed the German temple of the muses were increasingly
gaining followers (569 f.).

* * *

A third factor affecting the depiction of women in literary histories of
the period was the sheer increase in the number of women who sought
to gain access to the literary enterprise, a phenomenon upon which
almost all literary historians feel compelled to comment.[6] Although the
widespread acquisition of literacy by women that began in the eighteenth century had already destabilized the notion of learning and scholarship as a male preserve, their perceived invasion of the literary sphere
evoked vehement expressions of alarm, disapproval or derision. While an
early critic such as Gervinus limits himself to a remark on "the epidemic
effect of the obsession with writing" [*Schreibsucht*] among women
(5: 328),[7] Johannes Scherr (1875) asserts, "that the female contingent
which is forcing itself so impertinently into the public sphere consists
either of ugly old maids ... or of slovenly housewives and negligent
mothers" (92).[8] Gottschall expressed his dismay in more eloquently drastic terms in 1892: "The nobility of poetry was not always upheld by
these maenades, who swarmed about the gates of the German temple of
the muses" (4: 570).

The response to this threat often took the form of moral arguments
about the "natural" barriers that women were not to transgress. The
chapter on "Litterarische Damen" to which Karl Barthel consigns the
"ladies' auxiliary" makes this point most emphatically:

6. I dealt with this aspect in a 1986 essay, "Women and the Literary Enterprise in
Nineteenth-Century Germany," calling attention to older reference works by Brummer,
Pataky, Nigg, and Gross that documented the thousands of women who had already
entered the literary sphere. At that time I estimated they "compromised from one-fourth
to one-third of the total number of literary authors in this period: a far cry from the
minuscle proportion of them who have survived in more contemporary reference works"
(79). In recent years Gisela Brinker-Gabler, Elke Frederiksen, and Elisabeth Friedrichs
have contributed valuable bio-bibliographies of German women writers that have served
feminist scholars well.

7. Quoted in Brinker-Gabler, "Die Schriftstellerin," (19).

8. Scherr also wrote a *Geschichte der Deutschen Frauenwelt*, the final chapter of
which, "Frauen und Dichter," concludes with a long and chauvinistic diatribe on the true
place of women in the new German nation. Unlike their sisters in New York, Paris, and
Russia, who have fallen into the abyss of immorality, politics, and scholarship, German
women are admonished, "[die] sittliche Idee vom Vaterlande zu einer Herzenssache zu
machen, sie ihren Söhnen einzugebären, sie ihren Töchtern mit der Muttermilch einzu-
flößen und beide zu Bürgern und Bürgerinnen zu erziehen, welche sowohl befähigt als
willig sind, mitzuschaffen an der Zukunft unseres Volkes" (2: 305).

Women's sphere is that of narrow domesticity, *the world of the family; women's first profession is and will always remain the duty to glorify it as the priestess of morality, order, and propriety, and her special talent is that of quiet, thoughtful observation.* If as writers they keep these limitations of their profession and their abilities in mind, their writings will always be acceptable as a supplement to the writings of men; if, however, they transgress them, they will straightaway fall into the category of emancipated females (923, emphasis in original).

Fret as they do about the sheer numbers of women who have taken up their pens, literary historians of the period accord little attention to the social and historical circumstances surrounding the unprecedented entry of women into the literary sphere. Beyond dramatic increases in literacy, these would include the commercial and technical developments that led to rapid expansion in the ability of publishers to print, distribute and sell books and magazines. Two factors in particular seem to have attracted widespread notice and comment. The number of women who were producing novels, a genre whose growing popularity coincided with their entry into the literary marketplace, was used to bolster arguments that women were "by nature" incapable of producing artistically serious literature. It is not coincidental that this occurred just at the time, as critics such as Gottschall and Robert Prutz noted, when the original willingness of educated women to serve as audiences for great male writers was yielding to their own claim to creativity.[9] Rather than take into account the power of the educational tradition to which women were denied access, critics traced women's affinity to the novel to a supposedly feminine lack of aptitude for other forms that were thought to require more discipline than prose narrative, thus justifying the fact that literary history was in the process of creating a male canon. Since the novel was less demanding intellectually, they claimed, it was more suited as a pastime or an outlet for female sensibilities. Again, Gottschall comments on the rise of women novelists in the latter part of the century:

One finds their novels in the most respected family journals, and a catalog of German novels now has a great deal of resemblance to an English one, in which the 'eternal feminine' predominates. Of course, only a few of these women writers have any significant intellectual profile; most have an appealing gift for storytelling, a judicious conception of life, and now and then, even a fine portrait of the psyche [*Seelenmalerei*] of female characters (4: 600).

Most literary historians who dealt with the question of the increasing number of women writers also felt constrained to take into account a

9. See Brinker-Gabler, "Die Schriftstellerin," 17.

second factor: the various social emancipation movements, including those that led up to 1848, as well as more contemporary efforts on behalf of women's emancipation. Prutz's famous comment, "Women have become a real power in our literature; like the Jews, you find them everywhere" (2: 250), may have been meant positively in 1859, but one cannot help overhearing the same current of apprehension which underlies more hostile remarks, even when he tries to be sympathetic:

> Among our women today, we have so many writers because we have so many unhappy women. In literature they seek the satisfaction which domesticity, this first and most natural ground of womanhood, does not allow them. They flee into poetry because life repels them (2: 252).

The very structure of most nineteenth-century literary histories can be read as a response to the threat posed by the emergence of unprecedented and ever-increasing numbers of women writers. Literary historians who do not ignore women altogether often attempt to resist their incorporation into the construction of a national literature by enclosing them in separate chapters or sections which are appended to treatments of "real" literature written by individual male authors as, for example, Gottschall's chapter on "Dichter verschiedener Richtungen und dichtende Frauen" [Writers of Various Sorts and Women Who Write]. Appended, as they often are, to the "back of the book," such treatments of women writers as a caste separate from the real citizens of the literary realm call to mind forms of segregation practiced on racial grounds in recent American history. Indeed, it is the attempt to segregate these women into a separate class that underlies the most bizarre attempts to define them out of national literary history.

These same literary historians also displayed considerable inventiveness in developing an inventory of terms which enabled them to avoid designating a woman as *Dichter/in*, the German term for authors of serious literature [*Dichtung*]. Beyond the more prosaic designation *Schriftsteller/in* [writer], they generally preferred circumlocutions such as *schriftstellernde Frauen* [women who write] (Kirchner), *litterarische Damen* [literary ladies] (Barthel), *Frauen der Feder* [ladies of the pen] (Pataky), or even *Sängerinnen* ["songstresses"] (Engel). And while the literary output of a (male) *Dichter* would never be called *Schriftstellerei*, terms such as *weibliche Schriftstellerei* and *weibliche Dichterei* [female scribbling], which carry pejorative connotations, were regularly employed in the attempt to avoid referring to their work as *Dichtung*. Not until the end of the nineteenth century, as Helena Szépe has shown, was the term *Frauendichtung* available to denote writing by women – and even then, she suggests, it indicates "a certain attitude [not of a positive sort! P.H.]

towards women's literature" (11). Silly as all of this may seem from a contemporary perspective, the legacy of another variant of this term in particular has endured into the late twentieth century: "Frauenliteratur," which one might be tempted to translate as the German equivalent of "women's literature," connoted a widespread perception that literature by and for German women belonged to a lesser genre with a dubious claim to a place in the national canon. That the term has yet to gain respectability may also be seen in the titles of the two most important histories of women's literature to appear in the postwar period: Hiltrud Gnüg and Renate Möhrmann's 1985 volume *Frauen Literatur Geschichte* (Women Literature History: note the pointed disjuncture of these three terms which would normally be written as one compound word!) and Gisela Brinker-Gabler's 1988 two-volume *Deutsche Literatur von Frauen* (German Literature by Women).

* * *

An examination of the depiction of German women writers by their contemporaries in nineteenth-century literary history would have little more than anecdotal value if the perceptions that we encounter there could be dismissed as comic, isolated instances. Indeed, they came to constitute the dominant discourse of the discipline which has affected the way German literary history has dealt with its "ladies' auxiliary" well into the present. But, as Gnüg and Möhrmann report, almost as soon as they declared their intention to produce their volume, they had to come to terms with the fact that the enormous range of what has been left out of literary histories – and not only in Germany – precluded the production of a coherent literary history. They decided against a strictly chronological approach, such as would be forced upon them by adherence to the traditional concepts of historical epochs and opted instead to make visible the "ruptures and new beginnings … , the discontinuities which necessarily occur" (ix). They thus inverted the strategies by which women had so long been confined within literary history by taking their inspiration from both Virginia Woolf's postulate of the necessity of a "room of one's own" for the creative writer and Jane Austen's depiction of the "creaking door" which figuratively and literally led to the concealment of writing by women. Just as significantly, they chose not to limit their understanding of women, literature, and history by national boundaries. Thus contributors to the volume were invited to investigate the writing-spaces [*Schreib-Räume*] which sustained women's literary enterprise, even when they worked in seeming isolation from one another. These loci might be concrete places, such as convents, courts and salons – or they might be social configurations, such as St.

Simonism, various liberation movements, or arenas of social upheaval where women's texts have been inscribed.

Constructed in the voids of the dominant political and aesthetic discourse, the spaces which have been inhabited by the ladies' auxiliary of German literary history have yet to be mapped in relation to the very institutional structures amongst which they are situated. The task is not merely one of documenting their participation in the literary life of their times but of recognizing how constrained our understanding of "literature" is by notions of gender and Germanness. With this preliminary sketch, I have tried to indicate only a few of the aspects of the relationship which still await a more detailed analysis.

Note

All translations from German are my own.

Bibliography

Barthel, Karl. *Vorlesungen über die deutsche Nationallitteratur der Neuzeit.* Ed. Emil Barthel and Georg Reinhard Röpe. 9th ed. Gütersloh: Bertelsmann, 1879.

Becker-Cantarino, Barbara. *Der lange Weg zur Mündigkeit: Frau und Literatur 1500-1800.* Stuttgart: Metzler, 1987.

Blackwell, Jeannine and Susanne Zantop, eds. *Bitter Healing: German Women Writers 1700-1830.* Lincoln: U of Nebraska P, 1990.

Brinker-Gabler, Gisela, ed. *Deutsche Literatur von Frauen.* 2 Vols. Munich: C.H. Beck, 1988.

_____. "Die Schriftstellerin in der deutschen Literaturwissenschaft: Aspekte ihrer Rezeption von 1835 bis 1910." *Die Unterrichtspraxis* 9.1 (Spring, 1976): 15-29.

Brinker-Gabler, Gisela, Karola Ludwig, and Angela Wöffen, eds. *Lexikon deutschsprachiger Schriftstellerinnen 1800-1945.* Munich: Deutscher Taschenbuch Verlag, 1986.

Brummer, Franz. *Lexikon der deutschen Dichter des 19. Jahrhunderts.* Leipzig: Reclam, 1885.

Cocalis, Susan, ed. *The Defiant Muse: German Feminist Poems from the Middle Ages to the Present.* New York: Feminist Press at City University of New York, 1986.

Engel, Eduard. *Geschichte der Deutschen Literatur von den Anfängen bis in die Gegenwart.* 2 vols. Wien: G. Tempsky; Leipzig: G. Freytag, 1912.

Frederiksen, Elke, ed. *Women Writers of Germany, Austria, and Switzerland: An Annotated Bio-Bibliographical Guide.* New York: Greenwood, 1989.

Friedrichs, Elisabeth. *Die deutschsprachigen Schriftstellerinnen des 18. und 19. Jahrhunderts: Ein Lexikon.* Stuttgart: Metzler, 1981.

Fohrmann, Jürgen. *Das Projekt der deutschen Literaturgeschichte.* Stuttgart: Metzler, 1989.

Gervinus, Georg G. *Geschichte der deutschen Dichtung.* 5 vols. Leipzig: Engelmann, 1853.

Gnüg, Hiltrud and Renate Möhrmann, eds. *Frauen Literatur Geschichte: Schreibende Frauen vom Mittelalter bis zur Gegenwart.* Stuttgart: Metzler, 1985.

Gottschall, Rudolf. *Deutsche Nationallitteratur des 19. Jahrdunderts.* 6th ed. 4 vols. Breslau: E. Trewendt, 1891.

Gross, Heinrich. *Deutschlands Dichterinnen und Schriftstellerinnen in Wort und Bild.* 3 vols. Berlin: Fr. Thiel, 1885.

Hermand, Jost. *Geschichte der Germanistik.* Reinbek: Rowohlt, 1994.

Herminghouse, Patricia. "Women and the Literary Enterprise in Nineteenth-Century Germany." *German Women in the Eighteenth and Nineteenth Centuries: A Social and Literary History.* Ed. Ruth-Ellen Boettcher Joeres and M. J. Maynes. Bloomington: Indiana UP, 1986. 78-93.

Hohendahl, Peter Uwe. *Building a National Literature: The Case of Germany, 1830-1870.* Trans. Renate Baron Franciscono. Ithaca, NY: Cornell UP, 1989.

———. "Germanistik als Gegenstand der Wissenschaftsgeschichte." *Internationales Archiv für Sozialgeschichte der deutschen Literatur* 21.2 (1996): 143-61.

Keller, Evelyn Fox. *Reflections on Gender and Science.* New Haven: Yale UP, 1985.

Kirchner, Friedrich. *Die deutsche Nationalliteratur des Neunzehnten Jahrhunderts.* 2nd ed. Heidelberg: Georg Weiß, 1894.

Kolkenbrock-Netz, Jutta. "Wissenschaft als nationaler Mythos: Anmerkungen zur Haeckel-Virchow-Kontroverse auf der 50. Jahresversammlung der deutschen Naturforscher und Ärzte in München (1877)." *Nationale Mythen und Symbole in der zweiten Hälfte des 19. Jahrhunderts: Strukturen und Funktionen von Konzepten nationaler Identität.* Ed. Jürgen Link and Wulf Wülfing. Stuttgart: Klett-Cotta, 1991.

Kord, Susanne. *Ein Blick hinter die Kulissen: Deutschsprachige Dramatikerinnen im 18. und 19. Jahrhundert.* Stuttgart: Metzler, 1992.

Meyer, Richard M. *Die deutsche Litteratur des neunzehnten Jahrhunderts.* 3rd ed. 2 vols. Berlin: G. Bondi, 1906.

Möhrmann, Renate. *Die andere Frau: Emanzipationsansätze deutscher Schriftstellerinnen im Vorfeld der Achtundvierziger Revolution.* Stuttgart: Metzler, 1977.

Newman, Louise Michese. *Men's Ideas, Women's Realities: Popular Science 1870-1915*. New York: Pergamon, 1985.

Nigg, Marianne. *Biographien der österreichischen Dichterinnen und Schriftstellerinnen*. Korneuburg: J. Kühlkopfs Buchhandlung, 1893.

Pataky, Sophie. *Lexikon deutscher Frauen der Feder*. Berlin: Carl Pataky, 1898. Rpt. Bern: Lang, 1971.

Prutz, Robert. *Die deutsche Literatur der Gegenwart, 1848 bis 1858*. Leipzig: Voigt & Gunther, 1859.

Riehl, Wilhelm Heinrich. *Die Naturgeschichte des Volkes als Grundlage einer deutschen Sozial*politik. Vol. 3: *Die Familie*. 12th ed. Stuttgart: Cotta, 1904.

Rosenberg, Rainer. "Das Selbstverständnis der Literaturwissenschaft: Zur Geschichte der deutschen Germanistik 1900-1933. *Weimarer Beiträge* 32.3 (1986): 357-85.

Salomon, Ludwig. *Geschichte der deutschen Nationalliteratur des neunzehnten Jahrhunderts*. Stuttgart: Levy und Muller. 1881.

Scherr, Johannes. *Allgemeine Geschichte der Literatur*. Stuttgart: C. Conradi, 1875.

_____. *Geschichte der Deutschen Frauenwelt*. 5th ed. 2 vols. Leipzig: Otto Wigand, 1898.

Schmidt, Julian. *Geschichte der deutschen Litteratur von Leibnitz bis auf unsere Zeit*. 5 vols. Berlin: W. Hertz, 1896.

Stern, Adolf. *Die deutsche Nationalliteratur vom Tode Goethes bis zur Gegenwart*. 2nd ed. Marburg: G. Elwert, 1886.

Szépe, Helena. "The Term 'Frauendichtung'." *Die Unterrichtspraxis* 9.1 (Spring, 1976): 11-15.

Weimar, Klaus. *Geschichte der deutschen Literaturwissenschaft bis zum Ende des 19. Jahrhunderts*. Munich: Wilhelm Fink, 1989.

Part III

VISUAL CULTURE

Chapter 10

EN-GENDERING MASS CULTURE

The Case of Zarah Leander

Lutz P. Koepnick

𝕴n one of the episodes of Edgar Reitz's *Heimat* (1984), the protago-nist Maria and her sister-in-law Pauline, after visiting a local movie presentation, fashion their hair in front of a mirror in imitation of the exotic coiffure of the star they have just seen on screen: Zarah Leander in Detlef Sierck's *La Habanera* (1937). Highly prominent in Sierck's mise-en-scène itself, the mirror for both women opens up the possibil-ity to graft the star's cosmopolitan appearance onto their own physiog-nomy; it provides temporary release from the burdens caused by the prolonged absence of their husbands. The symbolic inventory of prewar mass culture, relying on the magnetism of stars and melodramatic excess, empowers both women to articulate a notion of female identity that is clearly at variance with Nazi ideology and its images of women as the breeding machines of the nation. Inhabiting a niche seemingly unfet-tered by Nazi politics, Reitz's protagonists appropriate the symbolic material of mass culture, they appropriate what the German culture industry of the 1930s shares with Hollywood in order to enact poten-tially non-conformist gestures of self-expression and thus rechart their position within the topography of everyday life.

Reitz's ethnography of female spectatorship vis-à-vis Nazi mass cul-ture challenges dominant accounts that present Nazi culture as a highly functional engine of ideological alignment. Reitz's snaphot brings to view moments of heterogeneity at the center of Nazi culture; it sharpens our awareness of the fact that, in contradistinction to the Nazi renditions of the German folk and nation as the primary signifiers of social integration and subject formation, many of Hitler's subjects defined their relation to the Nazi state via structures of experience that already during the Weimar Republic had been discursively constructed and contested as part of the Americanization of Germany, a German fascination with American urbanity, speed, consumption, and mass culture.

For historians such as Hans Dieter Schäfer (1981), the contradictions between Nazi propaganda and the existence of a relatively unpolitical sphere of private consumption, diversion, and commodity display prove the schizophrenic nature of Nazi politics. But despite Schäfer's attempt to psychoanalyze the Americanist inclinations of Nazi Germany, it is necessary to understand this split consciousness not as a symptom but as a shrewd technology of power: Nazi cultural politics allowed for seemingly unpolitical spaces of American-style consumption only to reinforce the workings of existing political dependencies and identities. Ideologically dissident forms of Americanized consumerism restrained articulations of solidarity that would have been powerful enough to contest the legitimacy of Nazi politics: the cult of privatist consumption impaired alternative definitions of German identity coupled with notions of political autonomy and emancipation. With the help of the charisma of Americanism, Nazi politics tried to gain control over the transformation of nineteenth-century bourgeois culture into twentieth-century mass culture in order to engender its own fascist version. What appeared from the phenomenological perspective of everyday practices as a space of diversion free of politics was at closer inspection political through and through.

Nazi feature films were key to the many ways in which German fascism tried to address the demand for an American-style consumer culture. Responding to the crisis of the film industry around the middle of the decade, Nazi cinema, particularly during the years 1935 to 1938, was frantically concerned with replacing the continuous popularity of imported Hollywood films with the appeal of seemingly unpolitical products made in Germany. As it copied the Hollywood star cult as well as some of Hollywood's generic formulas, Nazi cinema hoped to achieve both at once: to engineer politically effective responses and to increase cinema's dwindling revenues. Dedicated to a "Germanified Americanism" (Witte 106), prewar Nazi cinema was often based on surprisingly contradictory concessions, on unwieldy interfaces between premodern mythologies and the hardly controllable signs of modern consumer culture, on gestures of cultural appropriation pregnant with fragile syntheses and glossed-over fautlines, gestures which "left the government caught in ludicrous forms of self-redress and strategic withdrawal before the commodity fetish" (Bathrick 48).

Nowhere is this ideologically ambivalent attempt to solicit and contain popular culture from above more obvious than in the ways in which the German film industry of the mid 1930s sought to construct and proliferate female star images. Not only did all of the most important female stars of the Third Reich – Zarah Leander, Marika Rökk, Lilian Harvey, and Kristina Söderbaum – enter the German culture industry from abroad; in the case of Leander and Harvey, they also deviated conspicuously from the politically desired typology of woman as the domestic soldier of racial reproduction; they projected onto the German screen cosmopolitan sensibilities and forms of sexual agency that infringed on the overall inhibition of visual pleasure so characteristic of Nazi cinema. Captivating popular desires for visual consumption and melodramatic identification, stars such as Leander became the trade winds of Nazi cinema: their aura gently reminded viewers of attractions beyond the domain of ideological mobilization and yet at the same time assisted in blowing the vessel of everyday culture into the harbor of an autonomous German distraction industry.

Georg Seeßlen locates the political moment of Nazi feature films in the fact that they were intended to offer not outright propaganda but individual strategies of survival and models of conformity under the condition of fascism (*Tanz*, 56). What was political about the products of the Nazi dream factory, in other words, must be seen not simply in internal textual characteristics, but rather in the context of the distinctive projection situation and a set of external systems of signification that attributed meaning to a visit to the cinema. These included the impact of general structures of experience as much as group-specific patterns of perception; the ritual of newsreel shows that literally framed individual screenings; the iconography of stardom as proliferated through the mass media and in advertising campaigns; the party galas meticulously staged for individual film premieres; and, last but not least, the transtextual dynamic of generic conventions and formulas. It is against such a broader notion of the politics of Nazi film that the making of the UFA star Zarah Leander around 1937 and her first appearance on German screens in *Zu neuen Ufern* (To New Shores, 1937) and *La Habanera*, both directed by Detlef Sierck (alias Douglas Sirk), take on particular significance. Leander's star persona constituted a discursive site for the negotiation of ideologically unstable relations between gender identity, modes of spectatorship, the location of mass culture in fascism, and the meaning of German identity. Understood in Seeßlen's sense as the intersection of textual and contextual registers of meaning, the image of Leander bears witness to the Americanist inclinations and perplexing syntheses of the Nazi culture industry, the contradictory ways in which it allowed cultural hybridity and ideologically ambivalent representations of sexual difference to enter the heart of a cinema whose implicit function was to suture the individual into the community of the folk through peculiarly modern modes of diversion.

* * *

Zarah Leander was born on 15 March 1907 as Zarah Stina Hedberg in Karlstad, Sweden. Although never promoted by Hitler to the elusive position of a state actress, Leander captivated the emotions of German mass audiences between 1937 and 1943 with her curious mix of renunciation and determination, exoticism and "German" faith, fatalism and autonomy, sensuality and spontaneity. As UFA's best paid star during this period, Leander in fact provided the film industry with a charismatic anchor for the entire star system. Even before she was seen in a German production for the first time, Leander's image was shaped into that of a metastar whose primary function was to endow Goebbels's project of a Germanified Hollywood with legitimacy and to demarcate a framework in which other stars and Hollywood-like elements could assume their respective operations.

What originally incited UFA to attract Leander to Germany and shape her into the metastar of Nazi cinema was her spectacular success in Ralph Benatzky's *Axel an der Himmelstür* (Axel at Heaven's Gate, 1936) in Vienna. Leander promised to provide German audiences once again with the image of a powerful *femme fatale* to fill the void left after both Garbo and Dietrich had turned their backs on the German film industry. From the moment of its inception, then, Leander's star persona was characterized, and jeopardized, by ostensible signatures of simulation: whereas film stars commonly derive their charisma from a peculiar jargon of individual authenticity, from presumed continuities between on- and off-screen persona, Leander entered the German film industry as a substitute, a mere copy measured against what she was supposed to replace. Hence the extravagant press campaign that accompanied her move to Nazi Germany: an attempt to naturalize her stardom, give her an aura of exceptionality, and make audiences forget that her stardom designated nothing other than the presence of an absence. "I was supposed to be found so high above the audience," Leander herself recalled the fabrication of her aura, "that it became possible to see me distinctly as the 'star' who I was, yet not so distinctly that the common man would be unable to fancy and add details according to his own desires" (138).

Finally projected on the screens of Nazi cinema, Leander's composite stardom did not embody collective mentalities so much as it offered a projection screen itself, an imaginary space open for multiple and often contradictory desires, commitments, and appropriations. For Sierck, Leander's face resembled Garbo's because of what he called its flatness. Accordingly, it required the work of the camera and the handwriting of the director to endow Leander's physiognomy – a silent mask and virtual "cow face" (Zumkeller 74) – with signifying power and allure. For an anonymous columnist in a 1938 issue of *Filmwelt*, however, Leander's face introduced to the German cinema not a malleable surface, but a perfect symbol for what the author considered the essence of Germanic femininity: "This incredibly impeccable and sculptured face mirrors everything that moves a woman: wistfulness and pain, love and bliss, melancholy and resignation. In her attitude as an actress, Zarah Leander is the epitome of 'spiritualized sensuality.' As dark as her low, undefinable alto – which is able to represent so excitingly the expression of hidden female desires – is also her essence" (cited by Seiler, no page number). Thus alternatively seen as an empty signifier or an archetype of eternal womanhood, Leander's face was discursively molded into a site of wonder that carried either less (Sierck) or more (the *Filmwelt* reviewer) than necessary to make her a sovereign individual and allow her convincingly to propagate the idea of self-authorship so central to the Hollywood star cult of the time (Dyer 10). From the moment UFA inaugurated and circulated Leander's aura, her face simultaneously meant nothing and everything: instead of simply giving form to the viewer's day dreams, its function was to define a liminal space in which it was possible to play out one's desire and imagination without being disturbed by the stubborn logic of the reality principle.

But more than her face and looks, it was of course Leander's voice that was seen as the hallmark of her stardom. Musical numbers and revue elements within Leander's films invited her audiences to consume intensely the physical and aural presence of their star. Significantly, the popularity of Leander's singing relied on an array of ambivalences similar to the one that concerned the discursive construction of her face: Leander's sounds allowed for multiple and potentially incoherent appropriations. Lodged between – as Helma Sanders-Brahms has argued rhapsodically – "man and woman, [and] pulling one towards the abysses of one's own double nature" (168), Leander's baritone probed given constructions of femininity and thus unlocked a space for modes of identification at odds with the Nazi's politics of gender (Seiler 28; von Praunheim). Her Swedish accent, by way of contrast, infused the rigorous idiom of the German fatherland with a *melos* culturally coded as feminine. Within the films' textual economy, Leander's innerdiegetic performances tended to provoke sexual mores and gender definitions that were typically corrected by the lines of narrative development. Her spectators, in other words, could have it both ways at once: Leander's Gloria Vane in *To New Shores*, for example, appears on stage as a lascivious and polygamous *femme fatale*, whereas beyond her performance she emerges as a faithful and melancholic lover. What should deserve our interest most of all, however, is the extent to which Leander popularized musical forms clearly at odds with the ideological itineraries of Nazi cultural politics. Only a few of her hit-songs during the UFA period really adhered to the musical vocabulary defined by Nazi ideologues as German music. Clearly dominating Leander's performances, "Foxtrot, tango, habanera, and czardas, strictly speaking also polka, were musical forms that had to be considered as 'racially degenerate' within the National Socialist ideology because of their Afro-American or Slavic origin" (Sanders 36). In most of her films, Leander's sounds transported the viewer beyond the boundaries of the National Socialist world view and its essentializing definitions of what it meant to be German. Typically, however, such moments of transgression summoned a variety of inner- and extra-diegetic devices in order to realign the performance's centrifugal force with the ideological orders of the day.

Intoned in the role of the Swede Astrée Stjernhjelm who becomes entrenched in a love triangle on Puerto Rico, Leander's musical numbers in *La Habanera* are a good point in case. Composed by Lothar Brühne, her most memorable song "The Wind Has Told Me a Song" unmistakably borrows from the popular Caribbean habanera tradition, while the song's orchestration entails the use of balalaikas, castanets, and stuffed trumpets, instruments that were on the official blacklist of the Nazi music board. Like jazz, the habanera originated as a popular musical response to the experience of cultural displacement, defining itself as an intrinsically hybrid mode of expression. In Sierck's film, habanera rhythms yield a recurring sonic background to the melodramatic action; they in fact bring into relief the Leander character's despair and melancholy, her desire to escape the burdens of her own desire, to break away from the despot Don Pedro and to return home to Northern Europe. Although the film's narrative is at pains to stage the triumph of European rationality and composure over what it presents as Southern lust and greed, Leander's numbers and the film's musical soundtrack reverberate with far more ambivalent tones and undertones. Leander's sounds in fact seem to reinstate what the film's narrative and imagetrack tend to denounce. Although her vision of the homeland is meant to counter the lures of the exotic, Sternhjelm's musical investments indicate that her notion of home and national identity is mediated through her very experience of cultural otherness and its hybrid modes of expressivity. While the film's narrative builds up the myths of the homeland as a sanctuary of monoculturalism, the soundtrack insists that cultures never appear in the singular, and that home is not a place of origins but the effect of a constant engagement with the other, a space of hybridity and in-betweenness itself.

In order to channel the popular demand for exotic distractions back into the Procrustean bed of ideological correctness, UFA's advertising campaigns for *La Habanera* mapped the film's ambivalent motifs of displacement onto the all-too-familiar topographical myth of North and South. Leander's delicate immersion into a "degenerate" musical idiom transmogrified into an Italian Journey, a journey that takes one beyond oneself, but does not revise existing formulations of cultural boundaries and collective identities. During a promotion of the film, two members of La Scala, "accompanied at the piano by Professor Renato Virgilio, the former accompanist of Caruso," presented Italian arias, songs, and duets. In a curious exercise of cross-cultural redress, UFA thus mobilized the vocabulary of high culture and spiritual refinement, Italian opera, in order to bring Leander's exoticism – her engagement with Caribbean popular culture – safely home to Germany and to stake out a space in which the audience could consume its star against all signs of ideological inconsistency.

According to Klaus Kreimeier, most stars of Nazi cinema were designed to fetter the dreams of the spectator, to immobilize a politically uncontrollable dynamic of subconscious desires and identifications (338). Shaped into a multivalent signifier, Leander at first seems to designate a moment of exception from the norm. Inner- and extra-diegetic constructions of her star persona invited the viewer's imagination to wander off in various directions at once, and in particular in her early films to transgress the orders of conformity. At closer inspection, however, as a star Leander inhabited a discursive site at which ideology and commodification struck a curious compromise. For fashioning her image into a repository of multiple and often contradictory emotional investments and affiliations, UFA succeeded in inflating Leander's meaning to such an extent that the star emerged as a wholesale market of spectatorial delight and consumption. Leander's fans got whatever they wanted, which at first sight was a lot, yet which in truth only extended an invitation to affective assimilation: the pleasure of consuming the star Leander – to modify Adorno and Horkheimer's famous dictum – promoted the resignation which it ought to help forget (Horkheimer/Adorno 142). For the German audience of 1937, the charismatic aura of Leander meant everything and nothing; as a screen of highly contradictory investments, the star Leander became indeed, as one critic has put it polemically, "the falsest woman of the century" (Seeßlen, *Zarah Leander*, E3).

* * *

Stars stimulate modes of spectatorship that tend to undermine what formalist film scholars consider the primary engine of a film's meaning and ideology, namely the regime of narrative unity, closure, and causality. The star's presence within a peculiar text, as Miriam Hansen argues, blurs the boundaries between an "address relying on the identification with fictional characters and an activation of the viewer's familiarity with the star on the basis of production and publicity intertexts" (246). The star's performance interrupts narrative progress in favor of spectacular interludes in order to exhibit the star's features to the viewers' consuming glance. Stars promote viewing pleasures that are often heterogeneous to a film's particular narrative: the star system encourages the viewer to become not a hermeneutic reader, but a textual poacher who knows how to isolate from the film's mise-en-scène those moments of spectacle when the image of the star can be consumed most intensely.

The elaborately choreographed mise-en-scène of Sierck's first film with Leander, *To New Shores*, indisputably caters to the logic of the star system and popular practices of textual poaching. Set first in England during the heyday of colonial capitalism and then in Australia, the film makes use of the narrative's shifting topographies to deliver the image of the new star to the audience's consuming glance. Whether we see Leander in the role of Gloria Vane on stage in London or as a prisoner in the Parramatta jail, whether we see her in moments of euphoria or melancholic suffering, Franz Weihmayr's cinematography conjures a panoply of perspectives that suspend the viewer from the thrust of the film's overall narrative only to supply him or her with intimate looks at Leander's body and face. It is not without irony that *To New Shores* at the same time, however, seeks to tell a story about the division of modern culture into the commodified spectacles of popular entertainment, on the one hand, and the highly exclusive domains of aesthetic refinement and social representation on the other. Helplessly torn between these two spheres, the Leander character senses the popular consumption of her stardom as a form of violence, while she experiences the elite's rhetoric of cultural refinement as hypocritical, as a strategy that links certain cultural practices to class positions in order to cement given architectures of power. In contrast to the film's visual surface, then, which provides the Nazi culture industry with a much desired cult of stardom, the film's narrative belabors the split of modern culture into the spheres of high art and commodified diversion, and wants to work through the effects of this great divide on the construction of individual and collective identities, the symbolic construction of gender and of the nation.

Both in England and in its colony Australia, the traditional institutions of cultural refinement operate as stages on which power represents

itself. Reserved as a practice for the colonial elite alone, the rituals of aesthetic cultivation transform the crowd into cultural window-shoppers
who consume their own exclusion from power as a spectacle of first
rank. Popular culture, on the other hand, following the narrative development of *To New Shores*, is far from promoting democratic participation and empowerment either; as the other face of the marred coin of
modern culture, it in fact exhibits deformations and duplicities similar to
the ones that mark the arena of high culture. Mass culture's regime of
diversion emerges as one of excess and exhibitionism, of aggressive sexuality and voyeuristic pleasure – a spectacular foreplay enticing desires
but endlessly delaying their gratification. While Gloria's performance in
the opening sequence challenges the moralism of the Victorian bourgeoisie, the viewer is soon to learn that her provocative stage persona is
only a pretense, a second skin catering to her male consumers. Gloria's
"Yes, Sir!," mocking her Victorian watchdogs, brings into relief anything
but Gloria's true backstage personality. Significantly, already during Gloria's performance Sierck's diegesis is at pains to provide the viewer with
a clear sense for the constructedness of her stage persona. The camera
follows and reframes her movements on stage from ever-changing points
of view and focal lengths. Frequent cuts and abrupt shifts between the
myriad of perspectives draw the viewer's attention to the fact that what
we see is not the recording of an artistic expression, but a truly violent
process of dismemberment – male desire mapped onto and exploiting
the surface of Gloria's body. Allowing us to see the star through the eyes
of her delirious onlookers, Sierck's editing ends up denouncing popular
diversion as empty spectacle and lie: Gloria's spell of personality, so central to the charisma of the star, is fake, a reflex of projective activities, a
male fantasy that reinvents as commodity certain vestiges of authenticity only to fall pray to its own illusionism.

Sierck's critique not only of Victorian moralism but also of popular
diversion becomes obvious in a later sequence when the Leander character performs in front of an Australian audience characterized by desires
similar to those of the London public. In contrast to the London spectacle, however, Gloria now rebuffs any attempt to transform her body
into a pleasurable commodity. Not surprisingly, her effort to render her
performance a screen of her true feelings meets with the rude rejection
of the audience, which is unwilling to endure Gloria's "I Stand in the
Rain … ," an aria of passive, suffering femininity. As if to endorse this
exercise in expressive authenticity, the cinematography and editing during this second performance avoids the feverish oscillations between various points of view from the audience. Instead, the camera immediately
zooms in on Leander's face in order to present her in long and motion-

less medium-close up shots that isolate her from the unruly innerdiegetic audience and redeem the melodramatic power of her artistic virtuosity for modes of spectatorship that valorize contemplative identification and concentrated absorption over distracted and tactile appropriation. If Sierck's camera work in the earlier London performance defined the popular dimension as one in which male mass audiences crudely exploit women, during the second performance it tries to reinstate for the film's audience a legitimate notion of mass culture that incorporates principles such as originality, authenticity, and attentiveness typically associated with the discourse of bourgeois high art.

The diegesis of *To New Shores* itself takes recourse to the vocabulary of religious experiences in order to encode its vision of a homogenous culture integrating aesthetic refinement and popular entertainment. When Gloria marries the faithful farmer Henry in the last sequence, the church's altar, the choir's "Gloria In Excelsis Deo," and the final close-ups of the choir boys, allegorically picture the end of the great divide of modern culture. However baroque they may seem, the film's final images and sounds encrypt Sierck's vision of a culture in which melodramatic pathos and contemplative attentiveness heal the rifts between high and low, sublate the hostile tracks of cultural modernization into a new synthesis, and thus renew the symbolic resources necessary for social integration and identity formation: mass culture becomes art, art mass culture, so that the formerly divided community may live and blossom again.

Narrative development and mise-en-scène in *To New Shores*, then, delineate what appears to be a strangely ambivalent force field. On the one hand, the diegesis clearly supplied Nazi consumer culture with a spectacular commodity; Sierck's highly controlled mise-en-scène unlocked a series of private windows on the new star. Focusing on the sight of Leander, the film's melodramatic intensity catered to the audience's consuming glance, and thus to modes of spectatorship associated with a Hollywood-like star system. At the same time, however, Sierck's narrative also seeks to undo the dialectics of modern culture and thus obliterate the very foundation of the star system. The film's narrative not only denounces the modern triumph of commodified spectacles over artistic expressivity as a step into a terrorist realm of inauthenticity, it also renders melodramatic sensibilities as catalysts for acts of spiritual purification: melodrama yields the power to redeem the individual from the respective excesses of both the popular regime of distraction and the elite's hypocritical discourse of aesthetic refinement.

Dominant scholarship suggests that such ambivalences are characteristic of Sierck's critical irony, a testimony to the subversive potential of his films and his melodramatic authorship (Willemen, Halliday, Silberman; for an aggressive critique see Klinger). It is difficult to see, however, how the film's simultaneous avowal and disavowal of the popular dimension, of distraction and consumption, could have really pushed the limits of Nazi politics. After all, not unlike Sierck, Nazi culture itself promoted a reconciliation of the split course of modern culture, a mutual – and illusory – absorption of high and low. While it responded to popular demand and granted private spaces of Americanist consumption, Nazi culture at the same time tried to resolve the ensuing ideological discrepancies in particular and the division of modern culture in general within the mold of what Benjamin has called the aestheticization of politics, i.e., the reconstruction of aura and cult in the age of mechanical reproduction (Benjamin 241-42). Instead of heroizing Sierck's ambivalences as signs of resistance, it therefore seems much more appropriate to read the negotiation of mass culture, gender, and community in films such as *To New Shores* as an instructive witness to prewar Nazi cultural politics. A composite of Sierck's melodramatic craftsmanship and Leander's star presence, the film evidences the often contradictory, albeit no doubt effective, ways in which the National Socialists in their pursuit of a homogenous community of the folk made concessions to the demand for the warmth of a private sphere of life. Furthermore, however, it bespeaks the Nazis' hope to refunctionalize depoliticized practices of cultural consumption – including the identification with ideologically inconsistent representations of gender and cultural hybridity – in the auratic shapes of their public spectacles, mass rituals that promised to the individual the unification of modern culture, only to drown ideological inconsistencies in an unprecedented surplus of signs and symbols.

* * *

According to Benjamin's famous thesis, fascism implemented technologically advanced communication technologies such as film in order to cast a mythic spell over the masses. Mass spectacles and their mechanical reproduction addressed a peculiar modern mode of experience, namely an ever-increasing hunger for distraction and scopic pleasure, yet solely to transfix the masses in mute gestures of emotional subordination, to give them expressions but no rights. Within the context of fascist mass culture, distraction and modern spectatorship constituted forms which reproduced as a sensational event what mechanical reproduction allegedly rendered obsolete: the authoritative charisma of auratic experiences.

Implicitly challenging Benjamin's account of modern mass culture, Patrice Petro in *Joyless Streets* has argued that the category of distraction as a peculiar mode of experiencing the topographies of modern life was far less universal and gender-neutral than Benjamin assumed. Benjamin's category of distraction, she argues, might encode the experience of those permitted to participate in the processes of social and cultural modernization, of rapid technological and industrial expansion, since the middle of the nineteenth century; however, it eclipses the structures of experience of those who, owing to given landscapes of power, remained at the margins of these processes, in particular women. Highly popular in Weimar cinema as a "female" genre, and preparing the grounds for Sierck's later generic voyages, the melodrama – according to Petro – bears testimony to the existence of modes of spectatorship different from those described by Benjamin under the rubric of distraction. In the context of the melodrama, mechanical reproduction addresses those for whom distraction has not become the norm, those whose "concentrated gaze involves a perceptual activity that is neither passive nor entirely distracted" (67), and who therefore desire for the long breath of contemplative identification and emotional intensity.

Petro's insistence on the diversity and gender-specificity of modern spectatorship, on the parallel existence of distracted and emotionally attentive modes of looking, should make us wonder about the accuracy of Benjamin's theory of fascist mass culture as well as his aestheticization thesis. If, following Benjamin, fascism musters distraction to engineer political homogeneity, then do we have to assume that those committed to contemplative structures of visuality, to melodramatic spectatorship and consumption, escaped the suturing effects of the Nazi spectacles and its concomitant definitions of German identity? One might be tempted at first to answer this question in the affirmative and thus attribute a rather ironic moment of resistance to those who found themselves positioned at the fringes of technological modernization in a patriarchal society. But such an answer, after a more careful consideration, would blindly fall prey to false alternatives suggested in the question itself, i.e., the definition of Nazi cultural politics solely in terms of the homogenizing rituals that Benjamin analyzed under the catchword of the aestheticization of politics. What it would overlook is the fact that – in contrast to Benjamin's model – Nazi cultural politics were marked by a striking gap between ideology and practice itself, that they relied on both at once, the power of public mass spectacles and the lures of privatized consumption, on the mass-mediated staging of political events as vehicles of symbolic integration, as much as on the appeals of a seemingly non-political, American-style consumer culture.

The making of the star Zarah Leander circa 1937, and the ways in which melodramatic sensibilities were central to the attempt to engender an autonomous German culture industry, urge us not to mistake the very existence of different and competing practices of cultural appropri-

ation during the National Socialist period for a sign of ideological opposition. Leander's melodramatic exoticism no doubt offered an incentive
for local acts of ideological incorrectness, but it also provided the opportunity to rehearse newly emerging desires for cultural consumption.
Given the assumption that the split between Nazi ideology and everyday
practice did not express a mere pathology but rather served as a tool of
domination itself, the decisive question as to the cultural status of Leander's star image is therefore not whether her stardom was able to
empower female spectators in particular to autonomous identities and
distinct modes of identification, but whether and to what extent German fascism succeeded in forging ideologically ambivalent strategies of
empowerment back into the mold of their political projects. Although
the sequence from Reitz's *Heimat* mentioned in the beginning leaves it
unsaid due to a crucial blind spot in the director's ethnographic method,
his protagonists Maria and Pauline remind us graphically that we should
not naively confuse acts of cultural empowerment and subject formation
with strategies of resistance or even political emancipation. Identifying
with the exotic image of Leander, the two women inhabit a place for
themselves at odds with the Nazi's archaic ideology of gender, but their
assumption of agency is indubitably also in accord with the ambitions of
Nazi women organizations to foreswear claims to public power, and in
exchange, to expect "greater influence over their own social realm"
(Koonz 13). Melodramatic attentiveness in fact prepares Maria and
Pauline ideally for the role the Nazis were to script for women only a few
years after the release of *La Habanera*, namely to defend solitarily the
fatherland at the homefront and supply the ammunition industry with
a skillful workforce.

Leander's work with directors other than Sierck magnifies what is
precarious about any redemptive approach to Leander's star image or the
power of melodramatic excess. In 1942 spectators such as Maria and
Pauline would be invited to transfer their melodramatic delight to the
image of Leander playing the role of Hanna Holberg in the UFA melodrama *Die große Liebe* (The Great Love). Directed by Rolf Hansen, this
film was to boast the morale of those waiting and working at the home
front; it has become famous for Leander's infamous songs of persever-
ance. The film's final shot links what Reitz presents as source of female
defiance directly to the German war effort. We see Holberg temporarily
united with the aviator Paul Wendlandt (Victor Staal), attentively watching the skies, not in order to discover shooting stars but to behold of a
bomber formation en route to the front. Far from experiencing war as an
antagonistic element, Holberg's melodramatic gaze detects in war a figure that fascinates: war emerges as the very condition that makes great

love possible in the first place. Leander's star persona, in this final shot, transmutes warfare into the *telos* of melodramatic attentiveness and female spectatorship. Watching Leander watching, the 1942 spectator in fact was asked to see war's dramas of separation and reunion as melodramatic spectacles of the first order. "I know a miracle will happen at some point," Leander proclaims in this film – both a consoling empowerment of those fighting at the home front and a tribute to Hitler's desperate but effective myth of the "Wunderwaffe," the vision of a miracle missile magically undoing all enemies.

Note

This essay was completed before the publication of Eric Rentschler's *The Ministry of Illusion: Nazi Cinema and Its Afterlife* (Cambridge, MA: Harvard UP, 1996) and I was therefore unable to discuss Rentschler's chapter on Zarah Leander.

Bibliography

Bathrick, David. "Inscribing History, Prohibiting and Producing Desire: Fassbinder's *Lili Marleen*." *New German Critique* 63 (Fall 1994): 35-54.

Benjamin, Walter. *Illuminations: Essays and Reflections*. Trans. Harry Zohn. New York: Schocken Books, 1969.

Dyer, Richard. *Heavenly Bodies: Film Stars and Society*. New York: St. Martin's Press, 1986.

Halliday, Jon. "Notes on Sirk's German Films." *Douglas Sirk*. Eds. Laura Mulvey and Jon Halliday. Edinburgh: Edinburgh Film Festival, 1972. 15-22.

Hansen, Miriam. *Babel and Babylon: Spectatorship in American Silent Film*. Cambridge, MA: Harvard UP, 1991.

Horkheimer, Max and Theodor W. Adorno. *Dialectic of Enlightenment*. Trans. John Cumming. New York: Continuum, 1995.

Klinger, Barbara. *Melodrama and Meaning: History, Culture, and the Films of Douglas Sirk*. Bloomington: Indiana UP, 1994.

Koonz, Claudia. *Mothers in the Fatherland: Women, The Family, and Nazi Politics*. New York: St. Martin's Press, 1987.

Kreimeier, Klaus. *Die UFA -Story: Geschichte eines Filmkonzerns*. Munich: Hanser, 1992.

Leander, Zarah. *Es war so wunderbar! Mein Leben.* Trans. Anna Liese
    Kornitzky. Hamburg: Hoffmann und Campe, 1973.
Petro, Patrice. *Joyless Streets: Women and Melodramatic Representation in
    Weimar Germany.* Princeton: Princeton UP, 1989.
Praunheim, Rosa von. "Die Baßamsel singt nicht mehr." *Der Spiegel* 19 June
    1981: 158.
Sanders, Ulrike. *Zarah Leander – Kann denn Schlager Sünde sein?* Cologne:
    Pahl-Rugenstein, 1988.
Sanders-Brahms, Helma. "Zarah." In *Jahrbuch Film 81/82.* Ed. Hans Günther
    Pflaum. Munich: Hanser, 1981. 165-72.
Schäfer, Hans Dieter. *Das gespaltene Bewußtsein: Deutsche Kultur und
    Lebenswirklichkeit 1933-1945.* Munich: Hanser, 1981.
Seeßlen, Georg. *Tanz den Adolf Hitler: Faschismus in der populären Kultur.*
    Berlin: Verlag Klaus Bitterman, 1994.
___. "Zarah Leander." *CineGraph: Lexikon zum deutschsprachigen Film.* Ed.
    Hans-Michael Bock. Munich: Edition Text und Kritik, 1984ff. E1-E3.
Seiler, Paul, ed. *Ein Mythos lebt: Zarah Leander. Eine Bildbiographie. Zum 10.
    Todestag.* Copyright by Paul Seiler. Berlin, 1994.
Silberman, Marc. "Probing the Limits: Detlef Sierck's *To New Shores.*" *German
    Cinema: Texts in Context.* Detroit: Wayne State UP, 1995. 51-65.
Willemen, Paul. "Distanciation and Douglas Sirk." *Screen* 13.4 (1972/73):
    128-34.
Witte, Karsten. *Lachende Erben, Toller Tag: Filmkomödie im Dritten Reich.*
    Berlin: Vorwerk, 1995.
Zumkeller, Cornelia. *Zarah Leander: Ihre Filme – ihr Leben.* Munich: Heyne,
    1988.

Chapter 11

NAZISM AS *FEMME FATALE*

Recuperations of Cinematic Masculinity in
Postwar Berlin

Barton Byg

Provocatively summarizing the "historians' debate" of the 1980s,
Clive James recently wrote of the historian Ernst Nolte, "He
stated that Nazi Germany, by attacking Russia, had simply got into the
Cold War early …" (50). Seeing the Nazis as allies in the Cold War is a
provocative concept since it allows us to recall that the origins of the
Cold War are inextricably tied to both sides' relations to the Nazis.

Given the vehemence with which the Cold War soon took hold, however, there is a striking absence of Cold War concerns in paradigmatic
films from the immediate postwar years. Instead, postwar film – especially *film noir* – makes it clear that this was a period of great anxiety:
anxiety over the stability of men's gender identity, anxiety over the presence of strong women in the context of a postwar crisis of masculinity,
and anxiety over the possibility that the postwar period could bring
political change – either in the direction of social democracy in the U.S.
or a return to the "feminine" seductions of fascism in Europe. All of
these anxieties, which will be illustrated in the following through the
major films of the postwar period, can be seen as paving the way for the
Cold War as a means of assuaging them. The structured self/other
dichotomy and restoration of an "enemy" as the focus of heroic effort
effectively restabilized masculine identities in crisis.

Part of the anxiety of the postwar era, visible in the films to be treated
here, arises over uncertainty over who or what was actually the enemy.

The wartime reification of Nazism into a seeming monolith – both for Germans and the rest of the world – ceased to function in 1945. Attention shifted from the literal battle over Nazism to the murkier – and still unresolved – question of its cultural origins. As the work of a number of feminist critics attests, often in dialogue with Siegfried Kracauer's *From Caligari to Hitler*, a durable complex of terms has long been interconnected in the popular imagination: the cinema and the city, the cinema and women, women and commodity consumption, the cinema and commodity consumption, cinema and prostitution, and all of these connected to fascism. (see Elsaesser, "Re-Constructions," 22; Fehrenbach 5; and Petro 17, 19, 109). The apex of this interrelation seems to have been reached in Weimar Germany, a "Golden Age" of the cinema marked by intense anxiety about, and fascination with, women's social roles, their representation as sexual commodities and a scintillating modern urban environment. As Linda Mizejewski has demonstrated, the film *Cabaret* and its history can stand as a key example of this conflation.

The following will examine the often contradictory ways in which a gendered construction of otherness functioned in cinematic representations of the city of Berlin as the site of the collapse of Nazism into ruins on the eve of the Cold War. The three principal films to be treated here are all important works in film history, filmed within months of each other among the ruins of Berlin: Wolfgang Staudte's *The Murderers Are among Us* (*Die Mörder sind unter uns*, 1947), Roberto Rossellini's *Germany Year Zero* (*Germania anno zero*, 1947), and Billy Wilder's *A Foreign Affair* (1948). By documenting so clearly the crisis of masculinity in the aftermath of World War II, these films actually demonstrate the need for the ensuing Cold War and the culture that accompanied it. The Cold War compensated for this social anxiety both by reasserting the masculine certitude that had been functional in total war and by way of Cold War culture – in this case, a rejuvenation of the cinema.

In regard to the former, the U.S. decision to use the atomic bomb stands both as the final, violent assertion of masculinity in the war against Nazism (the enemy for which the Bomb was intended), and as the first strike of the re-masculinized nuclear age, against the fear of giving in to "feminine" and "sentimental" impulses (Farrell 6; Alperovitz 449, 459). Regarding the latter, a cultural recuperation of masculinity emerged through *film noir* and the subsequent renewal of the institution of the cinema, propelled by male-oriented critical appreciations of *noir* and Italian Neo-Realism, and resulting eventually in the "new waves" of European cinema. In one sense, all these cinematic movements can be seen as narrative ways of restoring the vitality of a masculinity left vulnerable in the wake of the war and the abdication or disgrace of the "fathers." In another, as "modernist" movements within the popular context of the cinema, they are examples of the masculine impulse in art to resist the threats posed by the feminine aspects of modernity/modernism (see Huyssen; Lersch-Schumacher 329-31).

The first question to be raised is, "Why was there no German *film noir* movement?" Given the conditions of the immediate postwar period in Germany, especially the crisis of masculinity, and the German contributions to this film trend in the U.S., its relative absence demands scrutiny. The appropriateness of *noir* to the postwar situation is clear from Heide Fehrenbach's description of the German social context, and Frank Krutnik's analysis of the role of such films in the U.S. of the same period: Krutnik sees the "'tough' thrillers" of *film noir* serving as

> a generically-regulated response to the various upheavals of the wartime and postwar eras. In particular, the "tough" thriller seems to be driven by challenges to the mutually reinforcing regimes of masculine cultural authority and masculine psychic stability ... . These films will frequently offer an engagement with problematic, even illicit potentialities within masculine identity, yet at the same time they cannot fully embrace or sanction such "subversive" potentialities (xiii).

A rather untypical example of American *film noir* is Edward Dmytryk's *Crossfire* (1947) – in Krutnik's view, a blend of the tough crime drama and the returning veteran "social problem" crime film (26). The theme of the film relates very closely to the situation in Berlin in 1946, but resolves the gender conflict in a much more decisive manner. Like many *films noirs*, *Crossfire* is the story of returning U.S. veterans who threaten to bring the violence of the war home with them. Many heroes of the *noir* genre find the home environment disorienting – partly because it is now occupied by strong, sexually threatening women. In an atmosphere in which crime and violence seem unavoidable, the pulp-fiction-style plot often leads to the death of the threatening female (Kaplan 3). The male hero may regret this, but by way of this dramatic test of strength he either achieves some reconciliation between the warlike past and the domestic present or is destroyed in a stylized climax of hopelessness.

The plot of *Crossfire* deviates from this model inasmuch as the crime involved is the murder of a Jew by an antisemitic returning veteran. The antisemitic motive of the murderer is given no further explanation, and the themes of Nazism, Germany, or even war are not brought into play. All the more interesting then are the few characteristics of the murder victim that are represented. On the one hand, he is at first taunted by the murderer in a bar, because the murderer falsely assumes that the somewhat soft-looking man in civilian clothes is a "parasite" who did not serve in the war. On the other hand, the murder victim Samuels is the only person to show understanding for a young soldier who is unable to adapt to peacetime. The young man, who is later suspected of Samuels's murder, had become an artist before the war, thanks to the New Deal. But after the war, he cannot reconcile his artistic with his military identity. The scene of Samuels's sympathy and understanding, with his left-liberal interpretation of the function and psychology of war and hatred, is inserted into the film as a flashback just before the true murderer is discovered and thus suggests that such views, in addition to his Jewishness, make Samuels a target for murder (see Krutnik 210 for the dialog).

As in most *films noirs*, reconciliation in this film comes about through violence. The plot derives its suspense from the confusion engendered by masculinity run amok, the "feminization" of the young man, and the somewhat leftist politics represented by the Jew. The resolution of the suspense takes on the conventional form of the shooting of the true murderer as he tries to flee down a dark street on a rainy night. But more important is the fact that the truth has been exposed by a second man in civilian clothes – the figure played by Robert Young – whose authority surpasses that of the men in uniform. Young's role thus prefigures multiple images of masculine authority that would help sustain Cold War stability in film and television: the quintessential FBI agent (who once fought gangsters and soon would hunt Communists), the male head of the family, and the reassuring professional – later reaffirmed in Young's most enduring roles on U.S. television in *Father Knows Best* and *Marcus Welby, M.D.*

The German situation is very similar, but with a unique intertwining of national, cinematic and gender issues. As Fehrenbach remarks, "Post-war Germany seemed plagued by a crisis of masculinity. And since the crisis coincided with military defeat and occupation, it was intimately bound up with notions of national identity" (95). Both the U.S. and Germany experienced crises of masculinity, the one arising from victory, the other from defeat; their common dynamic emerges, then, not from the national situation, but from the fascination of the cinema with representation of the threat posed by women in either situation. The iconic location in Berlin for this "psychic instability" and its "subversive potentialities," connecting women, the city, sexual excess, commodity exchange, and cinematic spectacle is the Weimar cabaret. The bewitching seductions of the trope of the Weimar cabaret thus become paradigmatic in cinematic treatments of German history and identity in the twentieth century, even to the point of conflation with the fascism that ensued. Only an energetically re-masculinized assertion of film artistry – such as through *film noir* – could lure the *femme fatale* from her historical lair and defeat her with the weapons of violence and crime.

American *film noir* thus represents a successful attempt to recuperate both masculinity and the cinema: Even when it ends in hopelessness and self-destruction, the "tough crime" thriller represents a kind of purification ritual, capable of restoring strength to the male audiences who endure it, while inspiring awe and respect in female spectators. A further device for restoring images of strength is its important role in recuperating the credibility of the cinema itself. Although distancing itself from the cultural and political complexities of Weimar and Nazi Germany, *noir* still derives artistic legitimacy from its continuity with Weimar cinema in exile through the influence of Germans in Hollywood and the international legacy of the Expressionist style.

Even Siegfried Kracauer's theses on the early tendencies toward fascism parallel this dynamic of blaming the cinema while still looking to it for renewal. The two most important books on the fascination of the Weimar cinema appeared in the same period as the films treated here: Kracauer's *From Caligari to Hitler* in 1947 and Lotte Eisner's *The Haunted Screen* (*L'Ecran démoniaque*) in 1952. They thus share the impulse to redeem the cinema as an institution even while exploring the dangerous fascinations it awakens. The subsequent "discovery" and appreciation of *film noir* as a type occurred as part of a European project of recuperating the cinema as a social and artistic (and masculine) institution by drawing inspiration from the unpretentious, commercial, but supposedly "virile" U.S. cinema (see Elsaesser, "Pre-History of *Film Noir*"). The contribution of German émigré directors to the phenomenon is also central to its legitimacy, as opposed to the cultural ruin of Europe by 1945 (on the German influence see Thompson and Bordwell 259). Philippe Sollers referred to postwar European culture as "castrated" in his explanation of the 1950s attraction of U.S. culture (Kristeva 283-84). The "camera-stylo," "auteur theory" and the new wave impulse are typified by language redolent of masculine rejuvenation.[1] As in the case of the modernist avant-garde, this masculine celebration of cinema also includes a male appropriation of "feminism," as François Truffaut claimed for the films of Ingmar Bergman and Alain Resnais (*Tu n'as rien vu*, 115).

The success of this re-masculinization of cinema seems to rest in part on a certain political innocence (real or constructed) and a geographical distance from the thorny issues of how Weimar and Nazi culture are

---

1. I have discussed this in more detail in my comparison of Alain Renais' *Hiroshima mon amour* (1959) and Konrad Wolf's *Der geteilte Himmel* (Divided Heaven, 1964).

intertwined. In both East and West Germany, therefore, film movements could not so easily carry out a recuperation of masculinity, given the country's contradictory cultural and historical situation. Instead, Socialist *films noirs* had to be mitigated with the "feminine" voice of social optimism (as we shall see in *The Murderers Are among Us*) while any attempt at a West German new wave was marked by various masculine melancholy obsessions. Wim Wenders' work can serve as an example here, with the U.S. filling in for the absent father and the GDR – especially in *Im Lauf der Zeit* (Kings of the Road, 1976) – for the structuring inaccessibility of woman.

The ambivalent memories of the Nazi period in both East and West can perhaps account for the continuing male identity crisis, its representation in film, and an enduring mistrust of film spectacle as implicitly fascistic (Kaes 8). Filmmakers as different as Rainer Werner Fassbinder and Konrad Wolf, for example, have imagined Nazi Germany as a strikingly "feminized" space of plenitude, pleasure and even excess. This pleasure, as spectacle in such films as Fassbinder's *The Stationmaster's Wife* (*Bolwieser*, 1977) and Wolf's *Lissy* (1957), is confined to the tainted yet intact national identity of the past, but is not possible in the present. That there remains a particularly European view of this crisis of masculinity can even be seen in important post-Cold-War films of the 1990s, such as *Ulysses' Gaze* (*To Vlemma tou Odysse*a, Dir. Theo Angolopolous, 1995), *Before the Rain* (*Pred dozhdot*, Dir. Milcho Manchevski, 1994) and *Lisbon Story* (Dir. Wim Wenders, 1994). All three perpetuate the romance between self-doubting male artist-figures and images of woman, the city, and destruction. Like other films dealing with the contemporary European malaise, none of these has found a wide audience in the United States. Ambivalence still does not sell.

The European difficulty in adopting a *film noir* strategy for confronting the *femme fatale* is clear in the representations of Berlin in 1946. In Germany, although there were tendencies toward *noir* in the same period, the gender roles in the films take on different dynamics in the context of the destruction of Germany and the presence of the occupying powers. In the German films, the women cannot be shown as either physically weak or aggressive; instead their threat resides in the fact that the male characters are the weak ones. The women are thus often connected to art and civilization, nurturing and self-sacrifice as in Wolfgang Staudte's *The Murderers Are among Us*, Willi Forst's *Die Sünderin* (1951), and Kurt Maetzig's *Marriage in the Shadows* (1947).

Based on this connection, the difference from U.S. *film noir* becomes clear. While the American male may be wounded or tormented, he is still in center stage. German masculinity in postwar film, however, has been pushed even further to the margins. The two rejoin only in the evocation of the Cold War in politics and then in the cinematic "new waves" as a cultural basis for the restoration of male authority.

Uta Poiger has traced the continued transformation of the battle over Nazi guilt into a Cold War struggle. For Cold War purposes, a connection could be made between "femininity" and socialism on the one hand and "femininity" and capitalist consumption or even fascism on the other. The key connection between the two is the repeated reference to the cultural license originating in Weimar, especially in the form of the cinema, the cabaret and the *femme fatale*. In a conflation of the fate of Weimar politics in the disaster of Nazism with the fascinating cultural and sexual license of the same period, Nazism itself becomes the ultimate *femme fatale*. In connecting Nazism with seductiveness and with capitalism, films imply that the danger indeed does not come from outside, but arises from one's own desires.

An ideal framing pair of films that illustrate this are Wolfgang Staudte's *The Murderers Are among Us* and Willi Forst's *Die Sünderin*, since both employ Hildegard Knef in the role of a woman who attempts to redeem a debilitated German man. In the former, *noir* elements are mitigated by the romantic optimism embodied in the Knef character. In the Forst film, after she has shown her resourcefulness in surviving both Nazism and occupation, the woman still sacrifices herself when it becomes clear that her lover Alexander cannot be saved. The controversy over this character, both a prostitute and a murderer, is well described by Heide Fehrenbach (92-116). Her recourse to both prostitution and commodity exchange (dealing in her husband's art) resonates with the postwar historical situation in a number of ways, as Fehrenbach points out. In her role as muse and merchant for German art and as a melodramatic suicide, the Knef character embodies the fascination with women's roles, with the cinema, and with Nazism and its legacy. The author of the screenplay, Gerhard Menzel, had also written a Nazi film with strong ambivalence about female sexuality, *Hitler Youth Quex* (*Hitlerjunge Quex*, Dir. Hans Steinhoff, 1933) which also ends in a sacrificial death.

Die Sünderin thus suggests a complicity between sexual pleasure, Nazism, and popular entertainment that is present in the earlier "rubble films" as well. Significantly, *The Murderers Are among Us*, *Germany Year Zero* and Wilder's *A Foreign Affair* all evoke a connection between the legacy of Nazism in the postwar rubble and references to the cultural and sexual license identified with Berlin in the Weimar Republic. The cabaret is a key locus of this dynamic connecting Nazism with commercial and sensual excess.

In *The Murderers Are among Us*, there is a cabaret where illicit exchanges take place and where war crimes are concealed; the women working there represent the trade in both sex and black market goods, although their customers are never shown. But the turning point in the film occurs when Dr. Hans Mertens is diverted from a visit to this cabaret with his former commanding officer, the war criminal he is intent on murdering in order to restore his own honor. Just as he is about to shoot his former captain, he is called to save a suffocating child and thus rediscovers his physician's vocation.

With the psychological stylization of Expressionism, the scene contrasts three highly significant spaces: the rubble of Berlin where the murder is contemplated; the cabaret, where German women consort with former Nazis (replacing the occupying forces in this context!); and the domestic space of a humble kitchen, where the sick child is to be saved. The metaphorical relation between a physician's recovery of will and a belief in a German future is confirmed by other films dealing with the legacy of fascism, such as Peter Lorre's *The Lost One* (*Der Verlorene*, 1951) and Konrad Wolf's *Genesung* (Return to Health, 1956 [no U.S. release]). In the Staudte film, Dr. Mertens reenters domestic life by performing the tracheotomy using ordinary kitchen utensils and a piece of the gas tube from the stove. As he leaves the kitchen after the successful operation, the Expressionist lighting gives way to more diffuse and three-dimensional images, leading him back into a similarly transformed domestic space with Susanne Wallner. The merger of Mertens' masculine skill as a physician and Wallner's domestic and artistic roles is also visually conveyed by the X-rays from his pre-war practice, which replace missing panes in her studio windows.

Roberto Rossellini, by contrast, ignores the *femme fatale* in *Germany Year Zero*, partly due to the more matter-of-fact approach to film performance typifying Neo-Realism. Still, he is quite unsubtle in his conflation of Nazi cruelty and evil with purported homosexuality, and his depictions of Nazi "decadence" seem to draw heavily on the clichéd iconography associated with gay culture in Weimar. Also, the space of the cabaret (here, true to Neo-Realism, minus the musical performance) again shows women transgressing their domestic role and linking sexual with economic instability: they consort with occupation soldiers and trade for black-market commodities. A metaphorical black-market commodity present in all of the films considered here is, however, the German cinema of the Weimar era. Rossellini's script advisor, Max Colpet (Kolpe), for instance, began his career as a scriptwriter and songwriter during the Weimar era, and worked with both Wilder and Marlene Dietrich (Kreimeier 17, Zolotow 51). With such strong links to Weimar cinema, especially clear in the protagonist's visible alienation from his surroundings, the film may be a retelling of the story of another young boy tormented by cultural and sexual confusion in the waning days of Weimar, *Hitler Youth Quex*.

Nazism as *femme fatale* becomes most explicit in Billy Wilder's film *A Foreign Affair*, in the person of Erika von Schlütow as played by Marlene Dietrich. This postwar film comedy clearly links its own antecedents in Weimar culture with fascism's ability to seduce. The return to such German dilemmas is partly a "homecoming" for Wilder, Dietrich, and the songwriter Friedrich Hollander, more so than for the characters in the story. Wilder, born in Austria, had begun his career in Berlin, first as a journalist, as a publicist for the jazz band of Paul Whiteman, and then as scriptwriter. His first return to Germany, however, came not with this film project but rather with his work as film officer in the occupying forces. In this role he supervised the editing of the film *Death Mills* by Hanus Burger, shortening the work from over 85 minutes to 21. In his famous memo on film policy, Wilder further distanced himself from direct confrontations with the Nazi past and urged "reeducation" through entertainment instead (Willet 38, 40-44). It is thus significant that Wilder, who had made such a classic *film noir* as *Double Indemnity* (1944) should make his first film about postwar Germany into a light, ironic comedy.

The film's title itself indicates that it will treat the connection between sexuality and politics, and the context is clearly not yet the Cold War but rather the occupation of Nazi Germany. The romantic comedy is built around a love triangle made up of an American officer (Capt. Pringle played by John Lund) who is fraternizing with Erika von Schlütow (Marlene Dietrich), a night club singer with past Nazi affiliations, and the (initially) sexually repressed Congresswoman Phoebe Frost (Jean Arthur). On the one hand, the film criticizes the blindness of the Americans, who have achieved victory but do not understand the power they have defeated. As Loewenstein and Tatlock put it in regard to Dietrich as the German *femme fatale*, "defeat confers analytic power, the pleasure of knowledge" (435). The U.S. Congresswoman's grotesquely comic allergy to any sexual references contrasts sharply with Dietrich's seductiveness, based on cunning and experience.

The Americans err in two ways: the soldier, in believing that military power is sufficient, and the Congresswoman, in believing that the occupation is a purely administrative matter. Dietrich, who is not directly portrayed as a former Nazi but as the former lover of a fugitive war criminal, underscores with her every word and movement that all power relations have to do with sexuality, from ration cards to the black market to international politics.

The song performance "Black Market" can be seen as the meeting point for all of the issues raised by this film and its place in cinematic and political history. The text alludes to the commodification of both the female body and cultural values in bitter yet seductive terms – "You take art; I take Spam." The song that Dietrich sings was composed by Friedrich Hollander, who accompanies her on screen at the piano. The song is thereby an extension of earlier Hollander contributions to the *femme fatale*, such as "Falling in Love Again" from *The Blue Angel*, and "*Wenn ich mir was wünschen dürfte ...*" used to link cabaret and Nazi sadomasochism in Liliana Cavani's *The Night Porter* (*Il Portiere di notte*, 1973). But here the *femme fatale* explicitly invokes commerce in addition to sexual allure and, in the figure of Dietrich, self-consciously inscribes the combination within the institution and history of cinema. The figure of Erika von Schlütow as a collaborative creation of Dietrich, Hollander, and Wilder thus unites a number of dualities: the Nazi mistress von Schlütow *and* Dietrich the anti-Nazi entertainer of U.S. troops, the collaborator *and* the exile, the Jew *and* the gentile, the American *and* the German, and one could say, both the man *and* the woman.

Dietrich's performance is thus the key to the difference between this Hollywood film and DEFA's *The Murderers Are among Us*. The cabaret is not a temptation to be avoided, but stands at the center of Wilder's film, as the space where Dietrich sings her analytically seductive songs, where Phoebe Frost awakens her own sexuality through role-playing, and where the fugitive Nazi is finally lured and shot.

Underscoring just how irrelevant the Communist side of the Cold War was to Wilder's concerns, the Soviets play very little role in this film, except as antifascists who want to capture the Nazi criminals and as simple soldiers who delight in throwing people into the air to folk music. Although Wilder treats both Nazism and Communism as sources of humor, the latter always appears the more harmless of the two. Both the Cuban missile crisis and hidden Nazi pasts supply laughs in *One, Two, Three* (1961), for instance, but the Communists are seen as both guileless and easily seduced by consumer capitalism, while the Nazis remain part of the latter system yet continue to conceal their secrets.

Wilder's film, by relying on the devices of comedy to present the "threat" represented by Dietrich, betrays an unshaken confidence in the power of cinema to contain the threat, even if U.S. military might is not alone sufficient. Loewenstein and Tatlock stress the important fact that, although *A Foreign Affair* shares with the Staudte and Rossellini films the "authentic" location shots of the ruins of Berlin, the film was made in Hollywood with action placed in front of these images as back projections. The U.S. film apparatus, like the U.S. Cold War apparatus, is thus able to incorporate the legacy of Nazism's destructiveness as the film has been able to incorporate its attractiveness through the figure of Dietrich. And the plot resolution has Frost and Pringle preparing to embark in the most conventional of 1950s American marriages, while the catalyst for this heterosexual union has been the cinematic adventure represented by Berlin and Dietrich.

The equation of women, Jews, homosexuals with the threatening Other of modernity had its origins in turn-of-the-century Vienna and the Weimar Republic, and reached its extreme in Nazi Germany (see Harrowitz and Hyams 4-6). This is the "enemy within" that the West has been dealing with, and the externalization in the form of a Communist (and feminine, perhaps Jewish) "Other" for the duration of the Cold War may have been but a temporary detour. As these films show, the temptations toward commercial and sensual excess in the cabaret have more to do with masculine vulnerability than with any external threat.

The three films under discussion all make use of the ruins of Berlin as a representation for the physical and cultural destruction of Europe, but in strikingly different ways. This is apparent in the visual balance between setting and such elements as character and plot as Paul Schrader has described it in regard to *film noir*: "When the environment is given an equal or greater weight than the actor, it, of course, creates a fatalistic, hopeless mood. There is nothing the protagonist can do; the city will outlast and negate even his best efforts" (57). In the quasi-expressionist style of *The Murderers Are among Us*, environment does tend to take over – especially in the form of rubble and shadow. Even more significantly, the violent act of male revenge called for by film convention is thwarted by the woman's (and Socialist cultural policy's) restraining voice. Rossellini's Neo-Realist treatment, on the other hand, reaches back more to "Neue Sachlichkeit" in uneasily placing its young protagonist on equal footing with the unstable physical and social situation around him. Surrounded by war ruins as well as moribund, discredited or homosexual men, young Edmund finds no avenue to manhood, merely self-destruction, and the film ends with a woman cradling his lifeless body – a Neo-Realist Pietà. Wilder's *A Foreign Affair*, finally, leaves no doubt that the characters, the comedy, and by extension, the U.S. film industry are in complete control of the situation. As Joseph Loewenstein and Lynne Tatlock point out, the authenticity of the shots of Berlin is overshadowed by the technique of incorporating them into a studio product back in Hollywood (433-34). Captain Pringle escapes the seduction of the Nazi *femme fatale* by returning home; he does not defeat it on its own territory.

Despite these differences, however, all three films relate to the *film noir* project of recuperating masculinity in the postwar cultural void, and all three look back to images from Weimar culture both for the origins of cultural instability and the cinematic means to combat it.

Bibliography

Alperovitz, Gar. *The Decision to Use the Atomic Bomb and the Architecture of an American Myth.* New York: Knopf, 1995.

Byg, Barton. "Geschichte, Trauer und weibliche Identität im Film: *Hiroshima mon amour* und *Der geteilte Himmel.*" Trans. Thomas Nolden. *Zwischen gestern und morgen: DDR-Autorinnen aus amerikanischer Sicht.* Ed. Ute Brandes. Berlin: Europäischer Verlag der Wissenschaften, 1992. 95-112.

Eisner, Lotte H. *The Haunted Screen: Expressionism in the German Cinema and the Influence of Max Reinhardt.* (*L'Ecran Démoniaque.* Paris: Le Terrain Vague, 1952. Trans. Roger Greaves. Berkeley: U of California P, 1973.

Elsaesser, Thomas. "Re-Constructions: Narratives of History in New German Cinema." Ms. n.d.

_____. "Towards a Pre-History of Film Noir." Paper presented at the Society for Cinema Studies Conference. New York, NY. 4 March 1995.

Farrell, James J. "Making (Common) Sense of the Bomb in the First Nuclear War." *American Studies* 36.2 (Fall 1995): 5-41.

Fehrenbach, Heide. *Cinema in Democratizing Germany: Reconstructing National Identity after Hitler.* Chapel Hill: U of North Carolina P, 1995.

Harrowitz, Nancy A. and Barbara Hyams, eds. *Jews and Gender: Responses to Otto Weininger.* Philadelphia: Temple UP, 1995.

Huyssen, Andreas. "Mass Culture as Woman: Modernism's Other." *Studies in Entertainment.* Ed. Tania Modleski. Bloomington: Indiana UP, 1986. 188-207.

Kaes, Anton. *From Hitler to Heimat: The Return of History as Film.* Cambridge, MA: Harvard UP, 1989.

Kaplan, E. Ann. *Women in Film Noir.* London: British Film Institute, 1980.

Kracauer, Siegfried. *From Caligari to Hitler: A Psychological History of German Film.* Princeton, NJ: Princeton UP, 1947.

Kreimeier, Klaus. "*Germania, anno zero*: Eine Momentaufnahme." *epd film* 6/95: 17-25.

Kristeva, Julia. "Why the United States?" [A discussion between Julia Kristeva, Marcelin Pleynet and Philippe Sollers]. Trans. Seán Hand. *The Kristeva Reader.* Ed. Toril Moi. New York: Columbia UP, 1986. 272-91.

Krutnik, Frank. *In a Lonely Street: Film noir, Genre, Masculinity.* London: Routledge, 1993.

Lersch-Schumacher, Barbara. "Über Weiblichkeit und Modernität: Befragung eines Konzepts." *Das Selbstverständnis der Germanistik: Aktuelle Diskussion.* Ed. Norbert Ollers. Tübingen: Niemeyer, 1988. 320-38.

Loewenstein, Joseph, and Lynne Tatlock. "The Marshall Plan at the Movies: Marlene Dietrich and Her Incarnations." *German Quarterly* 65.3/4 (1992): 429-42.

Mizejewski, Linda. *Divine Decadence: Fascism, Female Spectacle, and the Makings of Sally Bowles.* Princeton, NJ: Princeton UP, 1992.

Petro, Patrice. *Joyless Streets: Women and Melodramatic Representation in Weimar Germany.* Princeton, NJ: Princeton UP, 1989.

Poiger, Uta G. "Rebels with a Cause? American Popular Culture, the 1956 Youth Riots, and the New Conception of Masculinity in East and West Germany." *The American Impact on Postwar Germany.* Ed. Reiner Pommerin. Providence, RI: Berghahn, 1995.

Schrader, Paul. "Notes on *Film Noir.*" *Film Noir Reader.* Ed. Alain Silver and James Ursini. New York: Limelight, 1996. 53-63.

Thompson, Kristin and David Bordwell. *Film History: An Introduction.* New York: McGraw-Hill, 1994.

Tu n'as rien vu à Hiroshima! Un grand film, "Hiroshima, mon amour", analysé par un group d'univérsitaires sous la direction de Raymond Ravar. Brussels: Editions de l'Institut de Sociologie / Université Libre de Bruxelles: 1962.

Willett, Ralph. *The Americanization of Germany, 1945-1949.* London: Routledge, 1989.

Zolotow, Maurice. *Billy Wilder in Hollywood.* New York: Putnam's, 1977.

Chapter 12

VISUALIZING THE NATION

Madonnas and Mourning Mothers in
Postwar Germany

Mariatte C. Denman

n 14 November 1993, Germany's *Volkstrauertag* (national day of
mourning), a remodeled Neue Wache was dedicated and inscribed
"Zentrale Gedenkstätte für die Opfer von Krieg und Gewaltherrschaft"
(Central Memorial for the Victims of War and Tyranny), thus replacing the
former East German memorial that had commemorated the victims of war
and militarism.[1] Located on Unter den Linden, the Neue Wache is a
national memorial built from 1817 to 1818 after the German Wars of
Liberation by Karl Friedrich Schinkel under the auspices of Prussian king
Friedrich Wilhelm III (Tietz 9 ff.).[2] Positioned at the center of the

---

1. All translations from the German are mine. I am grateful to Patricia Herminghouse, Magda Mueller, and Anna K. Kuhn for their constructive comments on earlier versions of this article. I would also like to thank my colleagues Cathy Byrd and Simone
Novak for their insightful suggestions, and Freja Koch for her photograph of Kollwitz's
sculpture *Mutter mit totem Sohn*.

2. Before Germany's unification in 1990, the Neue Wache was the East German
national memorial; in 1956 the East German municipal council in Berlin decided to
restore the severely damaged Neue Wache, except for the partially melted altar-like granite block designed by Heinrich Tessenow in 1931, which would bear witness to the war.
In 1960, the inscription, "To the Victims of Fascism and Militarism," was added. In
1969, the granite block was replaced by a glass cube housing a burning flame. Two hori-
zontal tombstones, which covered the urns containing the ashes of an unknown German
resistance fighter, an unknown German soldier, and soil samples from nine concentration
camps and nine World War II battle fields, were placed in front of the cube (Tietz 86). For
a detailed description of the history of the Neue Wache, see also Büchten.

redesigned interior is an enlarged replica of Käthe Kollwitz's sculpture *Mutter mit totem Sohn* (Mother with Her Dead Son, 1937). This slightly larger than life-sized sculpture depicts a mother embracing her dead son, who is lying in a fetal position between her knees (Figure 1). As the news magazine *Der Spiegel* polemically announced: "Enlarged Kollwitz Pietà in the Neue Wache: a Christian war memorial for murdered Jews" (Hohmeyer 268).

Figure 1

Photograph Freja Koch

The controversy surrounding the reconfigured Neue Wache began even before the government, without parliamentary debate or public competition, announced on 27 January 1993 its decision to install a replica of Kollwitz's Pietà in the Neue Wache. In February Walter Jens, the president of the Akademie der Künste (art academy), wrote an open letter to Chancellor Helmut Kohl protesting the commodification of the Kollwitz sculpture (189). Several newspaper articles subsequently expressed misgivings about the politics of commemoration displayed in the Neue Wache, which not only appropriated Christian iconography for a national memorial but also represented the victims of different historical causes such as war victims, victims of the Holocaust, and fallen soldiers as a homogenous group (Reichel 104 ff., Koselleck 96 ff.).[3] In May a group of art historians sent an open letter to the president of the Bundestag, Rita Süssmuth, opposing the representational nexus of motherhood alongside concepts of national sacrifice. They argued that the apotheosis of motherly sacrifice was rather cynical in view of the social reality of many women, who face discrimination in the work place and the increasing threat of unemployment (quoted in Feßmann 103).[4] These attempts to raise fundamental questions about the role of history and commemoration in unified Germany, however, did not impact the plans for the Neue Wache.[5] Why is a mother figure used to represent the mourning, recovering nation? And why does this seemingly innocent symbol stir such public outcry?

The intersection of visual representations of mourning mothers with configurations of German national identity participates in a problematic reading of national history. An analysis of the recent debate over the Neue Wache reveals that the Kollwitz sculpture incorporates the powerful nexus of motherhood and national iconography, a nexus that was also

3. Reinhart Koselleck suggested inscribing the national memorial "Den Toten – gefallen, ermordet, vergast, umgekommen, vermißt" [To the dead – fallen, murdered, gassed, killed, missing], (34).

4. See also Hoffmann-Curtius and Wenk on allegorical representations of mothers and femininity in national rituals of commemoration and images of the state. I am indebted to Silke Wenk who has generously shared her thoughts and her articles on the Neue Wache.

5. Christoph Stölzl, the government representative for the project, justified the plans for the Neue Wache by saying that decisions about the design of the flag and the national hymn of the Federal Republic were also made by the government without the input of the parliament, or the public (195). After the rededication of the Neue Wache, the controversy continued. A counter exhibition, *Im Irrgarten Deutscher Geschichte: Die Neue Wache 1818-1993*, problematizing the reconfigured Neue Wache was held at the Kleine Humboldt Gallery in November 1993 to January 1994. See the collection of essays for the exhibition edited by Daniela Büchten that assembles a spectrum of critical views on the history of the Neue Wache.

crucial in Germany's search for national identity in the immediate post-war period, as several examples of visual representations of mourning mothers in magazines of the late 1940s illustrate.[6]

In 1991, when debates about a site for the national memorial began, Germany's search for a new identity was a volatile issue. The second massive postwar German exodus from East to West was abating while the influx of Eastern European refugees and immigrants of German heritage increased dramatically. By then, tensions between East and West Germans had intensified and disappointment about slow economic progress in the East had become evident. Controversies surrounding the involvement of renowned writers such as Christa Wolf, Heiner Müller, and others with the East German secret police (Stasi) raised questions about Germany's Stalinist legacy.[7] Finally, xenophobic violence against foreigners, asylum seekers, and immigrants prompted a revision of legislation governing political asylum in 1992. The resurgence of xenophobia also mobilized citizens to reclaim the public sphere by organizing candlelight demonstrations.[8] But, as Jürgen Habermas noted, instead of seeking political solutions to ease the social and cultural tensions that followed German unification, politicians and voters sought refuge in the motto, "We have to become a normal people again" (93).

As plans for a national memorial site evolved, both the Neue Wache and the Kollwitz sculpture seemed to offer the necessary attributes for this return to "normality," since the Neue Wache was a well-known component of German collective memory and Kollwitz's depiction of motherhood evokes what many perceive to be "universal" sentiments. For Helmut Kohl the sculpture symbolized hope and indestructible humanity and connected national history to personal memories of fallen sol-

6. As space is limited, I will focus here on the issue of the representation of the National Socialist legacy. The reconfigured Neue Wache, however, also offers a specific reading of East German history and Stalinism by subsuming National Socialism and Stalinism under the general term *Gewaltherrschaft* [tyranny or despotism]. The inscription equates Stalinism with National Socialism and thereby obfuscates both the complex relationship between the former FRG and GDR and the history of the cold war.

7. I am referring here to what has become known as the *deutsch-deutsche Literaturstreit* [German-German literature debate], or the Christa Wolf controversy which revolved around Christa Wolf's novel *Was bleibt* (What Remains) in 1990. Wolf had written this book, which delineates her experience of being under Stasi surveillance, in 1979, but only released it in 1990. This was seen as an act of complicity with the East German system by West German critics such as Frank Schirrmacher of the newspaper *Frankfurter Allgemeine Zeitung* (FAZ). For further reading on the importance and complexity of the Christa Wolf controversy see Anz, Huyssen, and Anna K. Kuhn.

8. See the controversy surrounding German national identity in *Die Zeit*: "Die Nation gehört nicht der Rechten." *Die Zeit* 43 (1993); and "Es ist wieder modern, sich zur Nation zu bekennen … Mach's nicht noch mal, Deutschland!" *Die Zeit* 44 (1993).

diers, of air raids, and flights of refugees (Stölzl 215). In a similar vein, Christoph Stölzl, the director of the German Historical Museum and Chancellor Kohl's advisor, emphasized that a mourning mother would not only touch the emotions of the people, but would also be an appropriate symbol for Germany's new attitude toward the catastrophes of this century (196). The message conveyed by Kohl and Stölzl was that Germany should revise its history in order to normalize it.

In James Young's view, the problem with national memorial sites is not just the selectivity of public memory, which is inevitable to the process of remembering; rather "the real danger may lie in an uncritical approach to monuments, so that a reified and constructed memory is accepted as normative history – and then acted upon as if it were pure, unmediated meaning" (182). In his study on Holocaust memorials, Young suggests that the aim of examining public memorial sites is to focus on the manner in which historical events are mediated and produced through particular narratives (5). German history, as represented in the Neue Wache, is intertwined with the symbolism of the mourning mother that combines kinship sentiments implied by the mother-son constellation and an idea of the German national community. Moreover, Kollwitz's work, known for its frequent representation of mourning mothers and suffering communities,[9] evokes a notion of solidarity based on shared memories of the suffering caused by war. In a similar vein, a simultaneous reading of the inscription "Central Memorial for the Victims of War and Tyranny" and the sculpture suggests that the mother, as an allegory for the mourning nation, embraces the son who embodies both victims and perpetrators of the Third Reich and Stalinism equally. Yet as critics argue, the obliteration of the difference between victims and perpetrators that the memorial proposes conflicts with Kollwitz's anti-war stance and her critique of nationalistic political movements (see Feßmann). In the context of the socio-political tensions of reunited Germany, this problematic incorporation of different groups under one sign in the Neue Wache clearly propagates historical closure and transhistorical reconciliation.

* * *

The Kollwitz sculpture placed in the Neue Wache not only obfuscates a confrontation with the legacy of National Socialism but, as a symbol for humanity, also conforms to the tradition of West German national

9. Examples of Kollwitz's work are the lithography *Pietà* (1903), or the lithography *Bauernkrieg* (Farmer's War, 1903), the woodcut *Das Opfer* (The Victim/Sacrifice, 1922/23), and the sculpture *Zwei wartende Soldatenfrauen* (Two Waiting Soldier's Wives, 1943).

memorials after the World War II. In contrast to World War I memorials honoring fallen soldiers, sites of commemoration after 1945 remind the viewer of the effect the war had on the entire German population (Mosse 215-19). By adopting the Christian iconography of motherhood, by integrating a Kollwitz sculpture into the design, and by positioning all Germans as victims of the war instead of victims, bystanders, and perpetrators of National Socialism, the politics of memory established in the Neue Wache also seems to reiterate aspects of German nation-building from 1945 to 1949. During this period, the search for moral and cultural values – and for a narrative imputing meaning to the experience of war and National Socialism – dominated the discourse on German national identity.[10] As in the recent example of the reconfigured Neue Wache, this search was also interlaced in complex ways with the discourse on motherhood, as the following examples from the interregnum years illustrate.

In the first few years after Germany's defeat, madonna images and pictorial representations of mothers with their sons appeared frequently in newspapers, women's magazines, and election posters in East and West German sectors (Zur Nieden 75 ff.). In contrast to single women, mothers were rarely the target of caricatures.[11] When in 1946 the American-licensed newspaper *Die Neue Zeitung* published the caricature entitled *Das Mutterkreuz* (The Motherhood Medal), depicting a pregnant woman with her four children about to receive the National Socialist Motherhood Medal from a Hitleresque figure, readers wrote angry letters to the editor. Calling the caricature a public insult, one reader considered the demeaning depiction of the pregnant mother an act of violence. Erich

---

10. See, for example, the journals *Die Wandlung, Der Ruf,* and *Der Aufbau.* For further reading on the political and cultural formation of West Germany, see Glaser, Hay, Hallwirth, Koebner, and Malzahn.

11. The myth of motherhood and the virtues of the "motherly woman" stood in contrast to controversies surrounding the sexuality of single women, which converged with the discourse on Germany's defeat and occupation by the Allies. The fraternizing single woman in particular was a popular theme in journals, newspapers, and caricatures. Challenging male control over women's sexuality, single women epitomized a threat to the national cultural order. Caricatures and satirical comments about them reflect the underlying tensions of a nation in which the black market and the economic contributions of fraternizing women were essential for the survival of many. The scandal surrounding Will Forst's film *Die Sünderin* (The Sinful Woman, 1951), the story of a young woman who was drawn into prostitution and assisted the suicide of a painter who was gradually losing his sight, not only aroused a debate over the erosion of bourgeois norms regulating female sexuality; it was also considered by the religious establishment as a threat to postwar concepts of masculinity (Fehrenbach 110 ff.). See Maria Höhn's analysis of the postwar discourse on women in *Der Spiegel* and Elizabeth Heinemann's examination of the *Trümmerfrau* [woman of the rubble] in West German collective memory.

Kästner, one of the editors of *Die Neue Zeitung*, apologized, stating that his newspaper did not intend to mock motherhood. Those readers disturbed by the image, he insisted however, should not forget the popular support of the "production" of children that the National Socialist war machine enjoyed (3). The caricature clearly challenged the myth of motherhood that continued to exist in the immediate postwar period by underscoring the role of National Socialist pronatalist politics.

Readers favored representations of motherhood, such as the 1946 series of photographic representations of the madonna, from different countries in the American-licensed illustrated magazine *Heute*. These images were accompanied by conciliatory commentaries that praised the madonna's endurance of pain and her exemplary and timeless role as an emblem of love and peace. In the same year, the Soviet-licensed women's magazine *Für Dich* published a photo of Kollwitz's bronze sculpture entitled *Der Turm der Mütter* (Tower of Mothers, 1938). The bodies of several mothers tightly arranged in a circle form a unity representing mothers with "all their pain and kindness" as the text below the photograph states.

After her death in 1945, Kollwitz's art was hailed as exemplifying not only the mother's hardship, but also the suffering of the *Volk*. In 1947, in memory of Kollwitz (1867-1945), the Berlin dancer and choreographer Dore Hoyer, a student of Mary Wigman, and her group performed scenes based on some of the artist's drawings and etchings. In the scene *Mutter im Krieg* (Mother in War), kneeling and crouching dancers in black dresses with scarves covering their heads perform a cycle of female suffering in war times. Expressing gestures of mourning, sacrifice, and pleading, this scene reaches beyond an individual ritual of commemoration. As the Soviet-licensed journal *Theater der Zeit* stated, Dore Hoyer and Käthe Kollwitz represent the *Volk*: "They are the *Volk*, they are the passionate voice of its longing, the cry of humanity" (Palitzsch 17). Both Kollwitz's sculpture *Der Turm der Mütter* and Hoyer's performance inscribe a concept of history in which images of femininity represent the universal experience of loss and pain caused by war.

A similar theme can be found in a drawing of a 1946 issue of the American-licensed newspaper *Die Zeit* that shows a woman standing at the edge of a cemetery (Figure 2). She is holding a young boy's hand while pointing to an endless field of crosses. Entitled "Persecuted for their belief, their conviction, their race, or their ethnicity," the caption beneath the image comments:

> Last Sunday, all of Germany commemorated the unfortunate victims who had lost their lives in the fight against National Socialist dictatorship and who were murdered in concentration camps (*Die Zeit*, 12 September 1946: 1)

While the text refers to the victims of the resistance and the Holocaust, the crosses in the drawing allude to a military cemetery. This tension between the text and the image imbues the mother, the son, and the fallen soldiers with the status of victims of National Socialism, while the Christian iconography visually elides the commentary's reference to Holocaust victims. Besides creating a common memory rooted in a military war narrative, the text, with the statement *"all* of Germany commemorated …," also seeks to represent a united Germany in the face of emerging political and social tensions between the East and West German sectors governed by the Allied forces. As the images in the newspapers and magazines illustrate, it is the mother figure, a symbol of community which was shared by East and West Germans alike, that underscores this message.

Figure 2 Drawing by Szewczuk, courtesy of Die Zeit

Zeichnung: Szewczuk

Verfolgt wegen ihres Glaubens, ihrer Überzeugung, ihrer Rasse oder ihres Volkstums

Am vergangenen Sonntag wurde in ganz Deutschland der unglücklichen Opfer gedacht, die im Kampf gegen die nationalsozialistische Diktatur ihr Leben ließen und in den Konzentrationslagern ermordet wurden

The depiction of the mourning woman viewing the cemetery seems to also propose that women stand at the margins of history as observers. As many articles in West German publications during the immediate postwar period suggested, women as bystanders of political events were not held accountable for National Socialism.[12] Not only in debates about women's roles in the West German political arena did images of femininity and the family serve to restore the shattered social and cultural order (Moeller 21); many women also understood themselves as guardians of the eternal virtues, hearth, and home. Gertrud Bäumer for instance argues in *Der Neue Weg der Deutschen Frau* (The New Path of the German Woman, 1946) that because of women's specific inclination toward higher values and their innate difference from men, the "motherly woman" has a particular role to play in the reconstruction of the German family.

Bäumer was a representative of nationalistic social politics during the Weimar Republic and an influential figure in the bourgeois women's movement since 1899, and in the *Bund Deutscher Frauen* Vereine (Frauenvereine) (*BDF,* Federation of German Women's Association) until its dissolution in 1933 under National Socialism. During the immediate postwar period until 1947, Bäumer's books were banned by the British censors because of her publications during the Third Reich, in which she employed mythological imagery of a national community and essentialist assumptions about womanhood and the Volk along the lines of National Socialist ideology, although without its blood and soil tenets (Evans 261).[13]

After 1945, Bäumer did not critically reassess the premises of her ideals of femininity, which had supported National Socialist politics of motherhood. Instead she argued that National Socialism was a "men's state" that promoted professional opportunities for men while curtailing women's political influence and abusing their "natural instincts" in women's organizations. In Bäumer's vision of a postwar Germany, the "new path for German women" meant a reversion to the special status of mothers and women within the family as the source of healing powers that would eventually enable the "rebirth" of the German national community.

12. For articles documenting this view see Annette Kuhn, volume 2. My analysis of the intersection between concepts of femininity and political debates focuses on West German sectors. It is important to note that while many East German magazines such as those cited above also depicted motherhood as a value unscathed by history, the East German constitution implemented a concept of family and motherhood based on gender equality, which also included regulations regarding women's employment; see Ferree on the differences between East and West German legislation of gender equality.

13. See Evans (Chapters 5, 7, and 8) and Koonz (Chapters 4 and 5) as well as Stefana Lefko's essay in this volume on Bäumer's problematic role in the German women's movement before 1933 and during the Third Reich.

In a similar vein, a 1946 article in the West German magazine *Regen-bogen*, "Die Frau denkt mit dem Herzen" (Women think with their hearts), suggests that women, through their love, will succeed "in rebuild-ing a humble but happier new *Heimat* out of hardship and death, out of blood and tears, out of the ruins and rubble" (cited in Annette Kuhn 172). A representative of the World Organization of Mothers of All Nations (W.O.M.A.N.) even argues in 1949 that rather than fighting for women's rights, the mission of her organization was to contribute to an inclusion of the "feminine-motherly force" in a male world order whose imbalance had caused chaos (cited in Annette Kuhn 30).[14] As a symbol of reconciliation, consolation, and identification, motherhood became a utopian ideal that provided many women a sense of stability against the backdrop of a collapsed society (Moeller 33). However, the roles that motherhood and concepts of femininity had played in National Socialist ideology and social practices were simply excluded from this discourse. The same authors who viewed National Socialist mothers as being seduced into submitting themselves to a "perverse" [*entartete*] ideology – as Gertrud Bäumer argues in her book for example – did not examine the ways in which women were involved in what Hannah Arendt has coined "organized guilt" (Arendt 333 ff.): namely those National Socialist orga-nizations and institutions that either were complicit with or contributed to the extermination of millions, such as the National Socialist women's organizations, the SS and others, for which women had worked as secre-taries, doctors, and concentration camp guards.[15]

These idealistic postwar notions of femininity confined to the private sphere also stood in stark contrast to the dire social reality of many fam-ilies headed by women and to legal debates on women's rights from 1945 to 1949. While the newly drafted and promulgated West German Basic Law granted women equality in 1949, the *Bürgerliches Gesetzbuch* (Civil Code) regulating the status of married women and their work was not revised until 1953 because the family was considered the cultural foun-dation of the German nation. As a result, women as German citizens were given equal constitutional rights, whereas as mothers and wives they remained subject to their husbands' authority as household head.[16]

---

14. Many postwar West German women's organizations adopted similar premises, based on a complementary definition of gender difference, for their concept of women's roles in a new German nation. See Annette Kuhn (Vol. 2, Chapter 1).

15. For an analysis of women's complicity with National Socialist ideological and social practices, see Koonz, Evans, and Frevert. Research on female perpetrators, however, has remained a blind spot in feminist research until the present, as Gudrun Schwarz argues.

16. As Robert Moeller notes, "before setting out to define the particulars of the *Grundgesetz* (Basic Law, M.D.), the political leaders in the Parliament Council agreed that

Surprisingly, even in post-unification visual culture, the representation of the mourning mother is employed to produce and sustain a specific reading of national history. As an allegory for the mourning German nation, the Kollwitz replica in the Neue Wache, like the images in postwar German print media, unites remembrance of the war with a longing for a new beginning at a time of historical transition when national identity is at stake. By combining memories of the past with a utopian longing for unity and solidarity, these representations of mourning mothers function to establish a foundational mythology. As Roland Barthes argues, myths are not perceived as historically constructed cultural narratives, but as eternal, permanent, and untainted by ideology or history. By obliterating historicity, Barthes writes, "myth has the task of giving an historical intention a natural justification, and making contingency appear eternal" (142). As a form of national mythology, the images of mourning mothers contribute to a dialectic of remembering and forgetting, which Ernest Renan described in his famous essay "What Is a Nation?" (1882). According to Renan the "essence of the nation" is established via mutual memories and a shared attempt to forget, through which violent events of the past slip into oblivion (11). As these postwar and post-unification German examples illustrate, representations of motherhood play a crucial role in the effort not only to mold discrete memories into a unified narrative of the victims of the war, but also to circumvent confrontation with the memories of Germany's specific National Socialist past. For these gendered visualizations of Germanness unite a discourse on historical responsibility with a kinship narrative that seeks to generate a sense of solidarity, coherence, and meaning against the backdrop of political tensions.

---

the catalogue of basic rights should not touch upon specific social and economic policies or the structures of the 'cultural order' [*Kulturordnung*]" (62). See also Ferree and Böttgen for a discussion of the role of motherhood in the political debates about the Basic Law and the Civil Code.

Bibliography

Anz, Thomas. *'Es geht nicht um Christa Wolf': Der Literaturstreit im vereinten Deutschland.* Münich: Spangenberg, 1991.

Arendt, Hannah. "Organisierte Schuld." *Die Wandlung* 4 (1945): 333-44.

Barthes, Roland. *Mythologies.* Trans. Annette Lavers. London: Vintage, 1993.

Bäumer, Gertrud. *Der neue Weg der deutschen Frau.* Stuttgart: Deutsche Verlags-Anstalt, 1946.

Böttger, Barbara. *Das Recht auf Gleichheit und Differenz: Elisabeth Selbert und der Kampf der Frauen um Art. 3.2 Grundgesetz.* Münster: Verlag Westfälisches Dampfboot, 1990.

Büchten, Daniela and Anja Frey, eds. *Im Irrgarten deutscher Geschichte.* Berlin: Schriftenreihe Aktives Museum, 1994.

"Der Turm der Mütter." *Für Dich* 15 (1946): 17.

Evans, Richard J. *The Feminist Movement in Germany 1894-1933.* London: Sage Publications, 1976.

Fehrenbach, Heide. *Cinema in Democratizing Germany: Reconstructing National Identity after Hitler.* Chapel Hill: U of North Carolina P, 1995.

Ferree, Myra Marx. "Patriarchies and Feminisms. The Two Women's Movements of Post-Unification Germany." *Social Politics* 2.1 (1995): 10-24.

Feßmann, Jörg, ed. *Streit um die Neue Wache: Zur Gestaltung einer Zentralen Gedenkstätte.* Berlin: Akademie der Künste, 1993.

Frevert, Ute. *Women in German History: From Bourgeois Emancipation to Sexual Liberation.* Trans. Stuart McKinnon-Evans. Oxford: Berg, 1989.

Glaser, Hermann. *The Rubble Years: The Cultural Roots of Postwar Germany.* Trans. Franz Feige, Patricia Gleason. New York: Paragon House, 1986.

Habermas, Jürgen. *Vergangenheit als Zukunft.* Ed. Michael Haller. Munich: Piper, 1993.

Hallwirth, Uta. *Auf der Suche nach einer neuen Identität? Zum nationalen Selbstverständnis in der westdeutschen Presse 1945-1955.* Frankfurt: Peter Lang, 1987.

Hay, Gerhard, et al. *Als der Krieg zu Ende war: Literarisch-politische Publizistik 1945-1950.* Katalog Nr. 23. Stuttgart: Klett, 1973.

Heineman, Elizabeth Diane. "The Honor of the Woman: Memories of Germany's 'Crisis Years' and West German Identity." *American Historical Review* 101.2 (1996): 354-95.

Hoffmann-Curtius, Kathrin. "Ein Mutterbild für die Neue Wache." Büchten and Frey. 60-63.

Hohmeyer, Jürgen. "Mutter im Regen." *Der Spiegel* 46 (1993): 268-70.

Höhn, Maria. "Frau im Haus und Girl im *Spiegel*: Discourse on Women in the Interregnum Period of 1945-1949 and the Question of German Identity." *Central European History* 26 (1993): 57-90.

Huyssen, Andreas. "After the Wall: The Failure of German Intellectuals." *New German Critique* 52 (Winter 1991): 109-43.

Jens, Walter. "Offener Brief an den Bundeskanzler Dr. Helmut Kohl." Stölzl. 189-90.

Kästner, Erich. "Nochmals: Das Mutterkreuz." *Die Neue Zeitung* 28 January, 1946: 3.

Koebner, Thomas, et al. *Deutschland nach Hitler*. Opladen: Westdeutscher Verlag, 1987.

Koonz, Claudia. *Mothers in the Fatherland: Women, the Family and Nazi Politics*. New York: St. Martin's Press, 1986.

Koselleck, Reinhart. "Stellen uns die Toten einen Termin?" Feßmann. 27-34.

_____. "Bilderverbot. Welches Totengedenken?" *Frankfurter Allgemeine Zeitung* 8 April, 1993. Also in Feßmann. 96-99.

Kuhn, Anna K. "'Ist eine Königin köpfen effektiver als einen König köpfen': The Gender Politics of the Christa Wolf Controversy." *German Monitor* 31 (1995): 200-15.

Kuhn, Annette, ed. *Frauen in der deutschen Nachkriegszeit*. 2 vols. Düsseldorf: Schwann, 1986.

Malzahn, Manfred. *Germany 1945-1949*. London: Routledge, 1991.

Moeller, Robert. *Protecting Motherhood: Women and the Family in the Politics of Postwar West Germany*. Berkeley: University of California Press, 1993.

Mosse, George L. *Fallen Soldiers*. New York: Oxford UP, 1990.

"Offener Brief an die Bundestagspräsidentin Frau Prof. Dr. Rita Süssmuth." *Die Tageszeitung* 18 May 1993. Also in Feßmann. 103-4.

Palitzsch, Peter H. "Ursprung des Schöpferischen." *Theater der Zeit* 1 (1947): 15-18.

Reichel, Peter. "Täter und Opfer – im Gedenken gleich?" Feßmann. 104-7.

Renan, Ernest. "What is a Nation?" (1882). *Nation and Narration*. Ed. Homi K. Bhabha. London: Routledge, 1990. 8-21.

Schwarz, Gudrun. "Verdrängte Täterinnen: Frauen im Apparat der SS (1939-1945)." *Nach Osten: Verdeckte Spuren nationalsozialistischer Verbrechen*. Ed. Theresa Wobbe. Frankfurt am Main: Neue Kritik, 1992. 197-227.

Stölzl, Christoph, ed. *Die Neue Wache Unter den Linden*. Berlin: Koehler & Amelang, 1993.

_____. "Die Trauer der Mutter: Plädoyer im Denkmalstreit um die Neue Wache: Sprechendes Mitleid statt Sprachloser Stein." *Frankfurter Allgemeine Zeitung* 13 March, 1993. Also in Stölzl. 195-97.

Tietz, Jürgen. "Schinkels Neue Wache Unter den Linden: Baugeschichte 1816-1993." Stölzl. 9-93

Wenk, Silke. *Versteinerte Weiblichkeit: Allegorien in der Skulptur der Moderne*. Köln: Böhlau, 1996.

Young, James E. *Writing and Rewriting the Holocaust: Narrative and the Consequences of Interpretation*. Bloomington: Indiana UP, 1988.

Zur Nieden, Susanne. "Mütter des Herzens: Überlegungen zu einem Frauenbild in der Alltagsliteratur der ersten Jahre nach dem Zweiten Weltkrieg." *So nah beieinander und doch so fern*. Eds. Agnes Joester and Insa Schöningh. Pfaffenweiler: Centaurus Verlag, 1992. 75-89.

Chapter 13

FRAMING THE *UNHEIMLICH*

Heimatfilm and Bambi

Ingeborg Majer O'Sickey

In the beginning, the word *Heimat* [homestead, homeland] signified the male's right to inherit the land. The early nineteenth-century saying, "the youngest son gets the *Heimat*," launched the term
linguistically, gendered it, and attached property and social status to it.
As Gertraud Steiner points out, *Heimat* in the sense of "homestead"
began as a specific term that marked social and economic class, so that
finding oneself *heimatlos* [homeless] "did not only represent an emotional low point, but meant quite concretely the condition of poverty
and social insecurity." Ownership or lack of *Heimat* [homestead], in
rural Germany, sorted people into a master/servant structure (11).
Thereafter, *Heimat* stretched into a rubber band of multiple meanings,
as seen in such interpretations as Heinrich Heine's vision of *Heimat*
sharpened by distance ("Heimat aus der Ferne"); Walter Benjamin's
notion that *Heimat* constitutes a journey back to one's childhood, satu-
rated with a longing for the past *(Städtebilder);* and Martin Heidegger's
later ideas that language makes up the "Haus des Seins" [the house of
self/being] that constitutes that *Heimat*.[1]

Heimatkunst [folk art] and *Heimatliteratur*, which took hold shortly
after the term *Heimat* came into being, created romantic images of a
world untouched by encroaching industrialism. Idyllic images of "home-

---

1. See Iring Fetscher, "Heimatliebe – Brauch und Mißbrauch eines Begriffs"
(16, 31).

on-the-range" that would be recycled well into the late 1990s had their beginnings not only in Heinrich von Kleist's, but in Gottfried Keller's and Annette von Droste-Hülshoff's nineteenth-century works. The villages depicted in some of these works seem to come straight from Josef Knilling's canvas *Deutsches Dorf* (German village). Best-sellers, such as Ludwig Ganghofer's novels that reached sales in the millions in the late 1880s, transported readers to a *locus amoenus* they savored in the paintings of Caspar David Friedrich. Even contemporary makers of *Heimat* on celluloid derive their ideas of countryside and village life from these traditional images, which, as Elisabeth Eisert-Rost and others point out, were always already derivative images of a topical world that had less to do with reality than with the way the bourgeoisie imagined country folk around the turn of the century (21).

Even this necessarily brief sketch suggests that the corpus of literary, artistic, and philosophical production relating to *Heimat* is enormous and varied. Without suggesting that the social sciences offer a tidy definition for *Heimat*, two texts may nevertheless serve to ground a discussion of the concept. One is from a 1986 essay by the renowned cultural anthropologist Ina-Maria Greverus, the other from Freud's 1919 essay "The Uncanny" (which will be treated in the second part of this essay). In her first thesis of fourteen, Greverus writes:

> I believe that the territorial imperative is a *conditio humana*. In this sense, the territorial imperative as a basic human orientation toward a territory offering the gratification of need for safety, activity, and identity is both intentional and based on primary requirements for existence (18).

This description implies that *Heimat* as real-estate is not only charged with providing economic and physical protection, but that *Heimat* embraces an individual's definition of self, and is therefore an integral part of identity. By asking basic existential questions such as "who am I?" and "where do I come from?" a genealogical framework is invoked. This and similar postulates of *Heimat* as "territorial imperative" reverberate throughout German history, testifying to the pursuit of *Heimat* as a battle for white, masculinized subjectivity.

If notions of *Heimat* partook of sexist and racialist discourse by way of Germany's colonial policies in the nineteenth century, the Nazis' further racialization of *Heimat* with claims for *Lebensraum* [space to live] and *Blut und Boden* (signifying that the presence of German blood confers on Germans the right to a territory) only added to the ideological baggage attributed to *Heimat*. After World War II *Heimatfilm* continued seamlessly, often with the same directors and actors, and dominated West German screens unchallenged until 1962, when New German Cinema filmmakers declared war on *Opa's Kino* [Grandpa's cinema]. Side by side with the classical *Heimatfilm*, the *anti-Heimatfilm* appeared in the wake of the cultural revolution of the late 1960s. A number of remarkable films critical of the concept of *Heimat* and of the traditional *Heimatfilm* were made by filmmakers like Herbert Achternbusch (creator of more than a dozen *anti-Heimat* films), Peter Fleischmann, and R.W. Fassbinder.[2] These filmmakers revealed the construction of identity and the fabrication of tradition as interested discourses of *Heimat*. While challenging the legitimacy of such reconstructions they boldly foreground their own work as the result of their participation in the discursive apparatus of cinema. On a totally different track from his New German Cinema colleagues, Edgar Reitz's spectacularly engaging 16-hour family saga *Heimat* (1984; shown both on television and in the cinema) serves as the most striking example of a contemporary rehabilitation of West German *Heimat*.[3] Although technically more refined than the run-of-the-mill *Heimat* film, and thus an aesthetic break in terms of genre expectation, Reitz's film satisfies yearnings for an organic, homogenized culture. Reconstructing the years from 1919 to 1982 in the life of a family from Schabbach (located in the Hunsrück mountains) with painstaking attention to cultural accuracy, Reitz's film was to present an alternative to the depiction of German history in the American TV series *Holocaust*, which had created an unprecedented level of discussion when it was aired on German television in 1978. Although the years 1933-1945 comprise more than half of the film, *Heimat* brackets the Holocaust as a historical fact. One might say that the (non)treatment of the Shoah and its tacit approval and reproduction of *Heimat* within traditional gender roles practically guaranteed success at the box office and positive critical reception. *Der Spiegel*, for example, praised it for presenting history from the perspective of individual biographies, and used the film's success as proof of the rehabilitation of the long-despised term *Heimat* and as revelatory of newly articulated emotions about *Heimat* in West Germany in recent years (252).

Framing Classical *Heimatfilm*

Heimat and film seem a match made in cinematic heaven with the camera recording their marriage with idyllic or dramatic panoramas of snow-

2. They drew on works by Marieluise Fleisser, Ferdinand Bruckner, and Ödön von Horváth, who radicalized the genre of Bavarian folk drama in the 1920s and 1930s (Elsaesser 141).

3. For pragmatic reasons, discussion of post-World War II films is limited to the West German *Heimatfilm*.

capped mountains and luscious meadows as a background. Its unique ability to make films from *Heimatliteratur* and *Heimatkunst* resulted in successful adaptations of *Heimat* novels such as Ludwig Ganghofer's 1917 blockbuster *Schloß Hubertus* (Hubertus Castle) and Wilhelmine von Hillern's *Die Geyerwally* (Vulture-Wally, 1875).[4] But is the union of *Heimat* film quite as unproblematic as this portrayal implies? It would seem that film would drag *Heimat*'s tarnished image even deeper through the mud.[5] After all, film is vexingly polyvalent as a vehicle, from the pristine to the vulgar, and reeks of the forbidden in its solicitation of Peeping Janes and Toms as its customers. From the biblical twin-cities Sodom and Gomorrah on, vice has had its locus in the city. Ethnic and racial otherness, too, are portrayed as urban phenomena, at their most extreme in Nazi iconography, where Jews are depicted scurrying furtively through the city's labyrinth passages. In sum, the city is the place where, as Josef Goebbels's racialist slur infers, "volksfremde Asphaltkultur" [rootless and alienated culture] flourishes. Thus, when refracted through considerations of medium and thematic, and when framed as a politics of gender and race intersecting with the politics of representation, *Heimatfilm* is a compounded term whose pressure point lies precisely in the threat that the outside (citified film) poses to the inside *(Heimat)*.

Heimatfilm responds vigorously to threats to its naturalized homogeneity. Some films thematize this by way of parody (in *anti-Heimat* films), while others deconstruct and/or reconceptualize traditional notions of *Heimat* (the latter will be considered at the end of the essay). By far the most persistent response comes from the classical *Heimatfilm*: hundreds of enormously popular films defend the turf of *Heimat* by constructing Germanized and hyper-masculinized bodies stuffed into *Lederhosen* and hyper-feminized maidens laced into dirndls, persisting even to this day in disavowing sexual diversity and multiculturalism in German society. Icons such as traditional costumes are immensely important to this disavowal.

Of the films surveyed for this study, none uses *Trachten* [traditional regional costumes] more conspicuously to buttress the native/other opposition by championing Bavarian happiness and wholesomeness

4. *Schloss Hubertus* was adapted to the screen three times, modified to suit the tastes of each period (1934, 1954, and 1973) (Elsaesser 141). Operas also served as pre-texts for the *Heimatfilm*, i.e., *Schwarzwaldmädel* (Black Forest Girl, 1950) was based on Leon Jessel's 1917 opera; the film was seen by over 16 million people when it came out, compared to the average film seen by between three and four million people (Steiner 89).

5. How deep this mud could be was revealed with the Lederhosen-Sex-Films of the 1970s. In 23 years, 77 *Heimatsexfilms* were produced, beginning with *Pudelnackt in Oberbayern* (Dir. Hans Albin, 1968) and ending with *Drei Lederhosen in St. Tropez* (Dir. Franz Marischka, 1981).

(codes for racial and sexual purity) than the film *Heimatland* (Homeland, 1953). Engaging traditional folklorist art, the film argues that the biggest threat to *Heimat* is the erosion of traditional values. This idea is demonstrated conspicuously in Herr Schnabel's speech in the village pub, echoing Nazi *Blut und Boden* propaganda of a decade earlier and thematizing the dangers of "foreign" influences and corrosive "elements" that undermine "Bodenständigkeit" [rootedness]. Schnabel's official position as town clerk and chairman of the region's organization for the protection of traditional costumes lends institutional power to his "theories." Although he reiterates his message to the point of becoming ridiculous, other iconography combines with film-technical strategies to keep the message intact. For example, a series of jump cuts from Schnabel to Bachinger configure the latter as an unstable character, establishing the moral lesson of the film; only the steadfast gamewarden, Bergheim, will get the prize (Helga). Bachinger is portrayed throughout in contempt of laws governing the jurisdiction of hunting game, the conventions of courting women, and defiant of the authority of the village elders, so that by the time he ends up in prison and is shot and killed by the gamewarden, the connection between Bachinger's violation of traditional values and his downfall has been firmly established.

Noteworthy too for the ways in which the *Heimatfilm* industry uses traditional costumes in order to promote indigenous German culture is Hans Deppe's instrumentalization (in *Schwarzwaldmädel*; Black Forest Girl, 1951) of the annual local festival showcasing traditional Black Forest costumes. Other icons as well turn out to be artifice: since the Black Forest did not look "real" enough for Deppe, he imported truckloads of carved and painted folklore art, furniture, wooden crucifixes, statues of the Madonna with child, and other carved holy figures and positioned these on location for a look of authenticity. As Steiner writes, even the village pub, the central location for the film's action, is a montage of shots from various houses in the region (90).

Finally, the most bizarre use of folk costumes and the genre's stock native/stranger opposition: *Der Schandfleck* (Mark of Dishonor, 1956) opens with a view of several exoticized dancers with feather headdresses and flowered knickerbockers dancing on a raised wooden stage set up in the village square. The dance – which appears to be a mixture of Native American and Bavarian folk dance – is staged for the villagers at the annual *Volksfest*. There is no contact between the dancers and the Bavarians, nor any reaction from the Bavarian villagers to the spectacle staged for their entertainment. They simply continue to sit or mill around in their native dress, chatting, drinking beer, and engaging in *Hinterland* politics. The tableau is set up for the sole purpose of contrasting "foreign culture" to Germanness. Images such as the ones described above found receptive audiences, reproducing and sustaining a culturally widespread rejection of anyone considered "deviant."

The *Unheimlich* [Uncanny] in Heimatfilm

It will be obvious now that it is necessary to add to the discussion of medium and thematics a combination of psychoanalytic and socioanalytic categories in order to get a sharper view of the stakes that *Heimat* film invests in. In the oft-cited essay, "Das Unheimliche" ("The Uncanny," 1919), Freud explains *Heimat* in terms of woman's genitalia, declaring that "neurotic men" experience these as *unheimlich* [uncanny]. Freud's remarkable confession is preceded by a long etymological demonstration of the multiple meanings of the word *unheimlich* (which include uncanny, homey, familiar, secret) and a compelling analysis of E.T.A. Hoffmann's story "The Sandman." Almost as an *après-coup*, Freud makes this amazing observation:

> It happens frequently that neurotic men declare that woman's genitalia is uncanny [*unheimliche*] to them. But this uncanny [*Unheimliche*] is the entrance to the ancient home [*zur alten Heimat*] of the human child, the entrance to the site of our first habitation. "Love is homesickness," the old saying goes, and when the dreamer remarks to himself during his dream: I know this, I've been here before, then the genitalia or the womb of the mother may be substituted. So, the uncanny is in this case also the formerly homey, the familiar. The "un" before *heimlich* [secret] marks its disavowal (75).

This intricate chain of substitution hides its own operation by nesting concepts as tidily as so many Russian wooden dolls: *Heimat* as mother, mother as *Heimat*, mother as home, mother as *unheimlich*, and therefore no longer *Heimat*. But, of course, this paragraph, uncanny itself, manifestly demonstrates "neurotic" men's fear of the uncanny, in that Freud discusses woman's genitalia only in their function of child-bearing. Uncanny, too, is the quality of virtual reality of "neurotic" men's perception of woman, which twists in an impossible denouement: she might have been good (*heimisch*, comforting in her familiarity), and she can never be as good – as she never was – again. Added to the original masculinized dimension of *Heimat* is this feminized one: the physical (female genitalia) and the psychical (a promise and the fear loss of familiarity and plenitude).

Programmatically stated, the *unheimlich* is the "Other" that *Heimat* seeks to keep out. The *unheimlich* combines with motion (picture) to abet *Heimat* in its need to repress the abject of female genitalia and in its mission to displace certain things. What are these "certain things"? Laura Mulvey's depiction of disavowal in her path-breaking 1975 essay "Pleasure and Narrative Cinema" may be helpful here. Using Freudian and Lacanian psychoanalytic theory in a feminist key, Mulvey theorizes filmic constructions of feminine and masculine subjectivity within masculinist culture. For our purposes, her explanation of the two modalities in filmic representation is most important. The first, the voyeuristic modality, expresses the desire to control the woman; the second, the fetishistic scopophilic mode, works as a mechanism for disavowal. Mulvey explains that the woman in narrative film "connotes something that the look continuously circles around but disavows: her lack of a penis, implying a threat of castration and hence unpleasure" (64). This series of compelling psychosocial and specific cinema-technical elements identifies *Heimat* and the *unheimlich* as consummately cinematic because of cinema's ability to control spatial as well as temporal dimensions, creating, as Mulvey points out, illusions that fit the viewers's pleasures (67). The camera's ability to adjust its *Einstellung*,[6] to move out of the frame that which would reveal the *unheimlich* in *Heimat*, produces the illusion of escape from the *unheimlich*. Thus, *Heimatfilm* as genre can be seen to reiterate the axiom that Germanness is marked by psychosocial processes having to do with loss and retrieval and the gendered and racial discourses surrounding them.

Framing Woman[7]

Basic to a reconsideration of *Heimatfilm* in such terms is the double notion of the camera's framing and the frame-up of female figures. Since cinema's favored object/ive is to frame women, and since that frame is produced by, and itself reproduces particular cultural views of women, *Heimatfilm* depends upon a few very specific images of femininity. In shorthand, these are: physical attractiveness defined as hyper-femininity, youth and virginity, daintiness (certainly always less muscular and shorter than the male lead), and a look of shyness.[8] *Heimatfilm* roughly coincides

6. As Elsaesser explains, this term must be understood in the sense of camera focus *and* moral viewpoint (5).

7. When I use the term "woman," it is to stress essentialization of women.

8. A notable exception is Wally in *Die Geyerwally* (Vulture-Wally, Dir. Hans Steinhoff, 1940), who is fiercely independent and quite wild (for example, she refuses the man her father picks and chooses Bärenjoseph instead, and when she suspects her lover of unfaithfulness, she hires a hit man to kill him). For all of her rebellion, in the end, she

with Hollywood's frame-up of Bambi as feminine principle. Originally created by Siegmund Salzmann (a.k.a. Felix Salten) in his novel *Bambi: A Life in the Woods* (1926), the first Bambi was a dark and realistic figure, drawn in harsh tones, reflecting Salzmann's experience with antisemitic Vienna and his presentiments of persecution by the Nazis.[9] It took another fourteen years for a sentimentalized Hollywood lens to capture Bambi for world consumption in the first Disney version (1942).

A major breakthrough for cinema was its discovery that Bambi's qualities as an innocent creature in need of protection made it an ideal symbol that would satisfy dominant cultural notions about femininity, i.e., about woman's "nature." With the bambified woman, cinema had found a simple way to create woman as visual yet unseen. Bambi-like shyness and timidity are conveyed by way of the female protagonists's posture (closed legs when seated, narrow stance when standing), controlled gestures, and tilted head posture either to the side or upward-looking (usually when shot with the male protagonist). Many films about *Heimat* instrumentalize the deer hunt and the Bambi myth to represent the woman as sexual prey and the man as sexual predator. In figuring woman as passive target of the active male gaze, bambified femininity vacates female attributes that are *unheimlich*. For example, in the enormously popular *Försterliesl* (Gamewarden's Liesl, Dir. Herbert Fredersdorf, 1955), Liesl is bambified in order to graft a particular femininity onto her. Indeed, framed with "Bambi" no less than twenty times, the female protagonist in *Försterliesl* offers a perfect demonstration that Freud's (and neurotic men's) creation of the ideal image of woman is always already a representation, a projection of masculinist needs. This echoes Mulvey's insight that woman is constructed as a passive object of the active male look, and is most consistently performed in narrative cinema in terms of a "to-be-looked-at-ness" which is based upon "an active/passive heterosexual division of labor" (62, 63). Bambification creates a masculinized viewing position that shields an embattled masculinity from fear of castration, fear of exclusion from the symbolic, fear of the Other, fear of ambivalence about origin. Cinematic maneuvers such as jump cuts and even reaction shots involving Liesl and the fawn plainly demonstrate woman's "to-be-looked-at-ness"; sound-bridging from one shot to another, and acting techniques involving body language that connote fragility, demureness, helplessness, and the like serve to connect woman to animal even if they are spatially separate, or were

meekly submits to Bärenjoseph after she realizes that he was innocent, and becomes the demure woman that *Heimatfilm* fosters.

9. I thank my colleague Sarah Elbert for leading me to Salzmann's work, which is housed in the Rheinhardt Special Collection at SUNY Binghamton.

previously unconnected thematically. An especially remarkable example is a sequence of shot-reverse-shots that show Liesl skipping through the meadow alternating with shots that show a fawn in a different location doing the same. Whenever such a sequence occurs, a number of panoramic shots of spectacular images of *Heimat* culminate in a zoom to the gamekeeper, marking the territory contiguously with the pair woman/ Bambi as part of *Heimat* possessed by the male.

This is exemplified in a sequence in which a hunting party from the city (headed by an absentee landlord, who vies for Liesl's favors) is prowling the forest. Liesl, who has run after an injured fawn, trips and sustains the same injury as the deer. The woman and the deer are thus not only linked in a shared impediment that makes them more vulnerable to the hunters, but following the formula of *Heimatfilm*, linked to the gamekeeper (the *Förster* of the film's title), who saves them. Thus, the unifying sign woman/fawn combines with the unifying discourse of (Bavarian) folk tradition to suture a message of "natural" purity as German.

The previously mentioned 1953 film *Heimatland*, too, constructs the female protagonist's vulnerability during "open season" by way of the poacher and the gamewarden, whose territory (Helga as *Heimat* and *Heimat* as Helga) is protected by law. In the second of two long sequences that are particularly revealing for the way in which the film conveys the woman as Bambi, Helga is whisked off in a driverless horse-drawn carriage on a hair-raising ride, during which she faints. After she is miraculously saved by Bachinger (the poacher), the camera performs a sequence that cuts from Bachinger propping up Helga against the carriage, to an image of a wobbly fawn in the meadow, and finally ends the sequence by zooming in on the arriving gamewarden. The zoom marks the gamewarden's claim on Helga. The metonymic slip from the feeble woman to the helpless fawn, infantilizes Helga, implying that, like the fawn, she is in need of protection. This sequence is preceded by Helga in her one-room school house, teaching the children the rules of the hunt. She tells them that a hunting license (issued by the village clerk, who is the same man who protects traditional costumes and customs) is required, that the gamewarden decides which animals are protected (fawns, does, and certain bucks), what the difference between a legitimate hunter and a poacher is. The courtship of Helga is framed in such a way that the viewer is very aware of the double entendre of her explanation of "hunting" rules. In their entirety, the two sequences thus manifest a double frame-up of woman: Helga is portrayed as submitting to being the hunter's prey and as upholding sexist traditions by teaching the rules of the sexual purchase to the children. By representing woman as happily participating in her own bambification, films can claim that "women like it." Helga's *Unheimlichkeit* (her sexuality and the secret of it) has thus been rendered (politically) ineffective for womanist interests. And indeed, the film shows that she serves patriarchal interests by vacating the position of power for the male. Given her place in the triangulated structure between the gamewarden and the poacher, she functions as a guarantor for white masculinist subjectivity. Socially and politically silenced, the feminine-as-reflection of masculinist projection protects the viewer of the *Heimatfilm* from too much femaleness. It is no accident that the word to 'screen' is used to mean 'project' when we talk about showing a film. As much as the *unheimlich* is banished from being seen, it strives to be *screened*, in this word's entire semantic range of to "project onto a screen," "shield," "shelter," "mask" and "erect a barrier."[10]

Revisions of Woman as *Heimat*

What then, of *Heimat* films of the 1980s and 1990s? How does the treatment of Germanness and gender in *Heimatfilm* evolve? Some films (besides the *anti-Heimatfilm*) deconstruct and/or reconfigure *Heimatfilm*. Compelling examples of this are Percy Adlon's 1990 *Salmonberries* and Michael Verhoeven's *Das schreckliche Mädchen* (The Nasty Girl, 1989/90). *Salmonberries* deconstructs *Heimat* as a key to identity from an "upside-down" geopolitical perspective: shot in Alaska and Berlin, Germanness and gender, Native Americanness and heterosexuality are interrogated from within and outside the borders of *Heimat*. Most of the film is shot in Kotzebue, an economically depressed town of about 3000 mostly Inupiaq Eskimo people, thirty-six miles north of the arctic circle. Even so, Germanness looms large throughout the film by way of Roswitha, who migrated to Kotzebue after she had escaped from East Berlin in the 1970s, and by way of the spectacular images of the fall of the Berlin Wall projected on Kotzebue television screens.

These events are refracted through the point of view of two women, Roswitha, the librarian (Rosel Zech) and the migrant mine worker, Kotz (k.d.lang). For all of their differences – Roswitha is a "straight," middle-class, educated, white East German; Kotz is "queer," lower-class, uneducated, white Inupiaq-Euroamerican – they share a very important structuring principle. Both women's identities are constituted in and by

10. The concept of "screen" also plays in the field of vision, to which belongs Lacan's famous remark, "If I am anything in the picture, it is always in the form of the screen" (cited in Silverman, 174). For a remarkable reading of Lacan's notion of the screen, see Silverman's discussion of the relation of the look, the gaze, and the screen in *The Threshold of the Visible World*.

historical trauma. Kotz, a lesbian in a world overwhelmingly ordered as heterosexual, was fathered in connection with the colonizers' migratory work and the exploitation of the Inupiaq people; an orphan, found in a card-board box in Kotzebue, she believes herself to be the direct descendant of Otto von Kotzebue. Roswitha's trauma is a result of the division of East and West Germany; fleeing from East Berlin, she was witness to her husband's brutal murder by East German border guards. The process of Roswitha's coming to terms with this trauma, and Kotz's discovery and coming to terms with her origins forges the women's friendship.

Both women seek to stabilize their identity by creating and uncreating fables of *Heimat*. They are aided in this by the media, a point made compellingly in the sequence that portrays Kotz watching CNN's live broadcast of the fall of the Berlin Wall. What she observes on the screen is both the continuation of Roswitha's story and the founding of the myth of an authentic national experience of unity. The constant repetition of citizens chanting "Wir sind ein Volk" ("We are One People") at the moment of revolution, confers an artificial unity upon the East Germans. But CNN's coverage not only creates a *Heimat* (defined by unity) but makes clear that such a narrative can only be constructed by the invention of an outside/r. The film frames this operation very nicely in the image of Kotz on top of the pinball machine in the *Grüne Linde* in East Berlin, and in her declaration to the crowded room "I understand you! I'm Eskimo. I'm Eskimo!" Her declaration serves to point to the tragedy (and impossibility) of residing in categories. Her declaration is met by two responses: a jeering one that says "Ick bin och en Eskimo" (Berlin dialect for "Yeah ... *right*. Me too") and a formal one in English, "We are all Eskimos." The first response is more appropriate, since irony seems the only possible response to Kotz's desire for commonalities based on equivalencies. Only laughter may be able to neutralize power differentials that inhere in the dichotomies of straight/queer, native/foreigner (Inupiaq-American/German), inside/outside (Berlin/Alaska), and so on. The remark "We are all Eskimos," which recalls John F. Kennedy's sound-bite "ich bin ein Berliner," is much closer to Kotz's own, of course, and along the trajectory of a CNN broadcast. Thus, made and released at a crucial point in German history (1989/90), *Salmonberries* more or less implicitly problematizes the notion that coming to terms with *Heimat* is a homogeneous process that can be legitimated by appealing to the authenticity of historical and/or personal narratives.

While Adlon's film deconstructs the entire notion of the redemptive possibility of *Heimat* for outsiders (lesbian and heterosexual women, East Germans, Inupiaqs) and posits living in categories pertaining to *Heimat* as an impossibility, Michael Verhoeven's 1989 *Das schreckliche*

Mädchen (The Nasty Girl) not only deconstructs classical *Heimat* film's mission to locate identity in white, heterosexual masculinity, but also constructs a feminist idea of *Heimat* for the protagonist, Sonja Rosenberger-Wegmus. The film is based upon the true story of Anja Rosmus, a schoolgirl who, responding to an essay contest titled, "Meine Heimatstadt im Dritten Reich" (My Hometown in the Third Reich), finds out about her town's support of, and collaboration with, the National Socialist regime. Verhoeven reconfigures the *Unheimliche* in *Heimat* (women) as the authoritative (moral) center of his film in ways that thematize the *unheimlich* in *Das schreckliche Mädchen* (the *unheimlich* as *schrecklich* [fear-inspiring])[11] as Sonja's relentless search for the truth of what "is" *Heimat*. Rather than punishing this *unheimlich*, Verhoeven reconfigures the bambified woman of classical *Heimatfilm* into a powerful woman who continuously reveals herself as she re-envisions and reconstructs *Heimat* through interrogation.

It is through this female figure that Verhoeven's film challenges commonly held ideas of *Heimat* as unassailable fact, highlighting the reality that *Heimat*, like all cultural narratives, is written to fill certain ideological needs. Thus, Verhoeven puts pressure on the belief that *Heimat* invariably offers ethical identity positions. This pressure is applied from the very beginning in the film's refusal to accept the conventions of the *Heimatfilm* genre by framing six beginnings. These are a Neo-Nazi toasting a beer stein to the audience; a written text "explaining" the origin of the film's story; a statue resembling Sonja placed next to the textual and verbal recitation of the first stanza of the *Nibelungenlied* (Song of the Nibelungs, ca. 1200); Sonja's explanation of her participation in the essay contest, "My Hometown during the Third Reich"; the film's credits superimposed upon the image of two "guest workers" attempting to wash off the question "Where were you between '39-45. Where are you now?" from a wall located opposite the cathedral; and Sonja standing under the hand of the statue of the Bishop overlooking the cathedral of Passau, explaining how Passau came to be her *Heimat*.

This narrative strategy at the very beginning of the film presages ways the rest of the film constructs the idea of *Heimat* as history and story [*Geschichte* and *Geschichten*] that must be interrogated. One of the six beginnings of the film illustrates this point: presenting a printed preface it situates viewers in a complex argument about history [*Geschichte*] and story [*Geschichten*]:

11. It is no small matter that the original title, *Das schreckliche Mädchen*, was sexualized for the English speaking market. "Schrecklich" does not have the sexualized connotation of "nasty."

This film was inspired by what happened to Anja Rosmus in Passau.
The story mixes fiction and fact and is pertinent to all towns in Germany.
The action takes place in Bavaria where I live.
All characters and events are fictitious.
— Michael Verhoeven

The text sets up a tension between competing constructions of personal story (biography), *Heimat* (authorized history outside the film frame), and story (the film's fiction) that mirrors the way in which the film itself negotiates *Heimat* throughout. The director first authenticates his film by claiming that it is based on a "true story," then raises the story to the level of *Heimat* (which, as story, is "pertinent to all towns in Germany"), and finally mediates this claim by calling it "fictitious." The bricolage of the protagonist's name (Anja Rosmus/Sonja Rosenberger-Wegmus) from real/fictitious fragments is mirrored in the pretense that the filmic story has been moved from Passau to Bavaria; Passau is in fact a town in Bavaria. The triple movement from Anja Rosmus' story to history to fiction and the dislocation and reinscription of place(s) challenge commonly held ideas of *Heimat* as a fixed category for identity positions.

On the other hand, the film confers "narrating authenticity" on the female protagonist. While the written preface can be seen as a strategy engaged to destabilize authority, the statue in the next frame (third beginning) functions to authenticate Sonja's place in history. The statue, with its realistic details such as pubic hair, nipples, and so on, is a lifelike reproduction of Sonja, all the while its pose references classical Greek sculpture. This linkage enables the viewer to imagine Sonja as a contemporary young woman, whose adventures span the period from the mid 1970s to the late 1980s, while at the same time allowing them to think of her in epic terms, going back to antiquity. Indeed, the view of the turning statue, accompanied by a female voice's recitation of the opening lines of the epic poem *Nibelungenlied* strengthens the impression of Sonja as an epic figure. Her attempts to uncover her town's dark secrets and its cover-up of collaborations of certain prominent citizens with the Nazis, locate Sonja in a *Heimat* linked to the poem's origin in an epic tradition located in Bavaria and Austria, going back to the Germanic-heroic poetry of the period of mass migration [*Völkerwanderung*]. Verhoeven's choice of the *Nibelungenlied* as a reference to his heroic figure's tale becomes clear when one considers that the *Nibelungenlied* differs from other heroic poems in that verifiable events and heroic deeds are honored here (rather than the realm of the fantastic, as in the idealized Arthurian tales).

Finally, the film presents this poem as a pre-text to Sonja's narration of her story. In this way it avoids a potential erasure of this particular woman's experiences in a gesture that would homogenize her into a "universal woman": Sonja's struggle is presented as a gender-specific struggle located in a particular cultural climate and political time, in a particular geographic location. As a consequence, *Das schreckliche Mädchen* implicitly recognizes the longstanding denial and repression [*Vergangenheitsverdrängung*] of the past history of patriarchal domination and women's oppression, without gliding over the fissures of both this struggle and the oppression. In this way *Das schreckliche Mädchen* does not simplistically suggest a privileged position for *Heimat*; indeed, very clear differentiations are made between the extent and the variety of ways that struggles with *Heimat* are undertaken or refused. For example, Sonja's grandmother, mother, and other female figures (Fräulein Juckenack, Sonja's mother and sister, as well as some of Sonja's friends) are configured in positions that oscillate between power and disempowerment by varying the degrees of their identification with patriarchal power.

At the end of the film, the statue in the third beginning is cast in yet a different light when it is reinvoked during the ceremony unveiling the bust that honors Sonja for her accomplishments in bringing Pfilzing's history to light. Sonja refuses this petrification of her attempts to forge a *Heimat* for herself and tells Pfilzing's citizens that she protests the attempt to silence her through public honors, and that she has only just begun to de/scribe *Heimat*. This seems true for the *Heimatfilm* genre of the end of this century as well. For the moment, films like *Das schreckliche Mädchen* revise the classical *Heimatfilm* to accommodate the construction of Germanness and female gender, and offer a reconceptualization of *Heimat* to accommodate a German identity based on difference.

Note

Unless otherwise noted, all translations are my own.

Bibliography

Benjamin, Walter. *Städtebilder*. Afterword by Peter Szondi. Frankfurt a.M.: Suhrkamp, 1963.

Eisert-Rost, Elisabeth. "Heimat." *Der Deutsche Heimatfilm: Bilder und Weltbilder*. Ed. Elisabeth Eisert-Rost, et al. Tübingen: Tübinger Chronik e.G., 1989. 15-31.

Elsaesser, Thomas. *New German Cinema: A History*. New Brunswick, NJ: Rutgers UP, 1989.

Fetscher, Iring. "Heimatliebe – Brauch und Mißbrauch eines Begriffs." *Heimat im Wort*. Ed. Rüdiger Görner. Munich: iudicium, 1992. 15-35.

Freud, Sigmund. *Das Unheimliche: Aufsätze zur Literatur*. Hamburg: Fischer, 1963. 45-84.

Greverus, Ina-Maria. "The 'Heimat' Problem." *The Concept of* Heimat *in Contemporary German Literature*. Ed. Helfried W. Seliger. Munich: iudicium, 1987. 9-27.

Mulvey, Laura. "Pleasure and Narrative Cinema." *Feminism and Film Theory*. Ed. Constance Penley. New York: Routledge, 1988. 57-68.

Salten, Felix. *Bambi: Eine Lebensgeschichte aus dem Walde*. Berlin, Wien: Paul Zsolnay, 1926.

"Sehnsucht nach Heimat: Das neue Heimatbewußtsein." *Der Spiegel 40.38.* 1 October 1984: 252-63.

Silverman, Kaja. *The Threshold of the Visible World*. New York: Routledge, 1996.

Steiner, Gertraud. *Heimat-Macher: Kino in Österreich 1946-1966.* Wien: Verlag für Gesellschaftskritik, 1987.

Chapter 14

RAPE, NATION AND REMEMBERING HISTORY

Helke Sander's *Liberators Take Liberties*

Barbara Kosta

𝕴t could be said that rape has not been given its history, and its story has yet to be told. Only since the women's movement and only since women have resolved to talk about rape has it become a public issue. It is no coincidence that Helke Sander, a prominent figure of the 1960s women's movement in Germany and articulate advocate of the politicization of the private sphere, should figure among the first to bring stories of rape to the screen in her film *Liberators Take Liberties* (*BeFreier und Befreite*, 1992). While other filmmakers have touched on this topic (Helma Sanders-Brahms and Edgar Reitz), no other German filmmaker has addressed so thoroughly the topic of war and rape. A brief review of Sander's career, especially in the early phase of the 1960s feminist movement, shows that she often pushes past thresholds of comfort in her choice of issues. One need only recall such films as *Does the Pill Liberate Women?* (1972) or *The Subjective Factor* (1981) to recognize her undaunted provocation of accepted sociohistorical assumptions, and her intense desire, in Sander's words, to "break things" with her films ("Feminism," 10). With her ambitious three-and-one-half-hour documentary film, *Liberators Take Liberties*, Sander's gaze rests on German women who were raped, some repeatedly, predominately by Red Army soldiers, the purported liberators, an irony which she evokes in her title.[1] Sander

1. Some critics have taken issue with the term liberators since not everyone shared this sentiment. For an excellent discussion on this topic, see Stuart Liebman and

uncovers an overwhelming number of rapes in her research. In Berlin and its surrounding areas an estimated 100,000 women were sexually violated, primarily in the period between 27 April and 10 May 1945, and in the first six months after the war. Through a montage of archival material that she and her assistant Barbara Johr excavated and of present-day interviews with the women, their children, soldiers and eye-witnesses, Sander seeks to break through the silence that has long beleaguered personal and public memory and prevented working through the trauma of wartime rape.

Sander's film provides a necessary starting point for the work of memory and, to some extent, it interrupts the standard discourses of wartime through the introduction of gender. As a feminist filmmaker, Sander carves out a public space for stories that bear witness to the sexual violence committed against women during war. She attempts to engage in the work of memory, in the sense that bell hooks calls the "politicization of memory," i.e., the conscious act of remembering events repressed by hegemonic discourses and representations in order "to illuminate and transform the present" (147). Yet, while *Liberators Take Liberties* initiates remembering, it simultaneously creates new barriers to understanding the experience of rape and war, since simply recalling experience does not automatically lead to its insightful processing. The material that testimonies provide, Shoshana Felman proposes, must be "reinscribed, translated, radically rethought and fundamentally worked over by the text" rather than merely "presented and reflected"(xiv-xv). The interpretive framework that Sander creates does not "radically rethink" the structures that initially produced the trauma of wartime rape because the recollections are not provided new lenses. Both the racial politics, which ill-fatedly resonate with right-wing representations of the rape of German women toward the end of World War II, and the narrative of rape that emerges from *Liberators Take Liberties* obscure the interrelationship of war, nation, and sexual violence.

Without a doubt, Sander's representation of mass rape adds a new dimension to the working through of Germany's past. Even her most ardent critics, who cite Sander for an appalling neglect of historical specificity, acknowledge the significance of her attempt to bring the topic of rape into the open.[2] This is not to say that the stories of rape never found their way into official registers or published memoirs, as historian Atina Grossmann points out. In the years immediately following World War II,

---

Annette Michelson. David Levin points out that those who experienced the Allies as liberators were predominantly people who were persecuted by the Nazis.

2. See *October* 72 issue.

they became an important part of the vernacular. Grossmann contends that women often spoke of the experience of being raped and officially testified to its occurrence if they sought an abortion (laws were relaxed to accommodate these women) (62). For various reasons, however, the accounts of rape all too soon receded from public discourse, and women were left without a forum for their very personal histories. Sander correctly insists that the mass rapes were "an open secret," but that they were deliberately excluded from public awareness ("Response," 86). With few exceptions, the testimonies were kept out of the historical record and certainly never before as extensively portrayed as in her film.

Why have the cases of rape remained sealed in the recesses of personal memory for such a long time, and, furthermore, why has the residual trauma of the rape experience in the generations that followed not been explored? This question becomes urgent in view of such chilling recollections as that of Wiltrud Rosenzweig, the daughter of a rape victim, who learned about her inception during an angry exchange between mother and daughter. She recalls: "She [her mother] brutally scolded me and said that I am a pig just like my father, who used to rape women .... . She said it with such hatred that it stunned me" (B&B, 156).[3]

There are a number of explanations for the culture of silence in both East and West Germany. Most compelling, the Holocaust and the atrocities committed against humanity during World War II make it difficult to assign the status of victim to Germans. This is especially true in a political climate that has consistently tended toward a revisionist writing of history as seen in the often cited "Historian's Debate" of the 1980s. In the West, remembering the past was viewed as counterproductive to the advent of German reconstruction and its heralded "Zero Hour," which was to usher in a democratic present and future severed from the past. Certainly during the 1950s, the personal narratives of rape found no place in the flurry of the economic miracle that sought to rehabilitate an ailing nation, to reinstate "normalcy" and to redefine German identity in the face of the horrific crimes committed in its name. Only the Right appropriated and exploited freely the memory of rape as a trope against Communism.[4] For the West German Left, the history of rape toward the

3. All translations from *Liberators Take Liberties* are my own and appear as B&B in the text.
4. Brownmiller contends that German professors "attempted to make nationalistic sense out of what they had found. The following is a quote from the document submitted by these German mandarins: 'It is clear that these rapings were the result of a manner of conduct and mentality which are inconceivable and repulsive to the European mind. One must partially attribute them to the traditions and notions in the Asiatic parts of Russia, according to which women are just as much the booty of the victors as jewelry ...'"(68-69).

end of World War II was lost to dogmatic identification with and sup-port of a Socialist state.[5] For the German Democratic Republic, address-ing the history of rape ran counter to ideological loyalties toward the Soviet Union and undermined the identity of the East German state.[6] At the same time, the reputation of the liberators and allies was at stake in both East and West Germany. Seen within these contexts, the failure to deal with the history of wartime rape arises from the overwhelming com-plexity of the issues involved in addition to the inadequacy of analytical approaches to this period in history. Consequently, a project like Sander's must proceed with extreme historical sensitivity while taking into account the personal histories revealed in the interviews. Admit-tedly, Sander must walk a fine line since the issues call for a perceptive analysis of the semiotics of violence and of the encounter of violence and national identity within the context of Germany's fascist past.

Since its premiere at the Berlin film festival in 1992, *Liberators Take Liberties* has received a mixed reception internationally. Reactions range in intensity from a passionate affirmation of the film's confrontation with wartime rape to a critical rejection of its anti-Russian undertones and its "transhistorical" elisions (Levin 71). Some critics have gone so far as to wonder about the political allegiances the women may have had.[7] In anticipation that the question of the role of women in the Third Reich may suggest a justification for rape, it is withdrawn while posed in one rhetorical breath. Still, the question awkwardly hovers at the periph-ery of some critiques. Keeping these critiques in mind, Sander deserves recognition for the wealth of material she collected and particularly for the oral histories and the insights they provide. Each woman's story con-firms the high incidence of rape and of the multiple rapes committed predominately by Red Army soldiers. Their testimonies communicate the terror of victimization and the long-term effects of rape on their lives. To the extent that Sander's film attempts to break the silence sur-

5. In the introduction to her book *BeFreier und Befreite*, Sander remembers how she first learned of the mass rapes through a neighbor who reported Sander and her friends to the police for allegedly printing communist flyers and conducting illicit meetings. The neighbor later revealed that Russian soldiers had raped her seven times and that other women in the building had similar experiences. Because she had been a "Blockwartin" during the Third Reich, the young people in the house hated her and tended to believe that she deserved being raped. It took years for Sander to revisit this topic.

6. 8 May was celebrated in the GDR as the *Tag der Befreiung vom Faschismus* [the day of liberation from fascism]. To commemorate 8 May, a Soviet monument in Berlin-Treptow portrays a powerful male figure in a military uniform carrying a child in one hand and a sword in the other. This image introduces a chapter in *Heimatkunde*, a third grade textbook used in the GDR.

7. See Round Table.

rounding the staggering incidence of rape, the question of what narrative emerges becomes of utmost importance. What does the narrative reveal, and what type of knowledge of rape culture, of rape and war is conveyed? What history of the time is produced? The overarching narrative that results is problematic at best.

As the film *Liberators Take Liberties* shows, silence is imposed upon the victims of rape largely because of the sociocultural meanings attached to it. They are revealed in statements such as Ursula Ludwig's, "We were used to being quiet and having to endure" (B&B, 175), or Dr. Lutz's, "One does not choose a broken cup" (B&B, 176), or Mrs. Hoffmann's, "There was no one there to protect us" (B&B, 109).[8] Such comments reveal much about the underlying motive of mass rape. They also shed light on the position of women within patriarchy and the interplay between sexuality and power, as well as the pervasive troping of nation and *Heimat* as female. Particularly the image of woman as nation, while diachronically anchored, gains synchronic fervor in a period that celebrates masculinity, promotes nationalism and identifies an outside threat. In patriotic rhetoric, the female body with its coded vulnerability, is used to symbolize the national body, whose boundaries are always in danger of being violated and thus need to be defended by men. In wartime, rape is thus deployed as a weapon to penetrate the innermost sphere of the national body, its home and traditions and to desecrate the values that women, as gender and social product, symbolically represent. As George Mosse observes: "Woman as a national symbol was the guardian of the continuity and immutability of the nation, the embodiment of its respectability"(18). Women serve as the bearers of cultural memory, and the trauma inflicted upon a nation is meant to live on in the female body.

While rape is used to defile and denigrate a nation, by extension, it also serves to strip a man who belongs to that nation of his honor, his masculinity, and what is seen as his exclusive right to woman as his sole property. Women thus become a vehicle by which male soldiers defeat the group with which they are in conflict. Not only is the female body as property violated and transgressed, but the male is emasculated and allegedly confronted with his own sexual inadequacy and his failure as protector. The insight that men use women to communicate with one another lends insight to the viciousness of sexual violence in times of war. Women are depersonalized to the point of becoming a signifier in the power struggle between men so that wartime rape essentially targets male identity. This explains the propaganda machinery's exploitation of

8. Sander addresses some people as Mrs. and Mr. and others by their full names.

women's bodies in newsreels and posters to arouse fear of the enemy who would rape "our" women and incite a crisis of masculinity. The excessive use of such iconography serves as an index to the centrality of gender in the configurations of war.[9]

In Sander's film, the perceived peril to masculinity is distinctly revealed in the recollection of men's reactions to the rape of their wives. One rape victim reports of her husband: "He thought I had deceived him and that I should have defended myself … . He said, 'You swore eternal loyalty … . If you only knew what you have done to me!' He was beside himself and it took about a year before we could talk to each other again in a friendly manner" (B&B, 173). The sense of powerlessness paradigmatically translates into betrayal. It is presumably the fault of the sexual woman who tantalizes the aggressor and who allegedly enjoys rape. Another woman recounts overhearing an officer declare that he would shoot his wife if she were raped. (B&B, 174)[10] It is implied that death offers a more feasible, that is, a more honorable alternative to the constant reminder of lost dignity and of property irreparably damaged. Contrary to what often is assumed, shame seldom prevented women's testimonies of rape; rather the fear of rejection, of being ostracized and blamed for inciting soldiers to rape (much as women are still blamed today) led to the suppression of their experiences and the deferment of healing. Mrs. Kleine, for instance, recalls the need to speak but "no one wanted to hear about it" (B&B 165) and remarks that women rarely were asked about their rape experiences. The unacknowledged threat to male subjectivity and the trauma of male disempowerment seem to have enforced women's reticence. Grossmann adds that it was only after men returned home that women fell silent (61).

Based on the explanations of the women interviewed, it could be said that the silence that has covered up these mass rapes and prevented the work of memory and mourning also has roots in the construction of masculinity. If rape aims to destroy female agency, and to restore masculinity, then this culturally enforced silence is the culmination of this same destruction of agency. Silence strikes at women's power in that it continues to disempower its victims and to sustain the asymmetrical power relation between genders. As Sander's film shows, over time, the experience of rape continues to define these women's sense of self, their relationship to their bodies, to the culture within which they live, and the relationship to the children of rape. At the center of such horrid

9. See Susan Gubar.

10. Seifert writes that rape as a "violent invasion into the interior of one's body represents the most severe attack imaginable upon the intimate self and the dignity of a human being; by any measure it is a mark of severe torture" (53).

defiling of women is a type of death that calls for mourning. "The trauma," Mrs. Rshevskaja perceptively reflects, "remains throughout her life and leaves behind a wounded psyche and repulsion toward sexual intercourse. It deprives her. It robs her of her past" (B&B, 132). Not working through the experience of rape allows for the experience of violation to wield its power from the unconscious for generations. It robs the future as well, as the children conceived through rape agree. The trauma of rape shapes their lives as the interviews with them show.

Oddly enough, the men in Sander's film, former Russian soldiers, explicate the phenomenon of rape during wartime. Their explanation retains power and their idiom is perpetuated. Male sexual aggression evolves as one of the dominant interpretive frameworks. For example, Gleb Dubrowo glibly contends that "the soldiers who raped German women did it out of sexual need and definitely not out of revenge" (B&B, 118). Curiously, many of the men interviewed, in contrast to Mrs. Rshevskaja, denied revenge as a motive for mass rape. Instead they were more inclined to cite "sexual need" and to echo the adage, "boys will be boys." Here the connection between gender, nation, and sexual violence is naturalized and war becomes the arena for unleashing a healthy libido. Such testimony upholds the "reactionary claim that rape is the inevitable result of a supposedly innate male aggressiveness coupled with an uncontrollable sexual need" (Woodhull 170). The understanding of rape as an integral by-product of war aims to normalize rape. Other less audible though more illuminating explanations submitted in Sander's film include revenge, retaliation, or reprisal for German atrocities against Russian women. Lew Kopelew suggests that the main perpetrators were ex-prisoners, that is, criminals who, owing to the shortage of soldiers, were released from prisons to fight. He also speculates that it could have been petty bourgeois soldiers who suddenly had license to do anything (B&B, 136). To illustrate Kopelew's statement, Sander includes documentary footage of Russian soldiers polishing their boots. The sequencing indicts these men as potential rapists. For many others who are interviewed and who attempt to make sense of rape, "it was war" becomes the resigned incantation.

Sander neither challenges the rationalizations and justifications nor ponders predicaments of speechlessness (except to impose her own formulation). She appears to lack the acumen to follow up in such a way as to shed light on views that have ossified as assumptions, or to probe the more insightful views offered. Unwittingly, many opinions that overlook historical specificity and call on biology to understand mass rape retain their power as explanations. Moreover, Sander appears unable to analyze the strategies through which the [official] truths of violence are produced and rendered commonsensical. Her stuttering and fragmented response on one occasion suggests that the topic became much too large for her to handle. When Iwan Stasewitsch recounts how Soviet soldiers were warned against sexual contact with German women because they used their infected bodies as weapons, Sander responds ineptly: "I think that a woman who is sick – that hurts – … .What I would like to say is that I don't see it as a means to defeat the enemy" (B&B, 121). On another occasion, Sander counters Fjodor Swerew's biologistic appraisal that men are more active sexually than women with "that is scientifically disproved. Women are actually more potent than men" (B&B, 124). Curiously, her response suggests a willingness to entertain Swerew's reasoning and betrays a sympathy for the basic premise of his misguided musings, albeit with her own scientific support.

While wartime rape aims to destroy a nation, it conversely serves to restore masculinity and the authority of the subject who rapes. Beverly Allen claims that violence against women may occur "wherever fear and insecurity are joined with power and immunity from prosecution in a sexist social system"(39). A number of testimonies recall multiple rapes performed for the gaze of fellow soldiers. Mrs. Hoffmann remembers the eagerness she witnessed among the soldiers who stood in line for their turn: "One of them would grab the next person's belt and say: "Come on, it's my turn" (B&B, 110). According to interview accounts, many soldiers were young, incited by older soldiers and, in numerous cases, the rapes occurred under the influence of alcohol. The high incidence of gang rape, despite the official criminalization of rape by soldiers, betrays a dynamic that is linked to the need to demonstrate invulnerability and virility, even at the risk of venereal disease and despite the warning that women use their infected bodies as weapons. While it is difficult to speak of gang rape within a wartime setting solely in terms of male socialization and the construction of masculinity in patriarchal societies, the correlation between social psychological research on group sexual assault and wartime rape is striking, in that the demands of the group powerfully influence individual behavior and increase the potential for aggression. "Sex as a competitive arena," Chris O'Sullivan asserts, "necessarily results in exploiting girls and women, because the motive is to 'score' to impress one's male friends rather than to relate to the female"(26). Although O'Sullivan refers to a much different context, namely to college fraternities, her insights may illuminate an additional factor within the context Sander explores. In his interview with Sander, Lew Kopelew cites the social pressure to participate in sexual violence as a likely motive. To refuse, he proposes, "was considered a breach of manliness and that was far worse" (B&B, 136). Mrs. Ludwig recalls a young officer who apologizes for having to rape her after three other soldiers already had sexually assaulted her. Paradoxically, she is escorted home afterwards because of the danger of being shot after curfew.

Feminists have long engaged in discussions on the culture of rape, and of rape and war, and have attempted to make transparent some of the systemic motivations. In *Mass Rape: The War against Women in Bosnia-Herzegovina*, Ruth Seifert offers a perceptive analysis:

> In fact, there are good reasons to assume that rapes do not have much to do wither with nature or with sexuality. Rather, they are acts of extreme violence implemented, of course, by sexual means. Studies show that rape is not an aggressive manifestation of sexuality, but rather a sexual manifestation of aggression (55).

In a summary of various positions, Teresa de Lauretis notes that while feminists like Susan Brownmiller viewed rape as "an act of aggression rather than a sexual act," Catherine MacKinnon pleaded for taking rape outside the realm of sexuality and for viewing it only as a criminal act of violence. Yet, as de Lauretis argues, this "allows one to be against it without raising any questions about the extent to which the institution of heterosexuality has defined force as a normal part of (hetero)sexual relations" (37). She quotes Monique Plaza, who maintains that "rape is sexual essentially because it rests on the very social difference between the sexes … . It is *social sexing* which is latent in rape" (37).[11]

The problematic representation of rape that emerges from Sander's film results largely from the very selective analytical lens she employs. For her, men are perpetrators and women are their victims; these two sides are often entangled in a battle of the sexes.[12] This facile syntax eclipses and suppresses the complex interplay of sexual violence and power, of masculinity, femininity and war, and the historical context in which power is taken and agency denied. Thus Sander's inquiry does not seem to have progressed beyond a feminist analysis of the mid-1970s. This is particularly visible in the film's disregard for the significance of the historical and cultural context that produces suffering and loss and that needs to be brought into the equation in order to understand and to work through the trauma of rape. So intent on producing an iconog-

11. See Copelon 200. The Geneva Convention does not recognize rape as a crime of violence but as a crime against honor and dignity. This distinction diminishes the criminal aspect of rape.

12. In the dialogues between Helke Sander and Roger Willemsen, Sander offers an extremely unnuanced analysis of the relationship between genders: "I think that men and women are strangers unto themselves. That is what is exciting about it. A man is just as foreign to me as a horse, a snake, or whatever else" (57).

raphy of woman as victim at the beginning of the film, Sander abandons the documentary mode and lapses briefly into docudrama. She exploits the genre's analogical realism to stage the scene of terror. A close-up fixes boots, the emblem of patriarchy, power, and violence, as they descend stairs into a basement; a light penetrates the darkness to reveal a woman who cowers in a corner. The high angle and close framing of her silent face emphasize the character's vulnerability and helplessness (in contrast to the animated faces of women recalling these events). This scene is followed by documentary footage of missiles, i.e., ejaculations, and of a city in ruins. While images of burning buildings, vacant streets, and piles of rubble fill the screen, Mrs. Ludwig, in a voice-over, relates the story of her multiple rapes by Red Army soldiers. The intersection of her memories with the visuals leads to an indictment of the soldiers whose entry into the city is purely sexualized. Within this constellation, the shelled-out buildings stand for women's mutilated and battered bodies and the allusion to the city as a defenseless feminized space suggests that Berlin, and by extension Germany, was raped and humiliated. Thus, the provocation intended by the capitalization of the "F" in the original German title *BeFreier*, which is supposed to call into question the integrity of the liberators, as well as the intended irony in the title *Liberators Take Liberties,* cast a dubious shadow on the end of the war. While the liberators were also those very troops who defeated the National Socialist dictatorship, in Sander's film they are marked exclusively as rapists.

Sander's reductive dialectic – reflected in her comments as well as in her montage of images – impedes the possibility of uncovering the elaborate network of issues raised within the film. She fails to seize the opportunities for analysis the testimonies could have provided. Grossmann, for one, calls attention to the manifold events whose intersection needs to be fleshed out in order to approach an understanding of this period in German history. This would include an examination of the referents available at the time to articulate the overwhelming occurrence of rape and of the way in which historical material is used to reconstruct the past ("A Question of Silence," 48-49).[13] Film critic Gertrud Koch attributes the tendency toward a reductive narrative in Sander's film to the biological essentializing that informed feminist analysis at the outset of the second women's movement, which has since shifted its focus to an understanding of gender as a social historical construct. Koch faults Sander for producing a "master narrative," which she cites as the prod-

13. Grossmann calls for looking at women's victimization as well as women's complicity with the Nazi regime. She also proposes to study the language women used to present their case for an abortion and their experience of rape in order to see how the ideology of the Nazi era and the Weimar Republic framed their stories.

uct of a "psychological-anthropological essentialism conceived ahistorically because it is purchased by the exclusion of women from history"(36). This tendency reaches its climax in an interview with Konrad Jahr, who is a child of rape. Sander probes: "Do you think that your violent beginnings have influenced your relationship to women or sexuality in any way" (B&B, 208). With analytical sophistication Jahr describes his journey from one foster home to the next and the missing sense of security and belonging that a stable environment may provide. Rarely did he experience tenderness or enjoy physical contact as a child. These factors, he reflects, may have influenced his relationship to women. All the while the camera focuses on his genitals, suggesting that this may be the scene of a potential crime. The shot raises the suspicion of a lineage of perpetrators and intimates that a child conceived through violence may be destined to repeat a similar violent act. Psychologically mapped out, the unreflected past sustains its power if the insights biographies offer are not provided an arena for personal and public reflection. Rather, the camera establishes a banal causality and seems to insinuate that biology is destiny.

Has Sander reached the end of her analytical rope because she has remained within the binary system of male vs. female despite feminist and poststructuralist resistance to the ideologically charged confines of polarizations? Bound by oppositions and reversals, the narrative is caught within a conceptual strait jacket that limits insight. In the train, on her way to Minsk, the filmmaker reports the intent of the journey: "Few people know that there were about one million women in the Red Army who were soldiers. I am going to Minsk now to ask them if, as soldiers, they ever said to a man, 'man come'" (B&B, 114)? This phrasing echoes women's recollections of male soldiers who in broken German repeatedly commanded their female victims to acquiesce. Yet, her counter-query only exemplifies the limited reach of Sander's investigation. Fixed on documenting the occurrence of the mass rape of German women, her project, at times, lapses into a prodigious insistence on numbers and so-called hard facts. "I wanted to know," she explains in the accompanying book, "what is meant when it is said that there were 'many' rapes in the last days of April and the beginning of May during the battle for Berlin. I wanted to know what 'many' meant for a city like Berlin that had about 1.4 million women at the time" (B&B, 14). Because the social and historical context of mass rape remains unexplored in Sander's representation, sexual violence is placed outside of history and outside the scope of social transformation.

Given the historical setting of *Liberators Take Liberties*, the relationship among nation, ethnicity, and gender becomes a significant complex of signifiers that numbers do not address. Within the context of the former Yugoslavia, Sander seems to recognize the weight that the various markers of identity bear as her essay in *Mass Rape: The War Against Women in Bosnia-Herzegovina* reflects: "The issue that must be clarified is whether the Muslim and Croatian women who are being raped in great numbers are raped because they are Muslims and Croats or because they are women" (xviii). In her own film, however, explicit questions of ethnicity or national identity play an all too minor role, if any at all. The privileging of gender, which seems to be Sander's sole preoccupation, leads to an analytical impasse and to an erasure of other significant markers of identity. Because she downplays the relationship of national identity and war, she paradoxically ends up repressing the very same historical context she wishes to examine.

Despite its relegation to the status of a backdrop, history, as always, sustains its presence. The selective attention to gender identity allows for slippages through which racial politics rears its ugly head and hazardously retains its power. The film inadvertently reinstates the discourses of revisionist historians and fuels what is referred to colloquially as "*Russenangst*" (a fear of Russians). In a documentary clip, presumably from the last days of the war, German women tell a reporter about Russian soldiers whom they describe as "bestial hordes," "who, telling from the way they looked, were Mongols" (B&B, 110). Another clip shows a wall that bears the message "protect our women and children from the red beasts." Its inclusion in combination with eye-witness reports of rape by "Asiatic hordes" (B&B, 131) not only racially vilifies but serves to cement the testimonies and affirm the sense of threat and the anxieties experienced at the time. One must wonder how these contemporaneous eye-witness accounts reconfigure the testimonies of the women Sander interviews in the present. In addition, the following documentary sequences of soldiers emphatically and denotatively fix the physiognomy of the perpetrator. The impression conveyed is that Russian soldiers were compelled by an uncontrollable libido, except for the officers who retained a modicum of civility and excused themselves before they raped. Without seeking to mitigate the blame for the horrific sexual violence against German women that Russian soldiers perpetrated, one must look at the historical knowledge constructed within the film which, in this case, peculiarly sustains ideological patterns that can be traced back to the Third Reich and even earlier.[14] As Koch observes, this becomes even

14. This representation becomes complex owing to the racial politics that called for relaxing Paragraph 218 in the last days of World War II in order to prevent the birth of children whose fathers were Russian. See Christiane Grefe.

more problem-ridden in Sander's indiscriminate use of newsreel clips that Nazis produced to incite hatred and dread (Koch 37-38). The montage of images supports the perceptions espoused and the language of propaganda lingers. At the same time, Russian folk music, a leitmotif throughout the film, becomes associated with pathology.

Whereby to intervene should not arouse the expectation that the women interviewed engage in critical self-reflection, but that the structure of the narrative lend itself to provoking spectatorial reflection and analysis, Sander never intervenes or unsettles the narrative. The very feminist demand of self-reflectivity on the part of the filmmaker is nowhere to be found. Instead her visible ennui, specifically in interview situations with men, or the spatial relationship she maintains in an interview, for instance, conducted back to back with a former Russian soldier, all convey miscalculated and misdirected manifestations of resistance or, more problematically, of aversion. Because Sander misses opportunities to investigate the relationship of gender, ethnicity, and war that structure the accounts of the women interviewed, she leaves undiscovered the intersection of biographical testimony, politics, and history.

The attempt to understand this time in history, and to find new ways in which to talk about German wartime experiences, fails in Sander's film. In other words, *Liberators Take Liberties* does not engage in the process of memory that liberates and challenges the structures that shaped the very history represented. The trauma of these experiences retains its hold on the generations that follow and its "psychic explosivity" persists in their biographies (Schmidt-Harzbach 21). The complexity of these histories remains undisclosed, as does an understanding of rape culture and of gender and sexual violence within the context of World War II. Although this may be a beginning, with *Liberators Take Liberties*, rape, in the last days of World War II, has not yet been given its history.[15]

15. The Japanese government, for instance, only recently acknowledged its debt to an estimated 200,000 women who were forced into brothels during the war.

Bibliography

Allen, Beverly. *Rape Warfare: The Hidden Genocide in Bosnia-Herzegovina and Croatia.* Minneapolis: U of Minnesota P, 1996.

Brownmiller, Susan. *Against Our Will: Men, Women and Rape.* New York: Bantam, 1975.

Copelon, Rhonda. "Surfacing Gender: Reconceptualizing Crimes Against Women in Times of War." *Mass Rape.* 197-218.

de Lauretis, Teresa. *Technologies of Gender: Essays on Theory, Film and Fiction.* Bloomington, IN: Indiana UP, 1987.

Felman, Shoshana and Dori Laub. *Testimony: Crises of Witnessing in Literature, Psychoanalysis, and History.* New York: Routledge, 1992.

Grefe, Christiane. "Flüsterkinder." *Wochenpost* 27.2. (1992): 8.

Grossmann, Atina. "A Question of Silence: The Rape of German Women by Occupation Soliders." *October* 72 (1995): 43-63

Gubar, Susan. "'This is My Rifle, This Is My Gun': World War II and the Blitz on Women." *Behind the Lines: Gender and Two World Wars.* Ed. Margaret Randolph Higonnet, et al. New Haven, CT.: Yale UP, 1987. 227-59.

Heimatkunde. Berlin: Volkseigener Verlag, 1987.

hooks, bell. "Choosing the Margins as a Space of Radical Opposition." *Yearning: Race, Gender and Cultural Politics.* Boston: South End Press, 1990.

Koch, Gertrud. "Blood, Sperm, and Tears." *October* 72 (1995): 27-41.

Levin, David. "Taking Liberties with Liberties Taken." *October* 72 (1995): 65-77.

Liebman, Stuart and Annette Michelson. "After the Fall: Women in the House of the Hangman." *October* 72 (1995): 5-14.

Mass Rape: The War Against Women in Bosnia-Herzegovina. Ed. Alexandra Stiglmayer. Trans. Marion Faber. Lincoln: U of Nebraska P, 1994.

Mosse, George. *Nationalism and Sexuality: Respectability and Abnormal Sexuality in Modern Europe.* New York: Howard Fertig, 1985.

O'Sullivan, Chris. "Fraternities and the Rape Culture." *Transforming a Rape Culture.* Eds. Emilie Buchwald et al. Minneapolis, MN.: Milkweed Editions, 1993.

Round Table: "Further Thoughts on Helke Sander's Project." *October* 72 (1995): 89-113.

Sander, Helke and Barbara Johr, eds. *BeFreier und Befreiter: Krieg Vergewaltigungen Kinder.* Munich: Antje K. Kunstmann, 1992.

Sander, Helke and Roger Willemsen. *Gewaltakte Männerphantasien und Krieg.* Hamburg: Ingrid Klein Verlag, 1993.

_____. "Prologue" *Mass Rape.* xvii-xxiii.

_____. "A Response to My Critics," *October* 72 (1995): 81-88.

_____. "Feminismus und Film: 'i like chaos, but i don't know whether chaos likes me.'" *Frauen und Film* 15 (1979): 10.

Schmidt-Harzbach, Ingrid. "Eine Woche im April Berlin 1945: Vergewaltigung als Massenschicksal." *BeFreier und Befreite: Krieg Vergewaltigungen Kinder*. Eds. Helke Sander and Barbara Johr. Munich: Antje Kunstmann, 1992. 21-45.

Seifert, Ruth. "War and Rape: A Preliminary Analysis." *Mass Rape*. 54-72.

Woodhull, Winifred. "Sexuality, Power, and the Question of Rape." *Feminism and Foucault: Reflections on Resistance*. Ed. Irene Diamond and Lee Quinby. Boston: Northeastern UP, 1988. 167-76.

Part IV

GERMANY AND HER "OTHERS"

Chapter 15

"GERMANY IS FULL OF GERMANS NOW"

Germanness in Ama Ata Aidoo's *Our Sister Killjoy*
and Chantal Akerman's *Meetings with Anna*

Barbara Mennel

itting in a Belgian coffeehouse, the film character Anne Silver describes West Germany of the mid-1970s with the words: "Germany is full of Germans now." This line of dialogue points both to the position of the speaking subject as outside Germany and to the historicity of her representation of Germany. The West German state, itself a consequence of German history, is both traversed and imagined from the outside. Because non-German texts concerned with Germanness perform an outsider position vis-à-vis Germany, their construction of German identity makes them especially productive for German Studies. Belgian filmmaker Chantal Akerman's film *Meetings with Anna* (1978) and Ghanaian writer Ama Ata Aidoo's prose poem *Our Sister Killjoy or Reflections from a Black-eyed Squint* (1977) offer images of West Germany in the 1970s that radically differ from the critical self-representations of the West German Left, women's literature, or representations of nation in New German Cinema, all of which were integral participants in the internal postwar debate about German identity prior to unification.[1]

---

1. For an overview of German film and literature of the 1960s to the 1970s, see McCormick.

In light of the heightened xenophobia and nationalism of the late 1980s and 1990s as well as recent debates about unified Germany as a multicultural society, the 1970s and early 1980s form a crucial period for investigating German national identity. This period figures in the public imaginary as the time between the political uproar of the 1960s, organized around the student movement, and the fall of the Wall, accompanied by a resurgence of nationalism and simultaneous attempts to live and theorize a multicultural Germany.[2] The space "in-between" was a time of self-reflective productivity, which, based on critical political and historical perspectives, produced new forms of writing and cinema. However, recent critics have demonstrated that these West German discourses produced a binarism of victim and perpetrator. New German Cinema tended to embody Germany in female victims; filmmakers portrayed themselves as victims vis-à-vis the state (for example *Germany in Autumn*); and feminist writings positioned women as victims of the patriarchal state.[3] *Meetings with Anna* and *Our Sister Killjoy* reflect critically on such simplistic binarisms of German national self-representation.[4] In addition to pointing to the silences and gaps in German representations of the Holocaust, colonialism, and racism, these texts offer a gendered perspective on the nation that entails post-Holocaust and postcolonial experiences of displacement. Their focus on gender and sexuality contrasts with German feminist representations of the Other as male and heterosexual, and indicates a conceptual problem in West German feminist discourse of the 1970s that subordinated the significance of race, sexuality, and nationality to notions of gender difference.[5]

2. For an overview of German national identity in relationship to the political and economic changes in the postwar period, see Knischewski.

3. For a critique of representations of Germany as victim in New German Cinema, see Santner and Rentschler. For an analysis of how feminist works, such as Verena Stefan's *Shedding* (1975) and Anne Duden's *Opening of the Mouth* (1982) rely on racial stereotyping to foreground the oppression of women, see Adelson, "Anne Duden's *Übergang*."

4. Neither *Meetings with Anna* nor *Our Sister Killjoy* has received any critical attention in Germany or in German Studies, and Aidoo's book is not available in German. Aidoo is an important feminist postcolonial writer of African literature, and *Our Sister Killjoy* occupies a central place in her oeuvre as the work through which she constructs her radical position vis-à-vis postcolonial Europe. The representation of Germany, however, has not received much critical attention in African literary criticism. Akerman, one of the most acclaimed feminist filmmakers, works in the tradition of Jean-Luc Godard and Andy Warhol and is generally discussed in relationship to postmodernity and psychoanalytic feminist film theory. The Jewish and German allusions in Akerman's films generally have been ignored in most feminist film criticism.

5. Angelika Bammer has argued that women's liberation appropriates "the historical significance of an anticolonial revolution and in fact in much feminist theory of the 1970s this analogy was commonplace. Verena Stefan, in a poetic-autobiographical mode, takes it metaphorically: the body of woman that has been occupied by male sexual desire

Reversing the conventions of the travel narrative, *Our Sister Killjoy* and *Meetings with Anna* displace Germany as the center and deconstruct the trope of the non-German exotic by integrating postmodern aesthetics and identity politics into their representations of Germany. While displacement and crossing of national boundaries are at the core of the narratives, neither work presupposes a lost whole, even though each presupposes a historical "before," that is, before colonialism, before the Holocaust, before exile. Both texts provide alternatives to the artificial split often posited between identity politics and postmodern aesthetics. The current privileging of nomadism as a trope of postmodern subjectivity ignores the historical and political specificities of the diasporas that these two works invoke. Nevertheless, their very existence (as well as their staging of encounters with Germans) acknowledges the specific political openness of West Germany in the 1970s. But because both texts allude to the ongoing legacies of the colonial and racist past, they offer readings of the 1970s that emphasize continuities rather than discontinuities with earlier German nationalist discourses.

The lack of interest in texts about Germany by non-Germans is persistent in *Germanistik* in Germany and German Studies in the United States. A recent example is Marc A. Weiner's suggestion that German Studies consists of "new-critical readings of canonical texts and *motivgeschichtliche* [thematic] examinations of canonized authors' works alongside projects more closely associated with the newer North American approaches" (vii). He leaves the definition of Germanness and German culture intact while foregrounding methodological questions. Jeffrey M. Peck articulates a more radical vision for German Studies that revolves around the question of German identity. He describes German Studies as a "topographical discourse" that draws "attention to intellectual *surfaces* and academic *contours*, critical *boundaries* and scholarly *fields* of demarcated interests, as well as the cultures that inhabit those territories – in short, *Germanistik* as well as Germany" (179). In his discussion of "what it means 'to be German'," (181) Peck points out that definitions of German citizenship based on passport and blood are inadequate because essentialist. According to him, *Auslandsgermanisten* [Germanists abroad] work in the "in-between" space "between Germany and America, majority and minority, strong and weak, or any two poles of an

---

is the terrain that has to be liberated" (Bammer 85). For a critique of the equation of "the 'colonized' with 'woman'" see Grewal and Kaplan (3). An important German critique of the representation of woman solely as victim is articulated in Christina Thürmer-Rohr's concept of *Mittäterschaft* (complicity), which entered the German feminist debate with her 1987 book *Vagabundinnen* (*Vagabonding*, 1991).

exaggerated or reified binary opposition that represent relations of power" (183). Finally, he calls for an expansion of the inhabitable space between these polarities. Unfortunately, his call for Germany to be displaced from the center of our field still leaves intact the binarism of inside (Germany) and outside (German Studies in the United States). Symptomatic of this troubling duality is that the shift from *Germanistik* to German Studies coincides with a move from literary texts to "topics such as film, feminism, and ethnic identity/minority discourse" (185), a distinction that relies on an identification of "German" with a homogeneous written culture, while coding as "American" the visual, political and multicultural. Despite the problems with Peck's model, the notion of "German" as a topographical entity is useful in analyzing the representation of Germany and Germanness in texts by non-German authors because it theoretically allows for considering non-German texts in the space of German Studies.

Concrete rethinking of the epistemological conditions of German Studies is offered in Leslie Adelson's article "Migrants' Literature or German Literature? TORKAN'S *Tufan: Brief an einen islamischen Bruder,*" in which she observes "that the notion of what is German in contemporary literature is as much contested on critical and scholarly terrain as is the designation of the Federal Republic as a *Vielvölkerstaat* in the public arena." Adelson is concerned with German-language literature written in Germany, and she argues that what is at stake is "the fundamental need to reconceptualize our understanding of an identifiably German core of contemporary literature" ("Migrants' Literature," 383). What should emerge, according to Adelson, is neither an affirmation of the center nor a topical addition to the self-perception of Germany, but instead a fundamental revision of the epistemological grounds of German identity and culture. This theoretical reconceptualization of German culture can be usefully applied to texts that are considered neither German nor migrant literature, and therefore do not fit into any of the categories put forth by German Studies to date. Their inclusion consequently opens the debate about the representation of Germanness beyond German-language texts. Expanding the boundaries of German Studies, such inclusions question current conceptualizations of the relationship between cultural representation and national identity.

Among such texts are Akerman's *Meetings with Anna* and Aidoo's *Our Sister Killjoy*. They allow us to pose anew the question of Germanness and to theorize the intricate implications of Germany's Others in German identity. *Our Sister Killjoy* refers specifically to Germany's National-Socialist past, although it also implicitly connects Germany to the European history of colonialism in Africa. *Meetings with Anna*, on the other hand, traverses Germany in the historical context of Jewish diaspora after the Holocaust. Both negotiate the representation of Germany in their own respective discourses (as a singular metaphor in the post-Holocaust Jewish imaginary and as part of the West in an African postcolonial discourse) as well as in the specific geographical and historical space of West Germany in the late 1970s.

Akerman produced her film *Meetings with Anna* in cooperation with the ZDF, a major West German television station in 1978. The film depicts its protagonist, the fictional filmmaker Anne Silver (later called "Anna" by her mother and an Italian woman), travelling through West Germany in the 1970s. Although we learn in the opening scene that she is undertaking this journey in order to present her films, we nevertheless see only her private encounters. The film depicts Anne's continuous journey through Europe, emphasized by long sequences of train rides, stays in hotel rooms and shots of train stations. Each city she visits – Essen, Cologne, Brussels and Paris – is marked by one meeting. In Essen she has a sexual relationship with Heinrich, a German, and in Cologne she encounters her mother's friend Ida at the train station. She meets her mother in Brussels and tells her about her desire for an Italian woman whose name is never revealed. Throughout the film Anne unsuccessfully tries to contact this unnamed woman in Italy by phone. The journey ends in Paris where Anne meets her male lover. After he becomes sick, she returns to her own apartment and listens to the messages on her answering machine, which include one from the Italian woman.

Similarly, Aidoo's *Our Sister Killjoy*, narrates a journey through West Germany in the 1970s. The text's main character, Sissie, is invited to visit Germany from her native Ghana, a former colony of Great Britain. She flies from Africa to Frankfurt and then travels to a small Bavarian town where she stays with an international group of young people working in a pine nursery. Sissie develops a friendship with a lonely German woman named "Marija" who is married to "big Adolf" and has a son "small Adolf." Marija makes sexual advances towards Sissie the day before Sissie departs for England; these are rejected by Sissie but initiate her reflections on colonial definitions of women's desire and identity. *Our Sister Killjoy* ends with a discussion about the moral imperative of returning to one's African homeland, and Sissie's letter to a male African lover written on her flight home.

Both texts focus on women's articulation of desire. *Meetings with Anna* ends with the voice of the Italian woman on the answering machine; *Our Sister Killjoy* ends with Sissie's letter to an unnamed male lover. While Aidoo's and Akerman's portrayals of West Germany are thoroughly gendered, gender itself is determined by a myriad of differences, such as national identity. Both texts present quotidian portrayals of "average" Germans and petit-bourgeois families who exoticize and silence Germany's Others. While *Meetings with Anna* points to the lacunae in 1970s West German self-representation through insinuation, the narrative strategy of *Our Sister Killjoy* fragments the prose poem into two interwoven parts: Sissie's encounters in Germany and her meditations on Ghana's colonial past in the inner monologues and poems. Both texts center on connections made in Germany, foregrounding language not as neutral system of signs, but as a reflection of the identity of those who enunciate it. German as national language is alienated [*verfremdet*] just as the main characters Sissie and Anne are alienated [*entfremdet*] from it.

Our Sister Killjoy reverses the conventions of the European travel narrative and its cultural production of exotic Others while it replays the colonial experience theorized by Frantz Fanon. At the outset of Sissie's journey to Germany we are introduced to temporal, geographical, and linguistic differences. "A cruel past, a funny present, a major desert or two, a sea, an ocean, several different languages apart, aeroplanes bridge the skies" (8). Instead of an introduction to the main character, we encounter "[o]ur sister," positioning the reader in proximity to the female protagonist and at a distance from Germany. Our sister Killjoy, Sissie, is addressed first as "Ja, das Schwartze [sic] Mädchen" [yes, the black girl] (12) at the train station in Frankfurt.[6] Aidoo's novel reflects the loudness and intrusiveness of the comment through bold print in the text, and by the fact that it is the only German sentence in the entire prose poem. The address "Ja, das Schwartze [sic] Mädchen" resonates with Fanon's description of the paradigmatic experience in which the black man from the colony recognizes himself in the fear of the white male child: "Mama, see the Negro! I'm frightened!"[7] Fanon reflects on the effects of the visual initiation rite through which he discovers his blackness and inscribes it on his body (112). Gwen Bergner has argued that in Fanon's account, "race is determined by sight, it is experienced profoundly in the body" which "shatters ... bodily integrity" (Bergner 78). Bergner likens "Fanon's emphasis on the visual field as instigating racial difference" to the "Freudian accounts of gendered subject formation" (78). While comparative discussions about race and gender easily reify the collapse of gender with white femininity and race with black masculinity, Aidoo's narrative portrays her main character's bodily and linguistic self-experience as always both racialized and gendered.

6. The sentence "Yes, the black girl" is written in misspelled German in the English text.

7. For an analysis of the black female as the "missing person in this 'race'/gender configuration," see Young (93).

In Aidoo's novel Sissie's racialized body is gendered feminine from the outset. Aware that "das Schwartze [sic] Mädchen" means the "black girl," Sissie looks for a black girl until she realizes that it is she who is meant. While the statement addressing the black man in Fanon's narrative expresses fear, the reference to Sissie reproduces the visual fascination, foreshadowing her later fetishization and sexualization in West Germany.[8] Learning to recognize herself in the racist gaze functions as Sissie's rite of initiation into West German society. As Sissie's recognition of race leads into the description of colonialism's reliance on racism as "[a] way to get land, land, more land" (13), the text connects the West German racist gaze with a history of colonial exploitation.[9] But while Fanon describes the internalization of the colonizer's racist gaze, *Our Sister Killjoy* reverses the gaze when Sissie realizes that the people surrounding her have "the colour of the pickled pig parts that used to come from foreign places to the markets at home" (12). Sissie's comparison racializes whiteness and makes it strange, a process generally absent in German cultural representations of race, where race is traditionally embodied by blackness. The connection between sight and race also characterizes Sissie's reflections about Marija's whiteness, especially her fascination with Marija's blushing, which she describes as "switching on and switching off like a two-colour neon sign." "[B]eing white" is perceived by Sissie as "a pretty dangerous matter," which leaves a person "awfully exposed" and "terribly vulnerable" (76).

Because Sissie meditates on Marija's whiteness in relationship to her blushing, a signifier of femininity in the West, the text points not only to the gendering of racial categories, but also to the racialization of Western constructions of femininity and the historical export of these concepts to the colonies. Sissie describes the position of African women as "a little more complicated than that of the dolls the colonizers brought along with them who fainted at the sight of their bleeding fingers and carried smelling salts around ..." (117). In Sissie's reflections on Western definitions of femininity, the choice of the word "doll" for these white women points, on the one hand, to the representational function of femininity and symbolizes, on the other, that women in this model are commodities of exchange. The colonial encounter, as Bergner has shown, is traditionally cast as a male/male encounter, in which a woman's function lies in her "trafficking."[10] Sissie's postcolonial travel to Germany thus reverses the colonial export of white femininity to the colonies.

8. On the interconnection of the stereotype and fetishization, see Bhabha.

9. For a theoretical overview of the connection between racist stereotypes and German colonial history, see Martin.

10. Bergner is referring to Gayle Rubin's term here; she also uses Luce Irigaray's concept of the "exchange of woman" (80-81).

Sissie is invited by the German government, for whom Sissie's journey holds out the promise of *Wiedergutmachung*, the German fantasy of "making good again" for the crimes of the Holocaust. Sissie as an African woman becomes a displaced token, rupturing the German-Jewish binarism that permeates German postwar history. Hence, this fetish character of the stereotype, embodied by her exotic blackness and Africanness, makes Sissie attractive to Germans in the Bavarian town: "As for the African Miss, ah … h … h … look at her costume. How charming. And they gaped at her, pointing at her smile. Her nose. Her lips. Their own eyes shining" (43). After she befriends Marija, the two women take walks together, and Marija feeds Sissie various German foods. Sissie's surprise, excitement, and disgust about certain foods invert the ethnographic colonial encounter. The other people in town (represented by the director of the local branch of a bank, the manager of a supermarket, and the insurance broker) become increasingly jealous of Marija's friendship with Sissie. They wonder, "So how was it that it was not them or their wives escorting the African Miss?" Because the officials in town cannot explain the friendship of two women who do not speak the same language, the interracial friendship becomes cast as lesbian.[11] The friendship between Marija and Sissie confuses the sexual structure of postcolonial Germany, and Marija's husband is called upon to restore order: "SOMEONE MUST TELL HER HUSBAND!! [sic]" (44).

Marija's character is offered for the reader's identification, integrating curiosity, friendliness and loneliness. However, her naive actions often initiate Sissie's reflections on the imperial relationship between the African continent and the West. When Sissie visits her the night before she leaves, Marija makes sexual advances by touching Sissie's breast, which Sissie rejects in a moment of awkwardness by accidently hitting Marija's cheek. In this key scene, Sissie identifies with Marija's loneliness and despair, but her identification is fractured by the persistence of the colonial past. The text focuses solely on the description of Marija's silent tear, through the vertical typesetting of the word loneliness on the left-hand side of the page:

> Marija was crying silently. There was a tear streaming out of one of her eyes. The tear was coming out of the left eye only. The right eye was completely dry. Sissie felt pain at the sight of that one tear. That forever tear out of one eye. Suddenly Sissie knew. She saw it once and was never to forget it. She saw against the background of the thick smoke that was like a rain cloud over the chimneys of Europe,

11. Casting an interracial female relationship as lesbian is, according to Judith Mayne "a long-standing iconographic tradition in Western art" (171).

L
O
N
E
L
I
N
E
S
S

Forever falling like a tear out of a woman's eye (65).

After enumerating icons of colonial exploitation (for example "slave traders" and "missionaries"), Sissie almost loses consciousness. "As the room began to spin around her, Sissie knew that she had to stop herself from crying. Why weep for them?" (65). Sissie's conscious disidentification demonstrates an awareness that identification of the colonized with the European's pain and despair is constitutive of colonial narratives.[12] While the text portrays Sissie's disidentification, it simultaneously makes it possible for the reader to sympathize with Marija's desperate desire for Sissie.

Our Sister Killjoy plays out Sissie's postcolonial negotiations in the West through her relationship with Marija, a German woman, focusing on the traces of colonial history in their relationship. After Marija's outburst of despair, Sissie recalls that colonial encounters with missionaries introduced the concept of sin for intimate relations among women, and thus exported not only definitions of gender but also of sexual identity. Marija and Sissie, however, are unable to overcome the gap that has opened up between them. Sissie later tells Marija that she is leaving. Aware that her departure hurts Marija, this moment reveals to Sissie her own pleasure in domination. The text strategically stands colonial structures on their head and lays bare colonialism's underlying dynamics of submission and domination through this reversal of roles.

As in *Our Sister Killjoy*, Anne, the main character of *Meetings with Anna*, traverses Germany in the 1970s. The narrative focuses on Anne's sexual, emotional and intellectual encounters, and relies on a lesbian "subtext." While *Our Sister Killjoy* explicitly foregrounds its references to colonial narratives, *Meetings with Anna* refers to Anne's displacement in Germany through a lack of explicit articulation. The film offers a specific perspective on Germany: that of a member of a Jewish generation born in central Europe after the Holocaust quoting a tradition of literary rep-

---

12. On the abjection of African women in colonial narratives, see McClintock, especially "Race, Mimicry and the Abjection of Black Women" (270-73).

resentation of Jewish and political exile. The fact that neither the term *Jewish* nor the term *Holocaust* occurs in the text corresponds to the absence that is in fact central to the film's narrative. A similar strategy prevails in regard to Anne's lesbian desire. The film visually and narratively portrays her encounters with heterosexual men, while its plot is motivated by Anne's desire to contact an Italian woman. Anne's heterosexual relationships are represented, but their romantic potential for the narrative is undermined because they are permanently disrupted and end in separation. Similarly to *Our Sister Killjoy, Meetings with Anna* presents the interaction of Germans in the space of the petit-bourgeois home. Just as Sissie accidentally slaps Marija's cheek, Anne spills the coffee offered to her in Heinrich's house and produces a slippage within the orderly setting. The accidental slap and the spill signify the displacement of the main characters in the setting of the German home, which is consistent with their larger displacement in each narrative as a whole.

Anne is repeatedly shown in hotel rooms, a motif that reflects the exiled person's situation. Heinrich's house is the only "home" to be visually represented in the film. It is, however, shown only from the outside where Heinrich and Anne are engaged in a dialogue. While Anne gains access to the German home on the level of the plot, we see her only outside on the porch – as if on a stage – apologizing for spilling her cup of coffee. In their dialogue in front of the house Heinrich positions himself as the authentic informer who represents a leftist, yet paradigmatic narrative of German history in which the German Left has been victimized by the state since the 1920s. His silence on the Holocaust positions Anne outside German history and silences her. At the same time, his narrative about his ex-wife's current lover, to whom he refers as "the Turk," makes the sexualized Turk stand in for all of Germany's Others and thereby ruptures the German-Jewish binarism.

The film captures the dilemma of Jewish subjectivity in relationship to post-Holocaust Germany: the injunction to identify as Jewish versus a rejection of the limited position of victim within the German-Jewish binarism. Instead of Anne's Jewish self-identification the film offers a discussion about exile, ruminating for example on the conditions that would be necessary for a return of exiled German Jews and how that return would affect language and identity. Anne's train rides from city to city echo a German-Jewish diaspora. In Brussels Anne meets her mother at the train station and talks with her in a café and in a hotel room, even though Anne's family must have an actual house in Brussels. Their meetings outside this "home" signify not only Anne's homelessness but her mother's displacement as well. The German-Jewish dialogue that traditionally forces Jews into permanent self-definition vis-à-vis Germany is inverted when Anne's mother asks her about Germany. Anne's answer, "Germany is full of Germans now," equates geographical borders with ethnicity and refers to the lack of an inclusive definition of "German." The suggestion that Germany might have once been less "German" integrates the unspoken past of the Holocaust and the extermination of so-called non-Germans into the spoken present of the late 1970s.

Anne's displacement as she travels from one hotel to the other is visually emphasized by shots of her lying or sitting on one of the two beds in the hotel room, while the other lies empty. The situation is momentarily resolved when the empty space is taken up by the mother and Anne tells her about the encounter with the Italian woman. This is cut to the farewell with the mother at the train station, where she addresses Anne as "Anna," the German-Jewish version of her name, which was translated into "Anne" in exile in French-speaking Belgium. In the final shot the audience hears the Italian woman speak, as her voice is recorded on the answering-machine in Anne's home asking "Anna dove sei?" [Anna where are you?] The Italian woman's voice is denaturalized through the answering machine and her question is rendered diachronic by way of the machine. Since the Italian woman speaks multiple languages, she translates her question into English, a language Anne understands, which thus is the only speech not subtitled in the English version of the film. She calls Anne by the Italian form of her name, "Anna," thus creating a connection between the female figures surrounding Anne: her mother and the Italian woman. The recorded voice does not close the narrative, but initiates a new reading of the film and its title *Meetings with Anna*. Moreover, Akerman's decision to use her own voice for the Italian character forecloses the exoticization and romanticization of the Other because it undermines the stereotypical association of Italian with desire and passion.

"Germany is full of Germans now" refers to Germany's history, but also to Anne's journey which has traversed Germany and left it behind. While *Meetings with Anna* reflects the consistent displacement of a Jewish woman filmmaker travelling through central Europe, *Our Sister Killjoy* explicitly refers to the movement from the periphery to the center: "but for the slave, there is nothing at the centre but worse slavery" (87). In the prose poem, England functions as the imperial center and Germany as its displacement, disrupting the binarism of margin and center. While Sissie's and Anne's journeys seem to leave Germany intact and behind, Aidoo and Akerman's narratives deconstruct the narrative foundations of German nationhood and alert us to the reciprocal implicatedness of post-Holocaust and postcolonial discourses in a definition of Germanness.

Note

I would like to thank Eleanor Courtemanche, Dana Luciano, Amy Abugo Ongiri, Bradley Prager, Bethany Schneider, and Jeffrey A. Schneider for reading and discussing earlier versions of this essay, and I am grateful to Leslie Adelson and the editors for their thoughtful comments.

Bibliography

Adelson, Leslie A. "Anne Duden's *Übergang*: Racism and Feminist Aesthetics: A Provocation." *Making Bodies, Making Histories: Feminism and German Identity*. Lincoln: U of Nebraska P, 1993. 37-55.

_____. "Migrants' Literature or German Literature? TORKAN's Tufan: Brief an einen islamischen Bruder." *German Quarterly* 63.3/4 (1990): 382-89.

Aidoo, Ata Aidoo. *Our Sister Killjoy or Reflections from a Black-eyed Squint*. London: Longman, 1977.

Akerman, Chantal. *Les Rendez-vous d'Anna* [Meetings with Anna], 1978.

Bammer, Angelika. *Partial Visions: Feminism and Utopianism in the 1970s*. New York: Routledge, 1991.

Bergner, Gwen. "Who Is That Masked Woman? or, The Role of Gender in Fanon's *Black Skin, White Masks*." *PMLA* 110.1 (1995): 75-89.

Bhabha, Homi K. "The Other Question: Stereotype, Discrimination and the Discourse of Colonialism." *The Location of Culture*. New York: Routledge, 1994. 66-85.

Braidotti, Rosi. *Nomadic Subjects*. New York: Columbia UP, 1994.

Doan, Laura, ed. *The Lesbian Postmodern*. New York: Columbia UP, 1994.

Fanon, Frantz. *Black Skin, White Masks*. New York: Grove, 1967.

Grewal, Inderpal, and Caren Kaplan. "Introduction: Transnational Feminist Practices and Questions of Postmodernity." *Scattered Hegemonies: Postmodernity and Transnational Feminist Practices*. Ed. Inderpal Grewal and Caren Kaplan. Minneapolis: U of Minnesota P, 1994. 1-37.

Kaplan, Caren. *Questions of Travel: Postmodern Discourses of Displacement*. Durham: Duke UP, 1996.

Knischewski, Gerd. "Post-War National Identity in Germany." *Nation and Identity in Contemporary Europe*. Ed. Brian Jenkins and Spyros A. Sofos. New York:Routledge, 1996. 125-55.

Margulies, Ivone. *Nothing Happens: Chantal Akerman's Hyperrealist Everyday*. Durham: Duke UP, 1996.

Martin, Peter. *Schwarze Teufel - Edle Mohren: Afrikaner im Bewußtsein und Geschichte der Deutschen.* Hamburg: Junius, 1993.

Mayne, Judith. *Cinema and Spectatorship.* New York: Routledge, 1993.

McClintock, Anne. *Imperial Leather: Race, Gender and Sexuality in the Colonial Contest.* New York: Routledge, 1995.

McCormick, Richard. *Politics of the Self: Feminism and the Postmodern in West German Literature and Film.* Princeton: Princeton UP, 1991.

Odamtten, Vincent O. *The Art of Ama Ata Aidoo: Polylectics and Reading against Neocolonialism.* Gainesville: UP of Florida, 1994.

Peck, Jeffrey M. "There's No Place Like Home? Remapping the Topography of German Studies." *German Quarterly* 62.2 (1989): 178-88.

Rentschler, Eric. "Remembering Not to Forget: A Retrospective Reading of Kluge's *Brutality in Stone.*" *New German Critique* 49 (1990): 23-43.

Santner, Eric L. *Stranded Objects: Mourning, Memory, and Film in Postwar Germany.* Ithaca: Cornell UP, 1990.

Schmidt, Ricarda. *Westdeutsche Frauenliteratur in den 70er Jahren.* Frankfurt: Rita G. Fischer Verlag, 1982.

Thürmer-Rohr, Christina. *Vagabonding: Feminist Thinking Cut Loose.* Trans. Lise Weil. Boston: Beacon Press, 1991.

Weiner, Marc A. "From the Editor." *German Quarterly* 68.1 (1995): vi-viii.

Young, Lola. "Missing Persons: Fantasising Black Women in *Black Skin, White Masks.*" *The Fact of Blackness: Frantz Fanon and Visual Representation.* Seattle: Bay Press, 1996. 86-102.

Chapter 16

BODIES FOR GERMANY, BODIES FOR SOCIALISM

The German Democratic Republic Devises a
Gay (Male) Body

Denis M. Sweet

> That which is unknown to the ruling self-understanding, the unexpressed,
> the unspeakable, is always to be found among the underprivileged, the mar-
> ginalized, among those declared incompetent and dispossessed.
>
> (Christa Wolf)[1]

Socialism's Homosexualities

The history of homosexuality in the German Democratic Republic
(GDR) is one of steadfast denial and rigorous suppression that
came to a dramatic end in the second half of the 1980s. Just a few years
before the Wall fell, what had hitherto been a taboo subject suddenly
became a widespread topic of public discussion in the state-controlled
media of the GDR. When homosexuality finally made (or was allowed
to make) its entrance into the public sphere, it was in a particular kind
of way to pursue a particular agenda, namely tolerance of homosexuals
(male homosexuals providing in general the subject of discussion, lesbians remaining largely ignored) and their integration into existing

---

1. Christa Wolf, "Berührung. Ein Vorwort," Wander (12).

socialist society. In this widespread and concerted public effort, gay men were constructed as victims. The argument called for pity and compassion from a normal majority for a minority that suffers on account of its "difference." This was the standard line taken in the media of the GDR toward what was in reality an increasingly recalcitrant gay male population, more and more of whom were applying to leave the country or joining the fast-growing gay liberation groups under the auspices of the Protestant church and thus formally beyond the state's control, though such groups were heavily infiltrated by the State Security apparatus (Stasi).

Of course there were other readings of homosexuality. Of the two most significant in the GDR of the late 1980s, one was put forward in published interviews with gay men and the other in a study done at the behest of East Berlin's internal security apparatus. Both adumbrated readings of homosexuality (exclusively male in both cases) that were defined by their own particular interests. The self-representations of gay men in the interviews elided inherent "difference" to pursue an assimilationist tack: respectability and loyalty to socialism were the name of the game. The Stasi study took recourse to older linkages between homosexuality and disease and identified gay men as sites of verbal and venereal contagion requiring stepped-up surveillance by the State Security organs. All of the constructions mentioned here, propagated by different interest groups, served an inherently conservative agenda: bolstering socialism in its final years. All were swept aside with the end of the GDR. What follows is an archaeology of these homosexualities of the former GDR. Empirical studies of the actual behavior and attitudes of gay men were not (could not be) published until after the GDR had ceased to exist (see Starke).

The Emblem of Suicide

In the last year of the existence of the GDR, in that remarkable year of lightning-fast changes when the old order was quickly vanishing and the new, reunified, order was not yet born, in the short final year between the mass street protests of the *Wende* that brought down the forty-year regime of the Socialist Unity Party late in the fall of 1989 and East Germany's formal accession into the Federal Republic of Germany on 3 October 1990, at a time when political events captured the national attention, it was rather peculiar that it should fall to a rather unassuming movie to take on the role of lightning rod for its times. Strange, that at a time when big Hollywood films were already flooding the market, an East German film should become the biggest box-office hit of the year. It had struck a nerve. But what was it?

Heiner Carow's feature film, *Coming Out,* about a young male teacher coming to grips with his homosexuality, scarcely seems the stuff to rivet the attention of a country caught in the grips of momentous political change. But here a film about the hitherto marginalized became a vehicle by which mainstream East Germans could grasp their predicament. Carow's film was about the struggle to assert one's own personhood despite unacceptance, social opprobrium, and marginalization. It was, for East Germans flocking to the movie theaters in that key year, a film not so much about homosexuality, as about the courage to stand up and be counted for what one really was. *Coming Out* is about putting an end to conformity, about the personal and social courage required for that process. It can be (and was) taken then as a narrative about the struggles of the East Germans as they sought to cast off repression and free themselves.

The film found little resonance in West Germany. The reasons why it was awarded a Silver Bear by the (West) Berlin Film Festival in February 1990 have nothing to do with the East German identification with the film's struggle for authenticity mentioned above, nor even with any intrinsic filmic merits; it was for its pluck, simply for its having broached the topic of coming out on the other side of the Wall, that *Coming Out* received its Silver Bear.[2] Film reviewers in West Germany, by contrast, who also foreshortened the film to a public service message about homosexuality, were less inclined to meet out such a well-intentioned, albeit patronizing, pat on the back. For them, *Coming Out* was an embarrassment that hearkened back to an earlier, more naive stage of development of gay liberation long since left behind in the dust of Western history. They had nothing but scorn or, at best, a kind of commiseration from the vantage point of their own perceived superiority for its manifest outdatedness.[3] In either case, the focus of both the festival judges and the film critics was on homosexuality, an underdeveloped homosexuality from an underdeveloped place. The film flopped at the West German box office.

Coming Out begins with an ambulance, blue lights flashing and siren howling, on its way to the emergency room of an East Berlin hospital.

2. The Silver Bear was awarded, in the words of the Berlin Festival jury, "for the sensitive treatment of the dilemma in which minorities – all minorities – find themselves and for the deep regard it expresses for human rights, humanity, and tolerance." Cited by Olaf Müller, who calls it "one of the stupidest reasons" he has heard for giving a film prize.

3. For example, the review by Oksana Bulgakowa in *tip,* one of West Berlin's popular entertainment listings, criticized the film as "didactic," an "alibi for other [socio-political] failures" [of the GDR] that serves up the viewer "treacly history lessons" [*menschelnder Geschichtsunterricht*]. "I'm happy to see," she concludes, "such unity

There – in graphic close-up – a tube is painstakingly inserted down a young man's throat and his stomach pumped out following a suicide attempt. Cut to him just afterwards lying on a gurney in the hospital corridor, sobbing. The attending physician walks up to him, and asks why he did it. "Ich bin schwul" [I'm gay], he says, then, as if the slang term *schwul* were not a formal enough category in this medical setting, repeats the cause of his unhappiness, more formally this time, "I'm a homosexual." All of this is most gripping, and yet these initial scenes of the film have nothing whatsoever to do with the ensuing story line. If the hospital sequence is meant as a flashback, it is left unclear what time it refers back to, for the character in question is an open and self-accepting young gay man throughout the course of the film. The attempted suicide that so graphically sets the stage at the beginning is simply dropped in the remainder of the film. It is quite puzzling.

While *Coming Out* was the first East German feature film to portray gay men's lives, it was not the first East German attempt to air issues connected with homosexuality. Indeed, *Coming Out* was merely a part – the notable highwater mark and, as it turned out, final installment (premiering in East Berlin the night the Wall came down, 9 November 1989) – of a much larger public tide of information aimed at furthering tolerance of homosexuals by the mainstream population and advocating their integration into socialist society. Such a campaign would have been unthinkable even a few years before, since homosexuality had been a taboo and unwanted subject in public discourse, an embarrassing area consigned to sexual pathology and the criminal code.

When homosexuality finally made its first public appearance, now tolerated or even furthered by the organs of the state in the last few years of the GDR's existence, it did so as a phenomenon rhetorically constructed with a particular end in mind, namely tolerance of a minority and its integration into existing socialist society. Homosexuality did not make its appearance on the public stage of that society as part of an interrogation of sexual hegemonies and hierarchies in socialist society, nor as an investigation into the construction of gender, or even as a means for discussing the control of sexualities at the hands of the state. No, none of this is undertaken, though some of it is certainly envisaged by some of the more liberationist gays who voice what is plainly a minority and isolated position.[4] No, the widespread and concerted public

---

among men, peoples, and continents, a 'sign of understanding' to use the customary politjargon – only it is of little help in enjoying this film as film."

4. Far-reaching social critiques and radical hopes for social transformation were articulated by some, particularly at the time of the *Wende,* critiques that burst the confines

efforts from 1987 to the end of the GDR move along different avenues
and actually have remarkably little to do with gender and sexuality.

Instead, two lines of argumentation predominate. The first concerns
integration and hails from an ideological provenance: no one should be
left out of socialist society. The nature of socialism is not exclusion but
inclusion of all its citizens.[5] The second line of argument has to do with
tolerance. This argument is framed on perceived difference – which is to
be answered by compassion. Homosexuals are put forward as people
who are different and who therefore suffer. The point of such argumentation is to ease their suffering by an act of compassion, i.e., by tolerance.
Let the lyrics of a song broadcast on East German radio to articulate this
message serve as a classic formulation of what was repeated endlessly in
the state-controlled print and electronic media:

> "They're scum,
> people like that should be shot.
> If that were my son, I'd know what to do!"
> Someone says, "He's a runaway."
> Someone says, "Beat it, get out of here."
> Someplace someone mumbles, "Ya fuckin' queer."
> Someone spits at his feet,
> someone throws food after him.
> A drunks grabs him and starts to pummel him.

Unjust suffering is the topic highlighted here, and it is left unclear
whether the figure in the song is really gay or is simply perceived as
such. Here, in a song ostensibly about homosexuality, homosexuality is
elided into a generic difference that is unjustly persecuted. It could just
as well be some other kind of difference. The refrain proceeds along the
same lines in a more sentimental and didactic fashion:

> When my yellow parakeet flew out the window,
> a pack of sparrows started to peck at him.
> He sang a bit different
> and wasn't as gray as they …
> Unacceptable things to a sparrow brain.[6]

---

of the generally adhered to constructions of homosexuality in the GDR's last years. See
the articles and interviews in *Die DDR. Die Schwulen.*

5. This is one of the fundamental themes of the two conferences on the "Psychosocial
Aspects of Homosexuality" held in Leipzig (28 June 1985) and Karl-Marx-Stadt (23 April
1988). An ideologically laden and yet typical formulation comes from Wolfgang Bradter's
paper entitled "Homosexuality, Human Dignity, and Tolerance in Socialism": "Only in
socialism can the dignity of working people be universally [allseitig] fulfilled" (Amendt 65).

6. "Der gelbe Wellensittich," transcribed from a transmission from GDR radio by
Gudrun von Kowalski. A slightly different version of this song is found on Gerhard
Schöne's album *Menschenskind* (Amiga, 1985) as "Wellensittich und Spatzen."

The argument, as it is posed in the lyrics of this song and as it was repeatedly formulated elsewhere in the GDR, appeals to moral rectitude in the face of the persecution and suffering of others, and as such continues on in a long (religious) tradition. Its listener/viewer/reader responds with a sense of moral outrage. The drama of this approach can be increased by increasing the suffering; the ultimate suffering being death – self-inflicted death. The public efforts to promote tolerance and further the integration of homosexuals into socialist society were characterized by an instrumentalization of suicide.[7] By tolerance (of the majority), suffering (of the minority) can be diminished. The issue here is suffering, not homosexuality. Such rhetorical constructions do not have, strictly speaking, anything to do with homosexuality. One can hate homosexuality but nonetheless be called upon to feel compassion for those who unjustly suffer. Love the sinner, hate the sin. This is the way by which homosexuality, a hitherto taboo topic, first entered public discourse in the GDR in the late 1980s.[8] It is a way to elicit a moral response without the specifics of homosexuality ever needing to enter the discussion. Suicide functions as the emblem for homosexuals' inherent suffering, brought about by their difference from the normal.

The off-camera attempted suicide of *Coming Out* and its gruelling clinical aftermath that so gut-wrenchingly ground the beginning scenes of the film, and that seemed to be out of place in the story line, reinscribe the by now familiar rhetorical construction. Here is a homosexual made recognizable: a suffering body threatened by its own hand. Compassion, please.

Authentic Voices

The emancipatory process heralded in the public efforts to further tolerance and integration took place on many fronts, from film and pop songs on the radio to television discussions by panels of experts, from articles in newspapers and popular magazines to books ranging from popular psychology to fiction and a gay diary. The single most important

7. See especially Ursula Hafranke's series of interviews and accounts of homosexuals' lives, including letters from readers, in *Das Magazin,* one of the most popular magazines with a mass readership in the GDR.

8. The appearance of homosexuality in the public sphere of socialist society had been preceded by at least five years of discussions, conferences, and forums within the Protestant church. This institution had been the first to address homosexuality as an issue of acceptance and social justice, beginning in February 1982 with a conference in the Evangelical Academy Berlin-Brandenburg on "Theological Aspects of Homosexuality." For a detailed account, see the essays by Günter Grau and Manfred Punge in *Und diese Liebe auch.*

book publication to result from it was a collection of interviews with gay men that appeared in the spring of 1989. Lesbians continued to remain more or less invisible to the public eye until Ursula Sillge's book, appropriately entitled *Un-Sichtbare Frauen* (Invisible Women) was published in 1991, a year after reunification. In the last year of the GDR's existence as a state, however, it was the gay male who was the object – and now with Jürgen Lemke's collection of interviews the subject – of demonstration. *Ganz normal anders* (literally "Quite Normally Different"; an English translation appeared under the title *Gay Voices from East Germany*) was to provide a voice for GDR gays. Here they were, or at least fourteen representative ones, from various generations and professions, city and country folk, speaking for themselves about their lives, not being spoken about. At the same time that an unusually large East German edition in an inexpensive paperback format appeared, a licensed West German edition came out with the added subtitle "Auskünfte schwuler Männer aus der DDR" (Gay Men from the GDR Talk). Yet the reception in the two German states could not have been more divergent, prefiguring and paralleling that of *Coming Out*.

Ganz normal anders struck a nerve in the East. Jürgen Lemke wrote a feisty stage version ("Men's Biographies in the GDR: I'm queer"), reinserting a colorful gay activist who had been deleted from the book, that proved a box-office smash throughout the GDR. An extraordinarily popular East Berlin production in the downtown theater (TiP – Theater im Palast) housed in the GDR's parliament building, in which that activist played himself, continued to draw crowds until the entire structure was closed down as a potential health hazard (asbestos). The theatrical and literary success in the East was sufficient to catapult Lemke into an overnight celebrity in the West. He appeared on talkshows and was featured in an interview with the West German newsmagazine, *Der Spiegel;* nonetheless all this signaled scarcely anything more than interest in then topical Eastern exotica. The production taken on tour of West Germany by the road company comprised of the same actors who had had such success in East Berlin never attracted much interest. The West German edition of the book of interviews was noticed even less and was eventually remaindered.

Authentic voices hitherto suppressed – that was what these interviews signaled, but the notion was no novelty. *Ganz normal anders* followed in well-established footsteps. Collections of representative interviews with the hitherto marginalized belonged to a popular genre in East Germany. Maxie Wander's spectacularly successful collection of interviews with women, *Guten Morgen, du Schöne* (Good Morning, My Beauty, 1977), was now followed by this most recent collection of interviews that sought to give voice to "that which is unknown to ruling conventions, that which has not been spoken, the unspeakable," to use Christa Wolf's formulation (Wander 12). This is precisely what Jürgen Lemke's collection of interviews with gay men proposed to accomplish twenty-two years later, in the last year of the GDR: to allow the voice of the silenced to speak their truth.

Yet representative interviews belong to a genre, at least as practiced by Maxie Wander and subsequently in East Germany, where authenticity is enriched after the fact. The spoken interviews provide the base material which is then literarily reworked. Readers have no guarantee that what they are reading was actually said in that form or in that sequence. One is simply presented with a text, reworked by the interviewer, a text that claims to be true to the interviewee's intentions and must be taken in good faith. The twenty-three questions that Maxie Wander posed the women she interviewed, for example, show up nowhere in the printed text, which is reproduced as an extended monologue rather than in the form of questions and answers. The same is true for Lemke's interviews. But let us suppose that this practice has distorted nothing, that the editor has simply clarified trains of thought, changed words for precision, deleted repetitions for the sake of a written text, then are we right in assuming that these are indeed authentic voices that speak an otherwise unadulterated truth?

Despite the attempt at representativeness by including young and old, educated and uneducated, those living in relationships and those not, men living in the country and professionals in the city, the representative (dissimilar) interviewees of this volume make for a remarkably similar end result, namely the image of utter normality that is projected. "Their life is, in many ways, like the life of everybody in this country, the GDR," writes the East Berlin sociologist Irene Runge in her introduction to the volume (Lemke 10). That is precisely it. There is nothing to give offense because there is nothing that might strike anyone in the mainstream as unfamiliar or different. Not much talk about sex, abnormal or otherwise, no desires voiced beyond those for love and intimacy. All of the men interviewed are rock-solid citizens. Their values are those of a German workers' state: work, dependability, duty. Pleasure is not at the forefront.

The message of compassion for suffering brought about by difference has been subtly but significantly transformed. These gay men do not suffer inherently, they are *made* to by those around them. Their difference is no longer inherent but lies in the eye of the beholder:

Our environment is hostile to homos, yes, that's so, we're discriminated against. Hatred of gays is all over the place; Joe Average reacts aggressively to us, that's my experience … . If they see some conspicuous guy on the street, you know, tralala, it starts up immediately. Castrate the sow, that's how they talk. It probably isn't meant as serious as it sounds, but that's what they say – often … They got it somewhere, you aren't born with attitudes like that (74).

If a particular kind of suffering homosexual had been put forward earlier as part of an argument for compassion, this volume describes men who are not different, who no longer suffer generically, and who realize full well the benefits that accrue to them from living in a socialist society that has overcome the horrors of persecution experienced under fascism. They voice this realization repeatedly:

I was sufficiently well-educated politically to know that [the spectre of Nazi-like terror against gays] was excluded under the new [socialist] conditions. Conflicts did not disappear, but life was no longer perilous (30).

Another man says:

I am fortunate to have progressed into an age in which living out my psyche no longer signifies death. Born a few years earlier, and I would have gone to the gas chambers. It's that simple (59).

Or this from a different interview:

You experience a state like the GDR as a blessing. This state enabled me to pursue new technical training in old age. I haven't forgotten. It's not something that I take for granted (199).

Sentiments like this run throughout the text as a kind of red thread. It goes much further than what might be an occasionally voiced personal gratitude for the new, socialist, social order which has made lives as responsible citizens possible. The gay men whose interviews appear in *Ganz normal anders* are respectable and hardworking citizens politically committed to socialism. They (not all by any means, but enough to cast this collection of interviews collectively in a certain vein) are members of the Party. They are involved in society, not withdrawn from it. For personal reasons connected with their homosexuality, but especially for ideological reasons, they are committed to their East German socialist state as a superior political and social order. One worker who is a Party member puts it most memorably, "The Soviet Union is my fatherland and the GDR my motherland" (38).

If these are representative interviews, then they are so with a vengeance, that is, they are not random but have been selected to construct a coherent and unified message about the homosexuality and political allegiance of gay men in the GDR. These men are positively identified building blocks of socialist society. In her introduction to the volume, Irene Runge had wondered what another selection of gay men might have said. One who might have been inclined to more critical utterances was the gay activist who had originally been interviewed for the project, but whose interview had been deleted from the published volume (to be reinserted in the successful stage version of 1990). One wonders which came first, the chicken or the egg – censorship by the Ministry of Culture through which the manuscript had to pass, or the logic of assimilation.

The authentic voices of the gay men whose interviews were published by the most respected publishing house of the GDR had been preselected, edited, and turned out under the sign of an assimilationist strategy, one that has deep historical resonances in Germany. In his study of outsiders, Hans Mayer characterizes Jewish strategies for assimilation into German culture since the Enlightenment as the attempt to emulate the path set out by the eponymous hero of Lessing's drama *Nathan the Wise:* assimilation through hypertrophy of wealth and education. In Jürgen Lemke's interviews with gay men two centuries later, the path laid out for assimilation into East German society is through a hypertrophy of respectability and political loyalty to the socialist order.

Security Risks

Of the three constructions of homosexuality put forward in the GDR in the 1980s mentioned in this article, the third was by far the most retrograde. Like the others, it had little to do with homosexual people, their actual lives, behavior, and attitudes, and more to do with the construction of a public rhetoric about homosexual men that handily furthered one's own agenda, in this case that of the State Security establishment. This study, a doctoral dissertation in criminology at Humboldt University in then East Berlin, can be seen as a maneuver on the part of the State Security apparatus to garner an academic cachet for its views, since the person who produced it was no run-of-the-mill criminology student, but a Stasi operative commissioned by the Stasi to carry out the study. Essentially it was an in-house product whose prestige was upped by the academic venue. The Stasi were now in the position to refer, if they so chose, to an academic study with its associations of objectivity and science to bolster the foregone conclusions of their policy-making.

If suffering was constructed as a vehicle to tolerance and integration into socialist society, and if a gay hypertrophy of respectability and loyalty were promoted to that same end, then the construction of homo-sexuality promulgated by Gerhard Fehr in his criminological study pursues a different tack altogether. Here there is no pity and commiseration for the suffering of those perceived as different, no conviction, no supposition that these people are loyal or even respectable. Far from it: gay men are security risks, and Fehr sets out to document why. Of the writings under discussion, this is the only one based on field research (interviews with gay men undergoing treatment for syphilis in the state treatment center for sexually transmitted diseases at Buch near Berlin), the only one to cite statistical evidence (from the confidential medical records of patients provided him by the medical director of that same treatment center), the only one to pursue a line of reasoning that does not segue into tolerance and integration, but rather into surveillance and control – stepped-up surveillance and tighter control.

Fehr's raison d'être was to sound the security alarm. His study pushes the security buttons of a state long obsessed with internal and external conspiracies by reading gay men as sites of infection in the body politic. Not only are they a "major source of infection" because of their promiscuity (ascribing high and increasing infection rates for syphilis and other sexually transmitted diseases to them), their very presence is a potential source for crime and social destabilization. Captivated by a glitzy lifestyle that places a premium on looks and ready cash (for purposes of entertainment, seduction, and sexual gratification), homosexuals who "often from an early age have behaved in a conspiratorial fashion toward their environment," steal on the job, practice fraud and cronyism (for sexual favors), so that if one is hired there soon ensues a whole little nest of them, especially in areas of the socialist economy that open the door to self-aggrandizement, "particularly gastronomy" (rich gay waiters!).

In their ravenous hunger for ever more sexual contacts, they take up with foreigners, "especially from capitalist countries, the FRG (West Germany), and West Berlin," and attempt to "expand" such contacts into "personal gain" and a possible way to leave the country *(Ausreise)*. Gay men whose attempts to "acquaint themselves with new partners at every occasion for sexual manipulations" make them into "an especially attractive group of people for the class enemy and his spy networks." Curiously (or perhaps it is not so curious after all), this catalog of medical, moral, and security threats ascribed to the nature of a group defined as different repeats the antisemite's insistent warnings about Jews – the connection to syphilis, hunger for glitz and the ingrown cronyism that produces little nests of them, the uncontrollability of one's own body (in the immoral and ineluctable search for ever more sexual partners), the questionable loyalty to one's fatherland: it is all prefigured there.

Under the guise of a criminological study, Fehr's enumeration of threats to the socialist body politic embodies a polemic for the strengthening of state security that culminates in the following call for vigilance:

> Fundamentally only with the cooperation of all organs and bureaus responsible for order and security in the capital, Berlin, can a successful battle be waged against these ... risk groups. It is necessary to observe and register the development and further behavior of homosexual persons in the capital and by means of constant surveillance and evaluation keep their activity under control. Furthermore, it is of the utmost importance for instances of order and security to be familiar with the meeting places, bars, and events of this group of persons and to undertake action to collect information ... Existing contacts to foreigners, especially from the capitalist states, must be registered and controlled in order to confront illegal petitioners [i.e., those applying to leave the GDR] and possible activities on the part of homosexuals for the enemy (this passage and the other quotations from Fehr above are cited by Thinius 18).

Yet even this catch-all catalog was curiously reticent. Two of the most pressing preoccupations of the Stasi at the time find no mention, at least no explicit mention. A now declassified internal Stasi document from 20 July 1984 makes it quite clear:

> In response to the death of a child in West Berlin resulting from a blood transfusion from a homosexual infected with HIV, a list of all known homosexuals [in the GDR] was compiled ... by the Central Office for Veneral Disease and provided to the Institute for Blood Donations ... This means that it will become known to a larger body of people that the names and addresses of homosexual men are archived (Grau, "Sozialistische Moral," 138).

The spectre of AIDS had already begun to loom on the security-conscious horizon. The policy of stepped-up surveillance espoused by Fehr for the security establishment melded with the more politic policy of tolerance and integration propagated by the political wing of the establishment. Rather than competing with each other, they enabled the state to play gay men off two prongs of contradictory policies of containment.

The same holds true for the second and then growing security preoccupation, namely the unchecked growth of the lesbian and gay liberation groups within the churches. Since these groups brought ever-growing number of homosexuals together outside the direct control of the state (the church alone was in a position to provide such a venue in the GDR, as all other organizations had to be state affiliated), surveillance was increased, large numbers of gay men and lesbians were induced to act as informants, mistrust of other members in the group (as potential Stasi informants!) was systematically sown following now-published Stasi guidelines on the *Zersetzung* [dissolution] of these groups (see Thinius; Sweet, "The Church, the Stasi …"). This was the response of the State Security apparatus following the logic of containment of the homosexual threat as sketched out in Fehr's dissertation.

The concurrent response of the political wing was to allow gay groups to constitute themselves for the first time outside the church, namely under the protection of sponsoring state organizations (Amendt 11). The socialist state itself thus provided its homosexuals with an alternative venue for organizing. This move was all the more curious, because the church had long since proven its usefulness as an instance of control. The Superintendent of Dresden, Christof Ziemer, admitted to me in an interview in his office on 18 June 1991 that the church had played a "domesticating role" in regard to its gay groups. The GDR was taking no chances in regard to its homosexuals: stepped-up surveillance of their activities, infiltration of their organizations, domestication of the church groups from within by means of the church itself, and a new policy of furthering gay groups and events outside the churches that was designed to siphon off their members. All of this characterized the policy of tolerance and integration into the status quo of socialist society. It was essentially a dual-pronged strategy of cooptation and containment, designed to neutralize perceived threats to socialism. By means of it, the GDR in its last years could appear progressive toward an historically persecuted minority that could now find a much publicized home in socialism.

The gay male bodies propagated in the German Democratic Republic were rhetorical constructs to certain ends. They reflect and embody the concerns of a (socialist) national security state confronted by issues of difference, organizational independence, and disease. These bodies were helpful for constructing particular arguments in keeping with policy guidelines. It is unclear whether their significance extends much beyond that.

Note

All translations from the German are my own.

Bibliography

Amendt, Günter. *Natürlich anders: Zur Homosexualitätsdiskussion in der DDR.* Cologne: Pahl-Rugenstein, 1989.

Bulgakowa, Oksana. "Der schwule Genosse." *tip* 20 (1990): 42.

Die DDR. Die Schwulen. Der Aufbruch: Versuch einer Bestandsaufnahme. Ed. Jean Jacques Soukup. Göttingen: Waldschlößchen, 1990.

Fehr, Gerhard. "Zu einigen Aspekten der Entwicklung der Risikogruppe der männlichen Homosexuellen und der Risikogruppe der kriminell-gefährdeten, nicht lesbischen, weiblichen Jugendlichen und Jungerwachsenen in der Hauptstadt Berlin." Dissertation, Humboldt-Universität zu Berlin, 1983.

Grau, Günter. "Beginn des Dialogs." *Und diese Liebe auch.* 18-22.

———. "Sozialistische Moral und Homosexualität. Die Politik der SED und das Homosexuellenstrafrecht 1945 bis 1989 - ein Rückblick." *Die Linke und das Laster: Schwule Emanzipation und linke Vorurteile.* Ed. Detlef Grumbach. Hamburg: Männerschwarm Skript, 1995. 85-141.

Hafranke, Ursula. "ungestraft anders?" *Das Magazin* Heft 1, 2, 5 (1989); Heft 2 (1990).

Lemke, Jürgen. *Ganz normal anders: Auskünfte schwuler Männer aus der DDR,* mit einer Vorbemerkung von Irene Runge. Frankfurt a. M.: Luchterhand, 1989.

———. *Gay Voices from East Germany.* Ed. John Borneman. Bloomington: Indiana UP, 1991.

Mayer, Hans. *Outsiders: A Study in Life and Letters.* Trans. Denis M. Sweet. Cambridge, MA: MIT Press, 1982.

Müller, Olaf. "Internationale Filmfestspiele Berlin 1990." *magnus 2* (April 1990): 60-61.

Punge, Manfred. "Das gebrochene Tabu: Zu Gang und Stand der Homosexualitäts-Debatte in den evangelischen Landeskirchen der DDR." *Und diese Liebe auch.* 92-108.

Sillge, Ursula. *Un-Sichtbare Frauen: Lesben und ihre Emanzipation in der DDR.* Berlin: LinksDruck Verlag, 1991.

Starke, Kurt. *Schwuler Osten: Homosexuelle Männer in der DDR.* Berlin: Ch. Links Verlag, 1994.

Sweet, Denis M. "A Literature of 'Truth': Writing by Gay Men in East Germany." *MKF - Mitteilungen aus der kulturwissenschaftlichen Forschung* 18 (August 1995) No. 36: 232-45.

———. "The Church, the Stasi, and Socialist Integration: Three Stages of Lesbian and Gay Emancipation in the Former German Democratic Republic." *Gay Men and the Sexual History of the Political Left.* Ed. Gert Hekma, Harry Oosterhuis and James Steakley. New York: Haworth, 1995. 349-65.

Thinius, Bert. *Aufbruch aus dem grauen Versteck: Ankunft im bunten Ghetto? Randglossen zu Erfahrungen schwuler Männer in der DDR und in Deutschland Ost.* Berlin: Bundesverband Homosexualität, 1994.

Und diese Liebe auch: Theologische und sexualwissenschaftliche Einsichten zur Homosexualität. Ed. Günter Grau. Berlin: Evangelische Verlagsanstalt, 1989.

Wander, Maxie. *"Guten Morgen, du Schöne": Frauen in der DDR. Protokolle,* mit einem Vorwort von Christa Wolf. Darmstadt: Luchterhand, 1979.

Chapter 17

PATTERNS OF CONSCIOUSNESS AND CYCLES OF SELF-DESTRUCTION

Nation, Ethnicity, and Gender in Herta Müller's Prose

Karin Bauer

The bland severity of her motifs, the sobriety of her themes, and the idiosyncracies of her style set Herta Müller apart from other writers on the scene of contemporary German literature. Inscribed in Müller's prose, which reflects her experience as a member of the German minority in Rumania, are the taboos, prohibitions, and rigorous codes of moral behavior imposed by the German community upon its members. Müller's texts are marked by a critical negativity that expresses itself stylistically in the monotonous rhythm of her sentences, the unrelenting bleakness of her imagery, and the "pathos of distance" of the narrative voice. Told from the perspective of the outsider who observes and experiences life from the margins of society, her stories relate the alienation of the individual from both the state and the community and the marginalization of women and those who do not conform to the norms of society.

Müller's texts tell of the isolation, cruelty, corruption, and hypocrisy of life in the German-Rumanian enclave and of the dreadful existence caught between two antagonistic, yet equally repressive orders, the Rumanian state and the German community. Müller distinguishes between two equally oppressive, male-dominated notions of homeland:

one is the "drunken homeland" of the German songs, the stifling tra-
ditionalism of the German community, and the other is the "mendacious homeland" of the Rumanian school books which turns teachers into executioners of a party-dictated feeling for the homeland
("Heimat," 70-1). The German songs, which convey antiquated
notions of morality and ethnic identity and a notion of Germanness
completely divorced from the social and political reality of life in postwar Germany stand in contrast but function similarly to the officially
prescribed love of country and its "father," Ceauşescu. "If we would
have won the war, this would be Germany," Müller's grandfather once
remarked resentfully (Müller, *Teufel,* 23). Neither the "mendacious
homeland" of the Rumanian Communist Party, nor the "drunken
homeland" of the German community succeed in constituting a positive model of national and ethnic identity, since both notions of homeland merely attempt to uphold a static image of nation and *Volk.*
Although antagonistic forces on the surface, the ethnic community
and the state are both marked by repressive nationalism and imposed
patriotism, and they employ concurring strategies through which they
affirm their claim to legitimation and power. In Rumania, Müller
stated shortly before the fall of the Ceauşescu regime, "your fate does
not depend on you. It belongs to Ceauşescu. He can do everything,
you can do nothing" ("Fatherland," 26).

Leaving no room for opposition, the totalitarian state was perceived
by Müller as a mere extension of the isolated little village of her childhood. In her portrayals of village life, she destroys all illusions about the
naiveté of country life, the nostalgic sense of community, and the solidarity amongst members of a minority group living in a hostile environment; instead, she lays bare the brutality and violence dominating
human interaction in general and male demeanor toward women in particular. Müller describes the pressure to conform and the tyranny of normality as an incessant "ticking of the norm" ("Ticken," 13). Closely
related to notions of order, discipline, hard work, and exclusionary categories – such as mad and sane, reasonable and unreasonable – the
abstract concept of normality determined who was included or excluded
from the community. Declared abnormal and marginalized were not
only those who could not model their lives according to what public
opinion deemed normal, such as the handicapped, but also those who
painted their houses a different color, combed their hair differently, or
left an unhappy relationship. The crusade of normality, Müller asserts,
never rests with the attainment of so-called virtues, it goes beyond the
exertion of social pressure by aligning itself to and functioning in accor-
dance with interests of power.

The patterns of consciousness that inform the constitution of the ideologies of nation, ethnicity, and gender in Müller's prose include the prohibition of self-reflection, the manipulation of representation, and the loss of historical perspective. As defining moments in both the formulation of national and ethnic identity and the marginalization of women, they propel cycles of self-destruction that lead to the virtual extinction of German culture in Rumania, on the one hand, and to women's descent into madness and self-denigration on the other. Müller focuses upon the – negative – dialectic of self-preservation and self-destruction and the German community's internal mechanisms of self-destruction, rather than the political causes for the low status of women and the virtual extinction of German culture in Rumania. The German community's prohibitions and taboos are staged in the mechanisms of self-destruction and the narrative techniques of Müller's novel *The Passport (Der Mensch ist ein großer Fasan auf der Welt)*, which reveals points of convergence between ideologies of nation, ethnicity, and gender. Connecting the dictates of authoritarian and totalitarian notions of national and ethnic identity and the subordination of women, the novel's narrative structure opens up questions about the textual representation and stylistic reproduction of these ideologies.

Müller's prose evolved out of the repressive and destructive order of her homeland and the "work on deception" [*Arbeit an der Täuschung*], which is a mechanism of conformity and an expression of the social and existential fear of being excluded or marginalized (*Teufel*, 13). Müller claims to have learned very early to deceive her family and community about her feelings, goals, and motivations. Deception became a strategy for the survival of a consciousness torn between the need for security within the collective and the demand for individual freedom. Paradoxically, the repressive order and the wish to conform and be part of the collective helped Müller to sharpen her ability to invent perceptions [*erfundene Wahrnehmungen*], the very ability that later marginalized her within the community. The "invented perceptions" of Müller's writing produce a subjective view of reality that differs sharply from the majority's view of reality and image of itself.

Originally an expression of the need of belonging, the "work on deception" and "invented perceptions" became a creative means to disagreeing and the only possibility of intervening in the reality and image construction of both the community and the state, because Müller's fictive reality was the only one she could control. However, Müller's prose is not a withdrawal into the realm of the imagination or an attempt to capture some form of authenticity behind the deceptive and hypocritical façade of norms, for the invented perceptions of Müller's narrative

voices are firmly grounded in the reality of existence and, simultaneously, deeply enmeshed in the social, political, and subjective context of
delusion. Her novels thus forfeit any hope for the discovery of a truth-
ful, authentic, or objective view of reality. Because of her representation
of village life within the Rumanian state, which neither conforms to the
self-image of the Communist state nor to that of the German community, she was harassed by the state and ostracized by the community.

Originally a proverb from her grandmother, "The devil sits in the
mirror" *(Der Teufel sitzt im Spiegel)* is the programmatic title of Müller's
critical reflections on writing and literature published in 1991. The
proverb is the leitmotif of the collection of essays, and it comes up,
explicitly and implicitly, in many of Müller's texts. The proverb has
many variations and shades of meaning; with the saying, the grandmother warns the grandchild against pride, vanity, narcissism, and
experiencing herself as a sexual being. Self-perception and self-reflection
in the mirror are seen as dangerous and destructive. "The devil sits in
the mirror," the grandmother said when the little child looked in the
mirror, humming a song. "The bird, which sings in the morning, is
later eaten by the cat," the grandmother continues *(Teufel,* 22). The
moment of self-reflection is followed by inevitable destruction: contentment with the self is a punishable offense. Self-reflection of the
body might also lead to promiscuity and disgrace, because nakedness
reflected in the mirror – the exposure of the body to oneself – bears the
danger of experiencing one's own body as an object of desire. "One
must only look in the mirror while naked or think of touching the skin
while rolling up one's socks. In clothes one is a human being, and without clothes one is not" *(Niederungen,* 60). The prohibition of self-perception and self-reflection is simultaneously the prohibition of precise
and meticulous observation, in which and through which perception
invents itself, proportions get distorted, and the detail becomes larger
than the whole: "The mirror is destructive ... The impression that precise observation means to destroy becomes more and more evident"
(Teufel, 23-4). By concentrating upon details, precise observation
deconstructs delusionary, globalized images and makes visible the vulnerability of the whole.

The prohibition of self-reflection has a decidedly political dimension;
it is a taboo imposed by those in power, for whom precise observation
brings the danger of doubts and self-doubts and thus a threat to their
position of power. Only those, Müller writes, who know the devil in the
mirror because they have often looked at him, can bear him. Perception
and its inventions by the reflecting individual are unpredictable and
therefore dangerous to the image and self-image of those in power. The

Rumanian State carefully orchestrated representations of itself through censorship, the display of official photographs of the dictator, and the use of national symbols, such as the red carnation. Most German villagers were enthusiastic supporters of National Socialism, which boosted their self-image as a supposedly superior ethnic group. Müller's father was a member of the SS, her uncle was the National Socialist village ideologue, and her mother would sing and knit for the men on the front: "Her knitting needles were guns during these evenings. The knitting, a march of the wool thread. This was one behavior, as member of the group. And the other behavior, when she was by herself: She heeded the warning: 'The devil sits in the mirror'" (*Teufel,* 24). Since self-reflection is based upon an awareness of present realities and of historical developments, it interferes with the construction of deceptive collective images and must be prohibited. Nationalist and ethnocentric ideology can only persevere through collective conformity to the myths of superiority and power, which, in turn, can only be maintained by observing the taboo on self-reflection.

For those in power and for the grandmother, who warns the granddaughter against nonconformity and who wants to affirm and protect the identity of the German community within a hostile environment, the devil lies in representation and reflection – in Müller's writing. In order to maintain the myth of superiority of Rumanian national identity and German ethnic identity, both entities must not only control the reflection and self-reflection of the individual as well as of the collective, but also the representation of their own bloody history. Self-glorification in censored representations (such as the homeland of the Rumanian school books and the homeland of the German songs) and repression of the violent aspects and times of their history (the German community's support of fascism and the Rumanian state's totalitarian rule) constitute only part of the manipulation of historical consciousness. Another important factor is the passivity and conformity resulting from fear and the feeling of helplessness and powerlessness, to which Müller referred when stating that one's fate was never in one's own hands but rather in Ceaușescu's.

Müller's image of the great black axle, which is turned by the dead villagers, reveals both the German community's submissive inertia and its patterns of interpretation, which are guided by superstition and a fatalistic view of history. Under the village well lies a great black axle with which the dead turn the years so that the others may die soon, too. As more people die, more help turn the axle and thus increase the passing of time and the number of the dead (*Barfüßiger Februar,* 6). In this image of history, time is propelled by the dead and not by the living. The historical process is not a progression toward a higher goal, it is also not a cyclical process of the eternal return of the same or a series of chance events, but rather an escalating cycle of self-destruction. The more people die and the faster the axle turns, the faster time passes – time consumes itself with an ever-increasing speed.

Demanding strict adherence to its rigorous code of morality and prescribed self-perceptions, the German community attempts to preserve a static collective identity. The patterns of consciousness perpetuating this forced identity lead to resignation in the face of history and, consequently, the abdication of responsibility for political and social action. Thus, this forced collective identity can survive only at the price of its involvement in the process of self-destruction. The attempts at self-preservation base themselves upon cycles of self-destruction rather than self-reflection, without which, however, there can be no understanding of historical processes past and present. The formation of historical perspectives depends upon the recognition that the present is, at least in part, the result of the past and that history is, as Walter Benjamin has pointed out in his "Theses on the Philosophy of History", not a static and completed event in the past; the past can only be interpreted from the perspective of the present, the moment of the *Jetztzeit* (258). However, in order to affirm their own position, the community as well as the state manipulate the representation and thus the perception of their own history. Both glorify their existence and celebrate their history through selective representation and by building a façade behind which lie poverty, violence, and censorship. The German minority not only represses part of its fascist history, but also leaves responsibility for the march of history to the dead rather than the living. This holds true, too, for the state, which seeks to validate its practices through the communist version of historical determinism and reverence to dead ideologues and static ideologies.

Müller's novel *The Passport*, published in German in 1986, shows the entwinement of the static notion of identity, the deterministic and fatalistic notions of history, and the ideologies of gender construction. Involved in perpetual cycles of violence, deception, and self-deception, the villagers in this novel are caught in an inescapable web of delusion. *The Passport* is written from the perspective of the miller, Windisch, who is waiting for the passport that will enable him to leave the country. Despite the fact that Windisch counts the passing of the days and years since applying for his passport, he lives in the seemingly timeless and static vacuum of the German-Rumanian community, and now "sees the end everywhere in the village" (7). Windisch registers the decay and the decimation of the village, and, in his fatalistic interpretations of events, he exhibits a preoccupation and heightened awareness of death. Images and metaphors of death and destruction abound as Windisch superstitiously interprets even chance occurrences as signs of a predetermined fate. His picture of reality is formed by irrational patterns of interpretation: the owl brings death to the one on whose roof it sits; an old woman dies because she cuts a dahlia; a calf shows whether a young woman is still a virgin. Windisch's idiosyncratic construction of reality is represented in a collage of empirically verifiable observations, invented perceptions, distortions, and projections. His reality constitutes itself within a web of male ignorance, superstition, prejudice, and preconceived notions of morality. For instance, Windisch and other men in the village are convinced that Dietmar, a young man who was accidentally shot during a manoeuvre, died because the young owl sat by the Danube and thought of the village. When Windisch's wife asserts that Dietmar's death was an accident and had nothing to do with the owl, Windisch gets angry and shouts: "Your understanding is tiny … . it doesn't stretch from your forehead down to your mouth" (79). Like the other men, Windisch is not open to new perspectives — especially not to a woman's — and merely integrates his experiences into pre-existing modes of perception. Therefore, every experiences serves as a mere affirmation of his picture of reality.

In the village, reality constitutes itself in truly mysterious but distinctly male ways. By privileging the male voice and by merging the male with the narrative voice, Müller's text reproduces on a narrative level the marginalization of women, the subordination of the female voice, and the repression of the female perspective. In this way, the text mimics the reality it portrays. Women's lives are the story behind his-story: ambivalent, marked by gaps, and subjected to male interpretations; there is no her-story in this text. Through its suppression of the female voice and the subordination of female history, the text reenforces on a narrative level the power of male interpretation and male authority over the representation of women. Women are deprived of the opportunity to counter men's construction of a feminine nature and the static and prejudiced projections of feminine character. Lacking rational means of interpretation, the men fall back upon their superstitions, enforcing their claims to power through verbal insults and physical abuse.

However, women and their bodies play an important role in the corrupt economy of the village. Employing their bodies as objects of exchange, women manage to obtain the passports necessary for emigration and a new life in the West. The women are:

> summoned to the priest because of the baptismal certificate, sometimes to
> the militiaman because of the passport. The night watchman has told

> Windisch that the priest has an iron bed in the sacristy. In this bed he looks for baptismal certificates, with the women. "If things go well," said the night watchman, "he looks for the baptismal certificate five times. If he's doing the job thoroughly, he looks ten times. With some families the militiaman loses and mislays the applications and the revenue stamps seven times. He looks for them on the mattress in the post office store room with the women who want to emigrate" (43).

Since Windisch's wife, who resorted to prostitution as a means of survival during the war, is now too old to be a viable object of desire and exchange, his daughter Amalie must make herself available to the village officials. The night watchman remarks to Windisch: "The priest makes her [Amalie] Catholic, and the militiaman makes her stateless" (43). The night watchman's speech masks the prostitution of the female body, which in his words becomes a bureaucratic formality. Furthermore, he speaks of the "women who want to emigrate" when, more precisely, he would have to speak of the wives whose husbands want to emigrate. His rhetoric demonstrates the male tendency toward denial and repression. When speaking about women, both the night watchman and Windisch also do not hesitate to demean them and ascribe to them essential characteristics, such as greed, stupidity, and uncontrollable lust. Significantly, nationalism, racism, and religious intolerance find their strongest expression in connection with the negative view of women, thus revealing the interconnection between racism, nationalism, and sexism. According to the night watchman, the women of the Walachian Baptists have an insatiable sexual appetite, but they cannot cook. The Walachian Baptists behave like animals when they worship, they howl when they pray, and "their women groan when they sing hymns, as if they were in bed. Their eyes get big, like my dog's … . On festival days they pair off. With whomever they catch in the dark … They do it on the carpet in the prayer house" (63). The religion of the Baptists comes, according to the night watchman, from America, "that's across the water," he adds, "the devil crosses the water too … . They've got the devil in their bodies. My dog can't stand them either. He barks at them. Dogs can scent the devil." Windisch remarks that the "Jews run America," an opinion the night watchman shares: "the Jews are the ruin of the world. Jews and women" (64). After speaking about the Walachian Baptists, the Jews, and women in general, the conversation moves on to West German women, who follow the latest fashion, are afraid of plucking chickens, smoke cigarettes, and "would prefer to walk naked on the street if they could" (64). Only in comparison to West German, Walachian, and Gypsy women are the men willing to assign some positive qualities to the women of the village: "The worst one here is still worth more than the best one there" (64). In order to maintain the larger myth of communal superiority, the men must assert their women's superiority in comparison to the women of the Others.

Like the other men who believe that, at bottom, all women are whores, Windisch is convinced that his wife "would spread her legs for a crystal vase" (39). Accepting and perpetuating her father's opinion, Amalie also calls her mother a whore. Katharina, who is called Windisch's wife throughout the novel except in the brief references to her life before marriage, was a prisoner in Russia for five years during the war. However, the narration of her past shows her not as an independent subject, but rather in subservience to men and male desire. While most of her fellow prisoners starved or froze to death, Katharina survived by engaging in life-preserving exchanges of clothing, food, and sexual favors: "She was shaved. Her face was grey. Her scalp was red-raw" (74), yet she went to the iron bed of a cook, who gave her potatoes, the iron bed of the doctor, who provided her with a sheet of paper and an "illness" that freed her from working in the mines for three days, and to the iron bed of the grave digger, who warmed her and gave her meat from the funeral meals in the village (75). Conveniently "forgetting" his exploitation of his daughter's body, Windisch holds Katharina's past, from which he supposedly rescued her through marriage, against her and does not see the prostitution of her body as a strategy of survival under extraordinary conditions, but rather as a freely chosen life style based upon an essentially flawed feminine character. He does not recognize that her behavior bears, as Adorno termed it, the "scars of social mutilation" and "the negative imprint of domination" and male violence (*Minima Moralia,* 95). On the contrary, he accepts his daughter's perpetuation of the very behavior for which he reproaches Katharina and from which he benefits.

Windisch wants to deny the present-day exchange of sex for passports. While Katharina and Amalie, aware of the workings of the male-dominated community, face the reality of their situation quite rationally, Windisch is afraid of the talk that Amalie's "visits" to the militiaman and the priest will cause in the village and refuses to leave the house to go to mass. This is his only acknowledgement of his daughter's involvement in the corrupt bureaucratic economy of the village. Following her departure to meet the militiaman, Windisch drinks and smashes the mirror which Amalie used to put on her make-up in preparation for her rendezvous. Windisch "sees," or rather invents the perception of the militiaman's and his own reflection in the mirror, and he "strikes the two small, despondent faces above the epaulettes dead" (71). The overlapping of the imaginary face of the militiaman with Windisch's own indicates that he for an instant recognizes himself in the militiaman, and his aggression turns against both reflections. By breaking the mirror Windisch conforms to the taboo on self-reflection, reflection, and representation. He can thus repress his knowledge of the corruption and sexual exploitation of his daughter and prevent interference from uncontrollable "invented perception." Simultaneously, demolishing the imaginary reflection of the militiaman in the mirror substitutes for a direct confrontation, and so the breaking of the mirror remains an expression of helpless frustration rather than an effective protest. He does not confront the disparity between his actions and his self-image and represses the momentary recognition of himself in the Other.

Despite their ability to look through and past male constructions of reality, the women, too, have internalized the taboo on self-reflection and the fatalistic attitudes resulting from the loss of historical perspective. They are both victims of and participants in the male order of things. Their existence is predetermined, and there are only a limited number of roles available to them within the community, where the stages of their lives derive from their function as sexual objects and their roles as daughters, wives, and widows. The younger women contribute their bodies to the village economy and the older women function as accomplices to male desire. For instance, Katharina assists her daughter, who looks in the mirror not for the purpose of self-perception but for the purpose of producing an image that is attractive to men, with the preparations for her encounter with the village officials, and the post woman brings the "invitations" and makes available the back room of the post office for the sexual encounters.

However, it is madness, not marriage, which offers a way for women to exclude themselves from direct or indirect participation in the corrupt village economy. The women's madness is described in terms of images of obsessive consumption and self-destruction: Crazy Widow Kroner is addicted to tea, "death was in the cups" (37), and eventually dies from the festering wounds on her body; the joiner's mother dies after consuming greedily and with hatred a melon resembling female genitalia. Yet another example of greedy and "devilish" self-consumption is the village's apple tree, which eats its own fruit. Like the great black axle, both the melon and the apple tree function as images of self-destruction, and the self-consuming performances of the mad women, who exist on the margins of society, enact and externalize the processes of self-destruction in the larger community. Their enactment of self-consumption holds up a mirror that makes obvious the hidden mechanisms of the community as a whole; as a mirror of madness, however, it falls outside of the acceptable forms of representation. Having internalized the taboo of self-reflection and the fatalistic attitude toward the present and the future, the descent into madness and self-destruction appears as the women's grotesque counter-impulse to their exploitation. Madness excludes them from the pressure to conform and from the mandate of participation in the corrupt system of exchange and thus offers them a measure of control. The image of the self-hating and self-consuming woman shows the impossibility of thinking or finding productive alternatives under the present conditions. "Liberation" and "emancipation," i.e., freedom from the ticking of the norm, are conceivable only as a process of self-destruction.

Müller's prose intervenes in these cycles of self-destruction by disregarding the pressures of conformity and censorship, for the very process of writing and representing is a gesture of defiance. Practicing the art of precise observation, her prose functions as a mirror that stands in opposition to the manipulative images and representations of her homeland. But Müller's prose also runs the risk of becoming itself involved in textual self-consumption, for her narrative mirror perpetuates the context of delusion in which her characters are caught, reflecting the position of women in society, their exclusion, marginalization, and subservience to male interests. By converging the narrative voice with Windisch's narrow perspective, Müller turns the narrative voice into his accomplice, just as the women in the village are turned into accomplices of male desire. Müller's narration reproduces the social relations of domination and the patterns of consciousness inscribed within social, political, and cultural practices by creating a forced identity of narrative voice and false consciousness. Since the narration inevitably reproduces the characters' lack of self-reflection and loss of historical perspective, the novel remains strictly within the limits of male, ethnic, and nationalist consciousness and forfeits any hope for a utopian Other.

In his essay "On the Question: What is German," Adorno writes that "the True and the Better in every people is much more likely that which does not adapt itself to the collective subject but, wherever possible, even resists it" (121). Resisting the pressures of conformity, censorship, and the attempts to control representation, Müller's writing certainly embodies the "Better," that which does not adapt to the collective subject, but on another level, it adapts to the coercive construction of collective identity. The lack of self-reflection and historical consciousness combined with the lack of narrative mediation in the reproduction of the images, preconceptions, projections, and ideological constructs shows Müller's prose to be a mirror of reflection rather than self-reflection. Her narrative voice heeds the taboo against self-reflection, and her negativity becomes, therefore, not a refusal to project a utopian "Better," but a symptom of the fatalistic view of history that thwarts any possibility for political and social action on an individual and collective level.

Müller's mirroring of the German community's self-destructive denial of realities past and present postulates the rigidity of collective consciousness as the cause for the decline of German culture in Rumania. The German minority's hypocrisy, objectivization of human relationships, commodification of women, and dogma of ethnic superiority parallel the repressive power structures of the Rumanian state. Clinging to German tradition is a gesture of protest against both the hostile attitude toward Germans in Rumania and the supposed moral decay inherent in contemporary manifestations of culture in Germany. However, because of the lack of self-reflection and historical vision, these gestures of protest become ritualistic reiterations of a static understanding of Germanness rather than dynamic gestures of resistance.

Note

All translations from the German are my own.

Bibliography

Adorno, Theodor W. *Minima Moralia.* Trans. E.F.N. Jephcott. London: Verso, 1993.

———. "On the Question: What is German?" Trans. Thomas Y. Levin. *New German Critique* 36 (Fall 1985): 121-31.

Benjamin, Walter. *Illuminations.* Frankfurt a.M.: Suhrkamp, 1977.

Eke, Norbert Otto. "Augen/Blicke oder: Die Wahrnehmung der Welt in den Bildern." *Die erfundene Wahrnehmung: Annäherung an Herta Müller.* Ed. Norbert Otto Eke. Paderborn: Igel Verlag Wissenschaft, 1991. 7-21.

Janssen-Zimmermann, Antje. "'Überall, wo man den Tod gesehen hat, ist man ein bißchen wie zuhaus.' Schreiben nach Auschwitz – Zu einer Erzählung Herta Müllers." *Literatur für Leser* 4 (1991): 237-49.

Krauss, Hannes. "Fremde Blicke: Zur Prosa von Herta Müller und Richard Wagner." *Neue Generation - Neues Erzählen.* Ed. Walter Delabar und Werner Jung. Opladen: Westdeutscher Verlag, 1993. 69-76.

Müller, Herta. "Heimat oder der Betrug der Dinge." *Dichtung und Heimat: sieben Autoren unterlaufen ein Thema.* Ed. Wilhelm Solms. Marburg: Hitzeroth, 1990. 69-83.

———. *Der Mensch ist ein großer Fasan auf der Welt.* Berlin: Rotbuch, 1986.

_____. *Niederungen*. Berlin: Rotbuch Verlag, 1988.

_____. *The Passport*. Trans. Martin Chalmers. London: Serpent's Tail, 1989.

_____. *Der Teufel sitzt im Spiegel*. Berlin: Rotbuch, 1991.

_____. "This is our Fatherland." *Index on Censorship* 8 (1989): 29.

_____. "Das Ticken der Norm." *Die Zeit* 21 Jan. 1984: 13-14.

Chapter 18

GERMANIA DISPLACED?

Reflections on the Discourses of Female Asylum
Seekers and Ethnic Germans

Magda Mueller

While positions of power are being actively negotiated within the Ger-man-German discourse, the new Germany is concomitantly engaged in European-wide discourses on the move towards a heteroge-neous and multicultural society. Over the last several years, united Ger-many has experienced a wide range of societal tensions, which are only partly grounded in the initially underestimated economic costs of unifica-tion. Beyond high unemployment, slow economic growth in the Eastern federal states, and the enormous costs of rebuilding the Eastern infrastruc-ture, another source of conflict is to be found in culturally expressed self-denial, which, it will be argued here, is one aspect of what Russell Berman has called "the labile character of German identity."[1] This weakened sense of identity is manifested in various ways, ranging from firebombing xeno-phobics to those who document their ambivalence about being German in films, essays, and literature. In fact, it could be said that much of the cul-tural production of postwar Germany has been occupied with producing a collective identity that is flawless in its humanistic trajectory.

---

1. Berman remarks: "I do not think that the perpetrators of violence on foreigners are doing that because they have a strong German identity. In fact, they do it because they have a weak identity, and this has to do with the cultural construction of German iden-tity – West German identity – since 1945. In other words, weakened particularism leads to xenophobia. Were it strengthened, it would probably lead to a more tolerant and lib-eral society" (89).

By contrast, this complex cultural postwar conceptualization is unknown to the large numbers of recently arriving ethnic Germans from Eastern Europe and the former Soviet Union who have not lived in postwar Germany. They thus retain different historical memories that challenge this weak sense of German national identity at its core when they utter the simple, yet highly charged statement "I am German." Due to xenophobic attacks on identifiable foreigners, the international and national media have reported primarily on the fate of asylum seekers in Germany and disregarded ethnic Germans. Germany has always been a heterogeneous society with regional identities firmly in place and with urban communities of Turks, Greeks, Italians and others. The current political tendency to focus only on asylum seekers undermines the process of integration by ignoring other newcomers to the society, such as ethnic Germans. Because they are already "German," members of the latter group are able to "come back" to a Germany that they have imagined as frozen in time. Their anachronistic understanding of their own Germanness, even when they do not know the language, is incompatible with the contemporary liberal rejection of traditional notions of German identity.

Even German feminists have done very little to come to terms with the tensions between asylum-seeking women, ethnic German women, and the female citizens of united Germany. The way in which the concepts of belonging, womanliness, and motherhood as held by the immigrant women clash with modern and postmodern views of contemporary German women becomes especially obvious in the contradictory discourses surrounding female asylum seekers and their supposed opposite, ethnic German women. This phenomenon shall be examined here in terms of two concepts: the notion of *Heimat* and the problematic construction of Germanness. The request to belong is shared by both groups, the asylum seekers whose lives in their country of origin are threatened because of political circumstances, and the ethnic Germans who claim a right to reside in Germany because of their ancestry and existing laws that recognize it. The degree of their belonging is ultimately decided by the Germans who already constitute the nation. The present analysis will seek to demonstrate what peculiar forms this specifically German dilemma can take when confronted with statements by ethnic German women who perceive their Germanness as a completely stable and integral part of their individual identity.

* * *

Although this is not the place to repeat the arguments for and against tightening the asylum laws, an understanding of the overall significance of this debate is necessary in order to grasp German resentment towards the "returning" of ethnic Germans. The history of the asylum laws is intertwined with Germany's Nazi past, as it was the exiles returning to Germany after the defeat of National Socialism, who, as a result of their own experiences in seeking political asylum, insisted upon the phrase that granted unrestricted right of asylum in the Basic Law, which simply stated: "Persons persecuted on political grounds shall enjoy the right of asylum" (14). In 1992 newcomers to Germany totaled 669,191 (438,191 asylum seekers and 231,000 ethnic Germans); in 1993 they totaled 540,599 (322,599 asylum seekers and 218,000 ethnic Germans), and in 1994 349,810 (127,210 asylum seekers and 222,600 ethnic Germans).[2] Such facts cannot be viewed in isolation or regarded as a temporary or transient change in the political landscape. While during the 1980s a constant stream of asylum seekers was arriving in Germany, the number of ethnic Germans emigrating to Germany increased dramatically because of political changes in Eastern Europe. While some argued that Germany had reached her capacity to accept any further refugees, asylum seekers, and ethnic Germans, others, driven by ethical and moral motives, maintained that Germany's open-door policy should remain firmly in place. In 1989 about 120,000 people applied for asylum, but by 1992 that number had almost quadrupled, causing the CDU to document that Germany had accepted four times as many asylum seekers as all the other member states of the European Union put together.[3] As a result, in 1993, the liberal legislation for asylum seekers was rescinded.

Whereas during the Cold War negotiating the right for ethnic Germans to "return" to Germany had been celebrated as a victory over the communist system, in the wake of *glasnost* and *perestroika*, this political justification had lost its legitimacy. Recognizing that not all German minorities living in the former Soviet Union and Eastern Europe could be successfully absorbed into the free market economy of the Federal Republic without causing more irritation among German citizens who were already experiencing high unemployment and an outbreak of xenophobia, the German government explored other avenues for improving the lot of the ethnic Germans and discouraging emigration, such as efforts to revive ethnic communities in Kazakhstan and other East European areas.[4] In 1990, for instance, the German government reached an agreement with the former Soviet Union to provide generous support to the ethnic Germans remaining on Russian territory by helping them to reestablish their German communities and strengthen their sense of cultural iden-

2. See *Almanach der Bundesregierung 1995/96*, (129 and 148-49).
3. See *Das neue Asylrecht*.
4. See Waffenschmidt.

tity.[5] Despite these efforts, some 200,000 ethnic Germans continue to seek reintegration into Germany each year. Since March 1996, another law now regulates the equal distribution of ethnic Germans across the entire Federal Republic in the hope of achieving more effective assimilation. The political privileging of ethnic Germans over asylum seekers has, however, provoked resentment and controversy, involving politicians of different political parties as well as the intellectual establishment, and producing quite heterogeneous, indeed contradictory statements concerning multiculturalism and the complex politics of belonging.[6]

The political discourse surrounding debates about asylum seekers' right to an unrestricted stay in Germany and the concomitant silence and uneasiness concerning ethnic Germans and their unrestricted "return" both reflect the deeply troubling nature of the term "Germanness." It is dubious whether it is possible to measure identity, and, if so, whether it should be done. Historical circumstances determine identity. Whereas Germans who grew up in postwar Germany rarely refer to their Germanness, in the case of ethnic Germans, this construction of identity is the characteristic that defines their sense of belonging, understood either communally or individually. In this context, "Germanness" has an ultimately different significance and may provide the key for illuminating the conflict. A woman from Rumania signals the tension: "I do not insist on my Germanness [*Deutschtum*] because I am conceited about it, but because it is simply part of my identity, and because I cannot behave differently" (Wendt 113).

Deutschtum is an especially loaded term within the German language, and, for that matter, within German Studies scholarship. It provokes anxiety within the German context by evoking the belief in racial purity of the Nazi era, that German past which does not seem to go away. Whereas the very specificity (the non-Germanness) of the asylum seekers is politicized in a way that enables liberal Germans to embrace their otherness as an escape from uncomfortably rigid constructions of Germanness, that very same notion of Germanness seems to be invoked by ethnic Germans and embodied in the premodern image of ethnic German women that circulates in the media and rhetoric of conservative politicians.

* * *

5. See *Zwischen Tradition und Zukunft*.
6. For instance, on 27 February 1996 the *Rheinische Post* commented: "Just in einer Zeit, da die deutsche Linke über ein Einwanderungsgesetz nachdenkt, das Flüchtlinge aus Afrika und Asien Eintritt nach festen Quoten in die Bundesregierung verschaffen soll, möchte Lafontaine Deutschstämmige 'draußen vor der Tür' stehen lassen." Cited in *CDU Argumente zur Aussiedlerpolitik*.

In analyzing these aspects of the complex nexus of otherness and belonging in the multicultural society that is now being inscribed in German publications, it is particularly instructive to observe the absence of national identity articulated in the texts of German women authors and, on the other hand, the unquestioned firm place that Germanness occupies in the identity of ethnic German women. A particularly useful document in this respect is an anthology of portraits of asylum-seeking women, "*Ich bete jeden Tag, bitte laß uns bleiben!*" *14 Porträts asylsuchender Frauen aus aller Welt*, ("I Pray Every Day, Please Let Us Stay!" 14 Portraits of Asylum-Seeking Women from around the World), one of numerous recent texts dealing with both asylum-seeking and ethnic German women.[7] Although rather journalistic in nature, this endeavor had an overtly political purpose within the societal climate of the 1990s in the Federal Republic of Germany. It was specifically planned to challenge changes in the asylum laws. Already the title of the volume signals emotionally charged territory in its plea for help, enforced by religious terminology. Contained in the notion of "praying" is an image of the helpless asylum-seeking woman on her knees, begging for help. Even though she prays to a higher being, *ipso facto*, she addresses citizens of the Federal Republic of Germany who are to become aware of her circumstances and recognize that, in this case, they can play God by pressuring German politicians to continue the liberal laws that governed the granting of asylum.[8]

In this unique collection of essays, well-known women writers (all but two of them native speakers of German) lend their communication skills to women who are seeking asylum in Germany, most of whom speak little or no German. The German authors not only inscribe their own (national and individual) concepts of class, race, and political involvement onto the texts they present, but also add some uniquely German baggage of their own, relating both to the historical origins of the asylum policy and the peculiar faith of German intellectuals in the power of the

---

7. See Ferstl and Hetzel, and Székely.

8. "Germany's willingness to open her doors to foreigners who have been persecuted on political grounds compares favorably with that of other countries. The new article 16a of the Basic Law, like the previous article 16, still guarantees protection from political persecution in the form of an individual basic right. In 1992, for instance, Germany alone took in nearly 80% of all people seeking asylum in the whole of the European Community. In 1989 the number seeking asylum in Germany was 121,318, in 1991 the figure rose to 256,112, and then to 438,191 in 1992. At the same time the proportion of those who could be recognized as genuine victims of persecution fell to less than 5%. In 1993, up to the end of August, some 260,000 asylum seekers entered Germany. Their number fell significantly when the new legislation became effective on 1 July 1993." *Facts about Germany* (16-17). See also Aziz, Benz, Leggewie, Gebauer, and Just.

written word. In Germany, the institution of literature has often been assigned a special role as a mediator of emancipatory discourses, which goes beyond its usual role in other nations. Its special function in the persistently incomplete project of "dealing with the Nazi past," is in turn connected to what Berman referred to as the "the labile character of German identity," and is reflected in texts on minorities in Germany.

Of particular interest in this anthology is the contribution by one journalist, Peggy Parnass, who thematizes the difficulties of the attempt to talk with an asylum seeker. The first hurdle to be overcome is to locate a partner for interviewing. This is not easy, since Parnass finds it impossible to approach an identifiable asylum seeker in the street and enter into a dialogue. She notes at the beginning of her essay that she would have preferred to speak with an African woman, but, unfortunately, no one was able to provide her with a contact. What might have been Parnass's image of an African woman? A woman from South Africa with the colonial experience of the colonizer? Most likely not. Rather, she imagines a black asylum seeker whose otherness is visible. The tokenism in her remark is typical of a liberal investment that can be subsumed in a "safe" otherness, one which does not impinge on German self-understanding. Parnass's well-intentioned slip in designating a certain kind of "otherness" as the most valued stigmatizes and reinforces the concept of race; as if on a scale from 0 to 10, a black female asylum seeker would be a 10. Given the reality with which she is confronted, Parnass has to settle for women from Albania, Bosnia, the Ukraine, and Russia.

In contrast to Parnass, Asta Scheib lets her own voice disappear behind that of her interview subject, Rita from the Sudan. She merely records details of Rita's life, restricting herself to functioning as a medium for Rita's terror- and torture-filled experiences. Introducing the reader to the conflicts between Africans with animistic and Christian beliefs, Rita describes her country as a hellish place, which has been devastated, raped, and destroyed. Nevertheless, her homesickness led Scheib to chose the title "I cannot live without my *Heimat*: Rita from the Sudan" (87). When *Heimat* is claimed in this fashion by asylum seekers, it provokes no resistance, while a German intellectual who participates in the assertion of *Heimat* within the German-German context would be ostracized by her/his peers and considered very much behind the times.

It appears that the volume *"Ich bete jeden Tag, bitte laß uns bleiben!"* was born out of the desire of the editor, Anne Rademacher, and the writers to enlighten and inform the German public about the situation of the asylum seekers. The particular historical situation of the female asylum seeker is constructed in terms of a reproach to the national conscience of a nation that is not willing to accept more asylum seekers. The anthology aims to counteract growing xenophobic sentiment in post-unification Germany by emphasizing the unique human predicament of these female asylum seekers. While the opponents of the liberal German asylum laws found their sole ammunition in current economic problems, the embarrassment caused by xenophobic actions and the reappearance of the "ugly German" dominates. Furthermore, "the labile character of German identity" emerges in the generally hostile attitude towards detectable foreigners in postunification Germany, and it is this identifiability of "otherness" in skin color or speech that is at the center of these essays. While some essays romanticize the construction of *Heimat* within the context of asylum seekers, others totalize their conceptualization of *Heimat,* and still others bear traces of their essentialistic origins, since in this collection only women write about women. Superficially one could argue that all of these essays are marked by sensitivity to the situation of the asylum-seeking women; however at the same time they lack acute self-reflection in their construction of the female asylum seeker as radically "other."

* * *

It is thus illuminating to analyze certain concepts and slips within the texts on asylum seekers that often do the opposite of what they claim in reinforcing anti-emancipatory discourses in their construction of "others" as exotic and non-German. Such exoticization reinforces the exclusion of other "others," such as the ethnic Germans whose focus on a German *Heimat* is something quite different from the notion of *Heimat* as the geographical place that the asylum seekers had to leave in order to save their lives. Through this exoticization these "others," i.e., the asylum seekers, are excluded and remain foreign bodies whose *Heimat* can only be the "elsewhere" they had to escape from. While the asylum-seeking women beg to stay in Germany, ethnic German women demand the implementation of their constitutional right to settle in Germany. The ethnic German women who assert that their *Heimat* is the "here" of Germany, to which they now return, can thus be seen in dialectic fashion as the "other" of the asylum seekers.

For ethnic German women the notion of *Heimat* remains vital; they are not tormented by an automatic succession of images that evoke the most problematic era of German history. Germany is perceived as "the old *Heimat* of their ancestors, of which they have been dreaming for decades and which now reveals itself as a foreign country" (*Die geteilte Heimat,* 29). This unbroken certainty of belonging enabled them to endure hardship during their relocation, for instance, to Siberia. One such ethnic German woman, Emma Resch, indicates that families received their emotional strength and hope from asserting this sense of belonging: "When we are free, we have to leave Russia. It is not our *Heimat,* we have to return to where we belong" (60). But their sense of belonging is not validated when they "return" to Germany, where they are perceived as "Russians," "Rumanians," "Poles," etc. For some ethnic Germans *Heimat* does not necessarily refer to Germany; it may also designate the place in one of the Eastern European countries where they had grown up and their families had lived. Another ethnic German, G. Wichary, sen., for example, states: "Berlin is not my *Heimat.* I have found a home. *Heimat* is where one is born and where one spends the best years of one's life" ("'Zu Hause, aber keine Heimat'," 100). For most, however, Germany is understood as the ancestors' *Heimat* where they can live as "Germans with Germans." While their individual concept of *Heimat* may differ,[9] their belief in cultural belonging is indisputable.

While West German society has been shaped by almost thirty years of feminist discourse and the implementation of feminist politics in administration and other areas, ethnic German women have little conception of that recent historical achievement. Their experiences stand in striking contrast to the societal realities of Germany today. The disparity is visible in many ways. For example, most ethnic German women come from rural areas or societies where having a large number of children is desirable and in which the socialization of women is strongly oriented towards the unquestioned value of motherhood and family. Their reports are either governed by an essentialist conceptualization of gender difference, which is exemplified when they thematize the exploitation of working women in Russian uranium mines during World War II (Lizz) or when they ignore the issue of gender altogether (Resch). Another area of difference concerns family ties. While in West German society the nuclear family is a familiar model for most women, it is alien to many ethnic German women. They are accustomed to living with extended families and maintaining close-knit relations for mutual support. Frequently, the entire extended family occupies a small apartment. "Returning" ethnic German women rarely live alone or away from their families, a custom which the German government policy of allowing families to be united facilitates. Thus there is much less concern about placing children in daycare or kindergarten, because the grandmothers are present to provide child care.[10] Other differences ethnic German women encounter

9. "Ich habe keinen Bezug zur Heimat, für mich ist Heimat die Welt." Such is the sentiment of another ethnic German, Gert Hoyer (Ferstl and Hetzel 138).
10. Erna Weber, a worker from the former Soviet Union, explains: "Bei uns sind die Eltern immer bei den Kindern, ja? In einer Wohnung, ja. Die gehen auf die Arbeit, und sie bleiben bei den Enkelchen. Die Eltern sind immer da" (Malchow 120).

involve sexual behavior. They are often shocked by Western standards. Women from Kazakhstan and Kyrgyzstan, for instance, were not used to leaving their houses without their husbands and were socialized to sub-ordinate themselves to the family rather than follow their own interests. Lastly, the anticipation – sometimes kept alive for generations – that they will finally "return" to the geographical place that their ancestors called *Heimat* provides a common bond between ethnic German women that transcends the factors described above.

Information provided by the German government on the issue of eth-nic Germans suggests that most of the ethnic Germans have been success-fully integrated into the societal fabric of the Federal Republic of Germany. Women's groups have been set up and *Frauenbeauftragte* [women in admin-istrative positions to further special interests of women] engage in dialogue with ethnic German women, encouraging them to understand that, based on their experiences in living between several cultures, they have brought what was referred to as a *Schatztruhe* [treasure chest][11] of cultural knowl-edge to Germany. Task forces, such as the "Pädagogische Initiative Darm-stadt," help them compare diverse roles for women and differing ways of life, so that they may ultimately integrate into German society. Thus, the clash of gender politics is softened by societal agencies that have been in place in the Federal Republic at least since the mid 1980s.

* * *

But there are other voices that vehemently challenge the very concept of ethnic Germanness based on loyalty to German ancestors, language, education, and culture.[12] An unnamed member of the city council for the Green Party bluntly states: "I cannot accept the fact that today these people bring back into the Federal Republic of Germany an ideology of Germanness that is one hundred or two hundred years old, when we in Europe are engaged in minimizing the ideology of the nation-state and nationality. They will have to unlearn all that very quickly because what they bring along as ideology is not harmless" (Stadtrat der Grünen 92). Such deeply held convictions are shared by a large number of German citizens, for whom the category of *Volkszugehörigkeit* is too reminiscent of Nazi ideology, especially since its essence is based on blood.

"For me, there exists no biology of Germanness," states the same member of the city council of the Green Party. "Being German does not derive from

11. See "'Larissas Schatztruhe'" (*Vorbildliche Intergartion von Aussiedlern* 128).
12. See Roland Tichy who maintains that united Germany should basically be open to all people willing to live and work in the Federal Republic of Germany, and that Ger-man law should not privilege one group over the other.

a German father or grandfather who at one time emigrated. I recognize that there are blood types O, A and B, but I do not recognize a blood type 'German.' German blood is not a natural basis [of identity, M.M.] but, as we know from our history, a dangerous ideology . Thinking about this is often so superficial that people can say they are German but no longer speak German" (92-93).

In the meantime, the Green Party is not alone in contesting the credibility of official policy towards ethnic Germans' unrestricted "return." In all political parties in Germany there are politicians who support and others who oppose current policies concerning ethnic Germans. In November 1996, Oskar Lafontaine, chairman of the Social Democratic Party (SPD), demanded a stop to the continuing arrival of ethnic Germans. He is opposed by a member of the same party, Manfred Püchel, the Minister of Interior of the federal state of Saxony-Anhalt, who argues that ethnic Germans would increase the constantly decreasing population in the Eastern parts of the Federal Republic, since most of its young people are moving to the Western states (see "Aussiedler"). The solution of the German government to alleviating the problems caused by the yearly integration of about 225,000 ethnic Germans into its society is to impose stricter language examinations rather than addressing the overwhelming number of admissions, as a recent article in *Der Spiegel* pointed out. However, the current emphasis that requires arriving ethnic Germans from Russia to speak German also ignores the fact that they were punished for doing this during Stalinism (see "Rußlanddeutsche"). In particular the younger generations of ethnic Germans are solidly grounded in the culture of their Eastern European origin, do not know German, and have only a superficial knowledge of German culture.[13] How this dual cultural experience will affect German culture as a whole remains to be seen.

The German government informed its citizens in detail about the history of ethnic Germans in order to promote their acceptance into German society.[14] In addition to the state's efforts, numerous volumes have been published with life stories by ethnic Germans from several Eastern European countries, covering a wide range of ages and social groups during the last several years.[15] Despite such attempts, many ethnic Germans are experiencing tremendous difficulties in adjusting to German society, which are often thematized in their stories. Also included are narratives of persecu-

13. See Heinelt and Lohmann.
14. Details are available in *Informationen zur politischen Bildung: Aussiedler*, and "Zahlen, Daten, Fakten."
15. See Knott, Malchow, and Székely.

tion during the Stalinist period, their deportation all over the Soviet Union from Siberia to Kazakhstan, the specific hardships to which women and children were subjected, and their longing to remigrate to Germany.[16]

* * *

Various aspects of belonging, longing for "*Heimat,*" and problems of integration and assimilation are portrayed in the texts of the Rumanian-German writer Herta Müller. In her work, both the ethnic German village and the Federal Republic of Germany are represented as places without a future. In fact, no geographical place has the potential for fulfillment of dreams for a better life. In *Reisende auf einem Bein* (A Woman Traveling on One Leg), Irene, driven by the longing for *Heimat*, emigrates to Germany, which in turn surprises her by its lack of *Heimat*. She perceives interpersonal relations in Germany as alienating and foreign. Müller claims that Irene's experience of unrelatedness, unconnectedness, and estrangement is one shared by many ethnic Germans emigrating from the East.[17] Furthermore, in Müller's text, gender boundaries are strictly defined, with certain spaces occupied solely by women and others by men. These strictly defined and gendered spaces function as an assertion of Germanness, captured in the constant cleaning of the houses (*Niederungen,* 123) that is intensified by allowing, for example, swallows to live in ethnic German villages and exterminating sparrows (74-5). While this practice might merely be a representation of rural life, Zygmunt Bauman characterizes this process of weeding out and selecting as one that ultimately ended in the Holocaust (*Modernity and the Holocaust,* 18).[18]

The envisioned *Heimat* Germany, meaning German culture in whatever form (which may be just the German language, or, due to the political persecution of ethnic Germans during Stalinism, just rudiments of it), this imagined Germany lived in the songs, poems, tales, stories, and customs of the ethnic Germans. Perhaps in this frozen image of Germany lies also buried a possible identity that disturbs those who feel defensive about simple statements of unalienated Germanness. Ilse from Rumania defines this identity:

> Germanness: I have to use this ominous word. As mentioned before, we thought of ourselves as Germans ... and then we had to prove our German-

16. See Székely (28-145) and Spevack (71-92).
17. "Ich wollte mit der Person Irene von mir selber weggehen und verallgemeinern. Aus diesem Grund habe ich beispielsweise vermieden, Rumänien im Buch zu nennen. Ihre Situation trifft auf viele zu, die etwa aus Ländern aus dem Osten hierherkommen." "Die Weigerung, sich verfügbar zu machen."
18. See Müller's own account of "dealing with the Nazi past" in *Frankfurter Rundschau* 8 August 1987.

ness to the authorities. We did that as well as we could. But beyond these simple administrative procedures, we discovered that especially people in Left circles were astonished that we insisted that we were Germans and not Rumanians (Wendt 113).

* * *

No doubt the influx of both ethnic German women with their specific relationship to tradition, i.e., the centrality of family values, prefeminist concepts of womanhood and womanliness, as well as asylum-seeking women has the potential to transform the intellectual and cultural climate in Germany. The direction this alteration might take has not yet been decided. The still-absent debate about a political philosophy that favors the return of ethnic Germans over the admission of asylum seekers needs to take place without getting mired in mere accusations. What else besides the mere fulfillment of legal obligations is hidden behind the German government's extraordinary mobilization for ethnic Germans? One might wonder if certain political interests in Germany hope for a renewal of traditional values by ethnic German women who are not yet infected by feminist thinking.

While the German women authors who advocate on behalf of asylum seekers see their endeavor in broadly humanistic and emancipatory terms, their project may actually enable the German reading public to legitimize the *"otherness "* of asylum seekers as an escape from a more rigid form of Germanness that is represented by the female ethnic Germans who have not yet experienced a modern Western society.

While asylum-seeking and ethnic German women share the desire to belong, both groups in their own way experience German society as alien and different. Citizens of Germany exoticize asylum-seeking women on the one hand and are embarrassed by the strong assertions of Germanness by ethnic German women on the other. While asylum-seeking women may still hope for a return to their *Heimat*, ethnic German women are often disappointed by the reality of their new German *Heimat*. The dilemma confronted by ethnic German women who discover that the central component of their identity, their "Germanness," is questioned by the Germans of their longed-for *Heimat* is not apt to be resolved soon: The new Germany is basically a postnational society.

Note

All translations from German are my own.

Magda Mueller

Bibliography

"Alles, was ich tat, das hieß jetzt: warten. Die ausgewanderte rumäniendeutsche Schriftstellerin Herta Müller im Gespräch mit Klaus Hensel." *Frankfurter Rundschau* 8 August 1987.

Almanach der Bundesregierung 1995/96. Ed. Presse- und Informationsamt der Bundesregierung. Bonn: Osang Verlag, 1996.

"Aussiedler: Sachsen-Anhalts Innenminister Manfred Püchel fordert mehr Rußlanddeutsche für die neuen Länder." *Der Spiegel* 11 (1996): 42.

Aziz, Namo, ed. *Fremd in einem kalten Land: Ausländer in Deutschland.* Freiburg i. Br.: Herder, 1992.

Basic Law for the Federal Republic of Germany. Bonn: Press and Information Office of the Federal Government, 1993.

Bauman, Zygmunt. *Modernity and the Holocaust.* Ithaca, NY: Cornell UP, 1989.

Benz, Wolfgang, ed. *Intergration ist machbar: Ausländer in Deutschland.* Munich: Beck, 1993.

Berman, Russell. Discussion contribution in "Nationhood, Nationalism and Identity" (89).

CDU Argumente zur Aussiedlerpolitik. Ed. CDU-Bundesgeschäftsstelle. Düsseldorf: Vereinigte Verlagsanstalten, 1992.

Facts about Germany. Frankfurt a.M.: Societäts-Verlag, 1993.

Ferstl, Lothar and Harald Hetzel, eds. *"Wir sind immer die Fremden": Aussiedler in Deutschland.* Bonn: Dietz, 1990.

Gebauer, Guido F., Bernhard H.F. Taureck, and Thomas Ziegler, eds. *Ausländerfeindschaft ist Zukunftsfeindschaft: Plädoyer für eine kulturintegrative Gesellschaft.* Frankfurt a.M.: Fischer, 1993.

Die geteilte Heimat. Neuanfang für die Deutschen im Osten oder Aussiedlung zu uns. Bonn: Aktion Gemeinsinn, 1994.

Heinelt, Hubert and Anne Lohmann, eds. *Immigranten im Wohlfahrtsstaat am Beispiel der Rechtspositionen und Lebensverhältnisse von Aussiedlern.* Opladen: Leske and Buderich, 1992.

Hoyer, Gert. "Die große Freiheit." Ferstl and Hetzel 135-40.

"Ich bete jeden Tag, bitte laß uns bleiben!" 14 Porträts asylsuchender Frauen aus aller Welt. Ed. Anne Rademacher. Munich: Goldmann, 1993.

Informationen zur politischen Bildung: Aussiedler. Ed. Bundeszentrale für politische Bildung. Munich: Franzis-Verlag, 1991.

Just, Wolf-Dieter, ed. *Asyl von unten: Kirchenasyl und ziviler Ungehorsam.* Reinbek: Rowohlt, 1993.

Kimminich, Otto. "Asylrecht in Deutschland und in der EG." Aziz 187-205.

Knott, Heidi et al., ed. *Heimat Deutschland? Lebensberichte von Aus- und Übersiedlern.* Paffenweiler: Centaurus, 1991.

Leggewie, Claus, ed. *Multi Kulti: Spielregeln für die Vielvölkerrepublik.* Berlin: Rotbuch, 1993.

Lizz, E. "'In die Urangruben.'" Ferstl and Hetzel 46-53.

Malchow, Barbara, Keyumars Tayebi, and Ulrike Brand, eds. *Die fremden Deutschen: Aussiedler in der Bundesrepublik.* Reinbek: Rowohlt, 1993.

Müller, Herta. *Niederungen.* Berlin: Rotbuch, 1984.

———. *Reisende auf einem Bein.* Berlin: Rotbuch, 1989.

"Nationhood, Nationalism and Identity: A Symposium." *Telos* 150 (Fall 1995): 77-111.

Das neue Asylrecht: CDU-Dokumentation. 18 (1992). Ed. CDU-Bundesgeschäftsstelle. Düsseldorf: Vereinigte Verlagsanstalten, 1992.

Parnass, Peggy. "'Gespräche?' Dunja, Azra, Sina, Rebekka und Ljuba." *"Ich bete jeden Tag, bitte laß uns bleiben!"* 145-64.

Rademacher, Anne, ed. *"Ich bete jeden Tag, bitte laß uns bleiben!" 14 Porträts asylsuchender Frauen aus aller Welt.* Munich: Goldmann, 1993.

Resch, Emma. "'Immer neu anfangen.'" Ferstl and Hetzel 59-63.

"Rußlanddeutsche: Sprache als Barriere." *Der Spiegel* 49 (1996): 60-63.

Scheib, Asta. "'Ich kann nicht ohne meine Heimat leben.' Rita aus dem Sudan." *"Ich bete jeden Tag, bitte laß uns bleiben!"* 87-97.

Spevack, Edmund. "Ethnic Germans from the East: *Aussiedler* in Germany, 1970-1994." *German Politics and Society* 13.4 (Winter 1995): 71-92.

Stadtrat der Grünen, "'Für mich gibt es keine Biologie des Deutschtums.'" Malchow 92-94.

Székely, Gisela, ed. *Lasst sie selber sprechen: Berichte rußlanddeutscher Aussiedler.* Frankfurt a.M.: Ullstein, 1990.

Tichy, Roland. *Ausländer rein! Deutsche und Ausländer - verschiedene Herkunft, gemeinsame Zukunft.* Munich: Piper, 1993.

Vorbildliche Intergartion von Aussiedlern in der Bundesrepublik Deutschland. 2. Bundeswettbewerb. Dokumentation 1994. Bonn: Bundesministerium des Inneren, 1994.

Waffenschmidt, Horst. "Aussiedlerpolitik mit Augenmaß." *Info-Dienst Deutsche Aussiedler.* 77 (March 1996). 2-8.

Weber, Erna. "'Jede Nation muß in ihr Land.'" Malchow 104-20.

"Die Weigerung, sich verfügbar zu machen: Herta Müller und Richard Wagner im Gespräch." *Zitty* 26 (1989): 68.

Wendt, Gunna. "'Die Sprache der Gefahren': Ilse aus Rumänien." *"Ich bete jeden Tag, bitte laß uns bleiben!"* 109-27.

Wichary, sen., G. "'Zu Hause, aber keine Heimat.'" Ferstl and Hetzel 98-101.

"Zahlen, Daten, Fakten." *Info-Dienst Deutsche Aussiedler.* 69 (July 1995). 2-27.

Zwischen Tradition und Zukunft: Situation und Perspektiven der Rußlanddeutschen in den Nachfolgestaaten der ehemaligen Sowjetunion. Ed. Otto Benecke Stiftung. Bonn: Otto Benecke Stiftung, 1992.

Chapter 19

GERMANIA – JUST A MALE CONSTRUCTION?

Gender, Germanness, and Feminism in East German Women Writers

Eva Kaufmann

As this volume's broad-ranging topics demonstrate, the word "Germanness," itself born of foreign perceptions and as such untranslatable into German, opens up a variety of issues. Such issues become particularly evident in texts where female authors of the former German Democratic Republic explicitly articulate their relationship to Germany (Federal Republic of Germany and German Democratic Republic). These young writers' relationship to Germany rests on different assumptions than that of women born around 1930. This younger generation of authors did not experience World War II and fascism and did not share the illusions of the older generation who had hoped to build a better world through socialism. They were either small children or not yet born when the Wall was erected. Nevertheless, their relationship to Germany reveals a pronounced sensitivity [*Problembewußtsein*].

The poetic texts of Annett Gröschner (born in 1964), Barbara Köhler (born in 1958), and Kathrin Schmidt (born in 1958) originated partly before and partly after the fall of 1989. In some instances, their texts reveal common ground in regard to issues concerning Germany. Such commonality cannot be attributed simply to a shared group identity in the strict sense. Their socialization in the GDR provided them with similar formational experiences so that when they began to write in the years just before the GDR collapsed, many images and poetic themes were "in the air."

Among the most interesting passages of their poems are those where concepts like "German / Germany / Germania / my country" are used in a variety of contexts. Unlike journalistic texts where individual words can often be understood literally, the poetic text demands that one scrutinize the complicated and many-layered associations in which a word may be embedded. If one pursues the implications of a given word, other words are of necessity ignored. Despite these difficulties (for translations too), the texts presented here contain rich material. Presumably, the reflection of Germanness in a poetic text is based on a long and thorough process of thinking and feeling. Less the result of external impulses like interviews, it may still be linked to current events, but nevertheless surely arises from a deep inner need of the authors. An examination of the following sample texts seems an appropriate way to gain some insights into the relationship between woman and Germanness for these three authors.

German Ancestors

All three authors share a connection to Friedrich Hölderlin who, not coincidentally, is often associated with the words "German / Germanness." The texts with which we shall be concerned here were written before the fall of 1989, including Schmidt's 1982 poem, with its alarming title "INS FELD, INS FELD MIT HÖLDERLIN" (To Battle, to Battle with Hölderlin),[1] whom she calls upon in support against "die alten Zöpfe des Zeitgeists" [old-fogy spirit of the times]. In her texts Schmidt borrows verses from Hölderlin's poem "DER GANG AUFS LAND" (Walk into the Countryside) with that summons, "INS OFFENE, FREUND" [into the open air, my friend, 2: 88], which suggests an atmosphere of a breaking open, an eruption. The underlying polemic directs itself against the stagnating, "closed society" of the GDR, against that which Hölderlin termed "die bleierne Zeit" [leaden times] in his poem. Schmidt writes:

> da kehrt ein deutscher vorfahr
> das schwarzweiß und rote, das braune und brandige
> gras des erinnerns hervor, das wächst ...
> aus unserer scheinheilen mitte.[2]

1. The poem originally appeared in *Poesiealbum 1979* (28). Quoted here from Kathrin Schmidt. *Ein Engel fliegt durch die Tapetentür* (10).
2. "a German ancestor displays / the black/white and red, the brown and burnt / grass of memory, it grows ... / in our shamperfect midst."

Schmidt views Hölderlin as someone who disrupts a stillness that is "scheinheil," a fitting neologism that combines "scheinheilig" [hypocritical] and "heil" [sound]. In the name of Hölderlin, different phases of recent German history are referred to by their symbolic colors (black/white and red, brown) – phases which are not to be repressed.

In Barbara Köhler's collection of poems *Deutsches Roulette*, which contains works from 1984-89, Hölderlin is included repeatedly with direct allusions to things German. In "Letztes Erinnern," which laments the separation from a close friend, the ending proclaims:

MEIN BELLARMIN /So
kam ich unter die Deutschen[3]

Annett Gröschner also alludes to Hölderlin's words in her poem "Friedrich im Schlaf" (Friedrich asleep) when she writes about her newborn son: "SO KAM er UNTER DIE DEUTSCHEN" [Thus he arrived among the Germans, *Herzdame* n.p.]. In both cases the Hölderlin quote stands as a code word for life circumstances which are perceived as unlivable. Not only Köhler, but also Gröschner apparently presume that like-minded individuals will link the key words, "So kam ich unter die Deutschen" (Hölderlin 3: 159) with that passage about the Germans towards the end of "Hyperion" which speaks of "barbarians since ancient times" and of "a battlefield where hands and arms and other limbs lie scattered about and the life blood that has been shed disappears [vanishes] into the sand, in a place where one can see craftsmen, thinkers and priests, but no people" (3: 160).

In one of Köhler's other poems, one of the few that are dated (April 1985), the title "Anrede zwo: "Diotima an Bellarmin" (Second Salutation: Diotima to Bellarmin) already refers to Hölderlin. In Hölderlin's epistolary novel, it is above all the men who communicate with each other. Hyperion and Bellarmin exchange thoughts about the fatherland, friendship, and love. In Köhler's works the woman addresses her friend Bellarmin about death and life and about the difficulty of establishing genuine human contact between the sexes. At the beginning of the text, she contrasts the concept of "German Roulette" to the commonly understood concept of "Russian Roulette," calling forth associations with that deadly game of empty and loaded cartridges. Here she is obviously not borrowing casino terminology, but rather inventing a term with its own meaning that refers to paradoxical and peculiarly German life circumstances, especially the difficulty of being heard by others. The line from which those two words were taken, which also lends the work

3. MY BELLARMIN / Thus / I arrived among the Germans (44).

its title, reads: "Sprache Ohneland. Deutsches Roulette endet mit Rien ne va plus" (Language withoutacountry. German roulette ends with *rien ne va plus*). While the concept of "Russian Roulette" is directly associated with fatal consequences, "Deutsches Roulette" poses the question of whether the "I" could play a new text to the old song: Diotima oder Die Wahre Liebe verreckt" (Diotima or True Love Perished, 12). It is traditional – thus the invocation of Diotima's death – that the woman dies of intolerable conditions. Unlike with men, not even a bullet is needed for her death. In the casino game of roulette, the words "rien ne va plus" signify the moment when the ball starts rolling and all bets are called. The gamblers can only wait and see. This is the basic situation that the poem suggests for the subject as well. She seems hopeless and helpless, suffers from the alienation of language and the lack of communication between the sexes. The direction in which the subject seeks a possibility for escape is sketched out in the sentence: "Und vielleicht sollte das aufhören: Wörter wie Mann und Frau einander vorzuwerfen" [And perhaps this should stop: holding words like "man" and "woman" against one another]. The subject does not give in and tries a "new" song, struggling against the tendency to confrontation – a typical German characteristic perhaps – and seeking human encounter. The early words "Sprich nicht weiter" [say no more] are countered twice by "Sprich weiter" [keep on talking]. This many-layered poem, which foregrounds lyrical reflections about personal relations (love and friendship), emphasizes the public context and the historical background implicit in the adjective *deutsch*.

For Köhler, Hölderlin is the one German poet who offers a frame of reference for her own voice in which she can move freely without the need for identifying or delimiting. He stands for those German writers from the late eighteenth and early nineteenth centuries who "rubbed their foreheads sore" on Germany's societal wall, as Anna Seghers pointedly wrote in 1935 (36). The reference to Hölderlin in Köhler's sonnet "Endstelle" lends its lament about loss and pain an even stronger impact. She effectively splices the last three lines from Hölderlin's famous poem "Hälfte des Lebens" ("Half of Life") into the opening lines of her own four stanzas:

Die Mauern stehn
Sprachlos und kalt, im Winde
Klirren die Fahnen[4]

---

4. The walls stand / speechless and cold, and in the wind / the weathervanes are rattling. *Gedichte* (121).

Eva Kaufmann

Sword in the Sheath

Gröschner's *Herzdame Knochensammler* (Queen of Hearts Collector of Bones), published in collaboration with the photographer Tina Bara, is a collection of poems written between 1983 and 1993. "Verlust und Gewinn" (Losses and Gains) ponders the recent historical upheavals from the standpoint of an East German woman and brings "Germania" into the game.

Was mir nicht gehörte
wird mir genommen im Namen
Deutschland ist gründlich
am Grund der Bodensatz Toter
stinkt nicht flüstert kaum noch
GERMANIA eine Erfindung der Männer
ist wieder
keine Frau nur ein Held
Kein Wort mir von Heimat
es war mir
ein heimeliges Gefängnis
ohne Licht zur billigen Miete
ein zu enger Schuh
und nun ist da nichts mehr
außer den Wänden
gegen die ich jetzt treten darf.[5]

She offers a sobering balance of the losses and gains that attended the end of the GDR and its absorption into the Federal Republic. Both states are viewed from a distanced perspective; criticizing the one does not automatically valorize the other. What is lost or gained remains on different levels. The subject is liberated from constrictions, from chains (cozy prison without light, shoes too tight). More difficult to interpret is the statement that "GERMANIA is once again not a woman." Why again? As if the allegorical character with the grammatically feminine sex were ever more than just a male hero. Moreover, the sculpted symbolic figure of the traditional Germania, (as she was recently depicted in the large exhibit "Marianne und Germania") is an exceedingly martialistic, heavy lady with a menacing look and a huge sword in her fist, ready to crush all *Erbfeinde* [arch enemies]. Such an image underlies the opposition: "not a woman, just a hero."

5. What never was mine in name / is taken from me / Germany has really / hit bottom the residue of corpses / has no odor, hardly makes a sound / Germania an invention of men / is once again / not a woman just a hero / don't talk to me about *Heimat* / for me it was / a cozy prison / without light for low rent / a shoe too tight / and now there is nothing left / but the walls / that I can kick against (n.p.).

- 294 -

This polemic against the heroism that nationalists so gladly identify with the German national character is similar to the description of a utopian landscape that is suited for human existence in Barbara Köhler's "Elektra. Spiegelungen VIII" (Electra. Reflections VIII): "dies ist der ort / zu gewinnen ohne siegen zu müssen" [this is a place / for winning without having to triumph, *Deutsches Roulette* 31]. Assuming that in no other country one can speak of a feminine creature, the question remains whether the central idea of this poem has, consciously or unconsciously, to do with a concretely futile hope. Behind the expression "GERMA-NIA … is once again not a woman" stands the loss of the ambitious, short-lived hopes of those who in the fall of 1989 believed that from the collapsing GDR a society could be reformed in which women could influence their own fates and the general course of things, not only gender relations. In the statement of principles that Ina Merkel delivered at the founding meeting of the Independent Women's Federation on 12 March 1989, she declared: "we should ask the political parties and movements which new life prospects this or that strategy will open up, so that our expectations, our questions regarding women can be realized politically in an alternative conception of society … The women have no Fatherland to lose, but rather a world to gain" (29, 31).

Such utopian conceptions corresponded to that explosive atmosphere that bloomed briefly in the fall of 1989 and with which Gröschner was also familiar. Her harsh dictum "kein Wort mir von Heimat" [don't talk to me about *Heimat*] is on the same level as that old statement of Ilse Frapan's "Wir Frauen haben kein Vaterland" [We Women Don't Have a Fatherland), which became the title of a novel in 1899.

In *Flußbild mit Engel* (Picture of a River with an Angel, 1995), Schmidt engages in an amazingly original wordplay, for example in the poem title "mein blähland mein blühland," characterizing her country as one that swells and blooms. In precisely this context the "my" sounds sarcastic. The expression "wo planjahrfünft getauscht in marksschein-quader" [where the five-year plan staggers into a block of Western mark notes, 13] marks the change from a planned to a market economy. The term "blähland" suits not only the puffed-up self-presentation of the GDR, but also the newly created Federal Republic, which bestowed West German Marks upon its voters boastfully promised "blühende Landschaften" [that the country would flourish]. What surprises is the consequence to which the text leads. Just like the official self-inflation and blooming, the belly of the subject swells, but

wie damals zu gebären
gelingt mir nicht

das land ist bläh und blüh
und für mein totgeborenes
ist es zu früh.[6]

The end of this poem calls forth many associations: in the most direct sense an actual miscarriage, in the conveyed meaning that this is not a country into which to bring children. Certainly this notion corresponds to reliable statistical figures regarding the drastically lowered rate of birth (more than 50%) in the new German federal states. Additionally it suggests doubt about whether this puffing-up and blooming is capable of anything productive at all. Besides this poem there is a series of others in which Schmidt complains that women and children cannot live well in this country. In "Hochzeit" (Wedding, *Flußbild mit Engel*) she mocks the official trend of persuading women demagogically into motherhood, domesticity, and marital bliss.

Schmidt also angrily dismisses other offers that "mein land" [my country] extends to East German women. For example "salami.pup-pen.barbie.taktik" shows how "unter deutscherlands kleinerem Flügel" [under more-Germany's smaller wing], somewhere in the flat lands of Mecklenburg, rural, strapping women try to shape themselves into Barbie dolls (32). And in the poem "preussisch alpin" (Prussian alpine) East German women who, according to Western men, never knew the good things in life, are lured to bed with "come on" and "komm auf den gipfel, carola" [come to the top, Carola] which refers to the pop song "Komm auf die Schaukel, Luise" (Come Swing with Me, Louise). Eastern women are advanced to the level of desired sex objects: "drolliger osten heißt: dralle verkosten" [fun in the East: check out the plump ones, 32] and also "wild geht der westen ins bette" [the west goes wild in bed, 12]. In these and other poems Schmidt defends women's interests against the various presumptions and manipulations that "mein land" bestows. That does not mean that she is now nostalgically characterizing GDR conditions as generally favorable to women and children;[7] however the sharp judgment she renders against changing conditions explains one thing: in the GDR she was able to have everything that was important: a job, her writing, and children. Later, though, any claim to such a full life was no longer tenable.

Schmidt's vita is exceptional: she had four children between 1979 and 1988; she worked most of the time as a psychologist; and she always

6. To give birth the way I used to / is no longer possible / the country is puffed-up (*bläh*) and blooming (*blüh*) / and for my still-born one / it's too soon (13).
7. She said that she did not feel discriminated against in the GDR when someone gave her a hard time in a job interview because of her three children—after all she knew that the law was on her side (personal communication, 7 October 1993).

wrote, even if at first she did not intend to publish her texts. Creating poems, however, was always possible for her, even while doing laundry. With her four children she is not at all the "Mutti-Typ" [mommy type] that some feminists make fun of.[8] Her texts do not indulge in any kind of motherhood myth, old or new. She once simply said that it had been a pleasure to be pregnant. Her situation is shaped by what life with four growing children brings, such as extensive paperwork with all kinds of bureaucratic officials.

Gröschner also viewed writing and having children as a unity. She writes in a letter in March of 1990: "when I decided to have my child, it was also because I thought I could manage without having to give up my dream of writing. Now I am not so sure" (Mudry 89). The fact is that she did somehow "manage." In connection with the much-discussed measures for providing work, she was able to earn her living from year to year with projects researching local history.[9] However, she hardly had time to write, let alone work on the planned novel. Like Schmidt, she does not allow pregnancy, birth, and childcare to sever her ties to the world. The previously mentioned poem about the birth of her son in January 1989 "Friedrich im Schlaf" (Friedrich Asleep, *Herzdame* n. p.), with Hölderlin's words "SO KAM er UNTER DIE DEUTSCHEN," affirms this. Written before the fall of 1989, this allusion is presumably directed not only at East Germans. Already in 1988, Gröschner – playing on the multiple meanings of "Scheide" – had transposed its meaning of "sheath" (for a sword) into that of "vagina," the side of infanticide in her poem "Jetztmorgengestern" (Todaytomorrowyesterday). The larger context of the poem concerns the precarious silence of women (in history) and its fatal counterpart in recent history:

ich seh den Trotz im Bild der Terroristin
Die Bomben legt am Kaufhaus der Geschichte
Jedoch am Ende ist es blanke Ohnmacht
Die neue Mauern baut: Sie heißt Germania
Steckt ihr Schwert in die Scheide
die kommenden Kinder zu töten: Blasse Deutsche ... .[10]

8. Helwerth and Schwarz allude to such controversies.

9. This project was completed and publicly introduced in 1994. For financial reasons a complete exhibition catalog could not be published. Instead the brochure "Augenblicke für später. Erinnerungen an 1945. Texte von Zeitzeuginnen, " (Moments for Later. Memories of 1945. Texts by Contemporary Witnesses) was published by the Kultur- and Socialamt Prenzlauer Berg, Berlin 1995.

10. "I see the defiance in the picture of the woman terrorist / who plants bombs in the store of history / but finally it is sheer powerlessness / that builds new walls: Her name is Germania / and she shoves her sword into the sheath / to kill the children who are on their way: pale Germans ..." *Herzdame* n.p.

As these poems originating both before and after the fall of 1989 demonstrate, Germania appears here as a murderous creature – the embodiment of negative tendencies in German history. Such imagery is linked to Gröschner's unusual sensitivity regarding war, which we will consider later.

Concerning the "Bloody Soil of German History"

Although she is much less polemical than Schmidt, Köhler also reacts quite pointedly to certain German historical and cultural traditions. Thus she takes on the concept of "*Tiefe* " [profundity, depth], which is traditionally tied to the notion of Germanness. In Part II of the poem "Papierboot" (Paper Boat), written before 1989, she writes: "Maybe it's a German story: The more meager the surface dimension, the more bottomless the depth. He who allows himself to fall goes under [*zu Grunde*]. In the mud which is hidden by the soil [*Grund*]. The bloody soil [*Grund*] of German history" (*Deutsches Roulette* 53). This drastic judgment relates to certain aspects of German Romanticism that are considered in Part I of the poem "Papierboot." What we find here is an allusion to a painting by Caspar David Friedrich which bears the title : "Zwei Männer in Betrachtung des Mondes" (Two Men Looking at the Moon). This image of cliffs, half moon, trees twisting in the wind, and two men could be understood as the essence of German, comtemplative profundity. Köhler begins her poem with the dedication: "für Eva Angela Ulrike Gudrun," who are referred to later on by the phrase "Vier Frauen in Betrachtung" (Four Women Looking). The scene depicts a conversation along the Elbe near Dresden, under a crescent moon. After the provocative statement "Die romantischen Bilder blättern ab" [Romantic images are flaking away], the text discusses what is there to be seen behind the "Kleister" [paste]. An anonymous voice refers to "Die giftige Schlammschicht am Grund der Flüsse" [the poisonous silt at the bottom of the rivers, 52]. This discussion rejects both the idyllic as well as its wholesale negation. If we assume that the four women are discussing history, we notice that they are not caught up in dreamy contemplation. Rather, they speak soberly about the connection between past and present.

The stiff immersion in a "grundlose Tiefe" [bottomless depth] is replaced with an image of spiritual motion and mobility. Köhler invites us, for instance, to see the Elbe not as an isolating border, but as a river that will eventually join the ocean. In *Blue Box* (1995), there is no explicit friction with Germany and Germanness. The joy of poetic reflection on new experiences of the world while traveling (to Iceland and Holland, for instance) outweighs any friction. However, the later prose poem "Rheinsberger Tristien" shows that she still feels challenged by provocative remnants of Prussian-German history. Köhler's text focuses on the castle Rheinsberg in the Mark Brandenburg where Frederick the Great had lived in the eighteenth century. Nationalistic tradition tends to portray him as the victorious field marshall, especially in the Seven Years War (1756-1763). In the GDR, this part of the Frederician past was less thematized, but the situation changed in the early nineties with the reestablishment of Brandenburg as a state in united Germany.

Köhler mocks "Brandenburgs Arkadien" (Brandenburg's Arcadia) when she writes: "HIER SOLL PREUSSEN SCHÖN SEIN" [Here Prussia is supposed to be beautiful, 17]. The text sharply denounces this sentiment by looking at the castle's architecture and the design of the park in images of dreary military training: "Die Bäume angetreten zu Alleen" [The trees line up into avenues, 17], "ringsum die Wälder ohne Unterholz Föhren und Buchen lange Kerls halten sich grade & die Stellung" [all around the forest without undergrowth, pines beeches tall guards standing straight at attention, 18]. This image of park and castle, both of which were restored with much effort after 1989, corresponds to other revived legends of Prussian kings where the "Fremdkörper Frau" [woman as foreign body] is only fit to be an allegorical decoration (18) – a jolt for readers who associate the East German tourist site with the lightness and loveliness rendered in Tucholsky's story *Rheinsberg. Ein Bilderbuch für Verliebte* (A Picture Book for Lovers). Each of the five stanzas ends with the words "IN FRONT DER SEE" [the lake in front]. The typeface may indicate that the phrase is quoted from an authentic source, perhaps from a tour guide, thus connecting the peaceful natural surroundings with the military front. Times may be changing, but here "die beste aller alten Zeiten" [the best of all the good old times, 19] seems reawakened. Merging the sayings "good old times" and "best of all possible worlds" derides "Brandenburgs Arcadia" all the more. Köhler's text reveals the Prussian essence as a type of behavior that has survived the centuries of Germany's various formations as a state. In this connection, "Tristien" calls to mind the connotations of that untranslatable English word "Germanness."

Köhler's remark that poems are "not a commentary on quotidian politics" (Dahlke 57) should of course be taken seriously. A poem like "Rheinsberger Tristien" may have its share of *Tagespolitik*, but it goes deeper and circles around the existential questions. Where Germany leaves its imprint in the way described above, there is no room for cozy feelings as Köhler expresses them in several poems about Saxonian landscapes, Dresden, and the Elbe. In the volume, *Deutsches Roulette* especially "Zwei Stück Heimat" (Two Pieces of *Heimat*) and "Niemandsufer. Ein Bericht" (No Man's Shore. A Report), as well as numbers 3, 7, and 8 of the cycle "ELB ALB," Saxon poet Köhler's feeling of regional affiliation and her anger at the Prussian tradition make all the deformations that result from Prussian German history seem especial, painful.

Köhler does better with her regional background. Unlike Prussia, Saxony's history is less encumbered by a tradition of absolute order. Yet her orientation toward the regional (which is also pronounced in the work of the Saxons Irmtraud Morgner and Kerstin Hensel) is not provincially anachronistic. Orientation toward the place where one grew up, had important experiences, and knew happiness and suffering are less shaped by ideology than by sensual impressions and concrete experience with the people and landscape.

Between River Borders East and West

Köhler's *Deutsches Roulette* has many a poem that articulates the pain caused by the border to the West, often signified by the image of the Elbe. "Rondeau Allemagne," for example, presents the problem of living and remaining in an isolated country. The peculiar title is confusing and telling at the same time – why "Rondeau Allemagne" instead of "Rondeau allemand"? *Rondeau*, the name of an old French round dance, provides the formal frame for Köhler's suggestive image of a fragmented and fragmenting life in Germany. By modifying the four lines of the first stanza in the second and third stanzas, she enhances the multiplicity of meanings in her material:

Ich harre aus im Land und geh, ihm fremd,
Mit einer Liebe, die mich über Grenzen treibt,
Zwischen den Himmeln. Sehe jeder, wo er bleibt;
Ich harre aus im Land und geh ihm fremd.[11]

The left-out comma in the fourth line which adds the meaning of the verb "fremdgehen" [to be unfaithful] to the verb "fremd sein" [to be estranged] pointedly expresses the dilemma of staying or leaving that occupied many young people of the GDR in the seventies and eighties. The phrase "die mich über Grenzen treibt" [that carries me over bor-

11. "I remain in the country and go, estranged, / With a love that carries me over borders, / Among the heavens. Let everyone look out for himself; / I remain in the country and yet unfaithful" (63).

ders] can refer to national borders (especially the German-German border), but also to the limits of one's feeling and thinking as well as the formal boundaries of the *rondeau* genre. Köhler inserts lines in the classically regular form that "step out of line." The traditional schema is used to find a structure that exceeds it.[12] This creates an inner tension appropriate for the "I" in its existence "zwischen den Himmeln" [among the heavens]. The movement of the rondeau is one of restless circling, just like the movement of the thoughts about remaining or leaving. This movement – which may not lead anywhere – is the form in which the tense, devastating existence between Germany and Germany would be endured.

Some of Schmidt's poems written after 1989 are not about the Elbe, which locked in GDR citizens on the Western side. They are about the Oder, which keeps people away who want to come to Germany from the East. "Grenzfluß" (Border River) speaks of the death of "die geheimen schwimmer die weit von süden / in den reichtum fliehen" [the covert swimmers from far in the south / who flee into affluence, 30]. The historical fact behind this image is what the media reported about numerous people who drowned trying to cross the river from the Polish side. As a new member of the "first world," Schmidt articulates in "landnahme" (land claim) her anger at those who deny people from developing countries access to her homeland with the saying "Das Boot ist voll" [No room in the boat]. This concern also appears in the poem "subverse," in the formulation "wie blondgänger schließen wir anderland aus, kraushaar und mandelblick" [like blondduds we shut other-country out, kinkyhair and almondeye, 31]. Disgust at xenophobic German tendencies is expressed in the satirical neologism "blondgänger," combining the (German) hair color with the word "Blindgänger," which is commonly used to belittle people perceived as deadbeats or duds. However in the role language of the poem, the language of the "silent majority," the word "Blindgänger" derives further meaning since it originated as a military term for an unexploded shell. It is precisely the sarcasm of such neologisms by which Schmidt historicizes the political tugs of war in *Tagespolitik*.

It's Always War

For Annett Gröschner, German history means war, war above all else and over and over again. Born in Magdeburg twenty years after World

12. See Dahlke 54.

War II, she did not grow up in the ruins of a city leveled by air raids. But there were still destroyed areas in the inner city. Certain events, such as the bells ringing on 16 January – the day of the bombing in 1945 – or the boom of fighter jets breaking the sound barrier, gave the child the feeling that the foundation of peace was precarious, with war lurking everywhere. In the 1960s, she repeatedly dreamed about war, much to the astonishment of the adults who said that a little girl could not possibly imagine "what war is" ("Der Krieg meiner Mutter" 137). In particular some inconsistent behaviors of the older generation made it clear to the girl how much people around her had been shaped by the war. On the one hand, her mother retained habits acquired in wartime, such as hoarding food in the basement – "You never know what might happen" (138). On the other hand, for a long time her mother refused to talk about the war because she repressed memories of being buried under rubble as well as what her own mother had told her about her grand-mother's death due to phosphorus bombs. Thus for Gröschner there emerges a female line (through her mother, grandmother and great-grandmother) with an experience of war that differs from the history of wars made by men.

Her unusual sensitivity toward war and its consequences soon led her to read Inge Müller (1925-1966) who, unable to come to terms with her own war experience, had committed suicide. Gröschner's long poem "Jetztmorgengestern" (Todaytomorrowyesterday 1988) opens with the line "Wir gehen 45 durch das tote Deutschland" [We traverse dead Germany in '45]. The dedication "with Inge Müller" indicates who is meant by this "we." With Müller, who had felt herself "UNDER THE RUB-BLE"[13] for all her life, Gröschner begins a search inside herself for the images of war, starting with her own mother's being buried under the rubble. By constantly thematizing women's experiences of war, Gröschner verbalizes the other view of war – the view of women, which fundamentally differs from that of men, who tend to subordinate their experience to military categories.

No World Lost, No World Gained

Despite the authors' different individual personalities and ways of writing, there are remarkable similarities among them. Unlike their male colleagues, they do not articulate their relationship to state and society in a genderless fashion. They adopt a distinctly female standpoint. Their

13. Müller writes about her traumatic war experience in the poems "Unterm Schutt I," "Unterm Schutt II," and "Unterm Schutt III" (20-22).

respective experience with both German states, FRG and GDR, foregoes the need for a national identity. These young women do not crave a fatherland with big shoulders to lean on. Their autonomous relation to the nation as a point of reference is dependent on their mature sense of history, their critical view of the German past, and especially the efforts of women who articulate their vital interests – then and now. It is also always the view from below. Being women from the East, they confront the contradictions of German and international developments without illusions or complaints. But the German condition incites a polemical kind of verse. In various ways, they use their mother tongue for ironic and satirical defamiliarization. Writing becomes a way to survive. The necessity of making a living, however, does not force them to submit to the constraints of the literary market. They refuse the fashionable dictate of arbitrariness. Their artistic ideal includes a decisive engagement born of self-respect and alternative values. This is what emancipates them from disapproval or applause – or the indifference of the literary marketplace. Literary success is not their primary source of personal pride. Their manifold longings, experiences and obligations expand the view of the world, its horrors and joys. For them, the world does not need a navel, especially not a German one.

Translated by Joachim Ghislain and Margaret McCarthy

Note

All poetry translation by the editors.

Bibliography

Dahlke, Birgit. *Die romantischen Bilder blättern ab*. Dissertation, Berlin, 1994.

Frapan, Ilse (Ilse Akunian). *Wir Frauen haben kein Vaterland: Monologe einer Fledermaus*. Berlin: Fontane, 1989.

Gröschner, Annett. *Ich schlug meiner Mutter die brennenden Funken ab. Berliner Schulaufsätze aus dem Jahr 1946*. Berlin: Kontext, 1996.

_____. "Der Krieg meiner Mutter." *Mütter und Musen*. Ed. Claudia Gehrke and Ingrid Schulze. Tübingen: Konkursbuchverlag, 1995.

Gröschner, Annett and Tina Bara. *Herzdame Knochensammler. Gedichte / Fotographie*. Berlin: Collektion Kontext, 1993.

Helwerth, Ulrike and Gislinde Schwarz, eds. *Von Muttis und Emanzen. Feministinnen in Ost- und Westdeutschland*. Frankfurt a.M.: Fischer, 1995.

Hölderlin, Friedrich. *Sämtliche Werke. Kleine Stuttgarter Ausgabe*. Vols.2,3. Ed. Friedrich Beißner. Berlin: Rütten and Loening, 1959.

Köhler, Barbara. *Blue Box. Gedichte*. Frankfurt a.M.: Suhrkamp, 1995.

_____. *Deutsches Roulette. Gedichte 1984-1989*. Frankfurt a.M.: Suhrkamp, 1991

_____. "Rheinsberger Tristien." *Moosbrand Nr. 4* . (1996): 17-19.

Merkel, Ina. "Ohne Frauen ist kein Staat zu machen." *Aufbruch. Frauenbewegung in der DDR. Dokumentation*. Ed. Cordula Kahlau. Munich: Verlag Frauenoffensive, 1990.

Mudry, Anna, ed. *Gute Nacht, du Schöne. Autorinnen blicken zurück*. Frankfurt a.M.: Luchterhand, 1991.

Müller, Inge. *Wenn ich schon sterben muß. Gedichte*. Berlin: Aufbau, 1987.

Schmidt, Kathrin. *Ein Engel fliegt durch die Tapetentür. Gedichte*. Berlin: Verlag Neues Leben, 1987.

_____. *Flußbild mit Engel. Gedichte*. Frankfurt a.M.: Suhrkamp, 1995.

_____. *Poesiealbum 179*. Berlin: Verlag Neues Leben, 1982.

Seghers, Anna. *Aufsätze, Ansprachen, Essays 1927-1953*. Berlin: Aufbau, 1984.

Tucholsky, Kurt. *Rheinsberg: Ein Bilderbuch für Verliebte* (1912). Berlin: Verlag der Nation, 1990.

Chapter 20

THE PRICE OF FEMINISM

Of Women and Turks

Leslie A. Adelson

𝔄s the tools and analyses of feminist scholarship have grown ever more refined over the last twenty years, feminist scholars of German studies have also revised their operative categories of women and gender to account for the embeddedness of womanhood in simultaneous constructions of race, class, sexuality, ethnicity, and nation. This phenomenon may be partly responsible for the increased acknowledgment of and interest in German literature written by women of non-German ethnicity or nationality. In this sector Turkish women writing in the Federal Republic have *as a group* attracted the most scholarly attention in a decade in which Turkish-related themes have been forcefully present in German news media and political debates (membership in NATO, the EC, and later the EU, the Gulf War, citizenship laws and asylum policies, violent xenophobia, Kurdish terrorism and human rights). It is particularly striking that U.S.-based scholarship on Turkish-German literature since 1985 has been propelled mostly by feminist concerns and has focused almost solely on texts produced by Turkish women writers, consigning literature by Turkish men in Germany to a footnote or two.[1] German-based scholarship on Turkish-German culture, most of which derives from an interest in intercultural pedagogy, seems to discuss male and female authors in roughly equal measure, albeit with no particular feminist or otherwise critical agenda beyond an

---

1. Gil Gott's dissertation is one exception to this.

often only vaguely articulated interest in issues of multiculturalism, integration, and intercultural understanding.[2]

Whereas the early 1980s saw a proliferation of publications that tended to associate a Turkish presence in Germany reductively with the phenomenon of the so-called guestworkers, the literary successes attributed since the mid-1980s to Turks living in Germany have stemmed largely from the pens of women writers, notably Aysel Özakin and, more recently, Emine Sevgi Özdamar, winner of the 1991 Ingeborg-Bachmann-Prize for Literature. Indeed this relates to an odd disjuncture in some of the most intractable commonplaces about Turkish-German culture and experience. While the hapless figure of the Turkish guestworker is presumed to be male and without speech, and Turkish migrants' literature is presumed to reflect this (and only this) situation, that Turkish-German literature which has been most widely received is by women authors. The general failure to receive works by Turkish male authors "confirms" a public sense of this alleged speechlessness, while the critical response to Turkish women writers tends to revolve, explicitly or implicitly, around the assumption that writing in Germany allows these women to find a voice denied them in Turkish culture and society.[3] One might say that the sociological counterpart to this is the notion that the casting off of the headscarf by Turkish women in Germany marks, not only their liberation from a putatively oppressive culture of origin, but also their entry into the allegedly liberatory space of German values *qua* European values. Scholarly recognition that debates about the headscarf can mean widely divergent things in different contexts, even within the Turkish Muslim communities in Germany (see Mandel), has had little effect on the signifying power of the headscarf in German public discourse to connote the degree to which Turkish society does or does not qualify as civilized, democratic, and European.

This essay addresses some of the pivotal ways in which "feminism" has come to function in public and scholarly debates about the meaning of Turkish culture in Germany since roughly 1980. The tendency on the part of critics and scholars of literature to associate Turkish-German culture primarily with women writers skews the analytical perspective on Turkish-German culture such that *woman*, gender, and Turkishness (ethnic, national, or cultural) can be too easily conflated.[4] Too frequently

2. Thomas Wägenbaur's theoretically rigorous work is one notable exception.
3. Fischer and McGowan discuss this phenomenon (12). Unfortunately the volume in which their essay appears does little, generally, to counteract the prevailing sociological interpretive paradigm. For an excellent study of the Muslim woman and Turkish modernity, see Nilüfer Göle.
4. On a related phenomenon in the 1970s, see Fischer and McGowan 12.

Turkish-German literature is seen through a lens that reflects a double othering: the otherness of Turkish experience is "added" to that of female gender. Although African-American feminists have been arguing against "additive" models of women's experience since 1977, the most common approach to Turkish-German women writers is marked precisely by the additive notion of double othering. While the existing scholarship on this growing body of literature has established some degree of scholarly legitimacy for this field of inquiry (a trend much more evident in the U.S. than in the Federal Republic), an analytical dilemma must be addressed before feminist scholarship on Turkish-German culture can bypass the epistemological and methodological rut that the "double othering" approach represents. This entails grappling with something that goes deeper than the feminist dilemma noted by Sigrid Weigel, who commented in 1992 that "criticizing the Turkish cultural image of women"(223-24) often serves to reinforce the anti-Islamic prejudices of the German public sphere.[5]

The questions foregrounded here are these: 1) How do feminist arguments impede rather than foster an incisively critical understanding of the relationship between gender and nation as it is currently configured vis-à-vis Turks and German culture? 2) What possibilities exist for a feminist approach to gender and nation in postwar Germany that would yield trenchant insights into the kinds of questions obscured by the more conventional feminist model of double othering? 3) To what extent does the opening up of Germanist feminist scholarship to issues of race, ethnicity, and nationality call for a revision of gender as a privileged category of analysis? 4) In what ways does this other type of Turkish-German dilemma prompt us to hone our interests in feminist and multicultural analysis to an even sharper edge?

Operative assumptions in this exploration are twofold. First, postwar discourses of German ethnicity are intricately bound up, not only in discourses of nationhood, but also in discourses of modernity and historical knowledge. Second, the signifying power of gender does not necessarily stand in a predictable relationship to any of the above. While these theoretical concerns provide the larger framework for this article, the immediate focus is a comparison of the function of feminist arguments and the intersections of gender and nation in three quite different textual arenas, all three of which raise troubling questions about the unpredictable relationship between gender and nation, particularly as it pertains to Turkish-German culture of the recent past. The comparison begins with the perhaps most unlikely pairing of Franz Schönhuber, the

5. Unless otherwise indicated all translations into English are my own.

founder (and until May of 1990, the leader) of the right-wing extremist Republican party, and Alice Schwarzer, a pioneer of radical German feminism and editor of *Emma*, the oldest surviving German magazine with a general feminist readership. Both have felt compelled to write publicly about Turks, the one, because he was concerned about perceived threats to the integrity of German national identity prior to unification, and the other, because she was enraged by the victimization of Turkish and German women since unification, a shared victimization (in Schwarzer's view) that crystallized in the firebombing murders of Turkish women and children in Mölln and Solingen (in 1992 and 1993, respectively).[6] My conclusion will consider how a pointedly "feminist" reading of Aysel Özakin's novel, *Die Preisvergabe* (The Prizegiving), obscures some of the more interesting questions that a critical reading of the text might raise about configuring the relationship between gender and nation.

* * *

As early as 1976 the German feminist magazine *Courage* published a report criticizing the West German government's bureaucracy for its complicity in the "patriarchal victimization of Turkish wives" (Wise 110). Nearly twenty years later Alice Schwarzer, writing for *Emma*, posits an even more radical linkage between patriarchy and Germanness. In her vitriolic essayistic response to the murders of Turkish women and girls in Solingen in spring of 1993, Schwarzer indulges in a universalizing feminist rhetoric, whereby all women are seen as victims of male violence and oppression. This dehistoricizing gesture – familiar to us from any number of feminist debates, projects, and preoccupations of the 1980s – entails some discursive acrobatics on Schwarzer's part. Because German men killed Turkish women in Solingen, she concludes that guilt and innocence are functions of gender, not nationality; for her, patriarchy is the root and only root of all evil. In a further dehistoricizing gesture Schwarzer specifically equates Islamic fundamentalism with fascism. "Fundamentalism is the Oriental variation of fascism. Both are men's domain [*Männersache*]" (35). Turkish and Islamic are treated in this instance as interchangeable signifiers, whereas the signification of Germanness is completely supplanted by the attribution of maleness. This discursive strategy renders German women themselves outside their national history to the extent that it displaces the twentieth century's defining nationalist experience of National Socialism onto the

6. Since Schwarzer's perspective is fundamentally ahistorical, my phrase "since unification" positions only the timing of her publication, not a focus of her analysis.

flickering projection screen of culpable Islamic patriarchy and misogyny. Schwarzer's particular privileging of gender seeks to deny the significance of nation, while the displacement that such privileging entails inadvertently reasserts the primacy of an historically specific experience of an en-gendered yet also national (that is to say, German) history.

Taking a reverse approach, Franz Schönhuber published his book on Turks in 1989, four years before *Emma's* dossier on fundamentalism, one year prior to national unification, and one year before Schönhuber lost control of his own political party, just as it was itself losing political steam. In stark contrast to Schwarzer's rabidly racist erasure of national particulars, Schönhuber's avowedly conciliatory arguments seem at times measured, even moderate. How is it, good liberals and feminists wonder, that a former member of the *Waffen*-SS and the (then) leader of an extremist right-wing party known for its anti-immigration platform can appear more compassionate and more "reasonable" (and specifically, less racist) than one of the country's most prominent feminist spokespersons? All the more startling is the realization that Schönhuber deploys pseudo-feminist strategies to achieve this effect *and* to argue for separate but equal German and Turkish national identities, which, he contends, are best sustained in separate but equal national territories.

Whereas Schwarzer posits German women outside history and only Turkish women as positioned in terms of ethnicity, Schönhuber explicitly cites Bodrum as the "birthplace of the father of historiography, Herodotus" (29). Schönhuber also claims to be adamantly opposed to racism in any form, something he holds responsible for "the greatest catastrophe of history" (213). This is a slippery slope because Schönhuber never clarifies whether he means the Nazi genocide of the Jews or the Germans being forever burdened with the expectation of atonement. The particular ways in which Schönhuber invokes Turkish and German national histories are indeed as dizzying as Schwarzer's erasure of these histories. They are as well thoroughly en-gendered, imbued through and through with constructs of both masculinity and femininity.

For Schönhuber the ultimate personifier and historical enabler of Turkish masculinity is Kemal Atatürk, whom the German Republican conjures as the actual father and figurative guardian of a noble (that is to say, masculine) Turkish identity ensuing from Turkey's birth as a nation in 1923.[7] The body of Schönhuber's text begins with an Atatürk quotation "I am happy to be a Turk!" (11). The absolute pride in independent Turkish national identity that Schönhuber associates with Atatürk, who

---

7. Schönhuber is hardly alone in this view of Atatürk, which – in these points – corresponds to the view that Kemalists have cultivated throughout the life of the Republic.

thus functions in this discursive mapping as the ultimate measure of authentic Turkishness, provides Schönhuber in turn with his rationale for rejecting the presence of Turkish guestworkers in Germany as well as Turkey's proposed membership in any European community or union. If Atatürk were alive today, he argues, there would be no guestworker problem (167) because no self-respecting Turk would relinquish national pride and grovel for German acceptance. Schönhuber has especially little patience for second-generation Turks in Germany who, in this account, blame "long dead fascism" (140) for their personal failures. Male Turkish guestworkers and their offspring thus appear as whining, insufficiently masculinized traitors to Atatürk's national ideals. The picture gets murkier when Schönhuber describes the influx of Turkish guestworkers as a kind of reverse crusade (66). The sense of threat that Schönhuber associates with this (12) is nonetheless not construed as masculine, since the guestworkers are portrayed at every turn as breaking faith with Atatürk, who solidly occupies the space of national masculinity for Schönhuber.

Articulating his ideal of separate but equal (equally masculine?) German and Turkish national identities, Schönhuber simultaneously posits "that there is hardly a people with whom we Germans are so bound in fate as with the Turks, in the good and the bad" (9). By this he means that both Turkey and Germany suffer from bad world press – "not without self-incurred culpability" – because of the genocide of Jews and Armenians. The fact that he adds this phrase "nicht ohne eigene Schuld" here seems relatively weightless when he claims in the next breath that Jews and Armenians now control "the opinion industry" (14). Schönhuber's aim in this book is not to justify Nazi atrocities or German antisemitism but to undermine what he sees as a major obstacle to Germany's ability to be done with that past. For him this obstacle stems from the Turkish presence in Germany, specifically that of the (Turkish) guestworkers.

> In our country the guilty conscience that Germans have cultivated for decades finds a type of wailing wall in the description of and commentary on German-Turkish events. At this wailing wall we can beat our breast, arduously debrowned, in order to achieve the expected production, mostly overproduction, of mourning demanded of us. Tone: the wretched guestworkers! (13).

For Schönhuber, then, both Turkish and German national identity are impeded by the ongoing presence of insufficiently masculinized Turkish guestworkers and their offspring in Germany.[8]

8. By treating the guestworkers as beyond the pale of historical change, Schönhuber holds them responsible for what he sees as Germany's inability to move forward *in* historical time.

Schönhuber's discursive invocation of femininity plays a structurally supporting role in the construction of this polemic. This is not because he deems Turkish society or the Islamic religion to be fundamentally hostile to women. On the contrary, he contends that there is no uniform treatment of women in Turkey or Islam (145, 147). His own belief in equal rights for women is conveyed primarily via the discursive space he accords his wife in his own narrative. On four separate occasions he literally relinquishes his narrative to her, about whom we learn not her name but that she is an accomplished lawyer and avowed "legalist" (181) who once specialized in Turkish matters on behalf of a foundation associated with the CSU, a conservative Bavarian Christian party (171). Schönhuber's wife clearly stands in here for the acceptable, self-realized Western woman, since Schönhuber elsewhere mocks what he calls "complex-laden Western women" who engage readily in sexual intercourse with Turkish men as "Wiedergutmachung" (compensation, usually for the Holocaust) for Germans' alleged hostility to Turks (34). Here we see another gendered example of what Schönhuber must regard as a perverse kind of *Vergangenheitsbewältigung* (coming to terms with the past). Schönhuber's faith in women's rights as a measure of civilization, predicated on a gendered narrative of twentieth-century history, is therefore universalizing in its intent and particularizing in its discourse.

* * *

This comparison of Schönhuber and Schwarzer sets the stage for a revised look at Aysel Özakin's novel *Die Preisvergabe*, which first appeared (1979) in Turkish in Turkey under the title *Genç Kız ve Ölüm* (Young Girl and Death), and was first published in German in 1982 by the now defunct Buntbuch-Verlag and republished in 1989 by the Luchterhand Literaturverlag. One of the most frequently reviewed and studied Turkish women authors of German literature, Özakin has consistently rejected both the national (Turkish) and the gendered (female) optics through which virtually all of her works have been read by scholars and critics alike.[9] An analysis of *Die Preisvergabe* may reveal what is to be gained if – instead of arguing that Özakin denies the obvious – one considers some of the blind spots that feminist discussions of Turkish-German culture and possible readings of the novel share. Let us look specifically at the tendential "feminist" erasure of both Turkish

9. Responding to Günter Wallraff's impersonation of a generic Turkish guestworker and his subsequent journalistic exposé of systemic racist exploitation in 1985, Özakin ("Ali") chastised the German Left in particular for its infatuation with Turks as a "symbol of suffering." This was the moment when she decided that it had become necessary for her to leave the Federal Republic. Since 1990 she has been living in England.

national histories and international modernist legacies as they figure in the text.

Nuray İlkin is Özakin's female protagonist who travels from Istanbul to Ankara in the late 1970s to be awarded a coveted literary prize for the publication of her first novel. Periodically interrupting the flow of the narrative about this journey and the author's strained encounters with the wealthy members of the Club of Fine Arts, excerpts from the prizewinning autobiographical novel recount the struggles of a secretary who chafes against societal norms and finally abandons her marriage to an engineer with whom she had previously been deliriously happy. Frequent references to women's plight in both strands of the larger novel stress, not explicit domestic violence, but implicit male hostility inherent in men's control over women's lives, even in the name of love. This theme of strong women whose spirit reaches beyond the domestic roles that society accords them is reinforced by the protagonist's obsession with her mother and her daughter. The former had been a beloved high school teacher and a seemingly self-realized devotee of Atatürk's national reforms, many of which had liberated women from Islamic dress codes and governmental bans on education. Her suicide is never fully explained in either part of the novel, though the protagonist surmises that marriage forced her mother to subordinate her dreams to her husband's interests. The protagonist's daughter is, by contrast, a young leftist intellectual who has no patience with the preoccupations of bourgeois individualism and seems to have renounced all personal desire. Much of the framing narrative is itself preoccupied with two questions that concern this daughter. One is whether the protagonist can convince her that the novel about women's liberation is worthwhile. The other is whether the daughter will survive the political demonstration that dissidents have called for the day after the awards ceremony, a demonstration banned by the government. The fact that violent and even fatal state suppression of political dissidence is an everyday occurrence is manifest as the prizewinning protagonist bears repeated witness to raids, arrests, brutality, and terror perpetrated by soldiers and police against the civilian populace. While she accepts the prizemoney but rejects the hypocrisy of the social elite that has awarded it to her, nothing is ever resolved with regard to state violence or the daughter's fate.

The German title of the novel evokes only the framing narrative, which revolves around the prizegiving. We may thus ask what prize a conventional feminist reading of *Die Preisvergabe* bestows on the text *at what price*. If one persists in reading this novel as a testimonial to the oppression of women under Islamic patriarchy, then how are we to grasp the relationship between Nuray İlkin's dilemmas and Turkish national history? Does a conventional feminist reading render both the feminist question and the Turkish nation "outside history"?

One could easily argue that an analysis foregrounding the alleged representation of Turkish women suffering from the constraints of Islamic patriarchy simply ignores many if not most of the textual details. The Muslim aunt who raises the young girl after her mother's suicide does wear a headscarf and punishes her for behaving like the boys. In virtually all other respects, however, the protagonist's dissatisfaction with her lot as a woman stems from her confrontations with the lifestyles and values of the secularized bourgeoisie. What then can we learn from this novel about alternative modes of conceptualizing relationships among gender, nation, ethnicity, culture, and the state?

* * *

There is at least one analytical alternative to the Eurocentric model that understands Turkish feminism only as a byproduct of Turkish women's encounter with liberal German or European values. For the evolution of Turkish feminism cannot be adequately grasped without some acknowledgment of complex intersections among the signification of gender, rights of women, constructs of nationhood, and politics of state. Although this essay cannot pretend to elaborate all the relevant intersections, a nod in this analytical direction will at least yield hitherto unexplored interpretive options for addressing *Die Preisvergabe* and the relevance of feminist analysis for a critically invested German Studies.

Since feminism was largely appropriated as an ideology by the early Republic in the name of the Turkish nation (Tekeli 40), an independent women's movement had little room for development. The military coup of 1980 seems to mark a watershed in this regard. Tekeli comments on a peculiar linkage between the spurt of feminist discussions in the 1980s and the brutal suppression of leftist dissidents. Some intellectuals believe, she notes, "that if the Left had not been fatally affected on 12 September 1980, the women who later turned to feminism would never have been able to break the ideological hegemony of leftist men and find their own language. Precisely this discussion contributed to feminism being branded by some within the Left as 'Septemberism'" (42). While this political and moral devaluation of Turkish feminism is certainly not the only possible reading of this 1980s phenomenon (Tekeli argues that 1980s Turkish feminism can also be seen as spearheading democratic opposition to a government that had brutally suppressed most other forms of political dissidence, 43), it does point to the fact that a contextualizing discussion of postwar Turkish feminism has to negotiate some type of relationship to both government politics of state and leftist concepts of revolution. *Die Preisvergabe* is therefore not simply about three women struggling for liberation and self-definition in modern Turkish society. Rather, it concerns different ways of conceptualizing political thought and action, each of which has potentially fatal consequences for understanding women, feminism, nation, and state.

Özakin herself opted for political exile in West Germany three months after the 1980 coup (Wierschke 43), but *Genç Kız ve Ölüm* was published in Turkey before the coup that was about to take place. The Turkish novel was thus written before the burgeoning of public feminist discussions in the 1980s, while the German translation was originally published both after the coup and at a time when the West German women's movement was still obsessed with Woman as gen(d)eric victim (see Adelson 37-55). The protagonist of *Die Preisvergabe* operates, not in a vacuum, but on a political and discursive cusp. Her mother and daughter represent opposing modes of understanding women's struggle for human rights and self-determination. The mother identified her cause with that of the state; her suicide suggests that this option may have failed her. The daughter identifies her cause completely with leftist ideology, against the existing state. Although this character seems rather dull and lifeless, the protagonist's concerns about her daughter's ability to survive political persecution and her judgment of the mother's novel lend a great deal of affective weight to scenes involving the daughter. One might say that Nuray İlkin and her writing self struggle to articulate a politics of gender and nation for which no adequate discourse existed in Turkey in the 1970s.

The textually pivotal military coup, the aftereffects of which color all the protagonist's ruminations about women's plight, is not the September coup of 1980 but the March coup of 1971.[10] The novel never delves, however, into the substantive politics of this event but focuses instead on the pervasive sense of vulnerability and danger that ensues from it. This reign of terror forms part of the backdrop for the novel within the novel when Nuray leaves her husband and affiliates with members of a left-wing newspaper cooperative, who introduce her to many new books and ideas. Though she and several of her neighbors are once seized from their homes by security forces in the middle of the night, the text divulges few details of the episode. The narrative about the prizewinning, on the other hand, occupies a later period in the 1970s, when political violence between Left and Right was compounded by the government's tendency to support violence by the Right against those suspected of leftwing inclinations (Zürcher 276).

10. Brief reference is also made to the 1960 coup, which the young protagonist and the intelligentsia generally greeted with enthusiasm (see also Zürcher 253).

But Özakin tells us none of this. As Nuray moves through the public spaces of Ankara, she is equally shaken by seeing a poor street musician, a young amputee, and an arrest that may be politically motivated. Forgetting them all, she "decided to go to the Club of Fine Arts" (40). Similarly, scenes of public brutality by police or soldiers emphasize her role as witness, not in the sense that she really documents what transpires, but in the sense that the violence and injustice around her act as a filter through which we watch the prizegiving unfold and through which we trace her thoughts on the subjugation of women.

After Nuray has collected her prize money and demonstratively turned her back on those celebrating her success, she is struck by a car. Her bruises are compounded by the fact that the driver fails to recognize her from television coverage of the awards ceremony. The narrator asks, "Why didn't anyone recognize her?" (207), an issue underscored when the protagonist reflects, "How insignificant I am!" (210). Since her novel about women's liberation is frequently referred to as that which will compel others to respect her as an author and *hence* as a person, the accident serves to highlight the linkage posited between legitimacy of the text and personhood of the author. The comment on Nuray's insignificance of self is therefore also a comment on the perceived insignificance of the novel. Since the daughter continually challenges Nuray to write about something other than bourgeois individualist desires and frustrations, the question as to the legitimacy of the novel within the novel is indeed the central question in the text.

One cannot assess this question simply by pointing to frequent statements within the text about the pervasiveness of men's control over women's lives. Instead one must consider how various tensions between women's issues and state politics function within the text. Since the novel within the novel addresses both presumed poles, we cannot claim that the interior novel concerns only women's issues while the frame novel addresses only politics of state. Because the two narratives tend to bleed thematically into each other, one wonders if the references to violent government suppression of politicial dissidence are meant to contest the significance of Nuray's drive for women's liberation. Or does the political violence function on the other hand to legitimize her quest to the extent that it appears more significant *because* the thwarting of her desire is *comparable* to the suppression of the dissidents' ideals? As previously indicated, Nuray's primary concerns (about her daughter's judgment of the novel and about the daughter's safety) are never resolved.

The novel's dramatic penultimate scene offers no resolution, thus exacerbating our sense that Nuray's claims to moral and political legitimacy are shaky at best. On the previous day Nuray had experienced a tension-ridden reunion with her ex-husband Cemil, who is now a self-pitying alcoholic. Her feelings for him are extremely ambivalent. After a troubled night she awakes feeling guilty and assuages her guilt by imagining resuming a friendship with him. Her revery in front of the mirror interrupted by "metallic noises" (250) coming from the hotel patio beneath her window, she looks out on a chaotic scene of policemen attacking a crowd of hotel guests. When four of the policemen begin beating one young man in particular, Nuray watches in horror from above as Cemil tries to intervene on the young man's behalf and is himself then beaten and carted off with many of the young people. This is an unexpected turn, for the novel's moral highground is suddenly occupied, not by Nuray or her leftist daughter, but by a pathetic drunk. The author standing at the window does nothing, and readers are left to wonder whether Cemil hadn't deserved better treatment from her after all. The dissident movement appears in the novel, in the end, just as ineffectual as Nuray's attempts to liberate herself as a woman.[11]

Measured against the textual and affective weight of state violence against perceived leftists, Nuray and her novel about her struggles as a woman do appear insignificant – the daughter's original verdict is left implicitly to stand. And yet, there is another theme running throughout the novel as a whole that casts the question of significance in a somewhat different light. This theme entails a metareflective question, not about the significance of Nuray's novel *per se*, but about the power of books more generally to establish a public sphere or to assert or challenge legitimacy, including the legitimacy of a given critical question. One might of course want to argue that Özakin's novel is about how the novel within the novel – the novel that revolves *primarily* around women's liberation – is not enough. I would argue instead that the text's many references to competing *functions* of other books as well as its own avoids this kind of reductive privileging of one political agenda, just as it also rejects the reductive conflation of one form of political oppression with another.

Although political violence perpetrated by men in uniform permeates the text, the narrative invokes the power of books in several different arenas. This is not always cast in a positive light. In a pivotal way Nuray realized that she had to read all the books that Cemil read in order to approximate equality within their relationship (140, 248). Reading Euro-

---

11. This scene is particularly important in that it functions as a corrective to an earlier moral failure on Cemil's part. While working as an engineer for a disreputable building contractor, he had kept silent about conditions that ultimately led to the death of a young laborer. This same building contractor just happens to be sitting within eyesight of Nuray when she has drinks with the representatives of the Club of Fine Arts. Again, the prizewinning is framed by something that seems to put its ultimate value into question.

pean modernist and existentialist texts together with Cemil also fosters the young couple's sense that they are different from all the conventionalists around them (191, 212). This sense of a shared literary experience as the foundation for a romantic cocoon is both shattered and reinforced when an old friend of Cemil's introduces Nuray to a different sort of books, those that entail explicit political critiques or descriptions of proletarian lifestyles. This political liason becomes the catalyst for Nuray's break with Cemil and bourgeois values. For a time she then devotes herself to all those books that members of her newfound political community deem important (112-116). These are also the leftists who resent the influence that Europe has exerted on Turkey through literature and call for a culture oriented "toward national values" (152-3). Although Nuray's personal experience with leftists is part of the narrative past, the daughter cultivates a similar model of community in the present. She and her friends try to pattern their personalities after the books they read, and Nuray's daughter is described as using no cosmetics, only soap, books, and paper (10, 217).

Given that Nuray's desires for freedom *as a woman* are thwarted by political activists and romantic aestheticists alike, what function accrues to her prize*winning* and her prize*giving* narratives? From the beginning the notion of a woman writing is depicted as something that sets her apart from other women, as Nuray en route by train to Ankara observes another woman writing something that she hides from the other women in the compartment. This act of self-differentiation is reinforced on several occasions when the writing of a novel makes Nuray feel different from, even superior to other women. She clearly feels that her novel will not only garner her respect and success, but also justify her very existence (57-58). The ambivalence entailed in writing passionately for women's liberation while deriving legitimacy from being *unlike* other women echoes subtly when the president of the Club of Fine Arts praises her with the words, "'You will become the Simone de Beauvoir of Turkey'" (73). Ambivalence is key here, as the wealthy men who fund and run the club *fête* the prizewinning author while their wives congratulate her in one breath and in the next confide that they haven't read her book. Nuray's acceptance speech on art as a path of resistance is textually juxtaposed with her reflections about having sold her soul in exchange for love and luxury in her second marriage, such that neither she nor the reader can escape the suspicion that she has sold her novel as an aesthetic commodity that brings her social recognition in exchange. Meanwhile we are constantly reminded of her drab clothing, which renders her both less attractive as a woman and less legitimate as a citizen when compared with the stunningly attired company that bestows its magnanimous stamp of legitimacy on her novel.

Leslie A. Adelson

Again, it would seem that her novel is hardly enough. But not enough for what? Not enough for a political critique? Not enough for a feminist intervention of any sort? These are not useful conclusions. For this novel does not so much make a political statement as it negotiates the politics of reading and writing at a time in postwar Turkish history when no broad public sphere existed for independent feminist debate and when dissident political thought, especially that from the Left, was brutally suppressed. In the sense that no novel can ever be interpreted only in relation to itself, no novel is ever enough. Reading *Die Preisvergabe* in the German context of the 1980s forces us to ask what relations our readings of it acknowledge or mobilize. When this novel is reduced to a statement of double othering, one that serves implicitly to assert the cultural superiority of European civilization, then our reading follows a very narrow line of analysis that posits gender and nation, once again, outside history.

* * *

The "prize" that a conventional feminist reading bestows on *Die Preisvergabe* comes at too high a price. A bifurcated approach to gender and Turkishness and to what that dyad means for understanding gender and Germanness reveals little indeed about specific intersections of gender, culture, ethnicity, nation, state, and history. As this analysis of Schwarzer, Schönhuber, and Özakin demonstrates, these phenomena should not be seen as collapsing into one another any more than they should be understood to exist independent of each other. Most importantly, the exact nature of these relationships and their ability to foster critical insights are not predictable, least of all when we think we know what we are reading and why. Finally, a refined feminist approach to Özakin's work compels us to consider what it means to recognize some Turkish writers' indebtedness to European modernism.[12] What bearing does such recognition have on how we assess the relationship between Turkish and German culture in Germany? Is it possible that one of the potential contributions of Turkish-German literary production to German culture is to point to what might be construed as a *shared* cultural history? This question, a positive answer to which would mark a radically different starting point for analysis than that usually applied to Turkish-German literature, cannot be asked by a feminist approach that perceives the gender of Turks only through the lens of ethnicity.

12. I am not able to do justice to this aspect in this abbreviated format. My book in progress on Turkish-German literature will address this and other issues in more detail and will expand the discussion of *Die Preisvergabe* by exploring the significance of Camus's *L'étranger* for Özakin's text.

Bibliography

Adelson, Leslie A. *Making Bodies, Making History: Feminism and German Identity.* Lincoln: U of Nebraska P, 1993.

Aufstand im Haus der Frauen: Frauenforschung aus der Türkei. Ed. Aylâ Neusel, Şirin Tekeli, Meral Akkent. Trans. Meral Akkent & Karin Ayche. Berlin: Orlanda Frauenverlag, 1996.

Çağatay, Nilüfer and Yasemin Nuhoğlu-Soysal. "Frauenbewegungen im nationalen Vereinigungsprozeß: Die Türkei und andere Länder des Nahen Ostens im Vergleich." *Aufstand.* 202-13.

Fischer, Sabine and Moray McGowan. "From *Pappkoffer* to Pluralism: On the Development of Migrant Writing in the German Federal Republic." *Turkish Culture in German Society Today.* Ed. David Horrocks & Eva Kolinsky. Oxford: Berghahn, 1996. 1-22.

Göle, Nilüfer. *Republik und Schleier: Die muslimische Frau in der Moderne.* Trans. Pia Angela Lorenzi. Berlin: Babel, 1995.

Gott, Gil. "Migration, Ethnicization and Germany's New Ethnic Minority Literature." PhD dissertation, University of California at Berkeley, 1994.

Kandiyoti, Deniz. "Patriarchalische Muster: Notizen zu einer Analyse der Männerherrschaft in der türkischen Gesellschaft." *Aufstand.* 315-29.

Mandel, Ruth. "Turkish Headscarves and the 'Foreigner Problem': Constructing Difference Through Emblems of Identity." *New German Critique* 46 (1989): 27-46.

Özakin, Aysel. "Ali hinter den Spiegeln." *literatur konkret* (October 1986): 6-9.

———. *Die Preisvergabe: Ein Roman.* Trans. Heike Offen. Frankfurt a.M.: Luchterhand Literaturverlag, 1989.

Schönhuber, Franz. *Die Türken: Geschichte und Gegenwart.* Munich: Langen Müller, 1989.

Schwarzer, Alice. "Hass: Wir gedenken der Opfer von Solingen." *Emma*, no. 4 (July/August 1993): 34-35.

Tekeli, Şirin. "Frauen in der Türkei der 80er Jahre. *Aufstand.* 27-46.

Wägenbaur, Thomas. "Kulturelle Identität oder Hybridität? Aysel Özakins *Die blaue Maske* und das Projekt interkultureller Dynamik." *Zeitschrift für Literaturwissenschaft und Linguistik* 97 (1995): 22-47.

Wallraff, Günter. *Ganz unten.* Cologne: Kiepenheuer & Witsch, 1985.

Weigel, Sigrid. "Literatur der Fremde – Literatur in der Fremde." *Gegenwartsliteratur seit 1968.* Ed. K. Briegleb & S. Weigel. Munich: dtv, 1992. 182-229.

Wierschke, Annette. "Schreiben als Selbstbehauptung: Kulturkonflikte und Identität in den Werken von Aysel Özakin, Alev Tekinay und Emine Sevgi Özdamar." Ph.D. dissertation, University of Minnesota, 1994.

Wise, Gail E. "Ali in Wunderland: German Representations of Foreign Workers." Ph.D. dissertation, University of California at Berkeley, 1995.

Zürcher, Erik J. *Turkey: A Modern History.* London/NY: I.B. Tauris, 1993.

Part V

FATHERLAND
AND MOTHER TONGUE

Chapter 21

LANGUAGE IS PUBLICITY FOR MEN – BUT ENOUGH IS ENOUGH!*

Luise F. Pusch

The process of language change set in motion by women during the last twenty years is the most significant and far-reaching linguistic innovation of the century. Not just in German-speaking areas, but worldwide. Far-reaching, because women did not stop with the lexicon (the usual arena of language change), but went straight to the core, to patriarchal grammar itself. There used to be almost no space for woman in this *man*or house, but she has meanwhile spread out comfortably and settled in. This makes it somewhat narrower and less comfortable for the master, who no longer has the entire terrain to himself. We women have long known that the feminization of language brings the human race a step closer to humanity. Woman is glad that this has now been acknowledged by some men as well, including such a highly regarded institution as the Wiesbaden Gesellschaft für deutsche Sprache [German Language Society]. For it is not so long ago that professors at German universities used to advise enthusiastic women students wishing to write their M.A. theses (then called Master's theses) on sexism in the German language that they had better not because the topic was only a passing fad.

Magazine editors occasionally ask me if I can produce an article on women's language. "Possibly," I usually reply, "and what did you have in

* Originally published in *Persönlich: Das Magazin für Werbung, Markt und Medien*, Rapperswil (Switzerland). Special issue on language, 19. 33 (6 October 1995): 32-33.

mind?" – "Perhaps something like 'Is women's language passé?' After all, one does not hear anything about it these days, don't you agree?" Well, maybe "one" does not, but women certainly do. Specifically, women hear a lot of ignorant griping from the masculine side of the house. Good, we say to ourselves, the guys are taking the subject more seriously now, because things are starting to get serious. Even in Mexico, one of the stubbornest bastions of machismo, there has reportedly been a legislative decision to abolish linguistic machismo in schoolbooks. The new Oxford Bible was cleansed of all sexist usages and other forms of linguistic discrimination. Many political bodies, from city governments and provincial legislatures on up to the German Bundestag, have yielded to pressure from women, resolving that the section in the German basic law guaranteeing men and women equal rights should be implemented with respect to language too. Some like to play dumb, arguing: "The right way is 'He's an *Ingenieur* [engineer], she's an *Ingenieur*, and they're both *Ingenieure* [engineers]' – you can't get any more equal than that! So, who needs this idiotic feminine suffix *-in*?"[1] Well, women think equality could also be achieved by saying "She's an *Ingenieurin*, he's an *Ingenieurin*, they're both *Ingenieurinnen*." This idea finds scant support among men in our master culture, where feminization means becoming declassed, pure and simple, because the feminine is in second place. If not last – it appears that the typical male is much fonder of his car or his livestock than his wife. In California, you can get up to a year in jail and a $1000 fine for abusing your wife, but abuse of animals is punished by up to a year in jail and $20,000 in fines.

Women's language is not passé but alive and getting better all the time. It has gained wide acceptance, so that in many areas following its guidelines has become simply a matter of politeness and good style. In fact, at a hearing in the provincial court of Lower Saxony seven years ago, a German professor remonstrated with me: What was our problem? After all, using double forms of nouns (i.e., *Leserinnen und Leser*, female readers and male readers) was long since totally taken for granted – we women were simply beating down doors that are already open. The fact that the doors have been open a very short time and that what is "taken for granted" was only recently dismissed by his colleagues as a "passing fad" is something he forgot to mention. This is a favorite tactic: When women have struggled to gain ground, essentially having wrested some-

1. Translation note: In German, a great many feminine nouns are formed by adding the suffix *-in* to the masculine noun; each noun also has its own plural form: *der Ingenieur* [engineer, masc.; plural *Ingenieure*]; *die Ingenieurin* [engineer, fem.; plural *Ingenieurinnen*]. Not unlike English, standard German grammar specifies the masculine noun as the generic or (supposedly) gender-neutral form.

thing away from men, they are regularly met with the explanation that they have had it all along anyway. In this view, it is not the men who have suffered a defeat, but the women who are hysterically fighting the wrong battle, running like chickens with their heads cut off to beat down doors held open by men, generous cavaliers that they are.

So, we and the German Language Society maintain: Women's language is not passé by any means; indeed, it is making excellent progress. Now that this has been officially recorded, I would like to summarize, for those who have slept through the debate up to now, why women's language is inescapable. The language we inherited from our fathers is a language that eliminates women. Concepts and images are overwhelmingly and most persistently generated by words. Every woman who is acquainted with talk therapies knows that words become realities via our imaginations. The best-known example is probably autogenous training. You tell yourself "My right arm is warm" and in a short time your temperature rises measurably. The most horrifying example is the murder of the European Jews. First they were defined as vermin by a perfidious discourse, by words, and then they were treated like vermin – exterminated. And us women? We are and were literally not worth talking about, which is exactly how we are treated. What do you think of when you hear or read words like "actor," "poet," "street sweeper," "reader," "passer-by," "Swiss citizen"? These words, patriarchal grammar assures us, are gender-neutral. But can you picture a gender-neutral Swiss citizen? Just try it. See, it does not work. You are picturing men. And because this is true, women have all but disappeared from the human imagination. It is especially difficult for women to think about themselves. The man of course thinks this is fine – woman is supposed to think about him, after all, and possibly also "his" children. As we know, the female Swiss citizen was denied the right to vote until 1971. A favorite argument was: "The law says that every *Schweizer Bürger* [Swiss citizen] is eligible to vote; it says nothing about *Bürgerinnen* [female citizens]." So much for the gender neutrality of masculine nouns. The concepts are interpreted according to the master's pleasure. If we are talking about rights, woman is excluded; when it is a question of responsibilities or punishment, naturally she is included.

The goal of all advertising is to anchor the product for which a suitable match is sought (see what I mean?)[2] firmly in the head of the consumer (are you visualizing a female consumer? If so, you are not normal).

2. The phrase glossed as "a suitable match" contains in German an untranslatable wordplay involving the word *Mann* [man or husband]. The expression *an den Mann bringen* means both "to find a buyer for" and "to find a husband for" – thus, "das ... 'an den Mann' zu bringende Produkt" can be read with both meanings – "the product for which a buyer/husband must be found."

Commercial and service industries pay enormous amounts of money to the various media for this. But the medium of the German language is organized grammatically in such a way that the image "male person" is generated by almost every sentence that mentions people. German grammars prescribe that any group of women, no matter how large, symbolically becomes a masculine group the moment that one single man joins it. Thus, ninety-nine *Sängerinnen* [female singers] and one *Sänger* (male singer) become in German one hundred *Sänger* [male singers]. It is up to the *Sängerinnen* to figure out what happened to them; the main thing is for the male to be linguistically present and accounted for.

Language is the medium of all media. Without language the other media would not exist – there would be no newspapers, no radio, no television, no Internet, no email, no multimedia. And this medium, the basis for all the others, is arranged such that women hardly appear at all. Men's language is a grandiose, ingeniously constructed publicity machine for men that operates totally free of charge. The women competitors have been crowded out to the margins. This propaganda works at a largely unconscious level, for most people are unaware of linguistic mechanisms and indeed must remain so in order for communication to work. As Hitler's propaganda minister Goebbels so clearly recognized: "Propaganda becomes ineffective the moment it is recognized. But at the moment when it hovers as a current in the background, it is effective in every respect." That most people are not aware of the propaganda for men known as language can be discerned from the deeply irritated sighs of many men and some women wondering if we don't have anything more important to do than make the German language unwieldy to the point of uselessness by adding feminine forms.

The publicity machine's success in maneuvering women to the sidelines can be seen in the circumstances of women worldwide, which were spelled out once again, and rightly so, at the International Women's Conference in China in 1995. Women do two thirds of the work in this world, for which they receive one tenth of the pay. And we possess one one-hundredth of the world's wealth. Ninety-nine percent of all the goods in this world are in the possession of men. In order that it not remain so, we interrupt the vicious cycle of power. We women have – as yet – little access to power, but we have access to language and we are using it. Language produces concepts, concepts influence our actions, actions influence our political and economic situation (our so-called reality), and this in turn influences language. If we change language, there is no doubt that we will change concepts too and thus, everything else. It is urgently necessary.

Translated by Jeanette Clausen

Chapter 22

THE NEW *DUDEN*

Out of Date Already*

Luise F. Pusch

𝔄pproximately every five years a new edition of the *Rechtschreibungs-Duden* (Spelling Duden) is handed down to the German people.[1] The latest one appeared at the end of August 1996, based on the newly revised official spelling rules which beginning in 1998 will apply to Switzerland and Austria as well as Germany. Formerly the *Duden* was touted as "authoritative in all doubtful cases," but today this proud statement is missing from the dust jacket, for the *Duden* is no longer authoritative. Its authority was always temporary anyway. The state had delegated this authority to the *Duden* until the Dreiländerkommission, the Commission of the three German-speaking countries, could agree on a new standardized spelling. The Commission went on and on – so long that we all believed the *Duden* was legally responsible for correct spelling. Endless committee work was necessary to hatch out the new reference work – though "hatch out" is a misplaced metaphor. The committee appointees were 100 percent male. The twelve-member Commission of the Institut für deutsche Sprache (German Language Institute) in Mannheim, which is now officially responsible for the *Duden,* also consists entirely of men: six Germans, three Austrians, and three Swiss. As a woman, you notice the male lineage right away. Therefore, I offer here a

---

* Originally published in *Das Argument* 217 (1996): 645-46.

1. The *Duden* is a standard German reference work named after the original publisher of the series, Konrad Duden.

few important hints for the self-confident user of the new spelling rules and all dictionaries based on them, including the *Duden.*

What does "authoritative" mean anyway? The state can prescribe binding grammatical rules to schools and public administrative offices, but otherwise spelling is a private matter. I, for example, am a supporter of lower-case spelling – which unfortunately has not gained universal acceptance – yet I still spell all kinds of words with capital letters, because others do. I would not have to, though – who could make me? For the last twenty years, women have used this freedom shrewdly – but the Commission has not caught on yet.

For women, it is not very important whether *Ballettänzer* [ballet dancer] is spelled with two or with three *t*'s, whether *Stengel* [stem] is spelled with *e* or *ä*, or *potentiell* [potential] with *z* or with *t*. If the commissioners think it is important for even the most innocent *Blumenstengel* [flower stem] to become *Stängel* so we are reminded of its relation to *Stange* [pole, staff], okay. How about "Jeder Mann ein potenzieller Vergewaltiger" [Every man is a potential rapist] – it is true, this controversial sentence does look more potent when *potenziell* is spelled with *z*.[2] I am not pleased that we are losing the distinction between "Miss" and the prefix *miß-*, between a *Miss Piggy* and a *Mißbrauch* (misuse). That is mischievous. Let us take advantage of the occasion to abolish the word "Miss" and all the Miss-pageants along with it.

But those are Peanuts – which by the way is one of the words in the new *Duden.* What is really disappointing is that in the entire dictionary, no consideration is given to women's critique of language. The process of language change that women have set in motion during the last twenty years is the most significant linguistic innovation of the century – I have said this before, but it can not be emphasized too often. We have reached the point where the generic masculine is not what it once was. Women are refusing to feel included by words like *Wähler* [voter], *Ballettänzer* [ballet dancer], or *Zuhörer* [listener]. That is why the use of double nouns, à la *Ballettänzerinnen und -tänzer,* has become widely accepted – whether spelled with two, three, or five *t*'s was pretty much all the same to us. For the written language we invented the short form *Ballettänz-erInnen,* with the nice tall capital *I* in the middle. This form, which has become an important part of contemporary German writing, is missing in the new dictionary. Because it is not there, it will still be possible to intimidate reform-eager *LehrerInnen* [teachers], *SchülerInnen* [pupils],

2. The German spelling reform requires that consonant alternations such as those between *z* in *Potenz* (potency, power) and *t* in *potentiell* (potential, latent) be eliminated in favor of the base word's spelling. Thus, the old spelling "potentiell" is to be replaced by "potenziell."

JournalistInnen [journalists] and others by using references to the Duden to put the brakes on their emancipatory zeal.

It is some consolation that we can write and speak German exactly as we please once we are out of school and away from the custody of authorities and their rule-rabid committee chairs. We women will keep on enriching the German language. This reactionary reference work showed us precious little gratitude for doing so, but the next century belongs to women and the next reform commission will surely come with it. Unique spelling rules already *domina*te in email and electronic chatting.[3] My sister writes to me as "Mein suses [süßes] Schnuckiherz!" [roughly, "my sweet cuddle-bunny"] and ends her letters with "herzliche Gruse [Grüße]" [warm greetings]. As you see, Germanic specialties such as the umlaut letter *ü* and the double *ss* or *ß* in *süß* and *Grüße* are out, because they so often are transmited in distorted form. A Germanist colleague in the USA asked me for help finding an article whose title appeared on my screen as "Wir m=FCssen [müssen] uns auf der Br=CKcke [Brücke] begegnen" [we must meet on the bridge]. I prefer *Brucke*. Well, as I said, the next reform commission is surely on its way.

In conclusion, let me add a word of praise for the new *Duden.* Though not voluntarily, and obviously under pressure from massive protests by women in the last twenty years, the *Duden* now lists more and more feminine nouns next to the masculine.[4] And so we find the *Demagogin* [demagogue, fem.] side by side with the *Demagoge, die Dänin* [Dane, fem.] and *der Däne, die Biologin* [biologist, fem.] and *der Biologe.* Occasionally, though, the feminine noun is missing. My cursory perusal turned up the following men as lonely singles: *Afroamerikaner* [African-American], *Bahnhofsvorsteher* [station-master], *Bajuware* [Bavarian], *Balljunge* [ball-boy (tennis)], *Ballonfahrer* [balloon pilot], *Bauunternehmer* [building contractor], *Bayer* [Bavarian], *Bazillenträger* [bacillus carrier], *Berliner* [resident of Berlin], *Blutsauger* [blood-sucker], *Bonner* [resident of Bonn], *Bonze* [bigwig], *Busspreiger* [Lenten preacher], *Druide* [druid], *Duckmäuser* [yes-man], *Dudelsackpfeifer* [bagpipe player], *Hairstylist* [hairstylist], *Hausfreund* [family friend], *Museumsaufseher* [museum administrator], *Minnesänger* [minnesinger], *Misanthrop* [misanthrope], *Modemacher* [fashion setter], *Mummelgreis* [old fogey], *Münsteraner* [resident of Münster], *Museumsdiener* [museum guard],

---

3. In this sentence, the author "feminizes" the German verb *herrschen* (rule, be master of) by replacing *herr* (master) with *frau* (woman) to coin *frauschen.* The gloss *domina*te is an attempt to render this word-play into English.

4. The long-standing practice of German lexicographers was to list in dictionaries only the masculine noun in all cases where the corresponding feminine noun could be predictably "derived" from it by adding the suffix *-in.*

Musikliebhaber [music lover]. I hope the next edition of the Duden will include the *Bajuwarin* [Bavarian, fem.], the *Bonzin* [bigwig, fem.], the *Hausfreundin* [family friend, fem.], the *Mummelgreisin* [old fogette], and all the other interesting women so we would not have to search in vain for them any more.

Translated by Jeanette Clausen

CONTRIBUTORS

Leslie A. Adelson is Professor of German Studies at Cornell University. She is the author of *Crisis of Subjectivity: Botho Strauss's Challenge to West German Prose of the 1970s* (1984); *Making Bodies, Making History: Feminism and German Identity* (1993); and numerous articles on contemporary German literature, feminist cultural theory, minority discourse, and interdisciplinary German Cultural Studies. *For Making Bodies, Making History* she was awarded the MLA's Aldo and Jeanne Scaglione Prize for an Outstanding Scholarship Study in the Field of Germanic Languages and Literatures (1994). For her overall contributions to the study of postwar German studies she received the DAAD Prize for Distinguished Scholarship in German Studies (1996). A book on Turkish-German literature is currently underway.

Ann Taylor Allen is Professor of History at the University of Louisville. She has taught at the University of Bielefeld and has held a Fulbright Teaching and Research grant at Humboldt University, Berlin. In the Fall semester of 1996, she was a Visiting Scholar at the Institute for Research on Women and Gender at Stanford University. She is the author of *Feminism and Motherhood in Germany, 1800-1914* and of many articles on various aspects of the history of women's movements in Germany and in international comparative perspective.

Karin Bauer is Assistant Professor of German Studies at McGill University in Montreal. Her main areas of research include critical theory and contemporary German literature. She has published articles on Herta Müller, Botho Strauss, Petra Kelly, Nelly Sachs and Christa Wolf. A book on Adorno, Nietzsche, and critical theory is forthcoming with SUNY Press.

Russell A. Berman is Professor of German Studies and Comparative Literature at Stanford University. He is the author of numerous articles and books on German literature and culture, including *The Rise of the Modern German Novel* (1986), *Modern Culture and Critical Theory* (1989), and *Cultural Studies of Modern Germany* (1993). He is currently completing a study on Enlightenment and colonial discourse.

Barton Byg teaches German and Film Studies at the University of Massachusetts, Amherst. He is author of *Landscapes of Resistance: The German Films of Daniele Huil-*

let and Jean-Marie Straub (1995) and a cofounding faculty member of the Interdepartmental Program in Film Studies at the University of Massachusetts, Amherst. As part of a research concentration on the cinema of the German Democratic Republic, he is director of the DEFA Film Library, also at University of Massachusetts, Amherst.

Jeanette Clausen is Associate Professor of German and Women's Studies at Indiana University-Purdue University Fort Wayne. She has published on Christa Wolf, Helga Königsdorf, and other German women authors. She coedited the anthology *German Feminism: Readings in Politics and Literature* (1984) and was coeditor of the *Women in German Yearbook* from 1986 to 1994.

Mariatte C. Denman received her Ph.D. from the University of California, Davis. Her article draws on findings of her dissertation, "Staging the Nation: Nationhood and Gender in Plays, Images, and Films in Postwar West Germany (1945-1949), " which examines gendered representations of West German national identity in the immediate postwar years. Her interests include contemporary German drama, Swiss literature, and visual representations of national identity.

Elke P. Frederiksen is Professor of German in the Department of Germanic Studies and an Affiliate Faculty member of Women's Studies at the University of Maryland at College Park. Her research and teaching focus on German and Austrian literature and culture of the nineteenth and twentieth centuries, with special emphasis on German women's social and literary history, as well as feminist theory. She has published four books and numerous journal articles and contributions to edited volumes. Her book edition *Women Writers of Germany, Austria, and Switzerland* was selected by *Choice* as an "Outstanding Academic Book of 1989." At the University of Maryland, she was named Distinguished Scholar-Teacher in 1986/87.

Sara Friedrichsmeyer is Professor of German and Head of the Department of Germanic Languages and Literatures at the University of Cincinnati. Her research has focused on the twentieth century. Her publications include *The Androgyne in Early German Romanticism* (1983) and the coedited volume *The Enlightenment and its Legacy* (1991). She is currently coediting (with Sara Lennox and Susanne Zantop) a volume titled *The Imperialist Imagination*. She has been coeditor of the *Women in German Yearbook* since 1990.

Joachim Ghislain completed studies in English and German at the University of Cologne and also studied comparative literature at the University of Rochester. His areas of research interest include literary and cultural theory. He recently completed an extended research project on Bakhtin and is currently a free-lance translator of technical and academic texts based in Davidson, North Carolina.

Eva Kaufmann, Professor of German at the Humboldt University in Berlin until 1990, has focused her teaching and research on literature of the nineteenth and twentieth centuries. She has published widely on writings by women, especially in the German Democratic Republic. In addition to her work on authors such as Anna Seghers, Irmtraud Morgner, and Helga Königsdorf, she has been particularly interested in women writers of the younger generations. She has also edited an anthology, *Herr im Hause: Prosa von Frauen zwischen Gründerzeit und erstem Weltkrieg* (1989).

Patricia Herminghouse is Fuchs Professor Emerita of German Studies at the University of Rochester. She has written widely on nineteenth- and twentieth-century

German literature in its social and institutional context, especially East German and women's literature. Editor of the textbook anthology *Frauen im Mittelpunkt* and a series of writings by nineteenth-century German political emegrés in the U.S., she also coedited *Literatur und Literaturtheorie in der DDR* (1976) and *DDR-Literatur der 70er Jahre* (1983). In addition to on going work on a book on literature in the GDR, she has been coeditor of the *Women in German Yearbook* since 1994. A volume with texts by Ingeborg Bachmann and Christa Wolf is forthcoming in the German Library series.

Lutz P. Koepnick teaches in the Department of Germanic Languages and Literatures at Washington University in St. Louis. He is the Author of *Nothungs Modernität: Wagners Ring und die Poesie der Macht im neunzehnten Jahrhundert* and of essays in *New German Critique, Critical Inquiry, Modernism/Modernity, Cultural Studies,* and *The German Quarterly.* He is currently completing a book on how German visual culture from the early 1930s to the present has worked through selected materials of Hollywood and American popular culture in order to create – often unwillingly – a progressively mediated sense of German national identity.

Barbara Kosta is Associate Professor of German at the University of Arizona. Her publications include *Recasting Autobiography: Women's Counterfictions in Contemporary German Literature and Film* (1994), a first-year German language textbook *auf deutsch!* (with Helga Kraft) and articles on German literature and film by women. Her interests are feminist theory, cultural and gender studies, German cinema, autobiographical writing, and twentieth-century German literature. She is currently working on modernity and the modern woman in the Weimar Republic.

Stefana Lefko received her Ph.D. in German at the University of Massachusetts, Amherst, with a dissertationon women's novels in the Weimar Republic. She is currently teaching at the University of Minnesota, Twin Cities.

Ingeborg Majer-O'Sickey is Assistant Professor of German at SUNY Binghamton, where she teaches German Studies. She writes on New German Cinema and is coeditor of *Triangulated Visions: Women in Recent German Cinema,* forthcoming at SUNY Press.

Margaret McCarthy completed her Ph.D. in Comparative Literature at the University of Rochester and is Assistant Professor of German at Davidson College, North Carolina. She has published articles on Jutta Brückner and Ingeborg Bachmann and is presently at work on a piece about Doris Dörrie. Her research interests include theories of autobiography, German film, feminist and cultural theory, and post-World War II German literature by women. She has received both Fulbright and DAAD research grants.

Barbara Mennel is a Ph.D. candidate in German Studies at Cornell University with a dissertation entitled "Seduction, Sacrifice and Submission: Masochism in German Postwar Literature and Film." She has articles forthcoming on Rainer Werner Fassbinder's *Ali: Fear Eats Soul* and Monika Treut's *Seduction: The Cruel Woman.*

Magda Mueller is Coordinator of German Studies at California State University, Chico. She has also taught at Stanford University and Columbia University. She is coeditor of *Gender Politics and Post-Communism. Reflections from Eastern Europe and* *the Former Soviet Union* (1993), and an editor of *TELOS.* She has published articles on topics of German intellectual history (Elmar Altvater, Peter Brückner, Urs Jaeggi, Michael Schneider, Robert Weiman), aesthetic theory (Ernst Bloch, Georg Lukács), GDR and contemporary German literature, film, culture, and feminist studies.

Brent O. Peterson is Associate Professor of German at Ripon College and the author of *Popular Narratives and Ethnic Identity: Literature and Community* in Die Abendschule (1991). He has published articles on German versions of Robinson Crusoe, popular authors such as Marlitt and Louise Mühlbach, cultural and ethnic studies, and the development of history and historical fiction. His current project is a book, Inventing Germany: Writing the Nineteenth-Century Nation.

Luise F. Pusch, Professor of Linguistics, has published books and articles on the theory of grammar and on the grammar of various languages. Her feminist publications include: *Das Deutsche als Männersprache (1984); Alle Menschen werden Schwestern* (1983); *Feminis-mus: Inspektion der Herrenkultur* (1983); *"Ladies first": Ein Gespräch über Feminismus, Sprache und Sexualität* (1993); as well as a coedited volumne, *Wahnsinnsfrauen* (1992, 1995) and *Handbuch für Wahnsinnsfrauen* (1994). She is well known for her trilogy of anthologies: *Schwestern, Töchter,* und *Mütter berühmter Männer* (1985-1994). She has published the popular feminist calender *Berühmte Frauen* since 1987.

Denis Sweet studied at Stanford and the Free University in Berlin before joining the faculty of Bates College in Maine, where he teaches German. His interests are cultural criticism centering on sexual politics and the functions of ideology, particularly in the former GDR. He has written on Nietzsche and Faust reception in the GDR and is currently preparing a book on East German gay literature.

Helga Schutte Watt is Associate Professor of German in the Department of Languages and Literatures, University of Denver. She holds a Ph.D. from the University of Massachusetts, Amherst, where she wrote a dissertation on eighteenth-century German travelogues. Her publications include essays on travel literature by nineteenth-century women and on Sophie La Roche's fiction and non-fiction. She is now working on a monograph on La Roche.

Susanne Zantop is Professor of German and Comparative Literature and Chair of the Department of German Studies at Dartmouth College. She has published a book on literature and history, *Zeitbilder: Literatur und Geschichte bei Heinrich Heine und Mariano José de Larra* (1988), edited a volume on painting and literature *Paintings on the Move: Heinrich Heine and the Visual Arts* (1989), and coedited an anthology of German women's writing *Bitter Healing: German Women Writers from 1700 to 1830* (1991). Her most recent book is *Colonial Fantasies: Conquest, Family, and Nation in Precolonial Germany, 1770-1870,* (1997).

INDEX

abortion, 122-23: and rape, 119, 228n14; opposition in Weimar Republic, 133. *See also*: Paragraph 218; reproduction, control of

Adelson, Leslie A., 108, 238

Adler, Hilde, 133

Adlon, Percy. *See*: *Salmonberries*

Adorno, Theodor W., 66, 80, 271: "On the question: What is German," 273

aestheticization of politics, (W. Benjamin), 171

Africans: (C. Meiners) 23-26, 25n7: asylum-seeking women, image of, 281; "natural" inferiority of "Negroes" (C. Meiners), 24-26; racial character of (C. Meiners), 24; and slavery (C. Meiners), 24

Aidoo, Ama Ata, *Our Sister Killjoy*, 235-45: Africanness in, 238-43; blackness and whiteness in, 240-41; lesbian subtext, 243

Akerman, Chantal, 235-40, 243-45: Jews and Germans in, 236n4; lesbian subtext, 243. *See*: *Meetings with Anna*

Allen, Ann Taylor, 148

Allen, Beverly, 224

Allgemeine Literatur-Zeitung, 30

Allgemeiner deutscher Frauenverein, 118

alterity. *See*: otherness

Americanization in Nazi Germany, 162

anatomy: and culture (C. Meiners), 3; and moral character (C. Meiners), 24; racial theories of, 24, 31

Anderson, Benedict, 55, 57

androgyny, ideal of (Romanticism), 58

Anglophilia, of Sophie La Roche, 39, 44, 46

Angolopolous, Theo. *See*: *Ulysses' Gaze*

Antel, Franz. *See*: *Heimatland*

anti-*Heimatfilm* (H. Achternbusch), 204

anti-Islamic prejudices in Germany, 307

antisemitism, 22, 22n1, 79-80: in Achim von Arnim, 53n6, 60n21; in BDF, 138-39; and feminism, 106; and homophobia, 258; in postwar German film, 178; (J. von Wickede), 92

Arendt, Hannah, 80, 198

aristocrats (J. von Wickede), 94

Arnim, Achim von, 51-65: antisemitism of, 53n6; 60n21; cross-dressing in, 61; on German language, 59n20; hopes for a German nation, 55-56, 62; ideal of marriage, 58; *völkisch* interests in 54. *Works*: *Die Gräfin Dolores*, 60; "Isabella of Egypt" ("Isabella von Ägypten"), 51-65; *Des Knaben Wunderhorn*, 57; *Die Kronenwächter*, 55, 57; "Der Wintergarten", 56

Arnim, Bettina von (née Brentano), 58, 107

Asians, "inferiority" of (C. Meiners), 23, 27

asylum laws, German, 277-78

asylum seekers in Germany, 107, 276-89: Africans, image of, 281; changed legislation of 1993, 278; exoticization of, 287; numbers of, 278; in media, 277; right to stay in Germany, 279. *See also*: women, asylum-seeking

Augspurg, Anita, 132n14

Aussiedler. *See*: ethnic Germans

Austen, Jane, 155

Austro-Prussian War, 94

Axel an der Himmelstür (Axel at Heaven's Gate, Dir. R. Benatzky), 164

Baader, Franz von, 58

Bachmann, Ingeborg, 103n1, 105, 107: "Literatur als Utopie," 105

Bachofen, J.J., 134

Bakhtin, Mikhail, 66

Bambi (F. Salten): film versions, 209-10

Bambi: as feminine principle, 209; and *Heimatfilm*, 202-16

Bammer, Angelika, 236n5

Barthel, Karl, 152-53

Barthes, Roland, 199

Basic Law (*Grundgesetz*), German: right of asylum, 278; status of married women, 198

Bauman, Zygmunt, 286

Bäumer, Gertrud, 132, 132n16, 134-36, 197

BDF (Bund Deutscher Frauenvereine). *See*: League of German Women's Organizations

beards, 26: as indicator of superiority and physical strength (C. Meiners), 28-29

Index

cosmopolitanism of, 36-39; and education of women, 42-43, 48; Francophobia of, 40-42, 46; and French Revolution, 44-46; German identity of, 38, 41, 43; nostalgia for the past, 41-47; patriotism of, 37-38, 40, 43. Works: *Briefe über Mannheim*, 47; *Erscheinungen am See Oneida*, 45-46; *Geschichte des Fräuleins von Sternheim*, 39-40, 48n6; *Liebe-Hütten*, 47; *Moralische Erzählungen*, 47; *Rosaliens Briefe an ihre Freundin Mariane von St.*, 40-43; *Schönes Bild der Resignation*, 45. *See also*: *Pomona für Teutschlands Töchter*

Lacan, Jacques, 211n10
Lange, Helene, 130, 130n7, 134
Langner, Margrit, 48n6
language: feminist critique, 223-30; and gender, 147-48; and German identity, 37, 59; as *Heimat* (M. Heidegger), 202; as marker of otherness, 59; masculine bias of grammar, 325-26; and propaganda, 326; spelling reform, 327-30
Laube, Heinrich, 73
Lauter, Paul, 101
Lavater, Johann Caspar, 32
League of German Women's Organizations (Bund Deutscher Frauenvereine: BDF), 122-24, 197
League for the Protection of Mothers (Bund für Mutterschutz), 122, 124, 133
Leander, Zarah, 161-75: biography and career, 164-65; face, 165; as *femme fatale*, 164, 166; in *Heimat*, 161; ideological nonconformity, 163, 165-67, 170; and Nazi film star system, 163-65, 170. *Roles: Die große Liebe*, 173-74; *La Habanera*, 161, 166-67; *To New Shores*, 168-71
Lemke, Jürgen: *Ganz normal anders*, 254-57; –, reception, East and West, 254
Lenau, Nicolaus, and gypsies, 57n17
lesbians: in East Germany, 248, 259; iconography of, 242n11
Lessing, Gotthold Ephraim, *Nathan the Wise* (J. von Wickede), 92-93
Lette Association (Lette Verein), 118
Levin, David, 217n1
Liberators Take Liberties (*BeFreier und Befreite*, Dir. H. Sander), 217-31
Lichtenberg, Georg Christoph, opinion of C. Meiners, 31
Limes, 2
Lisbon Story (Dir. W. Wenders), 184
Lissy (Dir. K. Wolf), 181
literature, German, by non-Germans. *See*: minority literature
literary history, German, 145-58: exclusion of women from, 145-55; feminist, 145,155; and national identity, 146-48; and natural sciences, 149-51; and women's emancipation, 154
Literaturstreit (German-German literary debate), 192, 192n7
Literaturwissenschaft, 146-50. *See also*: literary history
Loewenstein, Joseph, 184-85
Lorre, Peter. *See*: *The Lost One*
Lost One, The (Dir. P. Lorre), 183
Lukács, Georg, 66
Lyotard, Jean François, 102

MacKinnon, Catherine, 225
madonna, postwar images, 194-95
Maetzig, Kurt. *See*: *Marriage in the Shadows*

Manchevski, Milcho. *See*: *Before the Rain*
Mann, Thomas, and Gypsies, 57n17
Marenholtz-Bülow, Bertha von, 118-19
Marianne (symbol of France), 71, 294
marriage, Arnim's ideal of, 58
Marriage in the Shadows (Dir. K. Maetzig), 181
martial arts, and German power (C. Meiners), 29
Martin, Biddy, 106
Marx, Karl, *Critique of Hegel's Philosophy of Right*, 70
Marxism and Cultural Studies, 67
masculine identity, 176: re-masculization in cinema, 180
masculinity, 71, 76: and atomic bomb, 177; cultural "virility" of men, 149-50; and *film noir*, 178-79; in France, 30n9; in German discourse on Turks, 309-10; German, representation of, 78; and Germanness (L. Rellstab), 87; in Germany, 77; marked by beardedness (C. Meiners), 28; marginalization in postwar Germanfilm, 181-82; and national identity, 75; as negative quality of women writers, 151; in postwar Berlin, 176-88; postwar crisis of, 177-79; and rape, 221-25; recuperation of, 181
masculinization of women, debate on, 135
mass culture, Nazi, 161-75
maternalism, ideologies of, 113-28: and authoritarianism, 123; and National Socialism, 125
Maurer, Michael, 46
Mayer, Hans, 257
Mayne, Judith, 242n11
McClintock, Anne, 21
Meetings with Anna (Dir C. Akerman), 235-40, 243-45
Meiners, Christoph, 21-35: depiction of Africans, 23-26 25n7; – of American Indians, 26-27; public recognition of, 31; racial theories of, 23n3, 27; –, reception in France 31n15, 32n18; –, reception in nineteenth and twentieth centuries, 32, 30n11; in Russia, 31. *Works: Briefe über die Schweiz*, 21; *Geschichte des weiblichen Geschlechts*, 22; *Grundriß der Geschichte der Menschheit*, 23; "On the Colors and Shades of Different Peoples", 28; "On the Differences in Size Among Different Peoples", 28; "On the Growth of Hair and Beards among the Ugly and Dark-Skinned Peoples, 28; "On the Nature of the African Negroes", 24-27; *Revision der Philosophie*, 22
memory: cultural, women as bearers, 221; historical, of ethnic Germans, 277; –, of Nazi period, 181; politicization of, 218; of wartime rape, 217-31
Merkel, Ina, 295
Meyer, Richard M., 150
Middle Ages, idealization of (A. von Arnim), 53-54
migrants' literature, Turkish, German reception of, 306
minorities, German. *See*: ethnic Germans
minority literatures in Germany, 107-08: H. Müller, 286, 263-74; A. Özakin, 305-19
Mizejewski, Linda, 177
Möhrmann, Renate, 155-56
Mölln, murders of Turks in, 308
monarchy and *Gemeinschaft* (organic community) (J. von Wickede), 94
Mongolians, "mongolization" (C. Meiners), 23, 23n4
moral character: and anatomy (C. Meiners), 24; decline of, men held responsible for, 135; Protestant, 60; of women, 132

Moser, Friedrich Carl von, *Von dem Deutschen Nationalgeist*, 38-39
Mosse, George, 21, 57, 61, 221
mother: as Germany (H. Heine), 68; as *Heimat*, 207; and wife, juxtaposition (H. Heine), 71, 77-78
motherhood: as basis of social order (maternalism), 115-16; BDF ideology, 131; Christian iconography, 194; and citizenship, 139; and class, 132-33; concepts of, immigrant women, 277; discourses of, in early feminism, 113-28; East Germany, 197n12; ethnic Germans, 277, 283; identified with Germany (H. Heine), 69; metaphor of, 132, 138; myth of, 194-95, 194n11; National Socialist, politics of, 194, 197-98; in poetry of East German women, 296-97; representation of, in war memorials, 189-201; spiritual, 130-31, 148; and urban environment, 133
motherhood, social: in U.S., 120; and feminist maternalism, 113-28; in the English-speaking world, 120-21
motherly instincts, social value of 131
mothers: mourning (K. Kollwitz), 193, 193n9, 195; working, benefits for, 123; unmarried, in discourse of sexual reformers, 122
Müller, Heiner, *Germania Tod in Berlin* (*Germany Death in Berlin*), 3
Müller, Herta, 263-75, 286. Works: *Barfüßiger Februar*, 267-68; *The Passport* (*Der Mensch ist ein großer Fasan auf der Welt*) 265, 268-73; *Reisende auf einem Bein* (A Woman Traveling on One Leg), 286; *Der Teufel sitzt im Spiegel*, 264-67
Müller, Inge, 302, 302n13
Müller, Joachim, 68, 70
multiculturalism, 106: disavowed in *Heimatfilm*, 205; in Europe, 276; in German Studies, 306; in Germany, 106-08; literary approaches to, 107
Mulvey, Laura, 208
The Murderers Are among Us (*Die Mörder sind unter uns*, Dir. W. Staudte), 185-86
Mutterkreuz, 194

Napoleon, German resistance to, 84
Napoleonic Wars. *See:* Wars of Liberation
The Nasty Girl (*Das schreckliche Mädchen*, Dir. M. Verhoeven), 211-215
nation: conflict with religion and culture (J. von Wickede), 95; construction of, and gender roles, 95-96; figured as woman, 2, 221; ideology of, in literary history, 146-48; and masculinity, 32
National Association of German Housewives' Societies (Reichsverband deutscher Hausfrauenvereine), 137: withdrawal from BDF, 139
national consciousness, German: in nineteenth-century historical fiction, 83-89; lack of, in contemporary German women writers, 280
national ideology, German: and literary history, 146-49; and science, 149
National Socialism, 137: and BDF, 129; and cinema, 176-88; and feminism, 114-125; and feminist theories of Germanic women, 137; ideology of blood, 284-85; and maternalism, 125; racial purity, 279; and reproductive control, 124; in Rumanian German communities, 267; view of women, 140n32; women's role in, 140n32
National Socialist Motherhood Medal. *See*: *Mutterkreuz*
national unity, nineteenth-century longing for (L. Rellstab), 89
nationalism, 57-58, 137-38: condemned in East German poetry, 295; of G. Diehl, 136; ethnic, 55-56; German, 61-62, 83; in German women's movement, 131n12; and literary history, 146-49; in Napoleonic era, 84; and patriotism (J. von Wickede), 91; Polish (L. Rellstab), 87; and Weimar politics, 139; women's, 85; and xenophobia, 236
Nationalisms and Sexualities, 56-57
nationhood, German: narrative of, deconstructed, 245; Romantic longings, 57-62
nations, gendered conceptualizations of, 29, 32-33
Native Americans. *See*: Indians, American
Naubert, Benedikte, influence on Sir Walter Scott, 83
Naumann, Ursula, 40
Nazi culture and Americanism, 162
Nazi cinema, 161-75: cultural otherness, 166; depiction of Jews, 205; Germanness in, 166; Hollywood elements in, 164
Nazi Germany, 176-88: as "feminized" space, 181; film star system in, 164
Nenon, Monica, 47
Neo-Realism, Italian, 177
Neue Wache: controversy, 191-93; history of the memorial, 189, 189n2, 185n5, 192n6
New German Cinema, challenge to *Heimatfilm*, 203-04
Niederwalddenkmal (Niederwald monument). *See*: Germania; Rhine River controversy
Nietzsche, Friedrich, *Beyond Good and Evil*, 75-76
Night Porter, The (Dir. L. Cavani), 185
Nolte, Ernst, 176
Novalis [Friedrich von Hardenberg], 58, 70
novel: nineteenth-century, 84; as "women's genre," 153
NSDAP. *See:* National Socialism

oak tree (symbol of German strength): 3-4n4; (C. Meiners), 29
Oder River, in poetry, 301
Orientalism, 57
O'Sullivan, Chris, 224
otherness: 279, 282; double othering," 307; of female asylum seekers, 282; –, legitimated, 287; feminist constructions of men, 236; figured as urban phenomenon, 205; of Gypsies, 51; in Nazi film, 166; "safe" forms of, 281; sexualized Turks, 244
Our Sister Killjoy. *See*: Aidoo, Ama Ata
Özakin, Aysel: *Die Preisvergabe* (The Prizegiving), 311-18

Paragraph 218 (prohibits abortion), 123: BDF debate on, 122-23, 129, 133; and wartime rape, 219, 228n14; *See also*: abortion; reproduction, control of
Paris (Heine's reports), 78
Parnass, Peggy, 281
patriarchy: as basis of white superiority (C. Meiners), 24; Islam accused of (A. Schwarzer), 318
patriotism, German, 39, 88-89: of A. von Arnim, 54; of German Jews (J. von Wickede), 90-91; of German men (S. La Roche), 37, 47; of German middle class (S. La Roche), 39; of German women, (L. Rellstab) 86, (L. von François) 95; in Göttinger Hain, 40;

Index

Schneckenburger, Max, "Die Wacht am Rhein" (On Watch at the Rhine), 4
Scholem, Gershom, 79
Schönhuber, Franz, 307-11; and feminism, 309; views on women's rights, 311
Schrader, Karl, 119
Schrader-Breymann, Henriette, 118-19
Schreiber, Adele, 124
Schürer, Ernst, 54n11
Schwarzer, Alice, 308-09
Schwarzwaldmädel (Black Forest Girl, Dir. H. Deppe), 206
sciences, natural: gendered ideology of, 149-51; and German national identity, 149; and literary history, 149-51; relationship to poetry, 150
Scott, Sir Walter, influenced by B. Naubert, 83
Seeßlen, Georg, 163-64
Segebrecht, Wulf, 103
Seifert, Ruth, 222n10, 225
sexism in language. See: German language, feminist critique of
sexual difference, representation in film, 164
sexual reformers, feminist, turn-of-the-century, 122
sexual violence and power, 221-22
sexuality and national identity, 75-76
Seyhan, Azade, 52, 61
Shoah. See: Holocaust
Showalter, Elaine, 106n4
Sierck, Detlef (alias Douglas Sirk), 161, 163, 165-66, 168-73. Films: *La Habanera*, 161, 163; *To New Shores* (*Zu neuen Ufern*), 163, 166, 168-71
Sillge, Ursula, 254
skin color, 28: as indicator of beauty in women (C. Meiners), 28; as indicator of cultural superiority (C. Meiners), 28
slavery: emancipation of slaves (C. Meiners), 23-24; justified for Africans (C. Meiners), 24
social activism, nineteenth-century women's, 119
social purity movements and early feminists, 123
social welfare, turn-of-the-century, 122: for women, 120; and sterilization, 124; in U.S., 125
socialism, French utopian (Saint-Simonism), social values, 117
Solingen, murders of Turks in, 308
Sollers, Philippe, 180
Sömmerring, Samuel Thomas, 23n5-n6, 24-25, 31
Sonderweg, German, and feminism, 125
Soviet war monument, gendered iconography of, 220n6
spectatorship, female, 174; gender-specificity of modern, 172
Spengler, Oswald, 135
Spittler, L.Th., 23
St. Domingue (Haiti), 23
de Stäel, Germaine, 70, 76, 78; *De l'Allemagne*, 70
Stanton, Elizabeth Cady, 114
Stasi, surveillance of homosexuals in East Germany, 249, 257-60
State Security Organization, East Germany. See: Stasi
Stationmaster's Wife, The (Dir. R.W. Fassbinder), 181
Staudte, Wolfgang, 177, 181. See also: *The Murderers Are among Us*
Stefan, Verena, 236n5
Steiner, Gertraud, 202

Steinhoff, Hans. See: *Die Geyerwally, Hitler Youth Quex*
stereotypes, of race, 25
sterilization, advocated by sexual reformers: compulsory, 124; voluntary, 123. See also: reproduction, control of
Stöcker, Helene, 114, 133
Stolberg, Leopold von, attitude toward French, 46n5
Stölzl, Christoph, 191n5, 193
Strauss, Salomon, 73
subjectivity, Jewish, and post-Holocaust Germany, 244
suffrage, women's: Switzerland, 325; U.S., 120; German, 131-37; –, attempts to reverse (National Socialism), 140
Die Sünderin, (The Sinful Woman, Dir. W. Forst), 182, 194n11
Süssmuth, Rita, 8
Sweet, Denis, 83
Szewczuk, (artist), 195-96

Tacitus, *Germania*, 2
Tall Isaack. See: J. von Wickede
Tatlock, Lynne, 184-85
Taurinius, Zacharias, *Beschreibung einiger Seereisen nach Asien, Afrika und Amerika*, 55
Thiers, Louis Adolphe, 4
Thomson, James, 43
Thürmer-Rohr, Christina, 236n5
To New Shores (*Zu neuen Ufern*, Dir. D. Sierk), 163, 166, 168-71
Trachten. See: costumes, traditional
Trommler, Frank, 101
Turkey, feminism in, 313
Turkish and German histories, erasure of (Alice Schwarzer), 309
Turkish women: significance of headscarf, 306; writing in German, 305
Turkish writers and European modernism, 318
Türkish-German culture: feminist discussions of, 311; literature, 306, 318
Turks: in Germany, 306; as "guestworkers," 310; not considered European (C. Meiners), 28

UFA, 163-65, 167, 173
Ulysses' Gaze (Dir. T. Angolopolous), 181
Uncanny, the (*das Unheimliche*), 207-08; and otherness, 207-08
unification, German (1871), 22: literary concepts of, 94
unification, German (1990): and national identity, 1; social tensions, 276
Usborne, Cornelie, 124

Veit, Philipp, 3
Velsen, Dorothee von, 138
venereal diseases, 124. See also: feminism and prostitution
Verhoeven, Michael. See: *The Nasty Girl*
Vertriebenenverbände (associations of ethnic Germans), 2
Volkszugehörigkeit, 284

Vordtriede, Werner, 61
Wallraff, Günter, 311n9
Wander, Maxie, *Guten Morgen, du Schöne*, 254-55
war: and rape, 217-31; and sexual violence, 222-25; and venereal disease, 224